Critical Essays on
DON DELILLO

CRITICAL ESSAYS
ON
AMERICAN LITERATURE

James Nagel, General Editor
University of Georgia, Athens

Critical Essays on
DON DELILLO

edited by

HUGH RUPPERSBURG AND TIM ENGLES

G. K. Hall & Co.
New York

G. K. Hall & Co.
1633 Broadway
New York, NY 10019

Library of Congress Cataloging-in-Publication Data
Critical essays on Don DeLillo / edited by Hugh Ruppersburg and Tim Engles.
    p. cm. — (Critical essays on American literature)
  Includes bibliographical references (p.) and index.
   ISBN 0-7838-0458-X (alk. paper)
   1. DeLillo, Don—Criticism and interpretation.
  I. Ruppersburg, Hugh M. II. Engles, Tim. III. Series.
PS3554.E4425 Z6 2000
813'.54—dc21
                                      00-024507

This paper meets the requirements of ANSI/NISO Z3948-1992 (Permanence of Paper).

10 9 8 7 6 5 4 3 2

Printed in the United States of America

Contents

◆

General Editor's Note

◆

This series seeks to anthologize the most important criticism on a wide variety of topics and writers in American literature. Our readers will find in various volumes not only a generous selection of reprinted articles and reviews but original essays, bibliographies, manuscript selections, and other materials brought to public attention for the first time. This volume, *Critical Essays on Don DeLillo,* is the most comprehensive gathering of essays ever published on one of the most important modern writers in the United States. It contains both a sizable gathering of early reviews and a broad selection of more modern scholarship. Among the authors of reprinted articles and reviews are Christopher Lehmann-Haupt, Diane Johnson, Nelson Algren, George Will, David Cowart, Paula Bryant, Silvia Caporale Bizzini, and Thomas LeClair. In addition to a substantial introduction by Hugh Ruppersburg and Tim Engles, which surveys DeLillo's career and critical responses to it, there are also four original essays commissioned specifically for publication in this volume. Glen Scott Allen explores the unique manifestation of postmodern paranoia in *Ratner's Star,* while Mark Osteen concerns himself with the "marketing obsession" in *Running Dog.* Two new studies deal with *Underworld:* John N. Duvall is concerned with "baseball, aesthetics, and ideology," and Arthur Saltzman with the "awful symmetries" presented in the novel. We are confident that this book will make a permanent and significant contribution to the study of American literature.

JAMES NAGEL
University of Georgia

Publisher's Note

◆

Producing a volume that contains both newly commissioned and reprinted material presents the publisher with the challenge of balancing the desire to achieve stylistic consistency with the need to preserve the integrity of works first published elsewhere. In the Critical Essays series, essays commissioned especially for a particular volume are edited to be consistent with G. K. Hall's house style; reprinted essays appear in the style in which they were first published, with only typographical errors corrected. Consequently, shifts in style from one essay to another are the result of our efforts to be faithful to each text as it was originally published.

Introduction

◆

From the beginning of his career, Don DeLillo has received generally favorable attention from prominent reviewers and writers. Joyce Carol Oates and Nelson Algren reviewed his first novel. Anne Tyler, John Williams, John Updike, Diane Johnson, Millicent Bell, Fredric Jameson, and Anthony Burgess were among reviewers of his other novels. The *New York Times, New York Times Book Review, Los Angeles Times Book Review, Washington Post Book World, New Yorker, Nation, New Republic, London Review of Books,* and other major national and international publications have given serious sustained attention to his work. The *New York Times* in particular has reviewed each of his novels, including the one he wrote anonymously. It can hardly be said that he has not received sympathetic press from intelligent readers, many of them novelists themselves. Certainly, there have been negative reviews, especially in response to *Libra,* which both George Will and Jonathan Yardley in the *Washington Post* criticized for its treatment of the Kennedy assassination. While some of the early reviews pointed to flaws of various sorts in his novels, they found as well a great promise, often suggesting that DeLillo's "next" novel would finally and fully confirm his obvious talents. It is thus curious that his work was so late in winning a wider readership. Whatever he might have lacked in popular acclaim or in recognition by scholars of modern literature (only with *White Noise* in 1985 did he become a familiar name), unlike most new writers he did not struggle gradually out of the muck of obscurity and early on enjoyed support and recognition from writers and critics.

The critical reception of DeLillo's work divides into two phases. The first begins with *Americana* in 1971 and extends through *The Names* in 1982. During this phase reviewers began to recognize DeLillo's abilities as a novelist, his interest in "ideas," and his skill with language and humor. The popular and critical success of *End Zone* in 1972 labeled DeLillo a sports novelist, a reputation he could not shake though he never wrote another sports novel under his own name (the pseudonymous *Amazons,* published in 1982, was generally

1

recognized as his work; several reviews identified his hand in this novel, which helped keep alive his reputation as a sports novelist). The second phase began with *White Noise* in 1985 and has continued through his most recent novel, *Underworld,* in 1997. That DeLillo was deeply concerned with serious subjects—the failure of language, the state of the modern world, the Cold War, technology—had been evident as early as *Americana,* and what many reviewers seemed to like about *End Zone,* in addition to its humor, was its juxtaposition of the absurd and the serious. Such variously difficult later novels as *Ratner's Star, Players,* and *The Names* made clear that DeLillo was writing in the tradition of such novelists as Thomas Pynchon and Joan Didion (as well as Joyce, Dos Passos, and Faulkner) and that in his concern with international settings, terrorism, and science he was laying claim to a territory vastly different from the one his earliest novels would have seemed to predict.

With *White Noise* DeLillo secured his reputation as a leading contemporary writer in America. Not only did the success of this novel persuade readers to reassess the earlier novels, it also set a clear range of expectations for the later novels, *Libra, Mao II,* and *Underworld.* If in the earlier portion of his career DeLillo had to struggle against the desire of readers for a second or third *End Zone,* in the latter part he faced the challenge of having to surpass with each new book the achievement of its predecessor. Although *Mao II* was an interlude of sorts following *Libra,* reviewers greeted it as a major work. In the years preceding the publication of *Underworld* (especially after "Pafko at the Wall" appeared in *Harper's Magazine* in 1992), DeLillo was clearly expected to produce a masterpiece, a Great American Novel, the sort of work for which his entire career had prepared him and his readers. Although there were some critical reviews of *Underworld,* there were considerably more positive notices, and in general it was widely recognized as DeLillo's best work, a significant literary event, a major contemporary American novel, perhaps the most widely heralded book of the decade.[1]

REVIEWS

DeLillo's first novel, *Americana* (1971), received a major review by Christopher Lehmann-Haupt in the *New York Times,* who found the book "very much a first novel" but who praised "DeLillo's ability to write," his comic scenes, and his characters.[2] Nelson Algren, in *Rolling Stone,* admiringly summarized and quoted from the novel and then proclaimed, "Don DeLillo's swift, ironic, and witty cross-country American nightmare, as seen through a Scoopie 16 news camera, doesn't have a dull or an unoriginal line. If you dug Jack Nicholson's role in *Five Easy Pieces* or the fables of Donald Barthelme, Don DeLillo is your man."[3] Joyce Carol Oates, in the *Detroit Evening News,* praised the book for its sophistication, "which is amazing for a first novel, indeed."

The narrative technique is "beautifully executed" with "patches of writing . . . that are really striking. . . . DeLillo is to be congratulated for having accomplished one of the most compelling and sophisticated of 'first novels' that I have ever read."[4]

End Zone, which appeared a year later, was more widely reviewed. Lehmann-Haupt, again writing in the *New York Times,* praised the craft of the novel and noted its concern with "the terminologies of football and nuclear holocaust—the languages of end zones. The end zones of languages." He noted: "The suddenness of [DeLillo's] arrival places him among our best young writers. It makes one wonder whether there are any limits at all to his potential growth."[5] Nelson Algren, in the *Los Angeles Times Book Review,* recognized DeLillo's use of television as a window on the nation, praised the novel's humor and satire (which he compared to that of Evelyn Waugh) and its use of language, but found a loss of momentum: "Although there isn't a line in either *Americana* or *End Zone* that falters, it might be well if the author used his emergency before his motor starts sputtering."[6] Roger Sale, in the *New York Review of Books,* suggested that "DeLillo's essential engagement is not with people but with words, with modern jargon, with the almost torrential power organized and systematic language can have to invade and dominate a life, with the possibility that our country is unrecognizable to itself except when we are in the wombs of technical vocabularies." Though his review is generally positive, Sale faults the book's metaphor for contemporary American life—football—which, he argues, relieves DeLillo of having to delve into the inner lives of his characters, and which prevents action in the novel. Sale finds *End Zone* to be more an "idea orchestrated with sounds" than a book.[7] DeLillo's use of language and his development of plot and character have remained issues for reviewers throughout his career. A highly favorable review by S. K. Oberbeck in the *Washington Post Book World* viewed the novel as "powerfully funny, oblique, testy, and playful, tearing along in dazzling cinematic spurts of completely nutty writing, weaving and twisting and bobbing like Groucho Marx on a faked end run." Oberbeck compares the novel's bleak landscape to the surface of the moon in the film *2001: A Space Odyssey* and describes the football players as "quasi-madmen" and "massive mental retards." His view of *End Zone* as little more than a satirical sports novel remained the prevailing view of DeLillo's work for some years to come.[8]

Reviews of DeLillo's next novel, *Great Jones Street* (1973), suggested that readers had been spoiled by both the subject and the skill of *End Zone* and that DeLillo himself was struggling to identify and cultivate the landscape best suited for his fiction. Sara Blackburn, in the *New York Times Book Review,* complained that while the novel is "full of beautiful writing" DeLillo is unable to develop a fully realized plot in the rock-and-roll milieu of the novel and that his characters are "beyond redemption."[9] Christopher Lehmann-Haupt offered a similar assessment, complaining that although it has "so very many little things to like and laugh at" the novel is "disappointing and flat" and its themes "have very little to do with the hurdy-gurdy of a plot."[10] Webster Schott, in the *Washington Post Book World,* found the novel interesting and its themes compelling but suggested that "DeLillo needs a story, characters, and setting worthy of his gifts."[11] Nelson Algren described the novel with admiration and concluded approvingly that "DeLillo's books are never about what they appear to be about."[12]

Ratner's Star (1976), in many ways DeLillo's most difficult and interesting early novel, proved frustrating for Algren, who criticized its lack of humor and "gobbledygook" language and called it a "long, long book about brainpeople of the future."[13] Although J. D. O'Hara found the science fiction form unsuited for the "many ideas so satisfyingly raised, developed, and clarified in this fine novel," he also judged the work a "mind-expanding trip to the finish line, and full of wit and slapstick as well." DeLillo is, he wrote, "already the writer Vonnegut, Barth, and Pynchon were once oddly and variously taken to be, and he shows no signs of flagging, many signs of promise." *Ratner's Star* is "the American version of a European novel of ideas. Perhaps [DeLillo] most resembles Thomas Mann, lacking Mann's mysticism and long-windedness but sharing his remarkable ability to evoke and evaluate the ideas, language and attitudes of a wide range of intellectual disciplines."[14] Christopher Lehmann-Haupt, who has remained throughout DeLillo's career one of his most consistent and perceptive advocates, called the book DeLillo's "most spectacularly inventive" work, his "best meditation on the excesses of contemporary thought," and praised its "dazzling capacity to make fun-house mazes of the most abstruse passage of scientific theory" and its "lyric poetry."[15] Despite the praise of reviewers, and its cultivation of the soil already tilled by Pynchon in *Gravity's Rainbow* and *The Crying of Lot 49, Ratner's Star* has thus far attracted little attention from literary scholars.

DeLillo's fifth novel, *Players* (1977), gave occasion to assess the progress and course of his career. That DeLillo was receiving consistent and serious notice in such locations as the *New York Times* and *Los Angeles Times Book Review* and that he was being noticed by well-known writers was a measure of his rising status, despite the fact that with the modest exception of *End Zone* he had received little popular notice from readers. Stephen Koch, whose strongly negative review of *Players* appeared in *Harper's Magazine,* noted that *End Zone* was a best seller because "it was bought and read by people who loved not literature but football. I found *End Zone* a well written and extremely amusing novel." However, he found fault with *Players* on nearly every score, especially plot, character, theme, and prose style. Koch's basic objections seem to derive from a disagreement with the kind of novels that DeLillo writes, novels that eschew the traditional elements, the Aristotelian unities.[16] Other reviewers were more positive. Novelist William Kennedy praised DeLillo as a "spectacular talent, supremely witty and a natural storyteller," and found clear evidence of growth in his talent: "From his first book it was also clear that his control of the language was of a high order. The difference between that first book and the latest is what he leaves out. *Players* is half the size of *Americana,* but just as dense with implication of the meaning of the lives it presents to us."[17] J. D. O'Hara noted that DeLillo had not yet gained a wider audience and blamed this failure on the fact that he is mistakenly compared to such writers as Vonnegut, Pynchon, and Barth, writers who begin with a set of "Deep Truths" and then build novels designed to prove those truths, whereas DeLillo "characteristically accumulates heaps and windrows of material not to prove a *parti pris* but to demonstrate that there are questions" that are complex and cannot be easily answered. O'Hara agreed with Kennedy that *Players* is an advance over the earlier novels (it is shorter, simpler, more narrowly focused). Though it deals effectively with a wide range of people and themes, its characters are not always interesting, and they "block DeLillo from exploring the implications of his material in his usual exuberant fashion."[18] Diane Johnson gave the book its most intelligent review. Readers are not comfortable with DeLillo, she suggested, because he writes "deeply shocking things about America that people would rather not face." In its direct examination of "all the secret places in contemporary sensibility," she saw DeLillo as set apart from other contemporary novelists, who through excessive confessionalism or choice of subject generally manage to avoid looking at the modern world. Whereas Koch in *Harper's* thought the novel needed revision, Johnson suggested that "few recent novels have found so admirably congruent a form for their subject." The book has a "tight, carefully balanced structure" and a "masterful" attention to detail.[19] John Updike, writing for the *New Yorker,* reviewed the novel with a discerning ambivalence that found the two main characters so unlikable that he had difficulty mustering interest in them. Updike regards DeLillo as a novelist who has "class" and who is "original, versatile, and, in his disdain of last year's emotional guarantees, fastidious. . . . Into our technology-riddled daily lives he reads the sinister ambiguities, the floating ugliness of America's recent history."[20]

Running Dog (1978) received mostly favorable notices, though several reviewers expressed qualifications of one sort or another. An especially unfavorable review came from Thomas LeClair in the *New Republic,* who judged the novel as a minimalist exercise and "an experimental coda to a major writer's career." In it DeLillo reduces characters to "points on a graph, points nearly obliterated by the plot-lines that connect them."[21] Anthony Burgess, in the *Saturday Review,* perplexed and outraged by the America that *Running Dog* describes, wondered whether "the kind of fiction that Don DeLillo and other Americans are writing can be termed novels in the sense still current in Europe. Here [in Europe] it is legitimate to fictionalize the breakdown of civilization, but only from the viewpoint of a protagonist who holds on to the values out of which the novel-form was begotten. We need humanity to observe the death of humanity." Yet he found DeLillo's voice "harsh, eroded, disturbingly eloquent."[22] Michael Wood praised various elements of the novel but suggested that the reliance on conspiracy obscures the problem of evil and of human motivation.[23] Even the reviewer for the countercultural *Crawdaddy* found that "conspiracies are, after all, only incomplete systems" but suggested that their incompleteness is part of DeLillo's method.[24] Curt Suplee, in the *Washington Post Book World,* also recognized the focus on conspiracy and gave the book its most positive review, regarding it as a "richly understated, episodic but strangely coherent novel."[25]

DeLillo's next novel was one he has never acknowledged: *Amazons,* by "Cleo Birdwell" (1980), a risqué picaresque comedy about the first professional female hockey player. Although little is known about how DeLillo came to write (or, perhaps, cowrite) this book, it did receive several reviews. J. D. O'Hara, writing in the *Nation,* and Christopher Lehmann-Haupt in the *New York Times,* both commented favorably on its satirical portrait of the sports industry.[26] Both also recognized (or knew of) DeLillo's role as author of the book.

The reception of *The Names* (1982), DeLillo's seventh novel, was an odd mixture of respect for craft and theme and criticism of plot and character. Although most critics wrote favorably of the novel, few knew what to make of it, and most expressed reservations of some sort, especially about the plot, which was variously found to be "curiously static," "only intermittently compelling," "theoretical and empty," "closer to fable than to realistic storytelling," or marred by "too many dead-end lanes."[27] Michael Wood in the *New York Times Book Review* called the novel "dense, brilliant, ultimately rather elusive."[28] Many critics associated this difficulty with plot with the novel's concern with metaphysics and other abstract issues, such as global capitalism, conspiracies, language, and so on. Robert Towers found the novel's shape a deliberate strategy that creates "a sense of fragmentation, menace, and loose ends that seems appropriate enough to our experience of the final, ominous decades of this extraordinary century. What [DeLillo] loses is some of the potential force that a greater concentration of his effects might have produced."[29] Towers found the focus on external action and the more rapid pacing of the novel a welcome advance over earlier books. J. D. O'Hara, in the *Nation,* saw the novel as "a complex, mature, extended continuation" of *End Zone;* though "characters, settings, and styles are different; the elegance has a higher polish, the sensibility is subtler."[30] While Jonathan Yardley, J. D. O'Hara, Fredric Jameson, Christopher Lehmann-Haupt, and Frances Taliaferro recognized the novel's complex concern with language, Josh Rubins read it as a depiction of "the dynamics of alienation, the corruption of the American personality," and for Michael Wood it was a "meditation on the relation of this half-mythological America to the historical world."[31] Robert Towers echoes a number of critics in his conclusion that "nearly every page testifies to DeLillo's exceptional gifts as a writer—a writer who has not, in my view, published a novel whose total impact is equal to the brilliance of its parts." David Bosworth agrees: "Here is a man whose books should be read.

A novelist of high purpose, of rare ambition. . . . To say we expect more from him is an implicit if impatient compliment—a measure of this writer's special gifts."[32]

These high expectations, and the growing critical estimation of his ability, seemed vindicated in the 1985 novel *White Noise*. Although it received the same proportion of negative or ambiguous reviews as earlier works, this novel clearly satisfied those critics who had been waiting for DeLillo to write a "major" work. The American Book Award seemed to confirm the opinion of many that the novel was just that. A negative review by Robert Phillips in *America* took exception to the novel for its portrayal of "life in America today [as] boring, dehumanized and dangerous."[33] In the *New Criterion,* after surveying the earlier novels, Bruce Bawer lambasted *White Noise* for its shallow philosophizing and characters, for its "stylish, schematic view of modern America as a great big xerox machine. . . . DeLillo . . . in effect continues to write the same lifeless novel over and over again—a novel constructed upon a simpleminded political cliche."[34] These rejections of the novel are at least in part politically motivated (the *New Criterion* is markedly conservative in orientation), a trend that remains evident in the reception of DeLillo's later novels, especially *Libra* and *Underworld*.

Many reviews were more positive. Thomas Disch, in the *Nation,* called *White Noise* "as funny and as dramatically satisfying as a collection of the year's best *New Yorker* cartoons" and then criticized the absence of a story (because pain and death are reduced to "the category of media events") and the focus on the fear of death, which he could not take seriously because of the overwhelming humor of the novel.[35] Other critics were comfortable with the mixture of dark themes and comedy. Thomas DePietro, in *Commonweal,* called the novel a "truly Swiftian satire. . . . The only relief is laughter, pure and unabated—the kind DeLillo induces with apparent effortlessness. What we laugh at is ourselves in constant fear of oblivion. From the accumulation of consumer rot, DeLillo manufactures a wonderfully comic apocalypse—a genuine revelation."[36] Christopher Lehmann-Haupt, in the *New York Times Book Review,* called the novel "eerie, brilliant, and touching and as serious as death and puff adders." He added, "[F]or the first time in any of his fiction . . . Mr. DeLillo tells a story that is slightly more than just a vehicle for his brilliant writing and his gags."[37] Jayne Anne Phillips in a long appreciation of the novel praised DeLillo's portrayal of the family, of children, and of middle-class American culture.[38] Jay McInerney, in the *New Republic,* called it "a stunning performance from one of our finest and most intelligent novelists. DeLillo's reach is broad and deep, combining acute observation of the textures of American life and analytic rigor. . . . DeLillo is tremendously funny. *White Noise* is one of his most accessible novels."[39] Diane Johnson, in the *New York Review of Books,* deemed it a "meditation on themes of whiteness—the pallor of death, and white noise, the sound, so emblematic of modern life, that is meant to soothe human beings by screening out the other, more irritating noises of their civilization." She found "special pleasure" in "the extraordinary language, the coherence of the imagery, saturated with chemicals and whiteness and themes of poisons and shopping, the nice balance of humor and poignance, solemn nonsense and real questions."[40]

While *Libra* clearly seemed a significant advance over its predecessor, its publication, and its fictional treatment of the John F. Kennedy assassination, provoked considerable controversy. George Will, in the *Washington Post,* excoriated almost every aspect of the novel, from its "lunatic conspiracy theory" and "sandbox existentialism" to its "exercise in blaming America for Oswald's act of derangement." He took greatest exception to the novel's treatment of history: "Novelists using the raw material of history—real people, important events—should be constrained by concern for truthfulness, by respect for the record and a judicious weighing of probabilities." By portraying Oswald as a lone neurotic manipulated by an unlikely group of conspirators, DeLillo has committed "an act of literary vandalism and bad citizenship." Will calls DeLillo "a talented writer whose talent is subordinated to, and obviated by, puerile political stances."[41] Jonathan Yardley's review in the *Washington Post Book World,* echoing Will, sees DeLillo as a political novelist and a "writer of skill, wit, and ingenuity, but he employs these considerable gifts in the evanescent craft of pamphleteering rather than the durable art of fiction." *Libra* is an "act of exploitation" notable for "its lack of interesting prose, its deficiency of wit, and . . . its failure of the imagination."[42] Several reviewers seemed concerned with the novel's manipulation of fact and fiction and even discussed the plausibility of the conspiracy described in the novel. Cecilia Tichi, in the *Boston Review,* urged DeLillo to return to writing fiction, while Merle Rubin in the *Christian Science Monitor* complained that " 'Libra' presents a vision that is less engrossing than the purely fictional one in 'White Noise,' because of the reader's constant urge to check DeLillo's version of Nov. 22 against the known facts."[43] Richard Eder, in a review for the *Los Angeles Times,* suggested that most of the characters in the novel are denied independent existence by the facts of the story they are enacting, though he praised the portraits of Oswald and Ruby.[44] A reviewer in *Playboy* noted that while "*Libra* may be no more accurate than the Warren Report or a thousand other failed attempts to explain 11–22–63, . . . it captures the angry spirit of Oswald and his times."[45]

Though other reviewers expressed various caveats, the predominant opinion was that *Libra* was DeLillo's most ambitious effort yet. Terrence Rafferty in the *New Yorker* called it "his best novel," described the writing as "enthralled, as weirdly eroticized as prisoners' poetry," and suggested that "[f]or the first time, DeLillo's writing has the incendiary concentration of great fiction."[46] Christopher Lehmann-Haupt asked why, "lacking great suspense or tension, does the novel eventually work so powerfully," and he found his answer in DeLillo's use of details from his characters' lives, in "the seamlessness between the known and the unknown, between the actual record and what Mr. DeLillo has invented," in the powerfully conceived character of Oswald, and in the conspiracy itself.[47] For John Leonard this "cold and brilliant novel" was the culmination of "the peculiar art [DeLillo has] been perfecting since the antihero of *Americana.*"[48] Anne Tyler, in the *New York Times Book Review,* called the book DeLillo's "richest novel." Its intermingling of fact and fiction are part of its fascination: "At what point exactly does fact drift over into fiction? The book is so seamlessly written that perhaps not even those people who own both upstairs and downstairs copies of the Warren report could say for certain." Tyler found DeLillo's use of language, dialect, and characterization especially impressive.[49] Numerous other reviews echoed similar sentiments.[50]

Reactions to *Mao II* (1991) were largely favorable. Many reviewers saw in this tenth novel many of the standard DeLillo themes: "the terrorists and conspiracies, the obsession with media images, the off-kilter characters who act like survivors of a future that hasn't yet arrived."[51] Many reviewers also described it, for better and for worse, as a novel of ideas.[52] Robert Towers, for all his general admiration of DeLillo, found it "an overschematized work of realist fiction, theme-ridden to the degree that the novel's articulation becomes somewhat creaky. . . . [This] is the work of a major novelist writing almost, though not quite, at the top of his powers." Martin Amis, in the *Independent* of London, described DeLillo as "an exemplary postmodernist" but criticized the difficulty of judging ideas expressed by the characters: "DeLillo does better—does brilliantly—when he interprets rather than propounds."[53] Others identified the link of the reclusive novelist Bill Gray, and of DeLillo's central equation of novelists and terrorists, with the plight of Salman Rushdie, who had been marked for death by the Iranian government after the publication of *The Satanic Verses.*[54] DeLillo's use of language continued to receive praise, and in general he was accorded the sort of serious, respectful attention reserved for novelists of the first rank. Sven Birkerts, in the *Washington Post Book World,* judged *Mao II* one of DeLillo's best works; Lorrie Moore, in the *New York Times Book Review,* wrote that it "succeeds brilliantly"; Michiko Kakutani, in the *New York Times,* called it "disturbing, provocative and darkly comic. . . . [It] reads, at once, as a sociological meditation on the perils of contemporary society, and as a kind of new-wave thriller"; for Donn Fry in the *Atlanta Journal-Constitution,* it is a "riveting novel of ideas"; for Paul Skenazy in the *San Francisco Chronicle,* it is "brooding and solemn, even for DeLillo, yet it is a beautifully readable, haunting tale that jolts along at its own unsettling, disjunctive pace."[55]

Given the reception of *White Noise, Libra,* and *Mao II,* it is no surprise that many reviewers approached *Underworld* (1997) with high expectations. The novel was six years in the making, and many felt that it would confirm or deflate the high reputation DeLillo had achieved. Certainly its great length, and the time he took to produce it, suggested that the author himself had invested much time and energy in the book. *Underworld* was widely reviewed nationally and internationally, in venues that had paid attention to DeLillo since his first book and in others where he had never received notice (for instance, the *Economist*). For the most part notices were extremely positive and often perceptive and highly intelligent. Several negative reviewers were respectful in their dismissals and offered extended discussions of their objections. The most considered negative review came in the *New Republic,* where James Wood complained that the size and structure of the novel do not cohere and that DeLillo is too discursive, though "the book is so large, so serious, so ambitious, so often well-written, so punctually intelligent, that it produces its own antibodies and makes criticism a small germ."[56] Several negative reviews seemed politically motivated. James Gardner, writing for the *National Review,* called *Underworld* "a fundamentally serious work which never lapses into incoherence and which displays a tonic humility before the art of fiction" but found fault with its length, excess of details, and its "massive postindustrial sprawl with little discernible order and no real center."[57] Although some reviewers seemed to object to the notion that a Great American Novel was any longer possible or even a good idea, many seemed to feel that *Underworld* had made a serious claim on the title. Vince Passaro in *Harper's* found the novel DeLillo's most political and historical work yet and suggested that his use of these dimensions placed him among the finest writers in English, "Shakespeare . . . , Milton, Blake, Flaubert, George Eliot, Henry James, T. S. Eliot, James Joyce, . . . Samuel Beckett and Joseph Conrad."[58] David Wiegand, in the *San Francisco Chronicle,* judged it DeLillo's "best novel and perhaps that most elusive of creatures, a great American novel."[59] Paul Gediman, in the *Boston Review,* compared it to "such icons of excess as *Gravity's Rainbow* and *Ulysses.* Yet it has an integrity of voice and an accessibility that these behemoths lack."[60] Andrew O'Hagan in the *Village Voice,* John Leonard in the *Nation,* Tom LeClair in *Harper's,* Michael Wood in the *London Review of Books,* Paul Gray in *Time,* Blake Morrison in the *Independent* (London), Gary Lee Stonum in *Plain Dealer,* Millicent Bell in the *Partisan Review,* Luc Sante in the *New York Review of Books,* Irving Malin in the *Review of Contemporary Fiction,* Michiko Kakutani in the *New York Times Book Review,* Martin Amis in the *New York Times Book Review,* and Michael Dirda in the *Washington Post Book World* all gave *Underworld* positive assessments and identified the Cold War, the meaning of loss, the interconnectedness of apparently unrelated people and events, conspiracy, paranoia, and life in America as among its themes. Few contemporary American novels have been more widely and favorably reviewed.[61]

CRITICAL OVERVIEW

While some prominent reviewers were intrigued by the sprawled fragments of *Americana,* DeLillo's first novel did not receive significant scholarly attention until long after its release. As noted earlier, the ostensible subject matter of his second novel, *End Zone*, led many reviewers to consider him a sports novelist, a status that may have encouraged academics to dismiss his early work. However, by the late 1970s, the decade in which he published his first six novels, the tremendous range of his subject matter and themes began to prompt scholarly interest. Early critics concurred that the often dazzling surfaces of DeLillo's novels should not distract readers from their remarkably suggestive depths of meaning. The first scholarly analysis to appear was William Burke's discussion of *End Zone*, "Football, Literature, Culture." Burke compared the novel to Frederick Exley's *A Fan's Notes* (1968), describing both works as "fine novels . . . which treat the cultural importance of football" (391).[62] Burke drew connections between the novel's depiction of football as a reassuring field of order and the multilayered interest in language, war, and nuclear weapons. Two years later, in the *International Fiction Review*, Anya Taylor declared *End Zone* "no mere football novel," reading it instead as "a book about the decline of language under the bombardment of terms from thermonuclear warfare, and an attempt to revive language through an ascetic disciplined ritual of silence and self-loss . . ." (68).[63] In the only other critical analysis of DeLillo's work to appear in the 1970s, Michael Oriad surveyed the main characters of DeLillo's first four novels and found them similarly obsessed with discovering "the source of life's meaning" (6).[64] Oriad read these works as a thematically connected quartet that together constitute a larger novel, and he concluded that while these works do not provide answers to the big questions in life, they do "establish DeLillo as an important original voice in contemporary fiction" (23).

Another early treatment of DeLillo was an admiring chapter in Robert Nadeau's 1981 monograph *Readings from the New Book on Nature: Physics and Metaphysics in the Modern Novel*. Situating DeLillo amidst six other American novelists whose works concern the metaphysical implications of contemporary scientific paradigm shifts, Nadeau read DeLillo's work as expressive of the belief that the predominance of closed, binary modes of thought will ultimately lead to humanity's obliteration, and that reworking our use of language might effect a more genuine, accurate contact with reality. Adumbrating Tom LeClair's full-blown explication of DeLillo as a "systems novelist," Nadeau read DeLillo as an author who rails against "closed systems of abstraction that tend toward closure."[65] Nadeau offered a brief, useful overview of each of DeLillo's first six novels, but he concluded, diffusely, that DeLillo's "concern about the future is earnest and extremely thoughtful" (181).

Academic interest in DeLillo's work roused only on occasion during the early 1980s. Fredric Jameson, the eminent literary critic and cartographer of postmodernity, praised *The Names* in the *Minnesota Review*, where he described the novel as such a "delicious experience" that he read it twice,[66] but few full-scale analyses appeared. Tom LeClair published an extensive interview with DeLillo in a prominent literary journal in 1982, then reprinted the interview in a collection the next year.[67] Despite the depth and complexity of *The Names*, which appeared in 1982, only with the publication of *White Noise* in 1985 did scholarly interest in DeLillo's fiction begin to simmer. Many readers considered this novel the fulfillment of DeLillo's promise as a writer, and academic interest in his work has continued to increase ever since.

The first book-length analysis of DeLillo's fiction appeared in 1987, Tom LeClair's *In the Loop: Don DeLillo and the Systems Novel*. Echoing DeLillo's own wide-ranging ambition, LeClair attempts a comprehensive critique by positioning DeLillo in the context of the twentieth-century developments in science, philosophy, culture, and literature. After a review of Ludwig Von Bertalanffy's "systems theory," LeClair proceeds to place DeLillo within contemporary American literary trends, describing him (along with Robert Coover, William Gaddis, and Thomas Pynchon) as a "systems novelist." In his meticulous explication of DeLillo's first eight novels, LeClair demonstrates that their seemingly random, plotless nature is part of an intentional and ultimately hopeful critique of the twentieth century. DeLillo's avoidance of conventional plots, LeClair argues, is a metafictional strategy in his analysis of the open-ended, endlessly reciprocal nature of social systems. LeClair also examines many previously uninvestigated features of DeLillo's novels, as well as possible connections between the fiction and the author. LeClair discerns, for example, the influence of DeLillo's Catholic upbringing on his persistent depictions of what some readers identify as a quasi-religious mysticism in his novels. *In the Loop* thus lays much of the foundation for subsequent consideration of DeLillo's work. LeClair initiates as well a debate that still continues over whether DeLillo should be classified as a postmodernist or as a contemporary modernist (LeClair argues for the latter).

As previously noted, the acclaim accorded *White Noise* was amplified in 1988 by the release of *Libra*, which briefly enjoyed bestseller status and became a main selection of the Book-of-the-Month Club. In 1990, Frank Lentricchia edited an issue of the *South Atlantic Quarterly* devoted entirely to DeLillo's work. Subsequently published in book form as *Introducing Don DeLillo* (1991), the collection helped to secure a place for DeLillo in the contemporary canon of American literature. It includes Lentricchia's highly laudatory introduction and his essay on *Libra*, eight essays by other critics and historians on DeLillo novels, a chapter from *Ratner's Star*, and a previously published interview. Lentricchia makes an aggressive, insightful claim for DeLillo's importance in the introduction, where he writes of DeLillo's primary "mode" as that of "terrific [that is, terrifying] comedy": "It is the sort of mode that marks writers who conceive their vocation as an act of cultural criticism; who invent in order to intervene; whose work is a kind of anatomy, an effort to represent their culture in its totality; and who desire to move readers to the view that the shape and fate of their culture dictates the shape and fate of the self" (2).[68] Lentricchia effectively places DeLillo's work in opposition to predominant literary trends of the time, particularly those defined by regionally marked, heartfelt realism. (Ironically, *Underworld* has been praised for its realistic treatment of Italian immigrant life in the Bronx.) Lentricchia responds as well to conservative attacks against DeLillo leveled by Jonathan Yardley, Bruce Bawer, and George Will. Lentricchia's collection provides consistently excellent insight into DeLillo's novels, but its usefulness is marred by a lack of citations for quoted sources. Also in 1990, Cambridge University Press released another collection edited by Lentricchia, *New Essays on White Noise,* whose four essays implicitly argue for the novel's canonical stature (a stature recently reaffirmed by the 1998 publication of a Viking Critical Library edition of *White Noise,* edited by Mark Osteen, and by Penguin's 1999 reissue of the novel in its Great Books of the 20th Century series).[69]

Scholarly interest in DeLillo's work rose steadily during the 1990s in the form of book chapters, essays in major journals, and dissertations,[70] and on the Internet. In 1994, Johns Hopkins University's online journal *Postmodern Culture: An Electronic Journal of Interdisciplinary Criticism* published a "DeLillo Cluster" of four outstanding essays (two of which, by Glen Scott Allen and Bill Millard, are reprinted here).[71] An extensive, helpful Web site, "Don DeLillo's America," has been developed and dutifully updated by Curt Gardner.[72] Also, in 1993, Douglas Keesey's full-length introduction to DeLillo's work, *Don DeLillo,* appeared in Twayne's United States Authors Series.[73] In the fall of 1999, *Modern Fiction Studies* published *DeLillo II,* a collection of essays devoted entirely to DeLillo's work.

Keesey offers a chapter on each of DeLillo's first 10 novels, as well as a brief discussion of his plays, stories, essays, and the pseudonymously authored *Amazons.* After explaining DeLillo's consistent interest in mediated versions of reality, Keesey focuses his discussion of each novel on an analysis of the medium it foregrounds—film in *Americana,* language in *End Zone,* music in *Great Jones Street,* and so on. Keesey's introductions to these issues are consistently solid, but his discussion is grounded by a discordantly humanistic conception of the individual and experience. Most would agree with Keesey that DeLillo depicts the threats posed to individual autonomy and contact with reality by different sorts of media. However, many critics would disagree with Keesey's assumption that DeLillo depicts these media as getting in the way of some unadulterated access to one's "true" self and to "genuine" contact with reality—the critical tendency is to read DeLillo's work instead as a series of repeated assertions, despairing or not, that while release from controlled, dictated, and mediated experience and conceptions of oneself is desirable, escape into purified, unmediated identities and experience is impossible. Nevertheless, Keesey's book offers a useful introduction for readers unfamiliar with DeLillo's methods and themes.

Several other recent book-length critical works include useful chapters on DeLillo. In *Nobody's Home: Speech, Self, and Place in American Fiction from Hawthorne to DeLillo* (1993), Arnold Weinstein also addresses DeLillo's depictions of mediated identities, finding in DeLillo and a 150-year span of other American authors an assertion that a stable sense of self can be found through resistance to the constraints of language. Weighing in on the social constructivist side, Weinstein writes at the outset that "[o]ur culture and history bind us in ways beyond our control. . . . the individual as free agent is a tarnished notion, a fully discredited and perhaps dangerous myth."[74] At the same time, Weinstein reads in DeLillo a consistent desire for freedom, particularly a desire to realize an identity on one's own terms, a desire that works itself out through language. Weinstein eloquently unveils much in his rather freewheeling discussions of *The Names, White Noise,* and *Libra,* particularly in regard to DeLillo's obsessions with the shaping powers of language; he also demonstrates how brilliantly structured these three seemingly aimless, plotless novels are. Crediting DeLillo with ingeniously exposing the power of social forces to shape individuals' lives and personalities, Weinstein focuses finally on the depiction in *Libra* of Lee Harvey Oswald as "the definitive portrait of the American Nobody, the man seeking to construct himself while being constructed by forces beyond his ken" (314).

Paul Civello makes a more direct attempt to situate DeLillo's work within American literary tradition in *American Literary Naturalism and Its Twentieth-Century Transformations: Frank Norris, Ernest Hemingway, and Don DeLillo* (1995).[75] In three chapters, Civello places DeLillo's work both within and without the American Naturalist tradition. DeLillo's fiction, Civello writes, "undoes 'classical' naturalism, for in many ways the new physics and systems theory that DeLillo incorporates in his fiction undermines the basic scientific assumptions on which literary naturalism was based: classical physics, positivism, and various interpretations of Darwinian evolution" (112). Civello reads *End Zone,* for instance, as an exposure of the worn-out parallels between Christianity and classical science and of their ultimately fictive attempts to impose order on a chaotic, polymorphous reality. Emmett Creed, the football coach at Logos College, functions for Civello as the resident deity of a hermetically sealed system, lording over players who accept his orders as beyond their understanding. Protagonist Gary Harkness enjoys the simplicity of the closed system of football, but during his repeated trips into seemingly empty desert space, he comes to realize that much of what is "real" is left unaccounted for by humanity's limited epistemological constructs. Civello reserves his highest praise for *Libra,* whose depiction of Lee Harvey Oswald's inability to follow through on a conceived life-plot is a perfect undoing and rebuilding of the naturalist novel for postmodernity. Whereas the traditional naturalist characters operated in a universe driven by presumably knowable, measurable laws, DeLillo's Oswald demonstrates that the "individual must now try to locate himself in and reconcile himself to [a] new world of nonlinear causality and uncertainty, the comforts of the old order—knowability and the subsequent possibility of control or 'mastery' over the external world—no longer available to him" (141).

John McClure's *Late Imperial Romance,* with a long, perceptive chapter focused on the novels from *Players* to *Mao II,* views DeLillo in the context of postcolonial and global capitalism. McClure finds in DeLillo a novelist who both questions and rejects the premises of Western imperialism in the twentieth century but who also declines to endorse or even to recognize the struggle of its victims. DeLillo's refusal to take a "political" position against imperialism McClure takes to be either acquiescence to Western values and a rejection of the less civilized non-Western world or, in the case of *Mao II,* an endorsement of the Western world as the center of civilization and of all things virtuous. While McClure finds that the early novels critique the basic assumptions of Western hegemony, he finds *Mao II* a disturbing work that by identifying the East with religious cults, terrorism, and other amorphous sources of evil "tends to legitimate Western intervention and domination, rather than to interrogate it" and that treats in a reductive manner the voices, history, and problems of the East.[76]

A clear corpus of critical discussion has gathered around many of DeLillo's works, each with its own areas of interest and debate. Criticism on DeLillo's first novel, *Americana,* has focused largely on the novel's structure and its depictions of the incursions of mass media into human consciousness. The first extensive critique appeared in LeClair's *In the Loop.* LeClair argues that DeLillo's first novel is his most underrated and that it is much more carefully structured than it seems. Utilizing Gregory Bateson's concept of "the double bind," LeClair demonstrates that the novel draws incisive "analogues between the family system and the cultural system" and shows "how consciousness is furrowed and grooved by precisely those devices [the technologies of mass communications] that should set it free."[77] In "For Whom Bell Tolls: Don DeLillo's *Americana,*" David Cowart argues that protagonist David Bell's effort to capture America on film is an Oedipal quest to recover the lost connection with his mother, and that DeLillo comments in the novel on "the canker that rots the larger American innocence" by figuring America itself in terms of woman and/or mother.[78] In another illuminating essay on *Americana* and other early DeLillo works, Mark Osteen takes his cue from a comment DeLillo once made acknowledging filmmaker Jean-Luc Godard as an influence. Osteen effectively identifies the novel's concern with cinematic representation, demonstrating that it shows how film has "contributed to the commodification of consciousness that turns human agents" into automatized actors (439).[79]

While the ostensible focus of *End Zone* on football led many early reviewers and critics to consider DeLillo a sports novelist, subsequent criticism has centered on its complex meditations on language and epistemology. In a relatively early discussion of *End Zone,* Gary Storoff reads these meditations as ultimately nihilistic. Storoff regards DeLillo's depiction of the ordered fictional universe of football as representative of all of humanity's systems of meaning that we construct in our attempts to deny the irrationality of chaos.[80] Jill Benton agrees with those who would label *End Zone* "a quintessential football novel," but she places it in the genre of Menippean satire as well, then excavates many of its satiric inquisitions into oppressive forms of systematized discourse.[81] Similarly, Françoise Happe focuses on issues of genre by comparing the novel to Robert Coover's *The Universal Baseball Association, Inc., J. Henry Waugh, Prop.* (1971). Happe asserts that both novels subvert the narrative conventions of the sports novel genre in order to "contest the power structures that shape our world . . . by prodding us into an awareness of the way ideologies are relayed by popular culture" (175).[82] In "Deconstructing the Logos: Don DeLillo's *End Zone*," Tom LeClair offers (in a shorter version, reprinted here, of a chapter from *In the Loop*) a Derridean analysis of the novel, explaining how it deconstructs logocentric thought by demonstrating that such singlemindedness as that exemplified by Coach Creed makes "apparent a logocentric way of thinking that everywhere destroys nature."[83] In "Against the End: Asceticism in Don DeLillo's *End Zone*," Mark Osteen to some extent echoes LeClair's general contentions regarding the open-endedness of DeLillo's novels, asserting that in a metafictional mode, this novel exposes "the intimate connection between the need for fictional closure and the desire for the end of the world" (162). By writing about the deterministic drive toward endings in football and the stockpiling of nuclear arms in a work that does not end conclusively, DeLillo ironically, and hopefully, writes "a nuclear novel that is not apocalyptic" (163).[84]

Along with *Ratner's Star, Players,* and *Running Dog, Great Jones Street* has attracted relatively few analyses. Perhaps many agree with Nadeau's assessment of this tale of reclusive rock star Bucky Wunderlick as "DeLillo's least impressive, most transparent narrative . . ." (168). Anthony DeCurtis concurs in an essay in *Introducing Don DeLillo* that *Great Jones Street* is "not one of [DeLillo's] highly regarded novels" (131).[85] However, from his position as a senior writer for *Rolling Stone* (with a Ph.D. in English), DeCurtis interprets the efforts of nearly every character in the novel to capitalize financially from the woes of Wunderlick as an accurate allegory for the voracious appetites of American capitalism: "Everything is consumed, or it consumes itself. . . . After a decade [the eighties] of rampant market economics and amidst regular announcements of the worldwide triumph of capitalism—smug, dumb declarations of how the West has won—can the world DeLillo portrays in *Great Jones Street* not seem painfully familiar?" (140). In another of his several insightful essays on DeLillo's work, Osteen sees a parallel between Wunderlick's withdrawal in disgust from the morally repugnant excesses of American society and that of Henry David Thoreau in *Walden*. The crucial difference, though, as Osteen writes, is that Wunderlick's silence "comes to be seen as merely another form of excess. As his silence and even his suicidal impulses are appropriated by a commodity culture hungry for violence, he becomes the victim of his own and his audience's craving for sacrifices" (157).[86] Osteen also considers the irresistible parallel to be drawn between reclusive rock star Bucky Wunderlick and reclusive writer Don DeLillo.

Ratner's Star has repeatedly garnered favorable comparisons to Thomas Pynchon's work, not only for its ambitious, ostensibly similar immersions in the stuff of science fiction, but also for the intricate complexities of its structure, subject matter, and themes. As William D. Atwill writes, "*Ratner's Star* is linked to *Gravity's Rainbow* not merely by its encyclopedic aspirations, its deployment of recent theoretical and mathematical concepts, and its satirical wit, but also in the way both works question the wisdom of placing the world's fate solely in the hands of scientists and technocrats."[87] Nevertheless, despite the consistent respect this novel receives, few full-scale attempts have been made to critique it. As Tom LeClair wrote in the late 1980s (his own exhaustive chapter in *In the Loop* notwithstanding), "Unfortunately, DeLillo's most theoretically sophisticated and intellectually demanding book has received little engagement or understanding from academic critics who, if they write on DeLillo at all, usually dodge the monster that hulks at the center of his career."[88] There have been significant exceptions. Robert Nadeau offered an early assessment of the novel in 1981.[89] In "Don DeLillo's Perfect Starry Night," Charles Molesworth ponders some of the novel's less tangible features, including its many paradoxes, its jarring depiction of poverty as "less a privation than a separate source of plentitude" (156), and occasional moments of sublime lyricism amidst so much scientific, mathematical, and philosophical abstraction (as in a description of an anachronistic kite-flying competition).[90] Glen Scott Allen also explicates some of the connections to be made between this work and Thomas Pynchon's *Gravity's Rainbow.* Focusing in particular on the depictions in both works of paranoia and terror, Allen demonstrates that DeLillo's response to these phenomena "seems to argue for an almost romantic return to the sovereign powers of the individual—an entity considered essentially extinct in most theories of the postmodern subject."[91]

Of all of DeLillo's novels, his fifth, *Players,* has attracted the least scholarly interest. In a brief, early assessment, Michael Oriad reads *Players* as a bleak portrait of "disengaged people attempting to make life more than random interactions—and failing."[92] Crediting *Players* with being DeLillo's most subtle book, LeClair explicates the theme of doubles and argues that it reveals "to the careful reader mysterious motives of which the characters are unaware."[93] Most criticism of *Running Dog,* which depicts the search for a hypothetical pornographic film supposedly made in Hitler's bunker, centers on the novel's insights into the social roles played by cinematic representation. John Johnston reads the novel's quest for the hypothetical film as an example of "post-cinematic fiction." Such fiction, Johnston explains, "assumes a condition in which images define a new kind of reality in a world which seems to have entirely lost all substance, anchoring, or reference points, except in relation to other images or what are also conceived as images" (96).[94] Patrick O'Donnell agrees that cinematic mediation is central to the novel's commentary on the removed nature of contemporary experience; he also adds insightful consideration of literary mediation, reading the novel as an example of "hyperbolic intertextuality" that parodies the received generic formulae of such writers as Ernest Hemingway and Dashiell Hammett.[95] In a new essay included in this volume, Mark Osteen examines the connections in *Running Dog* between the depictions of history, pornography, fascism, the Nazi fascination with film, and the destructive realities of capitalism. As Osteen writes, "DeLillo mounts a complex contradiction of the enduring appeal of the fascist mentality, of the power of film to shape and record human subjectivity and history, and of the convergence of fascism and film in pornographic representation. The novel simultaneously investigates the fascinations of fascism and examines how such fascistic fascinations become marketable commodities."[96]

The general critical consensus regarding DeLillo's next novel, *The Names,* is that it represents an advance to a higher level of authorial maturity. Indeed, in 1987 LeClair wrote, "For all that *The Names* observes and connects, and for what its connections reveal about living on this round, large, and looping Earth, this novel is, I believe, DeLillo's best."[97] Weinstein also declares it "certain to gain in stature as DeLillo's novelistic stature becomes clearer to us in the coming years."[98] Critics have tended to read this novel's edgy portrayal of expatriates who encounter a cult that kills by matching the names of victims to the names of the locations where they happen to be as a meditation on the arbitrary strictures of language. In an essay included in this volume, Paula Bryant reads protagonist James Axton's travels abroad as a movement away from such strictures toward "an exuberant, unsettling demonstration of the potential for human freedom in the deliberate disordering and recreation of language," as figured in young Tap Axton's intriguingly garbled narrative fragment (16).[99] Matthew J. Morris takes a closer look at the novel's language itself. In so doing, Morris finds in it an assertion that altering our use of language can reduce its potential for political and sexual oppression, particularly by "celebrating" the words *and* and *all:* "such a celebration excludes only one thing: exclusion, the basis of sexism, colonialism, and cult murders."[100] Paul A. Harris also reads the novel as an ultimately hopeful statement on the emancipatory potential of "reshaped" language, "new forms that reveal something unseen within their makeup" (201).[101]

DeLillo's next two novels, *White Noise* and *Libra,* have provoked far more analysis than his earlier or subsequent works, more than can be summarized here. In *White Noise,* DeLillo takes on a wider range of themes and subject matter than ever before, and the critical responses have been correspondingly various. The first full-length analysis was LeClair's extensive treatment in *In the Loop,* which reads the novel's depiction of protagonist Jack Gladney poking through his family's garbage as emblematic of both the "glut and blurt" of contemporary American society and of the book itself as a "novelistic heap of waste. . . . [that] recycles American waste into art to warn against entropy."[102] Several critics have followed the example of John Frow, who examined themes in the novel by using the work of postmodern French cultural theorist Jean Baudrillard, who has delineated the "hyperreal" or the "simulacrum" (a notion charted as well in regard to America by Italian novelist and theorist Umberto Eco). Frow and others have argued that DeLillo depicts in *White Noise* a contemporary shift in attention from reality to representations of reality, so that it "is no longer possible to distinguish meaningfully between a generality embedded in life and a generality embedded in representations of life" (178).[103] John Duvall and Leonard Wilcox offer two further, particularly effective analyses of these concerns in the novel. Duvall demonstrates that a specific manifestation of the simulacrum depicted by DeLillo ("mediations that pose as the immediate") is the discernible resemblances of "multinational or late capitalism," with its flattening out of "the social, political, and the aesthetic," to Nazi fascism (128).[104] In "Baudrillard, DeLillo's *White Noise*, and the End of Heroic Narrative," Wilcox interprets Jack Gladney as a "modernist displaced in a postmodern world," particularly in his tendency to hold on nostalgically to outmoded conceptions of himself. For Wilcox, DeLillo depicts in Gladney "the emergence of a new form of subjectivity colonized by the media and decentered by its polyglot discourses and electronic networks," adrift in a landscape where "heroic striving for meaning has been radically thrown into question."[105] In an essay for *Modern Fiction Studies,* Tim Engles examines the depiction of individual identity in *White Noise,* focusing on Jack Gladney as an exemplar of particularly white, middle-class male subjectivity. Engles unveils another element within this novel's intricate cultural critique, showing that it contains a "subtextual portrait of white American modes of racialized perception" that illustrates the ironically relational conceptions of individualized, white American identities.[106]

The construction of American identities is also a major area of critical interest in analyses of *Libra,* which closely portrays a possible life, and a possible consciousness, for Lee Harvey Oswald, accused assassin of President Kennedy. In an essay written shortly after the novel's release, Frank Lentricchia calls the novel a "postmodern critique," then explicates its concern with the pervasive influence of television. In particular, Lentricchia writes, the novel portrays "the charismatic environment of the image, a new phase in American literature and culture—a new arena of action and a power of determination whose major effect is to realign radically all social agents (from top to bottom) as first-person agents of desire seeking self-annihilation and fulfillment in the magical third" (198).[107] In "Libra and the Subject of History," Christopher Mott plays on the word *subject* in his title by tying DeLillo's portrait of Oswald's self-image to the novel's investigations of American conceptions of history. Drawing on cultural theorist Louis Althusser's notion of socially indoctrinated individuals as "interpellated subjects," Mott excavates the novel's depiction of America's demands on its people, finding a "contradiction between the image of the free and self-determining individual from whose success America grows stronger and the interpellation of the individual into a regimented position in which she or he will be ordered to give up his or her life. This is the contradiction between the autonomous and unique person and the culturally determined subject position, both of which exist . . . in the ideology of American government."[108] In "The Fable of the Ants: Myopic Interactions in DeLillo's *Libra*," Bill Millard also discusses American notions of autonomous individuality, but he focuses on social connections at the micro and the macro levels. Using mathematician Alfred Bruckstein's conception of "myopic interactions" (drawn from a study of ant behavior), Millard illuminates DeLillo's portrayal of the disconnection between individual intentions and ultimate outcomes. In DeLillo's depiction of a Kennedy assassination plot, the conspirators "are all maintained in a state of myopia throughout the process; the initial message [to be made by the assassination] is replaced by an antithetical counter-message and never reaches its true intended receiver, the politically responsible public."[109]

While *Mao II* has won praise from academic critics, this more recent novel has received fewer full-scale analyses than the two novels that preceded it. Margaret Scanlan compares the novel's portrait of an ultrareclusive writer, Bill Gray, to the Salman Rushdie affair. Scanlan takes DeLillo to task for the book's apparent pessimism about the faded roles available to today's writers, and for failing to distinguish among contemporary global forces that threaten both the individual author's place in the world and individuality itself: "DeLillo seems so intent on reproducing the forces that homogenize the world that he gives up on the possibility of reproducing its heterogeneity. If Karen conflates the Ayatollah and Mao with her Korean Master [Reverend Sun Myung Moon, head of the Unification Church], so does the novel, in its own rigorously synchronic portrayal of the Christian cult, Chinese Communism, and Islamic fundamentalism" (247).[110] Silvia Caporale Bizzini examines how the novel explores the role of the intellectual, specifically of the writer as intellectual, in a society dominated by visual images.[111] In a comparison of *Mao II* to Pynchon's *Vineland* and Neil Jordan's film *The Crying Game*, Peter Baker explores differing conceptions of the postmodern in these works and specifically considers the role of the terrorist as an interpreter of modern culture (a view that diverges from that of Bill Gray in *Mao II*).[112] Jeremy Green's essay "Last Days: Millennial Hysteria in Don DeLillo's *Mao II*" provides an incisive reading of the importance of crowds in the novel, especially as they project concerns about the future focused on the loss of individuality and on global culture.[113] Thomas Carmichael's essay "Lee Harvey Oswald and the Postmodern Subject: History and Intertextuality in Don DeLillo's *Libra, The Names,* and *Mao II*" considers the role of the photographic image in *Mao II* in defining the "field of the postmodern condition."[114]

The previously discussed reviews of *Underworld* were so extensive and so often intelligent that many of them are well worth consulting as an introduction to DeLillo's 1997 novel. The three essays on *Underworld* in this collection represent the critical response that is just beginning to appear. John Duvall's reading of "Pafko at the Wall" in 1995 gave some indication of what the major concerns might be of the novel to which it would serve as a first chapter.[115] A lengthened version of that essay, revised in light of the publication of *Underworld,* appears in this volume. Peter Knight, in "Everything Is Connected: Don DeLillo's Secret History of Paranoia," explores the roles of conspiracy, paranoia, and interconnectedness in the novel, concerns that are crucial both to the themes as well as to its basic narrative structure. Both Knight and Duvall focus in different ways on DeLillo's depictions of the impact of the Cold War in American life. Arthur Saltzman, in "Awful Symmetries in Don DeLillo's *Underworld,*" takes a wholly different approach to the novel in his consideration of the importance of the sublime and of the possibility of transcendence in the novel, "an interest that," Saltzman finds, "extends throughout DeLillo's fiction."[116] These essays, and others soon to appear, are mapping out the themes, issues, and other concerns that will occupy readers and critics of DeLillo's most ambitious and expansive of novels for years to come.

Notes

The editors wish to thank Kellie Borders, Sandra Hughes, and Katherine Montwieler for their assistance with the preparation of this volume.

1. DeLillo has also been prolific in other genres; he has published 14 short stories: "The River Jordan," *Epoch* 10, no. 2 (1960): 105–20; "Take the 'A' Train," *Epoch* 12, no. 1 (1962): 9–25, reprinted in *Stories from Epoch,* ed. Baxter Hathaway, 22–39 (Ithaca, N.Y.: Cornell University Press, 1966); "Spaghetti and Meatballs," *Epoch* 14, no. 3 (1965): 244–50; "Coming Sun. Mon. Tues.," *Kenyon Review* 28, no. 3 (1966): 391–94; "Baghdad Towers West," *Epoch* 17, no. 3 (1968): 195–217; "The Uniforms," *Carolina Quarterly* 22, no. 1 (1970): 4–11, reprinted in *Cutting Edges: Young American Fiction for the '70s,* ed. Jack Hicks, 451–59 (New York: Holt, 1973); "In the Men's Room of the Sixteenth Century," *Esquire,* December 1971, 174–77, 243, 246, reprinted in *The Secret Life of Our Times: New Fiction from Esquire,* ed. Gordon Lish, 65–69 (New York: Doubleday, 1973); "Total Loss Weekend," *Sports Illustrated,* 27 November 1972, 98–120; "Creation," *Antaeus* 33 (1979): 32–46; "Human Moments in World War III," *Esquire,* July 1983, 118–26, reprinted in *Great Esquire Fiction: The Finest Stories from the First Fifty Years,* ed. L. Rust Hills, 572–86 (New York: Viking, 1983), also reprinted in *Lust, Violence, Sin, Magic: 60 Years of Esquire Fiction,* ed. L. Rust Hills, Will Blythe, and Erika Mansourian, 553–66 (New York: Atlantic, 1993); "The Runner," *Harper's* 277 (September 1988): 61–63; "The Ivory Acrobat," *Granta* 25 (1988): 199–212; "Pafko at the Wall," *Harper's* 285 (October 1992): 35–70, edited and reprinted as "The Triumph of Death," in *Underworld* (New York: Scribner's, 1997), 11–60; "The Angel Esmerelda," *Esquire,* May 1994, 100–109, reprinted in *The Best American Short Stories 1995,* ed. Jane Smiley and Katrina Kenison, 263–83 (New York: Houghton, 1995), also reprinted as a section of *Underworld,* 237–50, 814–24. DeLillo has also published four dramas: *The Engineer of Moonlight,* in *Cornell Review* 5 (1979): 21–47; *The Day*

Room, Special Insert, *American Theatre* 3, no. 6 (September 1986): 1–12, reprinted by Knopf, 1987; *The Rapture of the Athlete Assumed into Heaven,* in *Quarterly* 15 (1990): 6–7, reprinted in *Harper's* (December 1990): 44, also reprinted in *South Atlantic Quarterly* 91, no. 2 (1992): 241–42, also reprinted in *After Yesterday's Crash: The Avant-Pop Anthology,* ed. Larry McCaffery, 88–89 (New York: Penguin, 1995); and *Valparaiso* (New York: Scribner's, 1999). DeLillo has also published six essays, each of which helps to illuminate his literary efforts: "Notes toward a Definitive Meditation (By Someone Else) on the Novel *Americana,*" *Epoch* 21, no. 3 (1972): 327–29; "American Blood: A Journey through the Labyrinth of Dallas and JFK," *Rolling Stone,* 8 December 1983, 21–22, 24, 27, 28, 74; "Silhouette City: Hitler, Manson, and the Millennium," *Dimensions: A Journal of Holocaust Studies* 4, no. 3 (1989): 29–34; *Salman Rushdie Defense Pamphlet* (New York: Rushdie Defense Committee USA, 1994); "The Artist Naked in a Cage," *New Yorker,* 26 May 1997, 6–7; "The Power of History," *New York Times Magazine,* 7 September 1997, 60–63.

2. Christopher Lehmann-Haupt, "Old Story, Fresh Language," *New York Times,* 6 May 1971, 41.

3. Nelson Algren, review of *Americana, Rolling Stone,* 5 August 1971, 52.

4. Joyce Carol Oates, "Young Man at the Brink of Self-Destruction," *Detroit Evening News,* 27 June 1971, 5-E.

5. Christopher Lehmann-Haupt, "A Touchdown for Don DeLillo," *New York Times,* 22 March 1972, 45.

6. Nelson Algren, "A Waugh in Shoulder Padding," *Los Angeles Times Book Review,* 26 March 1972, 2, 7.

7. Roger Sale, "I Am a Novel," *New York Review of Books,* 29 June 1972, 28–31.

8. S. K. Oberbeck, "A Kick in the Head," *Washington Post Book World,* 16 April 1972, 15.

9. Sara Blackburn, "Great Jones Street," *New York Times Book Review,* 22 April 1973, 2.

10. Christopher Lehmann-Haupt, "DeLillo Runs out of Bounds," *New York Times,* 16 April 1973, 35.

11. Webster Schott, "Great Jones Street," *Washington Post Book World,* 15 April 1973, 1–2.

12. Nelson Algren, "Musical Chairs in a Rock 'n' Roll Throne Room," *Los Angeles Times Book Review,* 24 June 1973, 1, 8.

13. Nelson Algren, "Ratner's Star Just Fails to Twinkle," *Los Angeles Times Book Review,* 11 July 1976, 10.

14. J. D. O'Hara, "Your Number Is Up," *Washington Post Book World,* 13 June 1976, M3.

15. Christopher Lehmann-Haupt, "Kafka and Einstein Meet," *New York Times,* 27 May 1976, 33.

16. Stephen Koch, "End Game," *Harper's* 255 (September 1977): 88, 90.

17. William Kennedy, "The Flowers Are All Poison: Our Man in Ayer Hitam," *Washington Post Book World,* 21 August 1977, G1, G4.

18. J. D. O'Hara, "Two Mandarin Stylists," *Nation,* 17 September 1977, 250–52.

19. Diane Johnson, "Beyond Radical Chic," *New York Times Book Review,* 4 September 1977, 1, 16.

20. John Updike, "Layers of Ambiguity," *New Yorker,* 27 March 1978, 127–28.

21. Thomas LeClair, review of *Running Dog, New Republic,* 7 October 1978, 33–34.

22. Anthony Burgess, "No Health Anywhere," *Saturday Review,* 16 September 1978, 38.

23. Michael Wood, review of *Running Dog, New York Times Book Review,* 12 November 1978, 14, 76.

24. Debra Rae Cohen, "De Wild, De Wicked, De Fuhrer, and DeLillo," *Crawdaddy,* October 1978, 13, 16.

25. Curt Suplee, review of *Running Dog, Washington Post Book World,* 15 October 1978, E1, E4.

26. J. D. O'Hara, "A Pro's Puckish Prose," *Nation,* 18 October 1980, 385–86; Christopher Lehmann-Haupt, "Books of the Times," *New York Times,* 16 September 1980, C16.

27.   David Bosworth, "The Fiction of Don DeLillo," *Boston Review* 8 (April 1983): 30; Robert Towers, "A Dark Art," *New Republic,* 22 November 1982, 32–34; Frances Taliaferro, "Fiction," *Harper's* 265 (December 1982): 70–71; Josh Rubins, "Variety Shows," *New York Review of Books,* 16 December 1982, 46–48; Jonathan Yardley, "Don DeLillo's Terminology of Terror," *Washington Post Book World,* 10 October 1982, 3.

28.   Michael Wood, "Americans on the Prowl," *New York Times Book Review,* 10 October 1982, 1, 27.

29.   Towers, "A Dark Art," 34.

30.   J. D. O'Hara, "Analyzing the Risks," *Nation,* 11 December 1982, 630–32.

31.   Yardley, "Don DeLillo's Terminology of Terror," 3; O'Hara, "Analyzing the Risks," 630–32; Fredric Jameson, review of Don DeLillo, *The Names,* and Sol Yurick, *Richard A., Minnesota Review* 22 (Spring 1984): 116–122; Christopher Lehmann-Haupt, "Books of the Times," review of *The Names, New York Times,* 12 October 1982, C13; Taliaferro, "Fiction," 70–71; Rubins, "Variety Shows," 47; Wood, "Americans on the Prowl," 1.

32.   Towers, "A Dark Art," 34; Bosworth, "The Fiction of Don DeLillo," 30.

33.   Robert Phillips, review of *White Noise, America,* 6–13 July 1985, 16.

34.   Bruce Bawer, "Don DeLillo's America," *New Criterion* 3 (April 1985): 34–42.

35.   Thomas M. Disch, "Maximum Exposure," *Nation,* 2 February 1985, 120–21.

36.   Thomas DePietro, "Laughing through the Malls," *Commonweal,* 5 April 1985, 219–20.

37.   Christopher Lehmann-Haupt, "Books of the Times," *New York Times,* 7 January 1985, C18.

38.   Jayne Anne Phillips, "Crowding Out Death," *New York Times Book Review,* 13 January 1985, 1, 30–31.

39.   Jay McInerney, "Midwestern Wasteland," *New Republic,* 4 February 1985, 36–39.

40.   Diane Johnson, "Conspirators," *New York Review of Books,* 14 March 1985, 6–7.

41.   George Will, "Shallow Look at the Mind of an Assassin," *Washington Post,* 22 September 1988, A25.

42.   Jonathan Yardley, "Appointment in Dallas," *Washington Post Book World,* 31 July 1988, 3.

43.   Cecilia Tichi, "Walking the Line," *Boston Review* 13 (October 1988): 16; Merle Rubin, "More Fiction Than Fact," *Christian Science Monitor,* 12 September 1988, 18.

44.   Richard Eder, "Imagining the Kennedy Assassination: *Libra," Los Angeles Times Book Review,* 31 July 1988, 3–8.

45.   Anonymous, review of *Libra, Playboy* 35 (September 1988): 21.

46.   Terrence Rafferty, "Self-Watcher," *New Yorker,* 26 September 1988, 108–10.

47.   Christopher Lehmann-Haupt, "Pilgrim's Regress in Dallas, Late '63," *New York Times,* 18 July 1988, C15.

48.   John Leonard, "Scripts, Plots, and Codes," *Nation,* 19 September 1996, 205–8.

49.   Anne Tyler, "Dallas, Echoing down the Decades," *New York Times Book Review,* 24 July 1988, 1.

50.   See, for example, Eder, "Imagining the Kennedy Assassination: *Libra*"; Robert Towers, "From the Grassy Knoll," *New York Review of Books,* 18 August 1988, 6; Walter Clemmons, "Appointment in Dallas," *Newsweek,* 15 August 1988, 59; Lenny Glynn, "The Mind of an Assassin," *Macleans,* 29 August 1988, 50.

51.   Sven Birkerts, "The Future Belongs to Crowds," *Washington Post Book World,* 26 May 1991, 1–2.

52.   For examples, see Dennis Kucherawy, "Reign of Terrorism," *Macleans,* 12 August 1991, 43; David Homel, "Can the Writer Prevail over the Terrorist?" *Toronto Star,* 29 June 1991, F1; Louis Menand, "Market Report," *New Yorker,* 24 June 1991, 81–84.

53.   Robert Towers, review of *Mao II, New York Review of Books,* 27 June 1991, 17; Martin Amis, "Thoroughly Post-modern Millennium; *Mao II,*—Don DeLillo," *Independent* (Lon-

don), 8 September 1991, 28. Anthony Quinn notes the "masterly grip" of *Libra* but takes issue with the "rather shabby equation of novelists and terrorists" in *Mao II*, which "as a novel is wordy, windy and very, very dull." "Prisoner: Writer's Block, USA," *Macleans*, 14 September 1991, 28.

54.   Lorrie Moore, "Look for a Writer and Find a Terrorist," *New York Times Book Review*, 9 June 1991, 7, 49; Menand, "Market Report."

55.   Birkerts, "The Future Belongs to Crowds"; Moore, "Look for a Writer and Find a Terrorist"; Michiko Kakutani, "Fighting against Envelopment by the Mass Mind," *New York Times*, 28 May 1991, C15; Donn Fry, " 'Mao II' Author Probes Riveting World of Ideas," *Atlanta Journal-Constitution*, 14 July 1991, N10; Paul Skenazy, "DeLillo's Elegy to Language," *San Francisco Chronicle*, 9 June 1991, Sunday Review, 1.

56.   James Wood, "Black Noise," *New Republic*, 10 November 1997, 38–44. See also Walter Kirn, "Airborne Toxic Event: Don DeLillo's Latest Novel of Ideas," *Slate*, 23 September 1997, 1 September 1999 <http://www.slate.com/BookReview/97–09–23/BookReview.asp>.

57.   James Gardner, "The Los Angeles of Novels," *National Review*, 24 November 1997, 60–61. Gardner's criticisms grow out of his basic objection to the kinds of novels DeLillo writes, works that do not incorporate elements of the traditionally structured novel where developed plots and characters hold sway. A similar view is expressed by Daniel J. Silver, "Waste Management," *Commentary* 104 (December 1997): 63–65. See also Paul Elie, "DeLillo's Surrogate Believers," *Commonweal*, 7 November 1997, 19–22, where the novel is criticized for playing "fast and loose with the ideas about religion that [DeLillo] has humanized more successfully in earlier books." See also James Wolcott, "Blasts from the Past," *New Criterion* 16, no. 4 (1997): 65–70.

58.   Vince Passaro, "The Unsparing Vision of Don DeLillo," *Harper's* 295 (November 1997): 72–75.

59.   David Wiegand, "We Are What We Waste," *San Francisco Chronicle*, 21 September 1997, 1.

60.   Paul Gediman, "Visions of the American Berserk," *Boston Review* 22 (October/ November 1997): 46–48.

61.   Andrew O'Hagan, "The National Enquirer," *Village Voice*, 16 September 1997, 8–10; John Leonard, "American Jitters," *Nation*, 3 November 1997, 18–24; Tom LeClair, "An Underhistory of Midcentury America," *Atlantic Monthly* 280 (October 1997): 113–116; Michael Wood, "Post-Paranoid," *London Review of Books*, 5 February 1998, 3–4; Paul Gray, "How Did We Get Here?" *Time*, 29 September 1997, 89–90; Blake Morrison, "*Underworld* by Don DeLillo," *Independent* (London), 4 January 1998, 24; Gary Lee Stonum, "Seeking America's Secret Truths: Batting around Ideas from the Bronx," *Plain Dealer*, 21 September 1997, 11-I; Millicent Bell, "Fiction Chronicle," *Partisan Review*, 65 (Spring 1998): 259–72; Luc Sante, "Between Hell and History," *New York Review of Books*, 6 November 1997, 4–7; Irving Malin, "*Underworld*," *Review of Contemporary Fiction* 17 (Fall 1997): 217–19; Michiko Kakutani, " 'Underworld': Of America as a Splendid Junk Heap," *New York Times Book Review*, 16 September 1997; Martin Amis, "Survivors of the Cold War," *New York Times Book Review*, 5 October 1997, 7, 12; Michael Dirda, "The Blast Felt round the World," *Washington Post Book World*, 28 September 1997, 1, 10.

62.   William Burke, "Football, Literature, Culture," *Southwest Review* 60 (1975): 391–98.

63.   Anya Taylor, "Words, War, and Meditation in Don DeLillo's *End Zone*," *International Fiction Review* 4 (1977): 68–70.

64.   Michael Oriad, "Don DeLillo's Search for Walden Pond," *Critique: Studies in Modern Fiction* 20, no. 1 (1978): 5–24.

65.   Robert Nadeau, *Readings from the New Book on Nature: Physics and Metaphysics in the Modern Novel* (Amherst: University of Massachusetts Press, 1981), 173.

66.   Jameson, review of Don DeLillo, *The Names*, and Sol Yurick, *Richard A.*, 119.

67. Tom LeClair, "An Interview with Don DeLillo," *Contemporary Literature* 23, no. 1 (1982): 19–31. LeClair, one of DeLillo's most insightful and comprehensive critics, deserves credit for drawing academic attention to DeLillo's work in the eighties. In addition to *In the Loop: Don DeLillo and the Systems Novel* (Urbana: University of Illinois Press, 1987), he also published an argument for the significance of *Ratner's Star* ("Postmodern Mastery," in *Postmodern Fiction: A Bio-Bibliographical Guide,* ed. Larry McCaffery [New York: Greenwood Press, 1986], 117–28) and an illuminating essay on *End Zone* ("Deconstructing the Logos: Don DeLillo's *End Zone,*" *Modern Fiction Studies* 33 [Spring 1987]: 105–23).

68. Frank Lentricchia, "The American Writer as Bad Citizen," in *Introducing Don DeLillo,* ed. Frank Lentricchia (Durham, N.C.: Duke University Press, 1991), 1–6.

69. Lentricchia, "The American Writer as Bad Citizen"; Lentricchia, ed., *New Essays on White Noise* (New York: Cambridge University Press, 1991); Mark Osteen, ed., *Don DeLillo, White Noise: Text and Criticism* (New York: Penguin Books, 1998); Don DeLillo, *White Noise* (New York: Penguin, 1999).

70. The MLA bibliography lists more than a dozen dissertations on DeLillo.

71. "DeLillo Cluster," *Postmodern Culture: An Electronic Journal of Interdisciplinary Criticism* 4, no. 2 (1994), ed. Glen Scott Allen and Stephen Bernstein, 10 January 2000 <http://muse.jhu.edu/journals/postmodern_culture/toc/pmcv004.html#v004.2>.

72. *Don DeLillo's America* <http://www.perival.com/delillo>.

73. Douglas Keesey, *Don DeLillo* (New York: Twayne, 1993).

74. Arnold Weinstein, *Nobody's Home: Speech, Self, and Place in American Fiction from Hawthorne to DeLillo* (New York: Oxford University Press, 1993), 3.

75. Paul Civello, *American Literary Naturalism and Its Twentieth-Century Transformations: Frank Norris, Ernest Hemingway, Don DeLillo* (Athens: University of Georgia Press, 1994).

76. John McClure, *Late Imperial Romance* (New York: Verso, 1994), 122, 145.

77. LeClair, *In the Loop,* 33.

78. David Cowart, "For Whom Bell Tolls: Don DeLillo's *Americana,*" *Contemporary Literature* 37, no.4 (1996): 602–19.

79. Mark Osteen, "Children of Godard and Coca-Cola: Cinema and Consumerism in Don DeLillo's Early Fiction," *Contemporary Literature* 37, no. 3 (Fall 1996): 439–70. For further analysis of *Americana,* see Michael Oriad, "Don DeLillo's Search for Walden Pond," *Critique* 20, no. 1 (1978): 5–24; Neil D. Isaacs, "Out of the End Zone: Sports in the Rest of DeLillo," *Arete* 3, no. 1 (1985): 85–95; John Johnston, "Generic Difficulties in the Novels of Don DeLillo," *Critique* 30, no. 4 (1989): 261–75; Eric Mottram, "The Real Needs of Man: Don DeLillo's Novels," in *The New American Writing: Essays on American Literature since 1970,* ed. Graham Clarke (New York: St. Martin's Press, 1990): 51–98; Nadeau, *Readings,* 162–65; Daniel Aaron, "How to Read Don DeLillo," in Lentricchia, *Introducing Don DeLillo,* 67–81; Adam Begley, "Don DeLillo: *Americana, Mao II,* and *Underworld,*" *Southwest Review* 82, no. 4 (1997): 478–505.

80. Gary Storoff, "The Failure of Games in Don DeLillo's *End Zone,*" *American Sport Culture: The Humanistic Dimensions,* ed. Wiley Lee Umphlett, 235–45 (Lewisburg, Penn.: Bucknell University Press, 1985).

81. Jill Benton, "Don DeLillo's *End Zone:* A Postmodern Satire," *Aethlon: The Journal of Sport Literature* 12, no. 1 (1994): 7–18.

82. Françoise Happe, "Fiction vs. Power: The Postmodern American Sports Novel," in *Narrative Turns and Minor Genres in Postmodernism,* ed. Theo D'haen and Hans Bertens, 157–75 (Amsterdam: Rodopi, 1995).

83. LeClair, *In the Loop,* 119.

84. Mark Osteen, "Against the End: Asceticism and Apocalypse in Don DeLillo's *End Zone,*" *Papers on Language and Literature: A Journal for Scholars and Critics of Language and Literature* 26, no. 1 (1990): 143–63. For further discussion of *End Zone,* see Neil David Berman,

Playful Fictions and Fictional Players: Game, Sport, and Survival in Contemporary American Fiction (Port Washington, N.Y.: National University Publications, 1981); Nadeau, *Readings*; J. K. Higginbotham, "The 'Queer' in Don DeLillo's *End Zone*," *Notes on Contemporary Literature* 19, no. 1 (1989): 5–7; Mottram, "The Real Needs of Man"; François Happe, "Voix et authorite dans *End Zone*, de Don DeLillo," *Revue Francaise d'Etudes Americaines* 54 (1992): 385–93; Civello, "*End Zone*: The End of the Old Order," in *American Literary Naturalism*; Z. Bart Thornton, "Linguistic Disenchantment and Architectural Solace in DeLillo and Artaud," *Mosaic: A Journal for the Interdisciplinary Study of Literature* 30 (1997): 97–112.

85. Anthony DeCurtis, "The Product: Bucky Wunderlick, Rock 'n Roll, and Don DeLillo's *Great Jones Street*," in Lentricchia, *Introducing Don DeLillo*, 131–41.

86. Mark Osteen, " 'A Moral Form to Master Commerce': The Economies of DeLillo's *Great Jones Street*," *Critique: Studies in Contemporary Fiction* 35, no. 3 (1994): 157–72. For further discussion of *Great Jones Street*, see Oriad, "Don DeLillo's Search for Walden Pond"; LeClair, *In the Loop*; Nadeau, *Readings*.

87. William D. Atwill, *Fire and Power: The American Space Program as Postmodern Narrative* (Athens: University of Georgia Press, 1994), 153.

88. LeClair, *In the Loop*, 113.

89. Nadeau, *Readings*.

90. Charles Molesworth, "Don DeLillo's Perfect Starry Night," in Lentricchia, *Introducing Don DeLillo*, 143–56.

91. Glen Scott Allen, "The End of Pynchon's Rainbow: Postmodern Terror and Paranoia in DeLillo's *Ratner's Star*," p. 115 of this volume. For further discussion of *Ratner's Star*, see Burhan Tufail, "Moholes and Metaphysics: Notes on *Ratner's Star* and *A Brief History of Time*," *Imprimatur* 1, no. 1 (1995): 46–54; LeClair, *In the Loop* and "Postmodern Mastery."

92. Oriad, "Don DeLillo's Search for Walden Pond."

93. LeClair, *In the Loop*, 146.

94. John Johnston, "Post-Cinematic Fiction: Film in the Novels of Pynchon, McElroy, and DeLillo," *New Orleans Review* 17, no. 2 (1990): 90–97.

95. Patrick O'Donnell, "Engendering Paranoia in Contemporary Narrative," *Boundary 2: An International Journal of Literature and Culture* 19, no. 1 (1992): 181–204. Reprinted in *National Identities and Post-Americanist Narratives*, ed. Donald E. Pease (Durham, N.C.: Duke University Press, 1994): 181–204. For further discussion of *Players* and *Running Dog*, see LeClair, *In the Loop*; Steffen Hantke, " 'God Save Us from Bourgeois Adventure': The Figure of the Terrorist in Contemporary American Conspiracy Fiction," *Studies in the Novel* 28, no. 2 (1996): 219–43; Bill Mullens, "No There There: Cultural Criticism as Lost Object in Don DeLillo's *Players* and *Running Dog*," in *Powerless Fictions? Ethics, Cultural Critique, and American Fiction in the Age of Postmodernism*, ed. Ricardo Miguel Alfonso (Amsterdam: Rodopi, 1996): 113–39. On *Running Dog*, see also Patrick O'Donnell, "Obvious Paranoia: The Politics of Don DeLillo's *Running Dog*," *Centennial Review* 34, no. 1 (1990): 56–72.

96. Mark Osteen, "Marketing Obsession: The Fascinations of *Running Dog*," p. 135 in this volume.

97. LeClair, *In the Loop*, 177.

98. Weinstein, *Nobody's Home*, 289.

99. Paula Bryant, "Discussing the Untellable: Don DeLillo's *The Names*," *Critique* 29, no. 1 (1987): 16–29.

100. Matthew J. Morris, "Murdering Words: Language in Action in Don DeLillo's *The Names*," *Contemporary Literature* 30, no. 1 (1989): 113–27.

101. Paul A. Harris, "Epistemocritique: A Synthetic Matrix," *SubStance: A Review of Theory and Literary Criticism* 22, no. 2–3 (1993): 185–203. For further discussion of *The Names*, see LeClair, *In the Loop*; Dennis A. Foster, "Alphabetic Pleasures: *The Names*," in Lentricchia, *Introducing Don DeLillo*, 157–73; Thomas Carmichael, "Buffalo/Baltimore, Athens/Dallas:

John Barth, Don DeLillo and the Cities of Postmodernism," *Canadian Review of American Studies/ Revue Canadienne d'Etudes Americaines* 22, no. 2 (1991): 241–49, and "Lee Harvey Oswald and the Postmodern Subject: History and Intertextuality in Don DeLillo's *Libra, The Names,* and *Mao II*," *Contemporary Literature* 34, no. 2 (1993): 204–18; Weinstein, *Nobody's Home;* Paul Maltby, "The Romantic Metaphysics of Don DeLillo," *Contemporary Literature* 37, no. 2 (1996): 258–77; Maria Moss, " 'Das Schaudern ist der Menschheit bestes Teil': The Sublime as Part of the Mythic Strategy in Don DeLillo's *The Names,*" *Amerikastudien/American Studies* 43, no. 3 (1998): 483–96.

102.   LeClaire, *In the Loop,* 207, 212.

103.   John Frow, "The Last Things before the Last: Notes on *White Noise,*" in Lentricchia, *Introducing Don DeLillo,* 175–91.

104.   John Duvall, "The (Super) Marketplace of Images: Television as Unmediated Mediation in DeLillo's *White Noise,*" *Arizona Quarterly* 50, no. 3 (1994): 127–53.

105.   Leonard Wilcox, "Baudrillard, DeLillo's *White Noise* and the End of Heroic Narrative," *Contemporary Literature* 32, no. 3 (1991) 346–65.

106.   Tim Engles, " 'Who are you, literally?' Fantasies of the White Self in *White Noise,*" *Modern Fiction Studies* 45 (Fall 1999): 755–87. For further discussion of *White Noise,* see Michael W. Messmer, " 'Thinking it through completely': The Interpretation of Nuclear Culture," *Centennial Review* 32, no. 4 (1988): 397–413.

107.   Frank Lentricchia, "*Libra* as Postmodern Critique," in Lentricchia, *Introducing Don DeLillo.*

108.   Christopher Mott, "*Libra* and the Subject of History," *Critique* 35 (Spring 1994): 136 (p. 229 in this volume).

109.   Bill Millard, "The Fable of the Ants: Myopic Interactions in DeLillo's *Libra,*" *Postmodern Culture* 2, no. 2 (1994), paragraph 18 (p. 213 in this volume).

110.   Margaret Scanlan, "Writers among Terrorists: Don DeLillo's *Mao II* and the Rushdie Affair," *Modern Fiction Studies* 40, no. 2 (1994): 229–52. For further discussion of *Mao II,* see Christian Moraru, "Consuming Narratives: Don DeLillo and the 'Lethal' Reading," *Journal of Narrative Technique* 27, no. 2 (1997): 190–206; Adam Begley, "Don DeLillo: *Americana, Mao II,* and *Underworld,*" *Southwest Review* 82, no. 4 (1997): 478–505; Hantke, " 'God Save Us from Bourgeois Adventure' "; Gerald Howard, "Slouching towards Grubnet: The Author in the Age of Publicity," *Review of Contemporary Fiction* 16, no. 1 (1996): 44–53; James D. Bloom, "Cultural Capital and Contrarian Investing: Robert Stone, Thom Jones, and Others," *Contemporary Literature* 36, no. 3 (1997): 490–507; Thomas Carmichael, "Lee Harvey Oswald and the Postmodern Subject: History and Intertextuality in Don DeLillo's *Libra, The Names,* and *Mao II,*" *Contemporary Literature* 34, no. 2 (1993): 204–18; Howard V. Hendrix, "Memories of the Sun, Perceptions of Eclipse," *New York Review of Science Fiction* 46 (1992): 13–15; and Simon Hughes, "Don DeLillo: *Mao II* and the Writer as Actor," *Scripsi* 7, no. 2 (1991): 105–12.

111.   Silvia Caporale Bizzini, "Can the Intellectual Still Speak? The Example of Don DeLillo's *Mao II,*" *Critical Quarterly* 37, no. 2 (1995): 104–17.

112.   Peter Baker, "The Terrorist as Interpreter: *Mao II* in Postmodern Context," *Postmodern Culture: An Electronic Journal of Interdisciplinary Criticism* 4, no. 2 (1994): 34 paragraphs.

113.   Jeremy Green, "Last Days: Millennial Hysteria in Don DeLillo's *Mao II,*" *Essays and Studies* 48 (1995): 129–48.

114.   Thomas Carmichael, "Lee Harvey Oswald and the Postmodern Subject: History and Intertextuality in Don DeLillo's *Libra, The Names,* and *Mao II,*" *Contemporary Literature* 34, no. 2 (1993): 204–18.

115.   John N. Duvall, "Baseball as Aesthetic Ideology: Cold War History, Race, and DeLillo's 'Pafko at the Wall.' " *Modern Fiction Studies* 41, no. 2 (1995): 285–313.

116.   See p. 302 in this volume.

REVIEWS

Old Story, Fresh Language
[Review of *Americana,* by Don DeLillo]

CHRISTOPHER LEHMANN-HAUPT

I may as well toss the dead mackerel on the table at once and say that Don DeLillo's first novel, "Americana," is about an uneasy young television executive who quits his job to do what he really wants to do. That there are the obligatory executive-suite gags and the angst on wry sandwiches that go with the territory. That Mr. DeLillo's central metaphor of filmmaking is good in theory but weak in the knees. And that "Americana" is a loose-jointed, somewhat knobby novel, all of whose parts do not fit together and some of whose parts may not belong at all. I may as well get all this on the top of the table at once because when I start writing about the virtues of Mr. DeLillo's novel, I don't want it said that the fishy smell of unoriginality and amateurish plot construction is coming up from underneath the table. "Americana" is very much a first novel. I suppose it might even be said that it is very much a talented ex-advertising man's first novel (DeLillo spent five years with the firm that is now Ogilvy & Mather). But it has virtues.

LANGUAGE DOMINATES

The virtues have mostly to do with DeLillo's ability to write. I am not by nature a person much moved by pure language. Despite efforts to reform and see the printed page through William H. Gass's eyes, I remain a structure-and-character man who keeps trying to visualize the imaginary world that words represent (or that I imagine they do). But DeLillo made me the willing victim of his verbal assaults. He rearranged my brain cells to think the world his way and to continue composing DeLillo-like phrases long after I had laid his book aside. He had me soaring on his moods, scarcely caring about meaning at all.

"Then we came to the end of another dull and lurid year," he begins (and already one is coasting comfortably). "Lights were strung across the front of

Originally published in the *New York Times,* 6 May 1971, 41. Reprinted by permission.

every shop. Men selling chestnuts wheeled their smoky carts. In the evening the crowds were immense and traffic built to a tidal roar. The santas of Fifth Avenue rang their little bells with an odd sad delicacy, as if sprinkling salt on some brutally spoiled piece of meat. . . . The war was on television every night but we all went to the movies."

Further along, the novel's hero and narrator, David Bell, introduces us to Pike, who is the proprietor of an electrical appliance repair shop on 14th Street specializing in toasters with doors and prewar radios. Pike is drinking in an East Village bar. "He seemed drunk . . . or well on the way, and in an hour or so his head would tumble to his chest, and his entire upper body, with the sad and ponderous majesty of a dynamited mountainside, would pitch toward the table."

DeLillo affords himself opportunities. There are the scenes in which grown men play hilarious office games. There is a nonstop small-hours-of-the-morning radio broadcaster who never repeats himself and who was once thrown off television for announcing "that there was no weather in Los Angeles and there never had been. The weather was in ourselves." There is David's father, a pioneer advertising man who invented American-flag chic and whose religion is "move the merch."

There is Sullivan, a tall sculptress who tells David fantastic, lyrical bedtime stories about a Sioux mystic who outpredicts McLuhan (in jazzier language) and a black Irish uncle who sails the waters off Mount Desert Island, Me. There are others. A novelist trying to purge himself of slang. A tall, blue-haired hippie who spends his nights watching the UFO's in the Texas skies. They speak. They evoke DeLillo's prose. He can write.

PRODUCT OF AMERICAN LEGEND

David Bell's situation is roughly this: He has grown up with the American legend, personified by Burt Lancaster and Kirk Douglas. He had gone to prep school in New Hampshire and an experimental college on the West Coast. He had married because he liked the image of himself and his wife and divorced because he wanted to get closer to her. He had risen in his network. But the doors began opening in the dark room of his mind and control was no longer possible. So he set out for the middle country to examine the legend, his 16-mm. movie-camera in hand. And in the process of trying to make a film of his own life, he discovered—well, here:

"For years I had been held fast by the great unwinding mystery of this deep sink of land, the thick paragraphs and imposing photos, the gallop of panting adjectives, prairie truth and the clean kills of eagles, the desert shawled in Navaho paints, images of surreal cinema, of ventricles tied to pumps, Chaco masonry and the slung guitar, of church organ lungs and the state of empires, of coral in this strange place, suggesting a reliquary sea, and of the blessed semblance of God on the faces of superstitious mountains. Whether the novels and songs usurped the land, or took something true from it, is not so much the issue as this: that what I was engaged in was merely a literary venture, an attempt to find pattern and motive, to make of something wild a squeamish thesis on the essence of the nation's soul. To formulate. To seek links. But the wind burned across the creekbeds, barely moving the soil, and there was nothing to announce myself in the way of historic revelation. Even now, writing this, I can impart little of what I saw."

Not so.

It is a familiar story by now, flawed in the telling. But the language soars and dips, and it imparts a great deal. Exciting my . . . oh, my!

A Waugh in Shoulder Padding
[Review of *End Zone,* by Don DeLillo]

NELSON ALGREN

Americana, Don DeLillo's first novel, took the critics by surprise. While conceding its fluency and its fantasy, its wit and its precision, the character of David Bell, its blue-eyed protagonist, evaded them. As blue-eyed David Bell evaded himself. For Bell was a child of the cinema: a man afflicted with an objectivity so ominous that he could appraise his own flight from himself while running the projector.

"There are no old times," this icy manipulator concluded—after a sequence of jumpcuts and soft-focus tenderness fading into his own life's slow dissolve—"The tapes have been accidentally destroyed."

Feeling existence on tape or film to be more real than actual life, David Bell enjoyed his job, his status, his affluence and the offices where he produced TV commercials. "What the machine accepts is verifiably existent," he decides, "all else is unborn or worse." Then, equipped with tapes and films, he repudiates that belief by blowing friends, job, status and affluence by taking precipitate flight into that very Unborn or Worse.

This novel reduced the U.S.A., in scale, to a TV screen whereon we watched our own lives fading to a slow dissolve. We should have noticed sooner that that screen was really a window. And that blue-eyed Bell was not only a producer of TV commercials but the ultimate product of them.

As Gary Harkness is a man who lives to play football and, at the same time, regards it with the disdain of an intellectual—watching grown men playing a boys' game: "It's only a game but it's the only game."

End Zone is the kind of novel Evelyn Waugh would have written had he been 6-foot-2, weighed 196 without shoulder padding and had already fumbled football scholarships at Syracuse, Miami, Pennsylvania and East Lansing. Gary Harkness is now on his good behavior at Logos State of West Texas.

"We were a lean and dedicated squad run by a hungry coach and his seven oppressive assistants," he fills us in. "We did grass drills at 106 in the sun. We attacked the blocking sleds and strutted through the intersecting ropes and we went one on one, blocker and pass-rusher, and hand-fought

Originally published in *Los Angeles Times Book Review,* 26 March 1972, 2,7. Reprinted by permission.

each other to the earth. We butted, clawed and kicked. There were any number of fist fights. There were many times when I wondered what I was doing in that remote and unfed place, that summer tundra, being hit high and low by a foaming pair of 240-pound Texans. Being made to obey the savage commands of unreasonable men. Being set apart from all styles of civilization as I had known or studied them. Being led in prayer every evening by our coach, warlock and avenging patriarch."

Gary Harkness is neither the cold manipulator nor the ruthless womanizer that David Bell was. But he possesses the same camera-eye and the same urge somehow to trap himself disastrously. He blows up a whole stick of pot, secretly, before a game; but his subsequent action propels him into the co-captainship of Logos State. Yet, when advised by the Avenging Patriarch to "suck in his gut and go harder," he queries his coach:

"You're saying that what I learn on the gridiron about sacrifice and one-ness will be of inestimable value in later life. That if I give up now I'll almost surely give up in more important contests later on."

"That's it exactly, Gary."

"I'm giving up."

OTHER INTONATIONS

Harkness' 300-pound roommate, Bloomberg, isn't giving up. It's simply that he is more concerned with planning his past than his future:

"History is guilt," he advises Harkness. "I'm unjewing myself. You go to a place where there aren't any Jews. You revise your way of speaking. You take out the urbanisms. The question marks. All that folk wisdom. The melodies in your speech. The inverted sentences. Then you transform your mind into a ruthless instrument."

"Why don't you want to be Jewish any more?"

"I'm tired of the guilt. The enormous nagging historical guilt."

"What guilt?"

"The guilt of being innocent victims."

DeLillo's wit is so surgical you don't even know an artery has been severed. You don't laugh until you see you're bleeding.

". . . We started playing a game called Bang, You're Dead. Almost every child has played it in one form or another. Your hand assumes the shape of a gun and you fire at anyone who passes. You simply shout these words: 'Bang, You're Dead' . . . I died well and for this reason was killed quite often . . . shot from behind, I staggered to the steps of the library and remained there, on my back, between the second and seventh step at the middle of the stairway . . . it was very relaxing despite the hardness of the steps. I felt the sun on my face. I tried to think of nothing. The longer I remained there the more absurd it seemed to get up . . . I opened my eyes. Taft Robinson was sitting on a bench not far away, reading a periodical. For a moment, in a state of near rapture, I thought it was he who'd fired the shot."

Not Giving Up

Taft Robinson was the first black student to be enrolled at Logos: they got him for his speed. In time he might have turned up endorsing $8,000 automobiles and having his life story on the back of cereal boxes. But there were other intonations that year and so Taft Robinson no more than haunts this book. The Game That Means Everything is against Centrex and a coach gives the squad ample warning:

"You got five days to get ready. This isn't Snow White and the seven dwarfs you're facing. This is a bunch of headhunters. They like to hit. They have definite sadistic tendencies. This is a squad that's big and mean. You people got a long way to go in meanness. You think you're mean but you're not mean. Centrex is mean. They're practically evil. They'll stomp all over you. It'll be men against boys. They like to humiliate people. You better get ready for the worst."

Logos does get ready: with a beer party to end all beer parties. And Logos does get the worst. The game with Centrex must be the most exciting re-creation of an American football game in fiction.

In his second novel DeLillo sustains the fluency of his first yet has lost momentum. As if the momentum he picked up in *Americana* had propelled him onto the football field but had not quite carried him across the goal line. The book closes like a play on which the curtain has failed to descend. Not because the curtain wasn't ready but because the players had been in too much of a hurry to get offstage. Although there isn't a line in either *Americana* or *End Zone* that falters, it might be well if the author used his emergency before his motor starts sputtering.

Your Number Is Up
[Review of *Ratner's Star,* by Don DeLillo]

J. D. O'HARA

Author of two fine novels, *Americana* and *Great Jones Street,* and one dazzling novel, *End Zone,* Don DeLillo writes the American version of a European novel of ideas. Perhaps he most resembles Thomas Mann, lacking Mann's mysticism and long-windedness but sharing his remarkable ability to evoke and evaluate the ideas, language and attitudes of a wide range of intellectual disciplines. DeLillo also possesses an undercutting skepticism proper to the age of Beckett and Borges, an eye for rational absurdity as keen as Barthelme's and a sparkling comic inventiveness that fills his narratives with flashes of delight. He is already the writer Vonnegut, Barth and Pynchon were once oddly and variously taken to be, and he shows no signs of flagging, many signs of promise.

In *End Zone* one of DeLillo's many topics was the deceptive and incomplete nature of knowledge; another was the disparity between what we can manipulate intellectually, on the one hand, and "the untellable," on the other; a third was the contradictory temptations of complexity and simplicity; yet another was those unknowable, unspeakable fundamentals of existence, excrement and death. These topics recur in *Ratner's Star,* where excrement is pervasive and infectious, and death takes many forms, including decay, shadows, flooding, historical reversal, and cosmological black stars and black holes, as well as the moral and cultural death implied by corporate greed.

The areas of knowledge central to *Ratner's Star* are astronomy and mathematics. DeLillo develops them brilliantly so that the expert can wallow while even the layman can splash happily in the shallows or pick up pebbles on the shore. Billy Twillig, a 14-year-old Nobel-laureate mathematician from the Bronx, is summoned to Field Experiment No. 1, a huge think-tank, in 1979. A message has just been received from the vicinity of Ratner's star: 101 transmissions, 99 signals broken up by two pauses into 14 28 57. Mathematics is the only language potentially universal; Twillig must read this.

Originally published in *Washington Post Book World,* 13 June 1976, M3. Reprinted by permission of the author.

Field Experiment No. 1 provides characters whose elliptical speeches, cameo appearances and odd behavior compose a fascinating, funny and unnerving picture of life as seen intelligently. "All I know is one thing doesn't lead to another the way it should," as one character complains. Even at its best, existence is repeatedly and disturbingly dual. The binary world of computers is divided into 1 and 0; Ratner's star is shadowed by a black dwarf; the rational Twillig is set against his antipodal opposite, a nameless and magical Australian aborigine; and the clear world of mathematics is undermined by violence in the Bronx, the subway where Twillig's father works, human passion and irrationality, the "void core" at the center of Field Experiment No. 1's "Space Brain," and the black holes of the universe. Worse, this antiworld infects the world of intellectual clarity. When Twillig makes an error he hears "keep believing it, s*** for brains." Urine and feces become, as in grade school, "number one" and "number two"; and mysticism is wittily described as "science's natural laxative." Themselves decaying, the scientists here cannot face this world of corruption and excrement; they try to evade it with cosmetics and cute words. But words themselves are infected. Verbal ideas cannot compete with mathematical clarity; "the power of logic, so near to number and so distant," fills Twillig "with warped vibrations, as of a harp string plucked by monkeys."

No evasion or reconciliation of these manichean worlds is possible, and therefore no ultimate clarity is possible; DeLillo suggests this even in his central names. Twillig's name is Terwilliger with the "er" of doubt and ignorance removed, but what remains is still dual: "Twill" means "two-threaded." And why Ratner? The name of this astronomer (whom we meet, in a dreadfully comic scene) anagrammatizes into "errant terran ranter," which he certainly is. What's more, if you remove the *"er"* of ignorance from Ratner's, and then subtract star from what remains, you are left with n, which is "the well-known mathematical sign for an indefinite number"; "a sort of nth dimension, as the mathematicians say."

And more, more, more to come, including the meaning of 14 28 57. Unfortunately, DeLillo's choice of a science-fiction form ("fiction is trying to move outward into space, science, history and technology" he has said) obliges him to reach answers and to impose a dramatic conclusion on his discrete materials. The plot may be intended to appease those hominids still longing for the reassurance of cause and effect, but the many ideas so satisfyingly raised, developed, and clarified in this fine novel deserve a better fate. Still, what a mind-expanding trip to the finish line, and full of wit and slapstick as well. (There's a Fellini parade halfway through.)

End Game
[Review of *Players,* by Don DeLillo]

STEPHEN KOCH

Players is Don DeLillo's fourth novel, appearing five years after *End Zone,* which in the general view was a best-seller celebrated in its day for what are called "extraliterary" reasons: to wit, it was bought and read by people who loved not literature but football. Speaking as somebody who loathes and despises football, I found *End Zone* a well-written and extremely amusing novel.

DeLillo's next two books, *Great Jones Street* and *Ratner's Star,* were less satisfactory, and this latest is not, I'm afraid, very good at all. I hasten to add that there is nothing inexorable in this descent, no steady exhaustion of a subject, for example, no overmining of a given manner or style. It is hard to guess exactly what has gone wrong. Haste? Just a bad year? Possibly there is something about the subject. Football is a sport whose charms, such as they are, DeLillo has at his fingertips, whereas more digging is needed in *Players;* the very subject of the novel is unclear. It is a slack, shapeless work trying to tell a tale about a transformation in the lives of a stockbroker and his wife when a man they barely know is quite pointlessly assassinated by some entirely unconvincing "terrorists" in the New York Stock Exchange. I think (but am not sure) that all the characters work in the financial district so we will clearly see the dehumanized nature of their lives. But this suggests that the "lives" in question have some imaginative reality. Not so. There are no stockbrokers, terrorists, or wives—dehumanized or not—in *Players.* There are only words, inky squiggles on a page, telling us things that we do not believe.

Such as that after the shooting on Wall Street, Lyle the stockbroker—quite without the tiniest shred of motivation—drifts away from his sexy minx of a wife, Pammy (Pammy?), to join up with the uniquely dull coterie of non-characters who pulled the trigger and whom DeLillo keeps calling "the terrorists." Politics leads Lyle down the primrose path: his fate worse than death is only slyly hinted at, but it is (we are given to understand) both sexual and dicey, involving a girl with a dildo. So much for "politics." Meanwhile, the

Originally published in *Harper's* 255 (September 1977): 88–90. Copyright © 1977 by *Harper's Magazine.* All rights reserved. Reprinted by special permission.

estimable Pammy develops new interests of her own, entertaining herself by watching the auto-da-fé of a homosexual friend and sometime lover, sniffing the reek of gasoline in the smoky air, looking in bland affectless horror at the lump of charred flesh. Why—you may well ask—do Pammy and Lyle, until recently such a couple of sweeties, respond with such very strange violence to a shooting that on the page is so dull that the reader can barely remember it from paragraph to paragraph? Well, that—as the maid used to say in Thurber's stories—I don't know.

I'd be the last to insist that novels include characters who act through intelligible motives. I wouldn't insist they include characters at all. Though most novels have been accounts of intelligibly motivated characters, a good many of them have been nothing of the kind, several of the greatest among them. It does seem fair, however, to ask that the imaginative transaction that replaces such things on the page have something about it that the reader can find believable and interesting; I am afraid that this cannot be said of most of the writing in *Players*.

There are two exceptions. Every fifteen pages or so, some character decides to knock off a piece of intelligible motivation (it is usually the mercurial Lyle), whereupon he drops his pants and climbs into the sack with somebody—and we are treated to a brief, refreshing sex scene. Though none of these passages can hope for ultimate inclusion in the great erotic anthology in the sky, they do perk up an otherwise dreary landscape.

Some of DeLillo's passages about New York are likewise exempt from dreariness. New York is much on DeLillo's mind, and I gather the distortions of life in the behavioral sink are part of his point. Strangely enough, though he does his best writing about the city, he is not (in this book) a particularly good observer of it. For example, Pammy and Lyle venture out to dinner in SoHo one fine evening. There is nothing even slightly like SoHo in the passage. We could be in downtown Omaha. Still, accuracy is not the whole art of evocation, and a rather Baudelairean vision of the swarming city and its ever more frenetic sordidness keeps recurring, usually quite dissociated from the wooden characters and their tiresome nonadventures, but occasionally invested with a certain low-temperature prose poetry.

> Lyle stood in a phone booth in Grand Central . . . watching people heading for their trains, skidding along, their shoulders collapsed—a day's work, a drink or two causing subtle destruction, a rumpling beyond the physical, all moving through constant sourceless noise, mouths slightly open, the fish of cities.

This isn't bad, and near the end of the book (after her homosexual boyfriend has inexplicably burned himself to death) the bewildered Pammy is slipped into the arc-lit, teeming, black-and-blue landscape of Greenwich Village on a summer night in what are by far the book's best pages. The city and sex: dissociation is DeLillo's theme. Ever since Blake saw the soldier's sigh run in blood down palace walls, the city (the summer city especially) has provided a vision of the dissociative hell, if for no other reason than that pounding the pavement within touching distance of thousands of strangers can easily create a spectacle of pullulating life that is at once intense and unintelligible, vibrant and cut off.

I gather DeLillo's characters are intended to be pulled apart by an analogous imbalance between feeling and expression, between emotion and action. Apparently it is zombie time in old New York. But insofar as this adds up to anything but the oldest and most fraudulent cliché in the shop—Modern Life is Empty and Unfeeling—DeLillo has flubbed his point. Plain bad writing is partly the cause (I cannot resist the editorial, rather than genuinely critical, point that the book cries out for at least another draft), as is DeLillo's refusal to confront or explore the hot spots that are the obvious sources for the energy to which the book never connects: homosexuality, left-wing politics, and forms of sexual perversity.

DeLillo seems to justify these failures by suggesting that, after all, dissociated behavior is unmotivated. This is really very limp thinking, and of course quite the opposite is true. Dissociated behavior is usually motivated to the point of compulsion—and there lies the artist's theme. The compulsion may be bizarre and unattractive, and it may be the sort of thing that would bewilder and appall Louisa May Alcott. But it is not dead, not unreal, and not uninteresting. The same cannot be said for *Players*.

A Pro's Puckish Prose
[Review of *Amazons,* by "Cleo Birdwell"]

J. D. O'HARA

The title is misleading. There is only one Amazon here, Ms. Birdwell, and her martial weapon is a hockey stick. *Amazons* is her autobiography, with appropriately heavy emphasis on last year, when she made athletic history by being the first woman to play in the National Hockey League. Fans now look forward to her return under the New York Rangers' interesting new management, about which she says some perceptive things. Together, her play and her story should give our fall a lift: she bids fair to outshine current football stars and she certainly displays more wit and intelligence than our country's leading pushball teams, the Democans and the Republicrats. But Birdwell does not write primarily for sports fans, among whom the literacy rate is low. She writes for a higher audience—us—capable of appreciating such subtlety as that of her dust-jacket photo. In the picture she wears her Rangers uniform, but her flowing hair and a businesslike skate cover the end letters and reveal her as (in French) an angel.

There is something unexpected about an autobiography written, even by an angel, at such a fledgling stage. After all, we do not read such works for mere names, dates and places. We seek insightful, amusing and thought-provoking observations arising from experience and bearing valuably on life as we know it. And what of all this can we expect from a 23-year-old native of Badger, Ohio, who has spent most of her recent years playing hockey in distant leagues? Face it, all pucks look alike.

But it figures that any woman who survives an N.H.L. season must have some extra smarts. Birdwell shows hers even in her introduction: "Hockey is so fast it's practically nonlinear. What I have in mind is a book that's slow and sunlit and kind of meadowy. Reflections and meditations. I think my experience in the National Hockey League lends itself to some major thematic material." And she begins her memoir with a passage from the mystic, Wadi Assad. She will return to him, and to life in Badger. There's a lovely meditative survey of the four seasons, for instance, that should be quoted in

Originally published in the *Nation,* 18 October 1980, 385–86. Reprinted by permission.

its entirety. The introductory sentences will whet the appetite: "You knew it was midspring when you heard birdsong at dusk." "Summer was heat, stillness, and shade." "This was the holiday that led us into fall, when the light was soft and gold, and the leaves turned red, yellow, rust, winy dark, and amber." "Then one grayish day you'd get up and smell snow in the air." Of course her profession evokes a different tone:

> The world of men was a sound in my ears. Men on skates marching over concrete. Sticks tossed into corners. Men muttering matter-of-fact curses. The blast of hot showers. A hundred banging kinds of background noise.
> That's why these memoirs will be quiet, reflective, and thoughtful.

But Birdwell is not a professional author; her narrative follows no game plan. She experiences it as we do, moment by moment, and is sometimes equally surprised at the turns of events. Naturally, since she is a woman and full of small-town sociability, she writes mostly not about hockey action, in which every player is alone, or even about her happy youth. She tells about the people she lives among. And in the world of professional sport they are almost all men.

> I am more or less a connoisseur of the male form. . . . They are interesting bodies, the bodies of athletes, because of the wounds and bruises as much as the general excellence of form. The hurt is what gives these bodies their special emotional quality. Years of physical stress have made the players look noble and battered and antique Greeklike, except for goaltenders, who look like mounds of vanilla horsemeat, by and large.

The assurance of these generalizations and of the details given elsewhere indicates the modernity of these memoirs. Even her hymns to childhood include topics not traditional in the handling of that theme. Birdwell is a woman of the present. Many women are? Certainly lots of women publish books claiming that they are. But this is precisely where Birdwell differs. In such central areas as equality and sexuality, Birdwell . . . *Birdwell has no hangups. Nor has she overcome any.* This is not to say that she is a smug know-it-all. She is young. Much is new to her. She admits it:

> This is the second straight chapter that ends with sex and intimate fighting. There is a huge tradition behind this, but I'm not sure I want to be a part of it. There are other ways to end chapters and I'm determined to find some of them before too long.

She does. After all, she is attractive and suddenly famous in New York; she can be used to make money, and in other ways. She is besieged by lovers, promoters and other weirdos. All weirdos. Consider your own acquaintances. After narrating such encounters for a while Birdwell begins a chapter with the exhausted one-sentence paragraph: "All I wanted to do was play hockey."

She does not. In that chapter she leaves one man to visit another's apartment where she is phoned by a third. The chapter ends with some glumly appropriate observations: "I thought this would be a little book of meditations. . . . I'd like to develop a theme or find a shape for events. I didn't think major thematic material would be this hard to turn up." Then she recalls a childhood favorite, *The American Girl Book of Sports Stories.* "Those stories had themes, every last one of them. The events were shaped." But her own life is different, as she realizes: "That was Badger. This was Philadelphia, and the Spectrum was full of white-eyed, shining savages."

They are not the only savages. But space runs short. No time to speak of the Mafia and snowmobiles, the Arabs and hockey and real estate. Doom approaches. But women can find amusement even there; after all, theirs is a funny world by nature.

> Limp, the penis is a dubious item compared to the human hand. It just hangs there, backed by testicles, like a soloist with a rhythm section. Even the word is funny. . . . But women accept it as the force of nature and myth that it is. I don't think we want to change the basic principle.

Well, Birdwell possesses many qualities undemonstrated here. She is perceptive, she uses language so well that one wants to read the whole novel to friends, even on the telephone, collect, and she is marvelously funny even in crises. Order by the case. Christmas is coming.

The reader—you there—will have suspected something. A female hockey player? One would have heard, somehow. A funny female writer? Yes, it's possible; but her name is Ann Beattie. What's going on here? Who is this soloist really?

One can only intuit. Intuition reports that there are only two men alive capable of writing this book in English, and one of them didn't. So it must be the work of that terrific Athenian-American novelist Don DeLillo. Place your bets. And don't read the book in public if you have a shrill, whinnying laugh; people will complain.

The Fiction of Don DeLillo
[Review of *The Names,* by Don DeLillo]

DAVID BOSWORTH

Don DeLillo is one of the few American novelists to have emerged in the past decade who seems to have both the virtuosity and ambition requisite for greatness. Relentlessly contemporary, he has sought to explore the most modern face of America—its executive suites, its obsession with film and TV, its passion for football and fame and rock music and weapons technology. And, unlike so many of his fellow writers, indistinguishable in their anemic, retiring, quasi-ironic, white-wall-and-wicker prose, he has made these explorations in a language as distinctive and exuberant as the subjects described.

No review of DeLillo should gloss over this facility. When rigorously applied, his gift with words not only delights the ear and dazzles the mind, but searches out and revives those complexities and "deeper textures" (a DeLillo phrase) wherein the living truth is found to hide. Thus blessed, even his weakest books are redeemed to a degree by the brilliance of individual passages. The opening paragraph of *Great Jones Street,* for example, is in itself worth the price of admission. More wit and wisdom on the subject of fame are contained in its ten or twenty lines than in a library of monographs on Pop Art and TV.

The constant theme of DeLillo's work, the spiritual vacuum of modern life, is common to much American fiction; but no American writer has captured with his flair the flip and, to my mind, more fascinating side of contemporary despair—how meaninglessness stimulates as well as depresses, how it tempts and challenges the modern imagination. Rather than predictably passive and directionless characters, he gives us latterday spiritual questors. In a world bereft of sanctioned holiness, in a world of adamant relativity, they are mad jazz-monks, improvising their own ceremonies, their own strange gods, scratching frantic liturgical graffiti on the face of the Void.

In *End Zone,* for example, DeLillo's haunting and hilarious examination of college football, the hero's team is populated with young men given to odd exercises in spiritual self-discipline—one-arm pushups for the soul. One

Originally published in the *Boston Review* (April 1983): 29–30. Reprinted by permission of the author.

teammate memorizes poetry in German, a language he doesn't understand. The hero himself takes long walks in the desert and recites to himself the names of Presidents of the United States. That both of these self-created nonsense rituals are dependent on language is no accident; few authors are so obsessed with the religious and anthropological dimensions of everyday speech—language as display, language as social dance, language as koan or mantra, language serving some purpose beyond the meaning of its constituent words.

In particular, DeLillo has an infallible ear for the absurd inflations of rhetoric, that pseudo-knowledge, that verbal plumage, which so often attend the sects and subsets of American life. He has a comic knack *for* mimicking, whether in a football coach's halftime speech or an Air Force colonel's press release, the way we strangle our syntax with the graceless neologisms of technology, apparently hoping in the process to borrow some of the intellectual authority ascribed to Science, the twentieth century's minimalist god. But the invitation is not simply to laugh at fools, although laugh we do. Behind the satire lies a more serious and universal point, DeLillo's suspicion that *all* language, that of the poet as well as the pedant, serves the same desperate and self-defensive purpose. The costume we spin to hide ourselves from our nakedness. The pattern we use to fabricate a home, our imaginary womb in the infinite dark.

In *The Names,* DeLillo's seventh novel, most of his previous preoccupations reappear. Again he explores specific aspects of contemporary life, this time international business and cult fanaticism, and again language itself is central to the book's overall theme.

James Axton, the first-person narrator, has taken a job as a "risk analyst" for an international insurance company. An American stationed in Athens, he has accepted the position to be near his estranged wife, Kathryn, who is living with their son on a small Greek island where she works on a failing archeological dig. It is there, on Kouros, through Kathryn's boss, Owen, that Axton first learns of a wandering cult whose sole act of "religious celebration" is the selection and murder of a seemingly random series of victims. Never content to emphasize one plot thread, the novel keeps shifting, then, between these three realms of activity: Axton's life as an expatriate businessman, including a subplot concerning the CIA and Greek nationalism; his attempt to be reconciled to his wife and son; and finally his pursuit, more mental than physical, of the mysterious cult.

As we have come to expect from him, DeLillo uses the occasions of his novel's plot and setting to inscribe for us a multitude of precise and memorable observations—on old age, on Americans abroad, on airports, pleasure, and second wives. We're told, for example, that "military governments always plant trees. It shows their gentle side." At the end of a dinner party, we're offered this little gem: "Was this the point in the evening at which husbands and wives find each other again, suppressing yawns, making eye contact through the smoke? Time to go, time to resume our murky shapes. The public self is weary of its gleam." And this: "Self-depreciation is a language I don't think I understand. It's so often a form of ego, isn't it, a form of aggression, a wanting to be noticed even for one's flaws."

But when we draw back from this busy, varied canvas, with its plethora of small and vivid points, a larger pattern becomes clear. *The Names* is about "naming"—about language, about its irrational, emotive, almost mystical power: about how, beneath the pale skin of their meaning, words link up in a kind of geometric abstract art that soothes our deepest fears and satisfies our most urgent need to rescue order from the chaos of our lives. Owen—whose profession is the study of ancient inscriptions and who has become obsessed with the glyphs themselves, the "shapes" of the letters untranslated, apart from any context or explanation—warns Axton when he asks about the cult, "I wouldn't look for meaning, James." Later, Axton reports, "Owen and I had spent several hours building theories, surrounding the bare act [the cult murder] with desperate speculations, mainly to comfort ourselves. We knew in the end we'd be left with nothing. Nothing signified, nothing meant." As a monolingual American abroad who is constantly submerged in a sea of babble, of signs and sounds he cannot comprehend, James is led to wonder, "Could reality be phonetic, a matter of gutturals and dentals?" Even the comfort he takes in English conversation lies, we are told, not in "what is said," but in the "cadences," "the rise and fall of the ironic voice, the modulations, the stresses."

Time and time again, with perhaps excessive thoroughness but undeniable eloquence, DeLillo impresses upon us his view that what matters about language is its "pattern," its deeper rhythms and syntax, the design behind the signs rather than what they signify. His vision is that of an anthropologist, a cultural relativist, who upon surveying the variety of human societies refuses to endorse one system over the others, stressing instead mankind's unique capacity to make systems at all. All answers, he suggests, all explanations are ultimately false. Meaning is eternally elusive, but the search for meaning, the model worlds we continuously make with our words are all that we have to comfort ourselves—lullabies to mask the great white noise of the universe.

And the test case, the most extreme challenge to our talent for turning the entropy of experience into the arabesque of language, is represented in *The Names* by the cult itself. The apparent "senselessness" of its killing appalls and attracts us. Like Axton's, our minds pursue the members of the cult, desperate to find the hidden design that will explain their actions, believing that if we can just classify them, just find a name for what they do, it will somehow tame the horror we feel. But in an ironic twist, when a system is discovered—the cult is simply matching the initials of its victims' names with the initials of the town where they happen to be staying—our horror is not diminished by being defined; it is instead intensified.

"These killings mock us," Owen concludes. "They mock our need to structure and classify, to build a system against the terror in our souls. They make the system equal to the terror. The means to contend with death has become death."

Our means to contend with death, according to DeLillo, is, of course, language. Words are our defense against the one explanation for events we can never accept: randomness. The awful sacrilege of the cult is to use the very instrument of our protection—our names, our naming—as a weapon against us, just as, on a grander scale, the Nazis used all the instruments of higher civilization—medicine, technology, the intricacies of rational social planning—to perform the most monstrously uncivilized of acts, the maintenance of a bureaucracy of death. This profound if simple observation about the nature of terrorism is just one feature in DeLillo's complex metaphorical examination of contemporary life. Indeed, Axton himself can be seen as emblematic of the author's grim view of modern man: a stranger abroad, lost in a sea of incomprehensible signs, without beliefs, without metaphysical answers, forced by their absence to improvise his own theories, to surround the "bare act" of existence with his own "desperate speculations," aware though that these theories are "mainly for his own comfort," illusions to succor, aware that in the end he'll be "left with nothing"—"nothing signified, nothing meant."

Whether we accept this view as fundamentally true, as DeLillo appears to, or merely as an illusion characteristic of the times, it is nevertheless an accurate expression of this century's central spiritual dilemma. And there is much else to admire in this truly contemporary novel beyond the clarity and significance of its theme: a verbal vivacity, an almost effortless flow of witty conversation, an ease in depicting a variety of settings.

But it must be said, too, that *The Names* is a curiously static book. One would never guess that a novel about cult murders and CIA plots, written by a man of DeLillo's obvious gifts, could be a slow read, and yet *The Names* never quite acquires the pace or urgency its subject matter would seem to guarantee. Only the tension between Axton and his wife is rendered dramatically with emotional as well as intellectual resonance—and then, too abruptly it seems, Kathryn leaves. The cult, which is more a cerebral puzzle than a physical threat, more reported to Axton than experienced by him, and the CIA-terrorist subplot, which is evolved too late and indifferently paced, are strangely unexciting. They seem too frail a narrative skeleton, thin-wired hangers, upon which to drape the heavy flesh of DeLillo's theme. The author's talents, I think, undo him here. A lesser writer could not hold our attention, as DeLillo does with his sentence by sentence virtuosity, without more carefully attending to the theatrical rhythms of the novel's plot. But in *The Names* we read on anyway, tempted by the author's well-turned phrases, unusually lucid observations, gradually aware, though, that this performance, for all its flair, is somehow less than satisfying.

DeLillo himself senses the problem. At least three times, he has Axton, in his first-person narration, observe self-consciously that the reader will want less "reflection," more fast-paced scenes and dramatic action. But to prediagnose the complaints of one's readers is not to cure them. And to pretend so is, ironically, to mimic the error of the book's own cult members, their fixation on the totemic power of language, the author relying on magic instead of performance, hoping that through the mere act of "naming" his fiction's faults, he can, like demons, cast them out.

It is possible, I suppose, that the book's slow pace is a conscious strategy: that matching style to theme, DeLillo is striving to carve a kind of fictional glyph: a stately, static, abstract pattern, one of those "letter shapes" which so fascinate Owen. But fiction, unlike graphics, is a narrative art: it exists in time. Its pattern is not simultaneous but extended and rhythmic—it is by its nature inescapably dramatic. This does not mean that gunfire and ripped bodices are necessary; even the subtlest intellectual analyses can be dramatically rendered, as Henry James was fond of demonstrating. It does mean, however, that the subject matter, whatever its nature, must evolve over time. Ideas, if they are central to a novel's existence, must come into being; they must develop for the characters and for the reader with a growing sense of discovery, carry the force of a revelation. The ideas and analyses in *The Names,* despite the wit and cogency of their exposition, are less compelling because they are not successfully dramatized, because they are not developed so much as described . . . and described . . . and described again.

I stress this specific lapse because it relates to the one consistent weakness to be found in DeLillo's otherwise impressive work: the power of his individual prose moments too rarely seems to gain momentum; the cumulative affect of his book-length fiction always seems less than the prospective sum of its dazzling segments. Plots don't resolve, they spin out into space. Books don't surge so much as fade away. There is a certain honest logic to this situation; the occasional shapelessness of DeLillo's novels does, in a sense, reflect their subject matter—the age's air of spiritual chaos. No one would argue that our best writers should not be documenting this loss of faith, of vision, this fear we share that our lives are not ruled by any larger rhythms. But DeLillo, in his sincere depiction of the modern condition, seems too often to become its victim. His fiction, like his characters, is too often trapped in a kind of atomistic, moment-to-moment existence that strains even his considerable talent for improvisation.

To capture somehow the confusion and despair of contemporary life without in the process submitting to them, without committing the esthetic sin of the "imitative fallacy," is one of the most urgent challenges confronting fiction today. Because Don DeLillo dares to track the deepest sources of our discontent rather than merely to record its mannerisms, he has always seemed to me uniquely qualified to meet this challenge. If he hasn't yet, his failure arises from the difficulty of the task and not, as with so much fiction of the day, from an inexcusable lack of effort. Here is a man whose books should be read. A novelist of high purpose, of rare ambition, whose ongoing examination of our present-tense lives amuses and astounds us even as it educates. To say we expect more from him is an implicit if impatient compliment—a measure of this writer's special gifts.

Conspirators
[Review of *White Noise,* by Don DeLillo]

DIANE JOHNSON

The horrors of 1984 did not emerge quite in the form that Orwell imagined, reminding us that novelists are usually more gifted with hindsight than with prescience. Many novelists confess to feeling that there are certain things they dare not write, for fear they will come true, and can tell you of things they have written which have afterward happened, proving, if not prescience, the power of wishes. Novelists stay away from prediction. Not to make too much of the "airborne toxic event" in Don DeLillo's new novel, *White Noise,* and the Bhopal tragedy it anticipates, but it is the index of DeLillo's sensibility, so alert is he to the content, not to mention the speech rhythms, dangers, dreams, fears, etc., of modern life that you imagine him having to spend a certain amount of time in a quiet, darkened room. He works with less lead time than other satirists, too—we should have teenage suicide and the new patriotism very soon—and this must be demanding. But here, as in his other novels, his voice is authoritative, his tone characteristically light. In all his work he seems less angry or disappointed than some critics of society, as if he had expected less in the first place, or perhaps his marvelous power with words is compensation for him.

White Noise is a meditation on themes of whiteness—the Pallor of death, and white noise, the sound, so emblematic of modern life, that is meant to soothe human beings by screening out the other, more irritating noises of their civilization. The hero and narrator is Jack Gladney, chairman of Hitler Studies at a small eastern university:

> We are quartered in Centenary Hall, a dark brick structure we share with the popular culture department, known officially as American environments. A curious group. The teaching staff is composed almost solely of New York émigrés, smart, thuggish, movie-mad, trivia-crazed. They're here to decipher the natural language of the culture, to make a formal method of the shiny pleasures they'd known in their Europe-shadowed childhoods—an Aristotelianism of bubble gum wrappers and detergent jingles.

Reprinted with permission from the *New York Review of Books,* 14 March 1985, 6–7. Copyright © 1985 NYREV, Inc.

Jack is married to Babette, and they have a number of children from their former marriages. Babette, normally a wholesome, cheerful woman, has taken to sneaking a certain pill, and when challenged denies it. Next, a toxic leak obliges them to evacuate their house and exposes Jack to a chemical cloud which may or will kill him in an unknown length of time.

Now he is seized by the fear of death. He learns that mortality is Babette's preoccupation too, and that she has volunteered as an experimental subject to take a pill being developed to relieve this fear. She has been giving herself to the drug company man, in a shabby motel, on a regular basis, to ensure her continuing supply.

Will Jack be able to discover what Babette's taking? Will he be able to get a supply for himself? Is he really going to die of the whiff of Nyodene Derivative? Will he go through with his plan to kill Willie Mink, the drug company man, to revenge Babette and steal the Dylar pills? This is the armature upon which DeLillo hangs a series of observations, descriptions, jokes, and dialogues, approximately Socratic, on sundry great and lesser subjects:

"Did you ever spit in your soda bottle so you wouldn't have to share your drink with the other kids?"

"How old were you when you first realized your father was a jerk?"

"Exactly how elevated is my potassium?"

As we read fiction, we are always aware of the operative formal principle—it's either "life" (meandering, inconclusive) or "plot," as in this novel, where the fortune or fate of an individual is opposed to a conspiracy, to a plot within the plot, which serves as a metaphor for the world itself, organized against you, clever, wickedly determined on its own usually illegal ends, and in this mirroring the illicit desires of our own hearts. Thus the pirates, spy rings, smugglers, dope pushers, CIA, criminal organizations, high-up secret governmental department, terrorist cadre, heartless chemical industry we find in some of the most interesting recent fiction, conspirators representing in microcosm the hostile confusion and formless menace of the big world. A novel whose plot contains a plot might be *the* postmodern novel, an adaptation of an earlier model of fiction, from before the era of the fiction of the self, when we had novels of the person in society or the universe, making his or her way, and making judgments on it. It is a distinguished tradition from Gulliver to Greene, but harder than ever to succeed in, now that plots demand an extreme imagination if they are to surpass what is furnished by mere reality.

"Remember that time you asked me about a secret research group? Working on fear of death? Trying to perfect a medication?. . . Such a group definitely existed. Supported by a multinational giant. Operating in the deepest secrecy in an unmarked building just outside Iron City."

"Why deepest secrecy?"

"It's obvious. To prevent espionage by competitive giants. The point is they came very close to achieving their objective."

All of Don DeLillo's fiction contains the conspiratorial models of the world. In *Players* two Yuppies get mixed up with urban terrorists. In *Running Dog* a porn ring tries to get its hands on a dirty home movie reputed to have been made *in the bunker.* In *Great Jones Street* a drug syndicate pursues a depressed rock star who unwittingly possesses their stash. Chemical substances and commodities, like the conspiracies, and like the dustheaps in Dickens, embody the moral defects of the society that produces them.

In *White Noise* the conspirators try to find a drug that will take away the fear of death from a society that is fixedly preoccupied with producing death, but the motive is profit. Sometimes the desire for power, or to possess the substance for its own sake, moves the plot, but the Dickensian themes of mistaken, lost, or found identity, themes that have dominated novels ever since the nineteenth century, are deliberately effaced—another gloss on the modern situation. Perhaps a vestige of the struggle for place, that other Victorian obsession, can be seen in Jack's efforts to stake out an academic niche for himself as chairman of Hitler Studies.

One finds these plots, these themes, in other contemporary novels—by Robert Stone, or Gore Vidal (in his *Duluth* or *Kalki* mode), or Joan Didion, and however one might long for the affirmative charm of, say, Grace Paley, one can't but admit that these are powerful observers.

Our newspaper is delivered by a middle-aged Iranian driving a Nissan Sentra. Something about the car makes me uneasy—the car waiting with its headlights on, at dawn, as the man places the newspaper on the front steps. I tell myself I have reached an age, the age of unreliable menace. The world is full of abandoned meanings. In the commonplace I find unexpected themes and intensities.

Of course people are by no means agreed that the world is a suitable subject for fiction. The distinguished *Washington Post* critic Jonathan Yardley objects to DeLillo's agenda: "Could there be a more trendy catalogue of trendy political themes: radiation, addiction to violence, television as religion, the trivialization of suffering, the vulgarity of America?" But is topicality only transmogrified into art by the passage of time? Without a willingness to engage the problems of the world around him, we would not have the novels of Dickens, just as, without an acid tone and interest in abstraction, we would not have the novels of Voltaire, or Peacock, or Huxley. Yardley complains, like others, about "fiction as op-ed material. . . . a novel that simply does not work as *fiction,* which is the novelist's first artistic obligation." The difficulty seems to lie in the definition of fiction: "None of the characters acquires any genuine humanity."

Along with the novel of plot and the novel of character, certain old-fashioned theorists of the novel would sometimes speak of the novel of ideas, implying that it was a special taste, and that there is something distinct, if not antithetical, about ideas and the kind of narrative pleasure one derives from less abstract and more simply suspenseful stories: what will happen next? Perhaps the novel of ideas cannot be as exciting, if the ideas demand, like badly brought-up children, to be noticed. Perhaps, even, the reader's awareness of the restless and skeptical intelligence of the author may in some absolute sense operate against such reader responses as sympathy and identification. One is always slightly too aware of the efforts of, say, Bellow, another novelist of ideas, to try to combat their effect by putting in charming human touches, and DeLillo certainly tries to do that here, strewing the text with kids and endearing details of family life.

A first-person protagonist is at least a concession to our old-fashioned wish for heroines and heroes, somebody to stumble through the narrative, thinking the thoughts, experiencing the emotions, more reassuringly human than in satires like Vidal's equally trenchant but chillier *Duluth,* for instance, where all the jokes are the author's. Authors in their omniscience can be intimidating, and perhaps should be advised to conceal their intelligence, the way girls used to be advised to do. Anyhow, we are happy to have Jack Gladney, a diplomatic creation on DeLillo's part, and necessary to a fiction that could otherwise seem too programmatic or too abstract, a regular guy who, because an airborne toxic event and the fear of death are part of his life, convinces us that these unwelcome universals will soon be part of ours.

A more conventional hapless hero, like Jay McInerney's in his recent *Bright Lights, Big City,* may make us laugh by doing a bunch of bad-boy dumb things—too much cocaine before an office deadline—but he does them with minimum self-awareness, and a kind of irritating (male?) confidence in the total indulgence of his readers, among whom the men are expected to identify with him, the women forgive. But Gladney disarms by his penetration, even if he is a five-times married academic who goes around wearing his robe and dark glasses and has to pretend to know German. ("I talked mainly about Hitler's mother, brother and dog. His dog's name was Wolf. This word is the same in English and German. . . . I'd spent days with the dictionary, compiling lists of such words.")

All the characters are infected by Jack's high interrogative style. The novel is entirely composed of questions, sometimes ones you'd like to know the answers to: "Were people this dumb before television?" "Does a man like yourself know the size of India's standing army?" "What if someone held a gun to your head?" "What if the symptoms are real?"

What accounts for the charm of these serious novels on dread subjects? Perhaps Jack's eloquence is such that we are a little less harrowed by his author's exacting and despairing view of civilization. And he is very funny. Besides, there is the special pleasure afforded by the extraordinary language, the coherence of the imagery, saturated with chemicals and whiteness and themes of poisons and shopping, the nice balance of humor and poignance, solemn nonsense and real questions:

"What do I do to make death less strange? How do I go about it?"
"I don't know."
"Do I risk death by driving too fast around curves? Am I supposed to go rock climbing on weekends?"
"I don't know," she said. "I wish I knew."

Shallow Look at the Mind of an Assassin
[Review of *Libra*, by Don DeLillo]

GEORGE F. WILL

DALLAS—Don DeLillo's ninth novel, "Libra," asserts that what happened here in Dealey Plaza a quarter of a century ago became "the seven seconds that broke the back of the American century." If this hyper-ventilating book were merely what that sentence is—overwrought and unhistorical—it would not matter that "Libra" is a best seller. But the book, one of about 20 pouring forth on the Kennedy assassination, is an act of literary vandalism and bad citizenship.

DeLillo's attempt to "follow the bullets' trajectories" back into the minds of Lee Harvey Oswald and others becomes yet another exercise in blaming America for Oswald's act of derangement. It is valuable only as a reminder of the toll that ideological virulence takes on literary talent.

The story is that a cadre of CIA operatives, furious about the halfheartedness of the Bay of Pigs invasion, plan an "electrifying event" to galvanize the country against Fidel Castro. They decide on a "surgical miss" of President Kennedy by a gunman who would leave a paper trail to Cuba. But one thing leads to another, and to the man in the sixth-floor window of the Texas Book Depository.

DeLillo says he is just filling in "some of the blank spaces in the known record." But there is no blank space large enough to accommodate, and not a particle of evidence for, DeLillo's lunatic conspiracy theory. In the book's weaselly afterword, he says he has made "no attempt to furnish factual answers." But in a New York Times interview he says, "I purposely chose the most obvious theory because I wanted to do justice to historical likelihood."

DeLillo traduces an ethic of literature. Novelists using the raw material of history—real people, important events—should be constrained by concern for truthfulness, by respect for the record and a judicious weighing of probabilities.

History, says a DeLillo character, is "the sum total of all the things they aren't telling us." Of course. "They." That antecedentless pronoun haunts the fevered imaginations of paranoiacs. For conspiracy addicts like DeLillo, the utter absence of evidence, after 25 years of searching, proves not that there was no conspiracy but that the conspiracy was diabolically clever. He says that because of the seven seconds in Dallas, "we have been educated in skepticism." Skepticism? DeLillo is a study in credulity regarding the crudities of the American left. He says the assassination was "the turning point in consciousness" for Americans, that "we have been suspicious ever since" concerning "the secret manipulation of history." In Dallas we entered "the world of randomness," reminded by Oswald that "nothing is assured."

Spare us such sandbox existentialism. DeLillo rejects randomness. His intimation is that America is a sick society that breeds extremism and conspiracies and that Oswald was a national type, a product of the culture. From the unremarkable fact that recent assassins or would-be assassins (Sirhan, Ray, Bremer, Hinckley) have been marginal men, not social successes, ideologists of the left weave indictments of America.

DeLillo's indictment is interestingly uninteresting. It is the familiar, banal thought that Oswald was a lonely neurotic who tried to shed ordinariness by lunging into the theater of the Kennedys. And guess what? DeLillo has said: "Consumerism is a form of mass anesthesia. . . . It makes people lonely."

DeLillo's lurid imaginings will soothe immature people who want to believe that behind large events there must be large ideas or impersonal forces or conspiracies. It takes a steady adult nerve to stare unblinkingly at the fact that history can be jarred sideways by an act that signifies nothing but an addled individual's inner turmoil.

The mind of an assassin can be a deep and demanding subject. But the more DeLillo explains his work, the shallower it and he seem. In a burst of sophomoric self-dramatization, he says: "The writer is the person who stands outside society, independent of affiliations. . . . The writer is the man or woman who automatically takes a stance against his or her government." Automatically as in unthinkingly. DeLillo's celebration of the writer as unaffiliated "outsider" is hackneyed and unhistorical. (Henry James, Jane Austen, George Eliot and others were hardly outsiders.) DeLillo's celebration stops just a short step from declaring the writer as kin to Oswald, who, as a defector, was the ultimate outsider.

It is well to be reminded by books like this of the virulence of the loathing some intellectuals feel for American society, and of the frivolous thinking that fuels it. DeLillo is a talented writer whose talent is subordinated to, and obviated by, puerile political stances. What was unfairly said of a far greater writer (T. S. Eliot, born in St. Louis 100 years ago this Monday) must be said of DeLillo: he is a good writer and a bad influence.

Making Meaningful Worlds:
Self and History in *Libra*
[Review of *Libra*, by Don DeLillo]

Don DeLillo's cold, clear sentences in *Libra* feel not so much fixed to the page as suspended above it, like fields of force sent through space. These sentences echo, intersect with, and bounce off one another, producing complicated and often mixed messages about the permeability of terms—real and unreal, factual and fictional, true and false—through which people define their lives. This powerful yet peculiarly weightless quality of DeLillo's prose is perfectly attuned to the intense, yearning, detached figures who populate *Libra*, so many of them uncomfortable residents of private worlds outside history.

DeLillo's most absorbing characters, in *Libra* and in his earlier novels, are disenchanted men who derive from the contemporary American society that DeLillo sees and hears with bleak accuracy. But they also descend from alienated, solitary types treated by great American writers in the past— Stephen Crane's baffled negotiators of crisis, Ernest Hemingway's stunted stoics, Theodore Dreiser's amazed dreamers, Richard Wright's and Ralph Ellison's underground and invisible men, and Norman Mailer's seekers for a fame that only America's mass media can convincingly display and ratify. In this respect, *Libra* not only engages modern America by making John F. Kennedy's assassin the central character, but connects provocatively with American literary history by drawing upon and amplifying distinctively American texts, styles, and themes.

Indeed, *Libra* is an extraordinarily "literary" book, filled with allusions to (and sometimes jokes about) a host of writers and texts. When Lee Harvey Oswald writes answers to a series of questions put to him by his Russian interrogators, he finds that "the chair was too low for the table and he wrote for extended periods standing up." His posture while writing thus mimics the one made famous by Hemingway, a novelist whom Oswald in fact discusses with his Russian questioner, Kirilenko. As a Libran, Oswald is, we later learn,

First published in *Michigan Quarterly Review* 29 (1990): 275–87. Reprinted by permission of the author.

"capable of seeing the other side. He is a man who harbors contradictions: . . . he could play it either way." He is, one might say, close kin to Wright's Bigger Thomas, another angry, marginalized native son who harbors contradictions and is capable, Wright states, of going "either way," toward fascism or communism. Oswald's contradictions also link him to Whitman's speaker in "Song of Myself," a representative American full of contradictions and embracing multitudes, as boundless as Oswald is circumscribed and enclosed. Oswald read Walt Whitman "in hospital ruins" while stationed with the Marines in Corregidor.

Once one begins to note affinities between *Libra* and other books, it is hard to stop. Yet it is also the case that this wide-ranging novel, which glances at so many books and crafts intriguing relationships among them, is very concentrated in its attention to a fairly limited cast of characters. The allusions and references are prominent enough to be noticed and weighed, but subtle and restrained enough to allow DeLillo to maintain his (and the reader's) focus on the chief characters and their secrets, dreams, delusions, and reflections about where they fit in.

DeLillo's characters in *Libra*—Lee Harvey Oswald, of course, above all— wish to settle into a state of mind that will make their lives meaningful. They sense that they are excluded from history: they live insignificantly, quartered on the irritating margins of a world packed with activity that "others" have organized. *Libra* asks: How can an impoverished, isolated life be made real and recognized, and the self at last be given history's seal of approval? And the answer that the novel furnishes, taking the unpromising but pitifully emblematic Oswald as its material, is that life is made real when self and history happen—in this instance, murderously—to converge. This is destiny: when the circulation of carefully wrought plans, freakish coincidences, mere accidents, and unknown accessories aligns self and history, makes a "self" happen.

Perhaps DeLillo's clearest testimony to the hunger for a location in history occurs after Oswald concludes his meeting with Marion Collings, a forceful man—"so trim and fit he could snap his fingers and knock a picture off the wall"—intent upon recruiting Oswald for intelligence work:

> [Oswald] walked through empty downtown Dallas, empty Sunday in the heat and light. He felt the loneliness he always hated to admit to, a vaster isolation than Russia, stranger dreams, a dead white glare burning down. He wanted to carry himself with a clear sense of role, make a move one time that was not disappointed. He walked in the shadows of insurance towers and bank buildings. He thought the only end to isolation was to reach the point where he was no longer separated from the true struggles that went on around him. The name we give this point is history.

DeLillo portrays Oswald as a confused, pathetic, and abusive little man, yet also endows him with very American fears about anonymity (and the prospects for overcoming it) and in that sense sympathetically magnifies him. The "insurance towers and bank buildings" highlight the forces that oppress American outsiders, exiles, and outcasts from meaningfulness, and thus briefly dramatize the exploitative agencies that condition the lives led by burdened nowhere men like Oswald. But while *Libra* frequently mentions these large, omnipotent structures, it does not foreground them with the rapt, menacing detail that DeLillo supplies in earlier novels such as *End Zone, Players,* and *Running Dog.* Nor does *Libra* exorbitantly multiply analogies and fabricate, with runaway speed, mathematical and technological contexts for corporate power, as does *Ratner's Star.* To be sure, *Libra* does probe relationships between government, business, and espionage in the sections devoted to the conspirators' attempt on President Kennedy's life, but the focus is on Oswald, on the rhythm of the balked feelings and dim thoughts that traverse his zone of consciousness. *Libra* may seem to some readers to be less exuberant and spectacular than most of DeLillo's previous books, with all their spiralling analogies, but its power comes precisely from its astonishing conversion of Oswald into an absorbing character and thematic center for the study of the American self and its effort to find a home in history.

Oswald craves a role that will clarify his life and destiny. Sometimes he believes that he has at last fastened on the truth about how he fits in the world, especially when he traffics in Marxist theory. But generally he apprehends only that others have somehow managed to possess an important role—and hence a forthright presence for themselves in history—that has eluded him and that he must attain in order to bridge his vast distance from "true struggles." Oswald keeps trying on roles, imagining, for example, that after he returns to America from his stay in the Soviet Union he can sell his saga to the popular magazines: "He saw himself writing this story for *Life* or *Look,* the tale of an ex-Marine who has penetrated the heart of the Soviet Union, observing everyday life, seeing how fear rules the country."

Perhaps, Oswald later tells himself, he is, at bottom, a father, and can discover coherence in that role, amid the pleasures of the nuclear family:

When Marina told him she was pregnant he thought his life made sense at last. A father took part. He had a place, an obligation. This woman was bringing him the kind of luck he never figured on. Marina Prusakova, herself born two months premature, weighing two pounds, from Archangel on the White Sea, halfway round the World from New Orleans. He took her face in his hands. Fair-haired wispy girl. Full mouth, high neck, blue-eyed flower girl, his slender pale narcissus. Let the child look like her, even that little sulky curl of the mouth, her eyes showing fire when she is angry. He danced her around the room, promised to take better care of her than anyone ever had. She would be the baby until the real baby came.

This impoverished man is captivated by the joyous bourgeois family life and capitalist consumption—"stores in America were incredibly well-stocked, full of amazing choices," he says to Marina—that his Marxist views were supposed to enable him to shed. But DeLillo is not merely exposing the skewed lines between Oswald's political beliefs and domestic aspirations. The scene seems to solicit DeLillo's own support, as his fond, if still satiric, language reveals. Some of the phrases here reproduce what Oswald would speak ("this woman was bringing him the kind of luck he never figured on"), but others lyrically exceed anything likely to be found in Oswald's repertoire ("his slender pale narcissus"). DeLillo balances irony and parody with romantic tribute to the allurements that family life presents: these are fascinating and appealing to Oswald, and to the writer who tells his story.

For Oswald, the momentary family-man, his "days and nights" with the pregnant Marina were at first a "revelation": "He was a domestic soul, happy in the home, a householder who did the dishes, chatted with his wife about the wallpaper. It was wonderful to discover this." Once again DeLillo takes a great risk, reiterating and fleshing out the domestic contentment—the love of wife, child, and home—felt by the calculating killer of the revered JFK as he ironically acts out American dreams of tranquil family life in Russia. But such sweet feelings are finally more beguiling to DeLillo than to his ironized protagonist, and it is not long before Oswald chafes against the fact that "a family expects you to be one thing when you're another. They twist you out of shape." His family is too meager, and his own part as father/husband too sparse in its rewards, to heal the breach that divides him from the main currents of history. And so he abandons his family for fantasies of public renown and continues to drift, with intermittent periods of self-imposed discipline, toward political affairs.

Oswald is persistent, somewhat like the diligent madman comic in Scorsese's *The King of Comedy* who is determined to star on a late-night talk-show and who won't take "no" for an answer. (Oswald's disgust at the world's corruption and unfairness and his impulse toward violence and political assassination make him kin to another of Scorcese's anti-heroes, Travis Bickle in *Taxi Driver.*) But Oswald does not have a clear goal to which he can permanently rivet his energies; he has only a strong sense of not belonging, a long list of disappointments, and a string of deeds that with Beckettian pathos he fouls up or never undertakes. Late in the novel, in a typical instance of impasse, Oswald travels to Mexico City in an unsuccessful attempt to contact representatives of Castro's government: "Nothing has effect. He is turned down, frozen out. It's hard to believe the representatives of the new Cuba are treating him this way. It's a deep disappointment. He feels he is living at the center of an emptiness."

Situations like this one have a comic quality that DeLillo registers, but that he cannot fully elaborate without damaging the deathly context of the novel as a whole. His control remains steady, as he at once expresses and contains Oswald's thwarted efforts—"he is a zero in the system"—to transact business with the authorities and systems that exclude him.

Even when Oswald sojourns in his fantasies about how he might become integrated with history, he remains dissociated from the scenes he imagines: he sees himself seen. He believes that his acts will be significant and his life made real only when onlookers legitimate them. What he does will matter only when his dramatic performance is witnessed. When Oswald enters into the crowd that swarms around the neo-fascist General Walker, he imagines the shocked responses of the people who would observe Walker's death as well as the attentive audiences who would see photographs of the murdered man in the morning newspaper. "How simple," Oswald thinks, "how strangely easy it is to make your existence felt."

This meditative sentence carries a grim and eminently credible acknowledgment of the countless easy opportunities for violence that American society offers, and the bonds between brutal actions and fame: media and murderers go hand-in-hand. In *Running Dog,* one of the characters proposes that "when technology reaches a certain level, people begin to feel like criminals. . . . Someone is after you, the computers maybe, the machine-police." *Libra's* lesson is perhaps even more ominous, for it records the ease with which people can be objects of crime, struck down by the whim of a zero who resolves to make his existence felt. Paranoia about violence, conspiracy, crime, victimization, and death strike deep in the world described in *Libra.* "How do we know the motorman's not insane?", wonders Oswald as he rides the New York subway. Weird Beard on the Dallas radio asks his listeners: "Who is for real and who is sent to take notes? You're out there in the depths of the night, listening in secret, and the reason you're listening in secret is because you don't know who to trust except me. We're the only ones who aren't them."

Oswald's presence in history now seems so singular to us—he graphically counts in the system that ostracized him—that it may seem absurd to nominate him as an everyman. But DeLillo develops Oswald's conflicts and desires as simply more terrible versions of those that define other characters in the novel and that afflict Americans in postmodern times. One of the ways in which DeLillo humanizes (and typifies) Oswald is by giving him little successes that temporarily enthrall him but that, soon enough, illuminate the extent of his ongoing disappointment and sense of failure—and that also expose the paradoxical deep shallowness of his self-understanding. When, for example, Oswald studies Russian with Dr. Braunfels, he feels delighted about winning access to a new language and is pleased at the beginning of mastery: "Working with her, making the new sounds, watching her lips, repeating words and syllables, hearing his own flat voice take on texture and dimension, he could almost believe he was being remade on the spot, given an opening to some larger and deeper version of himself."

A rather expansive Oswald then addresses his teacher, in a passage that DeLillo presents bare of narrative comment:

He said to her, "A thousand years from now, people will look in the history books and read where the lines were drawn and who made the right choice and who didn't. The dynamics of history favor the Soviet Union. This is totally obvious to someone coming of age in America with an open mind. Not that I ignore the values and traditions there. The fact is there's the potential of being attracted to the values. Everyone wants to love America. But how can an honest man forget what he sees in the daily give-and-take that's like a million little wars?"

Like many of Oswald's statements, this one teeters between insight and idiocy, and it depends for its effect on the disparity between the grandeur of the claims and the smallness of the person and the superficiality of the knowledge about Marxism and Soviet society that he has achieved. Oswald has mechanisms for self-awareness and historical generalization; he knows that America has its attractions, and he is even-handedly sure to credit them even as he rejects them. But his words are laced with ironies that infiltrate his plain-spoken sentiments and that reverberate through the novel. What does it mean, after all, to say that one has an "open mind"? In DeLillo's scheme of things, as established in this book and in others, having an open mind does not denote an ability to inventory, categorize, and evaluate experience, but, rather, describes the mind's unending openness to the multitudinous messages of the culture. Messages from enveloping technologies are always streaming through minds, and so saturate the consciousness that they mock the prospect of any independent, open-minded appraisal of who one is and where one stands.

Oswald's story furnishes DeLillo with many opportunities for sardonic treatments of a world shot through with information and what we darkly suspect about the postmodern alteration of the mind. His analysis is crisply summarized when Marion Collings persuades Oswald to undergo debriefing:

> "A fact is innocent until someone wants it. Then it becomes intelligence. We're sitting in a forty-story building that has an exterior of lightweight embossed aluminum. So what? Well, these dullish facts can mean a lot to certain individuals at certain times. An old man eating a peach is intelligence if it's August and the place is the Ukraine and you're a tourist with a camera. I can get you a Minolta incidentally, any time. There's still a place for human intelligence."

"Intelligence" means, first, a fact that has been rendered meaningful, and, second, a person ("human intelligence") who recounts facts that may seem ordinary and uninteresting but that glow with significance for knowing listeners. Intelligence does not connote the power to think freely, make decisions, ponder alternatives, gain autonomy. It belongs to facts and their carriers, and to the agencies that relay and sift through them. And in American culture, there are always more facts, more intelligence. It is a restrictive system—no one can escape from its materials—but it is extraordinarily productive and, in this respect, ceaselessly changing. The irony is that the spread of information fails to lead to clearer meaning and more finely focused intelligence. People assemble knowledge, and its transmission from person to person and place to place does signify, yet the import of it all stays mysterious. It is possible to begin to record and classify ourselves and to collect items whose aura tells us something special (or so we trust), but the end result is always an incomplete montage.

A domesticated version of Collings's scenario exists in the Parmenter household, where Larry Parmenter, an operative for the CIA—the ubiquitous force that gathers, dispenses, and interprets "intelligence"—watches his wife clip articles from the newspaper:

> She said the news clippings she sent to friends were a perfectly reasonable way to correspond. There were a thousand things to clip and they all said something about the way she felt. He watched her read and cut. She wore half-glasses and worked the scissors grimly. She believed these were personal forms of expression. She believed no message she could send a friend was more intimate and telling than a story in the paper about a violent act, a crazed man, a bombed Negro home, a Buddhist monk who sets himself on fire. Because these are the things that tell us how we live.

In this scene and others, DeLillo shows an astute, off-beat, defamiliarizing curiosity about everyday life. What is a story in the newspaper? What makes it meaningful, and does it mean the same thing to everybody? Is the story typical or even true? Maybe not: it does not have to be true to remain a telling index to "how we live" and to bear weirdly tender witness to friendship. For Beryl Parmenter, "corresponding" with friends does not mean exchanging words with them in letters but, instead, means relaying images and stories that declare resemblances between the sender and receiver. What Beryl does affirms close kinships in understanding between friends: I know that you will see something in this clipping and will know why I sent it to you. People bond through bizarre, violent anecdotes and episodes that they share with one another.

Everything in this culture is potentially meaningful; "a thousand things" catch Beryl's attention. Image-laden America is random, prolific, and elusive, yet also strangely marvelous, for nothing in it is unmeaningful. Why not send the entire newspaper to a friend, and maybe—if one could lay hold of them—the reporter's notes and the editor's corrections and all of the endlessly connectable facts, details, and pieces of information and stabs at interpretation that the first clipped story draws to itself? Nicholas Branch sits alone in his room, swamped with data about a single event and immersed in the Warren Report, "the megaton novel James Joyce would have written if he'd moved to Iowa City and lived to be a hundred." But Branch is not really exceptional as a gatherer of information, even though he is writing about a shattering moment in history and is immersed in data about it.

The technologies of culture produce an unending flow of information that is subject to connections galore. All that is needed, DeLillo suggests with Swiftian keenness, is a place to start and an openness to the "dreamy sense of connection" between things in the world. "Once you start a file," says Guy Banister, "it's just a matter of time before the material comes pouring in. . . . It's all been waiting just for you."

Here, as so often, we glimpse the grotesque humor of American culture even as DeLillo contains it through the unextravagant, ominous pitch of sentences that are slanted toward satire and irony just enough so that we can feel the absurdities of the culture without being able to laugh them off. Branch "sits in the book-filled room, the room of documents, the room of theories and dreams," where he has already spent fifteen years sorting and annotating material on the Kennedy assassination sent to him by the CIA. Branch's job is to write a "secret history" of the assassination, but he realizes that the mountains of material are too massive ever to be levelled out and vanquished. He knows, too, that the material—all of it and none of it absolutely relevant—will never stop coming: "there's no end in sight."

The more facts that are assembled, and the longer that each fact is scrutinized, the more the status of the fact grows precarious:

> How can Branch forget the contradictions and discrepancies? These are the soul of the wayward tale. One of the first documents he examined was the medical report on Pfc. Oswald's self-inflicted gunshot wound. In one sentence the weapon is described as 45-caliber. In the next sentence it is 22-caliber. Facts are lonely things. Branch has seen how a pathos comes to cling to the firmest fact.

> Oswald's eyes are gray, they are blue, they are brown. He is five feet nine, five feet ten, five feet eleven. He is right handed, he is left handed. He drives a car, he does not. He is a crack shot and a dud. Branch has support for all these propositions in eyewitness testimony and commission exhibits.

> Oswald even looks like different people from one photograph to the next. He is solid, frail, thin-lipped, broad-featured, extroverted, shy and bank-clerkish, all, with the columned neck of a fullback. He looks like everybody.

Selves are facts and fictions, and are doubled with and crossed by other selves. A self, it seems, is disputed territory and a site where intelligence performs its work intensively but, in this instance at least, paralyzingly. Branch gazes at Oswald and finds him coalescing into other people: "he looks like everybody."

There are, however, epiphanies in *Libra*, heightened moments when sense-making and coherence momentarily occur. Usually these take place when a person resembles the images of himself or herself seen on film or television. Oswald's life is reassuringly touched in this way during his stint in the Marine Corps when he sees John Wayne, who has come to visit the troops in the mess hall. Oswald "watches John Wayne talk and laugh. It's remarkable and startling to see the screen life repeated in life. It makes him feel good. The man is doubly real. He does not cheat or disappoint." Oswald is pleasantly surprised that the movie star glimpsed in person is apparently an accurate representation of the figure that flashes on the movie screen. Generally, Oswald feels, there is a discomposing gap between the image and the reality, but not here: John Wayne neither cheats nor disappoints because he literally lives up to the man who occupies larger than life roles in the movies. DeLillo's point is that to Oswald, John Wayne is real on the screen and in life. Oswald does not perceive the movies as fiction or fantasy, but as another, maybe primary dimension of reality that John Wayne's appearance in the mess hall––in "real life"—happily replicates.

A similar instance of coherence blesses the crowds of people who come to see President and Mrs. Kennedy on the morning of November 22. Kennedy "looked like himself, like photographs, a helmsman squinting in the sea-glare, white teeth shining." As the motorcade travels down the Dallas streets, the crowd becomes especially excited and expectant, tense at the imminent arrival of the real: "The sight of the Lincoln sent a thrill along the street. One roar devoured another. There were bodies jutting from windows, daredevil kids bolting into the open. *They're here. It's them. They're real.*" This is a frightening moment, and not only for the obvious reason that we know in advance the next stages of the plot. DeLillo stresses the panicky ecstasy of people in quest of the real, as they rush to lose their loneliness in amazing spectacles. The roaring Dallas crowd in *Libra* recalls the frenzied, star-struck masses in Nathanael West's *The Day of the Locust,* who are also desperate to experience what's real. "Real" experience is born from images that the media generate—so much so that the real is only real when it confirms the radiance of images.

America's craving for and dependence upon images is one of DeLillo's preoccupations, and in *Libra* his activity as an explorer of this issue is complicated and enriched by the images of Oswald, Kennedy, Jack Ruby, the motorcade, and the Dallas streets that have entered the culture through display in books, magazines, television shows, and documentaries. There are many memorable images of these people, settings, and incidents—and they additionally circulate among and compete with representations popularized in movies (e.g., *Executive Action, The Parallax View*) and TV miniseries (John F. Kennedy as played by Martin Sheen). These are the images that DeLillo draws upon, develops, adjusts, and, at his most inventive and successful, overcomes and displaces. They constitute a crucial (and inescapable) part of the system within which he works as a writer, and the system within which the American lost souls he writes about tap into life and wander in the hope of finding themselves.

DeLillo's image-obsessed, lonely Oswald seeks the epiphany of entry into history: "History means to merge. The purpose of history is to climb out of your own skin." Through study and thought, Oswald trusts he will learn how he can break into the world that others have designed and in which they star. Early in the novel, in a typical scene, Oswald feels that "he wanted subjects and ideas of historic scope, ideas that touched his life, his true life, the whirl of time inside him. He'd read pamphlets, he'd seen photographs in *Life*. Men in caps and worn jackets, thick-bodied women with scarves on their heads. People of Russia, the other world, the secret that covers one-sixth of the land surface of the earth." One could gloss this passage as an account of American bovarism: the self glamorously estimates the self it should be, and could be if it were empowered to take pattern from the splendid forms displayed in books and magazines. This is the self thinking that it can become solidly entrenched in history—residing finally in a privileged world—when it can be judged to dwell in images.

As the novel moves steadily toward its climax, DeLillo provides signs of the imaged self that Oswald will become. During his stay in the Soviet Union, Oswald observes the downed U-2 pilot, Francis Gary Powers:

> It occurred to Oswald that everyone called the prisoner by his full name. The Soviet Press, local TV, the BBC, the Voice of America, the interrogators, etc. Once you did something notorious, they tagged you with an extra name, a middle name that was ordinarily never used. You were officially marked, a chapter in the imagination of the state. Francis Gary Powers. In just these few days the name had taken on a resonance, a sense of fateful event. It already sounded historic.

To Lee Oswald, becoming a historical figure means possessing a middle name in common parlance; it means being scripted in the book of the state, given a local habitation and a name that everyone knows. Oswald's destiny is to become Lee Harvey Oswald, a series of stark and fateful images of the man who shot President Kennedy—or who did not, or who did along with others—and who was himself shot by Jack Ruby.

In a daring act of writerly compassion, DeLillo grants Oswald a heightened understanding of himself after the police place him in a cell: "Lee Harvey Oswald was awake in his cell. It was beginning to occur to him that he'd found his life's work. . . . His life had a clear subject now, called Lee Harvey Oswald. . . . Everyone knew who he was now." The failed dyslexic writer of notes, essays, stories, and historic diaries now intends to devote his days to studying his own case and the details of the assassination, as Nicholas Branch will do later, and as DeLillo did himself in preparing for and producing the novel. Oswald at last has located himself in history, and he looks forward to the consuming project of self-scrutiny that awaits him: "Time to grow in self-knowledge, to explore the meaning of what he's done. He will vary the act a hundred ways, speed it up and slow it down, shift emphasis, find shadings, see his whole life change." Oswald strikingly casts his analysis of himself as a film, one that, like the film of Kennedy's killing taken by Abraham Zapruder, might be run and re-run endlessly, and at different speeds.

DeLillo portrays life in this book as a hypnotic transaction between selves that crave success and media that promise a lustrous place in history. This, he suggests, is what it means for a person to gain contact with himself and acquire the resolve needed to endure life in a small room. The introverted, formerly forsaken Oswald has identified himself as historic, and now can forecast the shape of his career. He is eternally wedded to the wealthy, attractive, beloved President ("he and Kennedy were partners"), and can now legitimately classify and brood upon his motives and acts for they are stunningly significant to everybody. In the past, he pored over who he was, and no one cared. Now he can devote all of his time and energy to such self-examination, and can do so purposefully, for he is Lee Harvey Oswald.

Oswald dies before he can embark upon the project of recreating himself (this is the project that DeLillo undertakes as his representative), but he enjoys the grim satisfaction of witnessing his own death represented on TV: "he could see himself shot as the camera caught it. Through the pain he watched TV. . . . He was in pain. He knew what it meant to be in pain. All you had to do was see TV." DeLillo bestows upon Oswald a fearful honor by allowing him to know the pain of his dying through the black and white images on the screen. These images mirror him; indeed, they are him, and they are captivating, as Beryl Parmenter's response to them testifies. Against her will, she is "held" to the TV screen that repeatedly broadcasts Oswald's murder:

> There was something in Oswald's face, a glance at the camera before he was shot, that put him here in the audience, among the rest of us, sleepless in our homes—a glance, a way of telling us that he knows who we are and how we feel, that he has brought our perceptions and interpretations into his sense of the crime. Something in the look, some sly intelligence, exceedingly brief but far-reaching, a connection all but bleached away by glare, tells us that he is outside the moment, watching with the rest of us. This is what kept Beryl in the room, this and the feeling that it was cowardly to hide.

This is DeLillo's greatest dare in the novel, and one wonders whether his characterization of Oswald finally can sustain the dreadful grandeur of such an interpretation. Oswald lives as a presence that we know and that knows us; his intelligent grasp of our lives is a fact about the culture that we cannot but acknowledge—and from which it would be cowardly to try to flee. "He is commenting on the documentary footage even as it is being shot. Then he himself is shot, and shot, and shot, and the look becomes another kind of knowledge. But he has made us part of his dying." Oswald achieves an awful transcendence at the moment of his death. His end is nightmarish yet wondrous, for somehow the killed killer has managed to oversee his own demise ("watching with the rest of us") and has ensured that Americans will be incorporated into it.

Possibly this moment in *Libra* is best perceived as a sinister vision of American oneness—America as a body of people who are linked by commonly witnessed images and who have shared in and partaken of Oswald's fateful emergence as an infamous self. We feel what Oswald did and all that it meant to our lives, but also recognize that we will never know the full truth about what he did and why and with whom he did it. In *Libra,* DeLillo traces a conspiracy in which Oswald figured and fathoms this assassin's character, and in these ways his book casts the random terrors of the past into patterns that readers can contemplate as their security against absolute panic and confusion. But ultimately the novel is powerful less for its temptingly persuasive explanations than for its evocation of mysteries about American selfhood and history that no explanation of Kennedy's and Oswald's deaths can wholly resolve. DeLillo tells us what might have been the truth—converting and redeeming brutalities by giving them a compelling, creditable form—even as he respects the layers of secrecy and mystery from which the whole truth never stands free. The far-reaching "something" that Oswald communicated to us when he died can never be named.

Market Report
[Review of *Mao II,* by Don DeLillo]

LOUIS MENAND

What most people worry about only at three o'clock in the morning, or after a very bad day at the races, Don DeLillo's characters worry about all the time. DeLillo invents people who don't know the luxury of having a psychology: they can't repress anything. And it's not just that they fear death, or stare hopelessly into the hollow drum of selfhood, or dread the stupefying materiality of the universe. They also never stop talking about it. They must be the most purely self-conscious characters in fiction.

The leading character in DeLillo's new novel, "Mao II," is a famous writer who has fled publicity and the public for a remote outpost in upstate New York, where he is writing his "next book," a novel he has been working on for twenty-three years. His name is Bill Gray, and when the story begins he has decided to end his isolation—or to temper it, at least—by having a photographer come to his hideaway and take his picture. Her name is Brita Nilsson, and she is equipped with an obsession of her own: she travels the world taking photographs of writers—not for commercial purposes, or even artistic ones, but because she has, she says, "a disease called writers." When she meets Bill, they have several DeLilloesque conversations, in which they say things like "When a writer doesn't show his face, he becomes a local symptom of God's famous reluctance to appear" and "I'll never make it to sixty. I see something coming and I see it complete. Slow, wasting, horrible, deep in the body. It's something I've known for years."

So that Brita won't be able to reveal the location of Bill's house, she is driven to and from it at night; her driver is Scott, a young admirer of Bill's work who devoted part of his life to tracking Bill down and persuading him that he needed an assistant, and is devoting the rest of it to organizing Bill's existence and guarding his reputation. He is so committed to this task that he happily shares his girlfriend with Bill; her name is Karen, and she is a former

Originally published in the *New Yorker,* 24 June 1991, 81–84. © Louis Menand.

Moonie who married a man she had known for fifteen minutes—and has not seen since—in a Unification Church wedding ceremony for sixty-five hundred couples at Yankee Stadium.

These four, with Bill at the center, are the principal characters in "Mao II." When I add that Bill's encounter with Brita precipitates his return to civilization (to New York City, and then to Cambridge, London, and Athens), where he becomes entangled in efforts to free a hostage held by a Maoist terrorist group in Beirut; that Karen goes to New York in search of Bill and spends most of her time in the squatters' village in Tompkins Square Park; and that news footage of the Tiananmen Square massacre and the funeral of Ayatollah Khomeini, a photograph of a mass trampling in a soccer stadium, and Andy Warhol's Mao silk screens make major thematic contributions to the novel (the book's title is borrowed from a Warhol drawing), it will be apparent to readers of DeLillo's work that all the familiar elements are here: fanaticism, obsession, and impending cataclysm.

How DeLillo contrives to fashion interesting novels from material like this is always a puzzle, since he seems so indifferent to most of the textbook principles of storytelling—things like "character development," plots that reward expectations, verisimilitude to ordinary experience. His people are cartoonish, puppets of their fixations, but they are often hard to forget. His stories tend to fizzle out inconclusively, but they are suspenseful. He often relies on implausible dialogue (children utter stunning aperçus, thugs engage in penetrating reflection on the ethical ambiguities of thuggery) to advance his themes; it sometimes seems as though his characters have simply become mouthpieces for authorial meditations. But he tends to give us choices about how we are to understand him. And although his world is not round or variegated or shaded, it has a certain unmistakable palpability: it's our world as it appears, perhaps, to someone who is not quite like us.

He does have several distinctive storytelling gifts. He is (as most admirers of his work have noticed) a close observer of detail and a precisionist with language. When he's not loading up his characters' speech with metaphysical speculation, he can be an uncanny mimic; every reader of "Libra" remembers Marguerite Oswald and Jack Ruby for their perfectly rendered colloquial voices. And he can be very funny, too, in a deadpan, Nabokovian fashion. Here is an example, from "White Noise" (1985), something a character observes out of the corner of his eye while chatting with a friend in a supermarket:

A woman fell into a rack of paperback books at the front of the store. A heavy-set man emerged from the raised cubicle in the far corner and moved warily toward her, head tilted to get a cleaner sightline. A checkout girl said, "Leon, parsley," and he answered as he approached the fallen woman, "Seventy-nine." His breast pocket was crammed with felt-tip pens.

Another writer might have ended the paragraph a sentence sooner, but DeLillo doesn't want us to miss the pathos of the breast pocket: the heart that finds a meaning in the sacred mysteries of supermarket pricing.

This sort of balance between doom and daffiness is not easy to sustain; if it went on too long, in fact, it would seem frivolous, as though horrors were being evoked simply in order to play straight men to the silly interchanges of ordinary life. Of DeLillo's recent novels, "White Noise" takes the greatest risks in this direction: its hero is a professor of Hitler studies at a small liberal-arts college—a conception that runs a little close to cuteness and kitsch. But much of "White Noise" succeeds as a dark suburban comedy about an ordinary American family that, through some unexplained accident of fate, has lost its faith in the consoling powers of the culture of plenty—supermarkets, shopping malls, tabloids, and television—and become possessed by an unshakable fear of death. (This is why supermarkets figure as religious places in DeLillo's novels: the frozen-food aisle is for him a *memento mori.*)

For DeLillo, though, such matters are not, finally, comic, and he has a tendency to press his points a little grimly, and to lose his balance slightly, as his novels draw to an end. In "White Noise" he doesn't need to insist quite so sternly that American consumer culture is only a whited sepulchre, or a flimsy distraction from the void. And in "Libra" he doesn't need to require us to think that the underground conspiracy he invents, which leads to the assassination of John F. Kennedy, is only the mirror image of the establishment it tries to overthrow. But he clearly wants us to think these things.

These strong views have made DeLillo a controversial writer among critics who hold strong views themselves. (This counts as a distinction on its own, since there are few enough novelists these days who provoke much controversy.) When "Libra" was published, in 1988, the columnist George Will and the Washington Post critic Jonathan Yardley complained that the novel was an anti-American political tract—"the evanescent craft of pamphleteering rather than the durable art of fiction," as Yardley put it. Partly, it seems, in response to this attack, Frank Lentricchia, a professor of English at Duke, has edited a collection of essays, "Introducing Don DeLillo," by critics sympathetic to what they understand to be DeLillo's take on American life. The volume makes, as advertised, a useful introduction: it includes an interview with DeLillo (who rarely submits to interviews); a chapter from an early novel, "Ratner's Star," published in 1976; some lively appreciative essays by Lentricchia, Charles Molesworth, and Daniel Aaron, among others; and a few essays that struggle to extract a coherent politics from DeLillo's novels. The efforts of this last group of essays meet with little success, for although DeLillo certainly has a take on contemporary life, it is much too unrelenting to sponsor a politics. He is not a writer who imagines that there is a handy exit from our condition. "I don't have a political theory or doctrine that I'm espousing," he remarks in the interview. "I follow characters where they take me and I don't know what I can say beyond that." It's a passage some of the contributors seem to have missed.

Where DeLillo's characters take him is a function of the sort of characters he creates, of course, and one of the objections to "Libra" by critics who didn't like the book was that by choosing to write about Lee Harvey Oswald, DeLillo was suggesting that there was something representatively American about him—that he was making Oswald stand for "us." (This was also, naturally, one of the things that some of the critics who did like the book chose to praise.) But this is like saying that Mailer is suggesting we are all like Gary Gilmore, or that Camus is suggesting we are all like Meursault, or that Flaubert thinks we are all like Emma Bovary.

A novelist who wants to take the measure of the quality of contemporary life needs a character who, for whatever demonic reasons, isn't able to block out impulses in the interests of surviving as comfortably as possible, the way the rest of us do. From the perspective of ordinary life, these characters are overreactors, transients, flakes. They approach the world with demands that are too serious; they are too easily affected by tiny changes in the cultural weather; they register deeply impressions that everyone else reflects. And their disappointment sometimes has violent or tragic consequences. In nineteenth-century novels, this character is often a woman who cannot subdue her nature to the requirements of domestic life. In twentieth-century novels, it is sometimes a criminal. In DeLillo's novels, it is usually a paranoid.

All the characters in "Mao II" are paranoids, but the chief paranoid is Bill. He has hidden his face for more than two decades to protect it from his fans, and he reenters the world out of the conviction that his struggle to preserve his individuality has become so ritualized that he has ended up imitating those paragons of self-effacement the Moonies. ("Once you choose this life, you understand what it's like to exist in a state of constant religious observance," he tells Brita.) He's a dinosaur, one of those old-fashioned writers who drink their dinner from a bottle of Irish whiskey and insist on using a manual typewriter. He says things like (to his editor): "Remember literature, Charlie? It involved getting drunk and getting laid." It's clear that his years of isolation are meant to confer a special authority: he hasn't become inured to contemporary culture yet, so he can see how badly the rest of us have degenerated.

Bill also holds the old-fashioned conviction that the novel was once "the great secular transcendence"; but now, he believes, it has lost its cultural authority and been displaced by "the new culture, the system of world terror." When he learns, during a visit to his editor, that a poet has been taken hostage in Beirut, this seems to him a perfect confirmation (it may seem to us a *too* perfect confirmation) of his deepest anxiety. "What terrorists gain, novelists lose," he explains to a representative of the terrorist group late in the story. "The degree to which they influence mass consciousness is the extent of our decline as shapers of sensibility and thought. The danger they represent equals our own failure to be dangerous." (This is, one feels, a little too obviously DeLillo speaking.)

The enemy of the word, which is worn and wrinkled by use, is the image, whose authority (as DeLillo sees it) seems absolute, as though it flowed from something not merely human—from something outside history. Karen, the Moonie, is a child of the image world: she watches disasters on the news with the sound turned off, defenseless against pictures of people swept up in inhuman frenzies, their individuality obliterated. And this effacement by the image is the tactic of the terrorist sect in Beirut: its members wear hoods to erase their own faces, but each of them has a picture of their leader pinned to his uniform.

The conjunction of terrorism with reflections on words and images recalls DeLillo's "The Names," which appeared in 1982—the story of a "risk analyst" stationed in Athens who becomes fascinated with a cult that roams the Middle East selecting murder victims on the basis of alphabetic coincidences. (They kill people whose initials match the initials of the name of the place they are in.) DeLillo's theme in "The Names" is not easy to summarize (the essay on the novel in "Introducing Don DeLillo" gets hopelessly ensnarled), because two notions about language keep switching places in the book: the notion that language has been corrupted in the contemporary world, and that its purity has to be relearned and respected; and the notion that too much respect for purity leads to fanaticism and murder, and that corruption is language's natural state.

DeLillo performs the same appealing trick of complication in "Mao II." Karen is a woman of the image, but then so is Brita, who photographs people not to efface them but to particularize them. Bill is a man of words, but so is Scott, who maniacally hoards Bill's writing and tries to control his life. Bill is the arch-individualist, who turns his back on other people; Karen is a human chameleon, whose empathy is boundless. And so forth.

This tension among possibilities is novelistic, but it does not, by itself, make a novel. It is only the outline of a novel, and most readers of "Mao II" are likely to feel that the scheme is too naked, that it lies too heavily on the story—something that is not true of "The Names," which is more thickly populated and richer with incident. "The Names" is also a lot longer. Although it's probably unwise these days to complain that a book is too short, "Mao II" has the spare quality of a parable or a cautionary tale. It isn't dense enough, and it therefore leaves us feeling uncomfortably exposed to the heat of DeLillo's own obsessions.

One of those obsessions, though it is never mentioned explicitly, is obviously the persecution of Salman Rushdie, and this accounts, I think, for the didactic tone. "Mao II" is a statement in defense of the writer against absolutism; and statements, even when they are presented in the guise of fiction, do not admit very much ambiguity.

The gesture toward Rushdie gives the novel's urgency a focus. DeLillo's other obsessions in the book, though, seem somehow dated—an odd effect in the work of a novelist so riveted on the contemporary. It's not only the Lebanese terrorists and their hostages, the Warhol silk screens, and the Unification Church that don't have the resonance they once did—that seem to belong to the pathology of a slightly earlier era. It's also the idea, emphasized repeatedly in the novel, that culture has become a huge machine for turning reality into a marketable image. "There's the life and there's the consumer event," says Bill to Brita. "Nothing happens until it's consumed. Or put it this way. Nature has given way to aura. A man cuts himself shaving and someone is signed up to write the biography of the cut." And Brita, later on, muses about the way that "everything that came into her mind lately and developed as a perception seemed at once to enter the culture, to become a painting or photograph or hairstyle or slogan."

This notion of the voracious transformation of everything into a simulacrum of itself—this fixation on the bottomlessness of contemporary culture—is what Warhol's art was all about, of course. (It's fitting, given this theme, that the title of the book doesn't simply allude to a Warhol title but reproduces it.) "Nothing is authentic!" is the despairing, traditionalist version of this idea. "Everything is only a representation of a representation!" is the enthusiastic, "postmodernist" version. In either version, it is the sort of stock that sells best in a bull market, when the economy is in full gear, everyone is racing to keep up, and the culture is wearing out styles as quickly as they can be invented. This is perhaps why Warhol's two moments came nearly twenty years apart: in the go-go years of the sixties, and again at the end of the eighties.

Things are more bearish today. Our feet feel more mundanely planted on the ground, and the idea that our souls are being sucked from us by the image-makers—that, as a dramatic sentence in DeLillo's novel puts it, "the future belongs to crowds"—is less persuasive than it might have seemed just a few years ago. This is, as our century goes, a fairly prosaic moment, and DeLillo is not a novelist of prosaic emotions.

The Blast Felt round the World
[Review of *Underworld,* by Don DeLillo]

MICHAEL DIRDA

Don Delillo's eagerly awaited new novel, *Underworld,* is extremely long, no question about it. But that's as close to a criticism as you'll find here: I'd have been happy if the book were the length of *Possession, Atlas Shrugged, Invisible Man* and *Studs Lonigan* combined.

That it recalls all these very different modern classics, as well as much of DeLillo's earlier work (*End Zone, Libra*), is a measure of both its ambition and quite awesome achievement. This is a novel, after all, that draws together baseball, the Bomb, J. Edgar Hoover, waste disposal, drugs, gangs, Vietnam, fathers and sons, comic Lenny Bruce and the Cuban Missile Crisis.

And that's just for openers. It also depicts passionate adultery, weapons testing, the care of aging mothers, the postwar Bronx, '60s civil rights demonstrations, populuxe culture, advertising, graffiti artists at work, Catholic education, chess and murder. And still we're not through. There's a viewing of a lost Eisenstein film, meditations on the Watts Tower, an evening at Truman Capote's Black & White Ball, a hot-air balloon ride, serial murders in Texas, a camping trip in the Southwest, a nun on the Internet, reflections on history, one hit (or possibly two) by the New York mob and an apparent miracle. Most amazingly, none of this seems jumbled or arbitrary: As DeLillo says and proves, "Everything is connected in the end."

Such richness. Think of *Underworld* as a great Victorian-style panoramic novel—*The Way We Live Now,* say—or even as a 12-part miniseries, titled perhaps "Cold War and Remembrance." For DeLillo's masterpiece provides both a cultural history of America during the Bomb era and a suspenseful journey into the past.

The main character is Nick Shay, in the 1990s an aging waste-disposal expert but in his youth a teenaged dropout from the Bronx. Nick is the common element in several of the novel's principal obsessions. In his rowdy youth he takes up briefly with a neighborhood housewife, Klara Sax, who eventually

Originally published in the *Washington Post,* 28 September 1997, 1, 10. Copyright © 1997, the *Washington Post.* Reprinted by permission.

remakes herself into a world-renowned artist, part Christo, part Georgia O'Keeffe. Nick also comes to possess what may be—doubts remain—the legendary baseball, homered by Bobby Thomson, that unexpectedly gave the 1951 pennant to the Giants. As it happens, on that very same day, October 3, the Russians set off a powerful atomic blast, thus heating up the Cold War. And sometime in his youth Nick seems to have committed a murder. Nuclear weapons, waste, the fate of that fateful baseball and the destinies of an ordinary man and his loved ones plangently intertwine for 800 pages.

In an interview Don DeLillo once asserted, "I want to give pleasure through language, through the architecture of a book or a sentence and through characters who may be funny, nasty, violent, or all of these." *Underworld* delivers on every count.

Consider a few sentences. The moody stand-up entertainer Lenny Bruce resembles "a poolshark who'd graduated to deeper and sleazier schemes." In one performance he maniacally sums up every other Swedish art film of the '60s: "Ursula Andress naked to the waist with a slain calf slung over her shoulder." When the formidable Sister Edgar is glimpsed, she is "diagramming a compound sentence, the chalked structure so complex and self-appending it began to resemble the fire-escaped facade of the kind of building most of the boys and girls lived in." After the Texas Highway Killer calls in to a news program to explain his crimes, he says: "I hope this talk has been conducive to understand the situation better. For me to request that I would only talk to Sue Ann Corcoran, one-on-one, that was intentional on my part. I saw the interview you did where you stated you'd like to keep your career, you know, ongoing while you hopefully raise a family and I feel like this is a thing whereby the superstation has the responsibility to keep the position open, okay, because an individual should not be penalized for lifestyle type choices." Toxic waste-disposal experts, we learn, spread tales about a spectral ship, filled with unimaginably poisonous material, that can never come into port: The Flying Liberian. Advertising is dubbed, with a kind of Japanese aptness, "the industry of vivid description."

Underworld crackles with such memorable formulations. "A museum was empty rooms with knights in armor where you had one sleepy guard for every seven centuries." Marilyn Monroe, we learn, hated being Marilyn, but Jayne Mansfield loved it. Nick shrewdly observes "how people played at being executives while actually holding executive positions . . . It's not that you're pretending to be someone else. You're pretending to be exactly who you are." Nick's brother Matt serves in Vietnam "where everything he'd ever disbelieved or failed to imagine turned out, in the end, to be true." The original bombheads, the scientists who worked at Los Alamos, flicker by as "all those emigres from Middle Europe, thick-browed men, with sad eyes and roomy pleated pants." One Hispanic character has "the reflective head of an elder of the barrio, playing dominoes under a canopy while the fire engines idle up the street . . . "

DeLillo can do voices—the Texas killer, a Jewish paranoid, Russian capitalists, artsy New Yorkers—as well as aphorisms. Here's a thrilling old black street preacher: "You see the eye that hangs over this pyramid here. What's pyramids doing on American money? You see the number they got strung out at the base of this pyramid. This is how they flash their Masonic codes to each other. This is Freemason, the passwords and handshakes. This is Rosicrucian, the beam of light. This is webs and scribbles all over the bill, front and the back, that contains a message. This is not just rigmarole and cooked spaghetti. They predicting the day and the hour. They telling each other when the time is come. You can't find the answer in the Bible or the Bill of Rights. I'm talking to you. I'm saying history is written on the commonest piece of paper in your pocket."

As should be evident, *Underworld* is rippled throughout with humor, from old ribaldries about Speedy Gonzalez to the guerrilla satire of the Terminal Theater. Just before the Black & White Ball, an earnest Clyde Tolson informs J. Edgar Hoover about a plot to steal the director's trash cans. "Confidential source says they intend to take your garbage on tour. Rent halls in major cities. Get lefty sociologists to analyze the garbage item by item. Get hippies to rub it on their naked bodies. More or less have sex with it. Get poets to write poems about it. And finally, in the last city on the tour, they plan to eat it . . . And expel it . . . publicly." That night, at the ball itself, the guests do the twist "with all the articulated pantomime of the unfrozen dead come back for a day." Even Clyde dances with a provocative young masked woman who suddenly whispers, "If you kiss me, I'll stick my tongue so far down your throat . . . it will pierce your heart."

Formidable characters, themes, language—there's almost none of that icy detachment for which DeLillo has occasionally been faulted. Even his fascination with conspiracy and paranoia fits not only the times but also his novel's intricate architecture. After an opening prologue, set in 1951, the narrative leapfrogs to the early 1990s, and then gradually works its way back in time toward explosions of sex and death in the summer of 1952. An epilogue eventually returns us to the present. In effect as we read, we penetrate beneath history's surface, gradually descending into the past, that underworld which shapes our lives.

Of course, DeLillo rings other changes on the meaning of underworld, associating it with crime, dreams, the afterlife, subway tunnels and even that lost film masterpiece by Eisenstein, "Unterwelt." Similarly, the novel creates numerous doubles and mirrorings: Moonman decorates subway cars; Klara paints old B-52s; Sister Edgar twins J. Edgar; a clip of a murder by the Texas Highway Killer prefigures a viewing of the Zapruder film of the Kennedy assassination. Public and private intertwine; the half-remembered fades into the wholly imagined. A nun in a burned-out ghetto screams at a busload of gawking foreign tourists: "Brussels is surreal. Milan is surreal. This is real. The Bronx is real." Periodically, DeLillo shows us our forgotten brethren, those who happened to live, figuratively or literally, downwind from the blast—the tortured damned of a Brueghel painting and the deformed experimental subjects in Eisenstein's movie, the lost souls of the barrio, the victims of atomic radiation in Kazakhstan.

But "everything's connected." Searching for the Thomson baseball, obsessive Marvin Lundy examines old photographs and bits of movie film, enlarging details, patiently studying the very pixels. "All knowledge is available if you analyze the dots." Everything's connected: Nick's brother interprets photo data for the bombing runs of Chuckie Wainwright, who inherited a certain old baseball from his ad exec father, who once planned an orange-juice campaign similar to the one used on the billboard where the face of the martyred girl Esmeralda miraculously appears. One eventually discovers that *Underworld* operates as a kind of hypertext, a never-ending series of narrative links.

Of all these, the sections set in the early 1950s possess a particular magic. The opening 60 pages thrillingly recreate that final game of the 1951 pennant race. The account of Nick's cocky adolescence—cigarettes on the stoop, nights at the pool hall, sex in stolen cars, fights with outsiders—seems like the purest Americana, to use the word with which DeLillo presciently titled his first novel. Appropriately Nick's part of *Underworld* ends with a paragraph redolent of loss and desire, echoing Whitman, recalling *Gatsby*. Nearing retirement, enjoying a comfortable life and a successful career, Nick yearns for his youth: "I long for the days of disorder. I want them back, the days when I was alive on the earth, rippling in the quick of my skin, heedless and real. I was dumb-muscled and angry and real. This is what I long for, the breach of peace, the days of disarray when I walked real streets and did things slap-bang and felt angry and ready all the time, a danger to others and a distant mystery to myself."

Last spring Thomas Pynchon brought out *Mason & Dixon*. This fall we have Don DeLillo's *Underworld.* Can you imagine the headache for the judges of the literary awards? But, I say, let 'em agonize. The rest of us can read and rejoice.

ESSAYS
◆

For Whom Bell Tolls:
Don DeLillo's *Americana*

David Cowart

Don DeLillo's 1971 novel *Americana,* his first, represents a rethinking of the identity or alienation theme that had figured with particular prominence in the quarter century after the close of World War II. The theme persists in DeLillo, but the self becomes even more provisional. The changing social conditions and imploding belief systems that alienate a Meursault, a Holden Caulfield, or a Binx Bolling do not constitute so absolute an epistemic rupture as the gathering recognition—backed up by post-Freudian psychology—that the old stable ego has become permanently unmoored. Whether or not he would embrace Lacanian formulations of psychological reality, DeLillo seems fully to recognize the tenuousness of all "subject positions." He knows that postmodern identity is not something temporarily eclipsed, something ultimately recoverable. DeLillo characters cannot, like Hemingway's Nick Adams, fish the Big Two-Hearted to put themselves back together. Thus David Bell, the narrator of *Americana,* remains for the reader a slippery, insubstantial personality—even though he claims to be able to engage with his self whenever he looks in a mirror (13/11).[1] Bell in fact stumbles through life, waiting for some change, some new dispensation, to complete the displacement of the old order, in which the fiction of a knowable, stable identity enjoyed general credence.

In psychoanalytic theory, one's sense of self originates, at least in part, in the early relationship with the mother. DeLillo, like Freud or Lacan, extends this idea beyond individual psychology. He knows that Americans collectively define themselves with reference to a land their artists frequently represent, in metaphor, at least, as female. In *Americana* DeLillo represents this female land as maternal—a trope common enough in Europe (where nationalists often salute "the Motherland") but seldom encountered on this side of the Atlantic. The author thereby makes doubly compelling the theme of the land violated, for he presents not the familiar drama of rapacious Europeans despoiling a landscape represented as Pocahontas, but the more appalling tragedy of the

Originally published in *Contemporary Literature* 37, no. 4 (1996): 602–19. Copyright © 1996. Reprinted by permission of the University of Wisconsin Press.

American Oedipus and his unwitting violation of a landscape that the reader gradually recognizes as Jocasta.[2]

By means of these and other allegorizing identifications, DeLillo participates in and wields a certain amount of control over the profusion of images by which America represents itself. More than any other contemporary writer, DeLillo understands the extent to which images—from television, from film, from magazine journalism and photography, from advertising, sometimes even from books—determine what passes for reality in the American mind. Unanchored, uncentered, and radically two-dimensional, these images constitute the discourse by which Americans strive to know themselves. DeLillo's protagonist, a filmmaker and successful television executive, interacts with the world around him by converting it to images, straining it through the lens of his sixteen-millimeter camera. He attempts to recapture his own past by making it into a movie, and much of the book concerns this curious, Godardesque film in which, he eventually discloses, he has invested years. Thus one encounters—two years before the conceit structured *Gravity's Rainbow*—a fiction that insists on blurring the distinctions between reality and its representation on film. Film vies, moreover, with print, for readers must negotiate a curiously twinned narrative that seems to exist as both manuscript and "footage"—and refuses to stabilize as either. *Americana,* the novel one actually holds and reads, seems to be this same narrative at yet a third diagetic remove.

In his scrutiny of the mechanics of identity and representation in the written and filmed narratives of David Bell, especially as they record an oedipal search for the mother, DeLillo explores the America behind the *Americana*. What the author presents is a set of simulacra: manuscript and film and book mirroring a life and each other, words and images that pretend to mask a person named David Bell. But of course David Bell is himself a fictional character—and six years too young to be a stand-in for DeLillo (though one can recast the conundrum here as the attempt of this other subject—the author—to trick the simulacra into yielding up a modicum of insight into the mysteries of the ego's position within the Symbolic Order). DeLillo makes of his shadow play a postmodernist exemplar, a dazzling demonstration of the subject's inability to know a definitive version of itself. Thus Bell's film begins and ends with a shot of Austin Wakely, his surrogate, standing in front of a mirror that reflects the recording camera and its operator, the autobiographical subject of the film. A perfect piece of hermeticism, this shot announces an infinite circularity; it suggests that nothing in the rest of the film will manage to violate the endless circuit of the signifying chain. It suggests, too, the complexity—indeed, the impossibility—of determining the truly authentic subject among its own proliferating masks.

One can resolve some of the difficulties of DeLillo's first novel by searching for coherent elements amid the larger obscurity of its action and structure. The central events of the narrative evidently take place some time after the Kennedy assassination (the American century's climacteric) and before the Vietnam War had begun to wind down. Recollecting the second year of his brief marriage, terminated five years previously, Bell remarks that the conflict in Southeast Asia "was really just beginning" (38/35), and subsequently the war is a pervasive, malign presence in the narrative. Inasmuch as the hero is twenty-eight years old and apparently born in 1942 (his father in the film mentions that the birth occurred while he was overseas, shortly after his participation in the Bataan Death March), the story's present would seem to be 1970. Yet occasionally Bell intimates a much later vantage from which he addresses the reader. He seems, in fact, to be spinning this narrative at a considerable remove in time, for he refers at one point to "the magnet-grip of an impending century" (174/166). He is also remote in space: like another great egotist who embodied the best and worst of his nation, Bell seems to have ended up on an "island" (16/14, 137/129) off "the coast of Africa" (357/347).

DeLillo structures the novel as a first-person narrative divided into four parts. In the first of these Bell introduces himself as a jaded television executive in New York. Presently he collects three companions and sets out on a cross-country trip—ostensibly to meet a television film crew in the Southwest, but really to look in the nation's heartland for clues to himself and to the American reality he embodies. In part 2, through flashbacks, the reader learns about Bell's relations with his family (mother, father, two sisters) and about his past (childhood, prep school, college). In part 3, Bell stops over in Fort Curtis, a midwestern town, and begins shooting his autobiographical film with a cast composed of his traveling companions and various townspeople recruited more or less at random. This part of the story climaxes with a long-postponed sexual encounter with Sullivan, the woman sculptor he finds curiously compelling. Subsequently, in part 4, he abandons his friends and sets off alone on the second part of his journey: into the West.

Bell's "post-Kerouac pilgrimage," as Charles Champlin calls it (7), takes him from New York to Massachusetts to Maine, then westward to the sleepy town of Fort Curtis, in a state Bell vaguely surmises to be east (or perhaps south) of Iowa. After his stay in Fort Curtis he undertakes a "second journey, the great seeking leap into the depths of America," heading "westward to match the shadows of my image and my self" (352/341). A hitchhiker now, picked up "somewhere in Missouri" (358/348), he travels with the generous but sinister Clevenger, himself a remarkable piece of *Americana,* through Kansas, through "a corner-piece of southeastern Colorado," across New Mexico, and on into Arizona. Significantly, he never gets to Phoenix. Instead, he visits a commune in the Arizona desert before rejoining Clevenger and heading "east, south and east" (372/362), back across New Mexico to the west Texas town of Rooster (where DeLillo will locate Logos College in his next novel, *End Zone*). Parting with Clevenger for good, Bell hitchhikes to Midland, where he rents a car and drives northeast, overnight, to Dallas, honking as he traverses the ground of Kennedy's martyrdom. In Dallas he boards a flight back to New York.

In his end is his beginning. Seeking the foundational in self and culture, Bell travels in a great circle that is its own comment on essentialist expectations. His circular journey seems, in other words, to embody the signifying round, impervious to a reality beyond itself. In this circle, too, readers may recognize elements of a more attenuated symbolism. As an emblem of spiritual perfection, the circle suggests the New World promise that Fitzgerald and Faulkner meditate on. As an emblem of final nullity, it suggests America's bondage to historical process—the inexorable *corsi* and *ricorsi* described by Vico (whom Bell briefly mentions). DeLillo teases the reader, then, with the circle's multiple meanings: vacuity, spiritual completeness, inviolable link in the chain of signification, historical inevitability.

That history may be cyclical affords little comfort to those caught in a civilization's decline. Like his friend Warren Beasley, the Jeremiah of all-night radio, Bell knows intimately the collapse of America's ideal conception of itself. He speaks of "many visions in the land, all fragments of the exploded dream" (137/129). The once unitary American Dream, that is, has fallen into a kind of Blakean division; and DeLillo—through Bell—differentiates the fragments embraced by "generals and industrialists" from what remains for the individual citizen: a seemingly simple "dream of the good life." But this dream, or dream fragment,

> had its complexities, its edges of illusion and self-deception, an implication of serio-comic death. To achieve an existence almost totally symbolic is less simple than mining the buried metals of other countries or sending the pilots of your squadron to hang their bombs over some illiterate village. And so purity of intention, simplicity and all its harvests, these were with the mightiest of the visionaries, those strong enough to confront the larger madness. For the rest of us, the true sons of the dream, there was only complexity. The dream made no allowance for the truth beneath the symbols, for the interlinear notes, the presence of something black (and somehow very funny) at the mirror rim of one's awareness. This was difficult at times. But as a boy, and even later, quite a bit later, I believed all of it, the institutional messages, the psalms and placards, the pictures, the words. Better living through chemistry. The Sears, Roebuck catalog. Aunt Jemima. All the impulses of all the media were fed into the circuitry of my dreams. One thinks of echoes. One thinks of an image made in the image and likeness of images. It was that complex. (137–38/130)

This passage is an especially good example of the DeLillo style and the DeLillo message. DeLillo's writing, like Thomas Pynchon's, is keyed to the postmodern moment. Inasmuch as this is prose that strives to become as uncentered and as shadow-driven as the peculiarly American psychological and social reality under scrutiny, one glosses it only at the risk of violating the author's studied indirection. But one can—again, without pretending to exhaust its ambiguity and indeterminacy—hazard a modest commentary.

"Almost totally symbolic," the dream of the good life is subject to "complexities" from which powerful ideologues are free. Focused, single-minded, exempt from doubt, the military and industrial powerful confront the "larger madness" of political life in the world (and especially in the twentieth century) with a singleness of purpose that, however misguided, at least enjoys the distinction, the "harvests," of "purity" and "simplicity." The reader who would convert these abstractions into concrete terms need only recall how for decades a Darwinian economic vision and a passionate hatred of Communism made for an American foreign policy that was nothing if not "simple." The irony, of course, is that simplicity is the last thing one should expect of dealings between nations, especially when those dealings take the form of war. But DeLillo evinces little interest in attacking the monomania of Lyndon Johnson and Robert McNamara or Richard Nixon and Melvin Laird. By 1971, their obtuseness had been exposed too often to afford latitude for anything fresh in a literary sense—and DeLillo has the good sense to know the fate of satiric ephemera like *MacBird!* (1966) and the contemporaneous *Our Gang* (1971). In *Americana,* by contrast, DeLillo explores the far-from-simple mechanics of life in a culture wholly given over to the image. The citizen of this culture, however seemingly innocent and uncomplicated, exists as the cortical nexus of a profoundly complex play of advertisements, media bombardments, and shadow realities that manage, somehow, always to avoid or postpone representation of the actual, the "something black . . . at the mirror rim of one's awareness." DeLillo, then, chronicling this "existence almost totally symbolic," sees the American mass brain as "an image made in the image and likeness of images."

But the real lies in wait, says the author, whose thesis seems to complement Lacanian formulations of the subject position and its problematic continuity. The subject cannot know itself, and language, the Symbolic Order, discovers only its own play, its own energies, never the bedrock reality it supposedly names, glosses, gives expression to. Hence DeLillo actually echoes Lacan—not to mention Heidegger, Derrida, and others—in speaking of "interlinear notes" to the text of appearances, a presence at the edges of mirrors, "truth beneath the symbols." *Americana* is the record of an attempt to break out of the endlessly circular signifying chain of images replicating and playing off each other to infinity. As such it is also the record of a growing awareness of the complexity with which a consumer culture imagines itself. For the author, this awareness extends to knowledge of the social reality beneath what Pynchon, in *The Crying of Lot 49,* characterizes as "the cheered land" (180).

Part of the agenda in the Pynchon novel, one recalls, is to bring to the surface of consciousness the disinherited or marginalized elements of the

American polity. *The Crying of Lot 49* functions in part to remind readers that enormous numbers of Americans have been omitted from the version of the country sanctioned by the media and other public institutions, and that is one way to understand what DeLillo is doing when a reference to Aunt Jemima follows a cryptic remark about "the presence of something black (and somehow very funny) at the mirror rim of one's awareness." For years, one encountered no black faces in that cornucopia of middle-class consumerism, the Sears, Roebuck catalog, but the semiotics of breakfast-food merchandising could accommodate a black domestic like Aunt Jemima. The reference to a familiar and venerable commercial image affords a ready example of a reality that the sixties, in one of the decade's more positive achievements, had brought to consciousness—the reality of an American underclass that for years could be represented only as comic stereotype. Thus the reader who needs a concrete referent for what DeLillo is talking about here need go no further than a social reality that was, in 1970, just beginning to achieve visibility.

Aunt Jemima metonymically represents the world of advertising, a world dominated by that especially resourceful purveyor of the image, Bell's father (the familial relationship reifies the idea that television is the child of advertising). The father's pronouncements on his calling complement the book's themes of representational form and substance. He explains that advertising flourishes by catering to a desire on the part of consumers to think of themselves in the third person—to surrender, as it were, their already embattled positions as subjects. But the person who laments "living in the third person" (64/58) is his own son, this novel's narrating subject. "A successful television commercial," the father remarks, encourages in the viewer a desire "to change the way he lives" (281/270). This observation mocks and distorts the powerful idea Rilke expresses in his poem "Archäischer Torso Apollos": "*Du musst dein Leben ändern* (313).[3] The poet perceives this message—"You must change your life"—as he contemplates the ancient sculpture. He suggests that the work of art, in its power, its perfection, and (before the age of mechanical reproduction) its uniqueness, goads viewers out of their complacency. The artist—Rilke or DeLillo—confronts torpid, passionless humanity with the need to seek a more authentic life; the advertiser, by contrast, confronts this same humanity with spurious, even meretricious need for change. The impulse behind this narrative, interestingly enough, is precisely that need to change a life one has come to see as empty—the need to return from the limbo of third-person exile, the need to recover, insofar as possible, a meaningful subjectivity.

Like the questers of old, then, Bell undertakes "a mysterious and sacramental journey" (214/204): he crosses a threshold with a supposedly faithful band of companions (Sullivan, Brand, Pike), travels many leagues, and descends into a Dantean underworld with the Texan, Clevenger, as cicerone. Indeed, the nine-mile circumference of Clevenger's speedway seems palpably to glance at the nine-fold circles of Dante's Hell (especially as Bell imagines, back in New York, a "file cabinet marked *pending return of soul from limbo*" [345/334]). When, from here, Bell puts in a call to Warren Beasley, who has "foresuffered almost all" (243/232), he modulates from Dante to Odysseus, who learns from Tiresias in the underworld that he must "lose all companions," as Pound says, before the completion of his quest. Alone and empty-handed, without the boon that traditionally crowns such efforts, Bell is a postmodern Odysseus, returning not to triumph but to the spiritual emptiness of New York before ending up in solitude on a nameless island that would seem to have nothing but its remoteness in common with Ithaca. Indeed, announcing toward the end of his story that he will walk on his insular beach, "wearing white flannel trousers" (358/348), he dwindles finally to Prufrock, the ultimate hollow man.

In attempting to understand the reasons for Bell's failure, the reader engages with DeLillo's real subject: the insidious pathology of America itself, a nation unable, notwithstanding prodigies of self-representation, to achieve self-knowledge. The novelist must represent the self-representation of this vast image culture in such a way as to reveal whatever truth lies beneath its gleaming, shifting surfaces. But the rhetoric of surface and depth will not serve: America is a monument to the ontological authority of images. DeLillo seeks at once to represent American images and to sort them out, to discover the historical, social, and spiritual aberrations they embody or disguise.

DeLillo focuses his analysis on the character of David Bell, a confused seeker after the truth of his own tormented soul and its relation to the larger American reality. One makes an essential distinction between DeLillo's engagement with America and that of his character, who becomes the vehicle of insights he cannot share. Marooned among replicating images, Bell loses himself in the signifying chain, as doomed to "scattering" as Pynchon's Tyrone Slothrop. In his attempts to recover some cryptic truth about his family and in his manipulation of filmic and linguistic simulacra, Bell fails to see the extent to which he embodies an America guilty of the most abhorrent of violations—what the Tiresias-like Beasley calls the "national incest." David Bell's existential distress seems to have an important oedipal dimension, seen in his troubled memories of his mother and in his relations with other women in his life. I propose to look more closely, therefore, at just how the relationship between David Bell and his mother ramifies symbolically into the life of a nation.

The emphasis, in what follows, on the Freudian view of the Oedipus complex is not intended to imply an argument for its superiority to those post-Freudian (and especially Lacanian) views invoked elsewhere in this essay. When the subject is postmodern identity, one naturally opts for Lacan's refinements of Freudian thought, but insofar as Lacan took little interest in pathology per se, and insofar as DeLillo's emphasis is on a nation's sickness, the critic may legitimately gravitate to the older psychoanalytic economy and its lexicon. It is a mistake to think that entry into the Symbolic Order precludes all further encounters with the Imaginary, and by the same token we err to view Freud's system as wholly displaced by that of his successor. Indeed, Lacan resembles somewhat the messiah who comes not to destroy the law but to fulfill it, and just as the theologian illustrates certain points more effectively out of the Old Testament than out of the New, so does the critic need at times to summon up the ideas of the Mosaic founder of psychoanalysis.

Throughout his narrative, Bell strives to come to terms with some fearsome thing having to do with his mother—something more insidious, even, than the cancer that takes her life. She grapples with a nameless anomie that becomes localized and explicable only momentarily, as in her account of being violated on the examining table by her physician, Dr. Weber (one recalls the similarly loathsome gynecologist in *The Handmaid's Tale,* Margaret Atwood's meditation on another rape of America). Neurasthenic and depressed, Bell's mother evidently lived with a spiritual desperation that her husband, her children, and her priest could not alleviate. Bell's recollections of his mother and his boyhood culminate as he thinks back to a party given by his parents, an occasion of comprehensive sterility that owes something to the gathering in Mike Nichols's 1968 film *The Graduate,* not to mention the moribund revels of "The Dead." The party ends with the mother spitting into the ice cubes; subsequently, the son encounters her in the pantry and has some kind of epiphany that he will later attempt to re-create on film. This epiphany concerns not only the mother's unhappiness but also the son's oedipal guilt, for Bell conflates the disturbing moments at the end of the party with his voyeuristic contemplation, moments earlier, of a slip-clad woman at her ironing board—a figure he promptly transforms, in "the hopelessness of lust" (117/109), into an icon of domestic sexuality: "She was of that age which incites fantasy to burn like a hook into young men on quiet streets on a summer night" (203).

Perhaps the remark of Bell's sister Mary, who becomes the family pariah when she takes up with a gangland hit man, offers a clue to this woman's misery: "there are different kinds of death," she says. "I prefer that kind, his kind, to the death I've been fighting all my life" (171/163). Another sister, Jane, embraces this death-in-life when she opts for Big Bob Davidson and suburbia. Bell's father completes the pattern: like the man he was forced to inter in the Philippines, he is "buried alive" (296/285). The death that his mother and sisters and father know in their different ways is also what David Bell, like Jack Gladney in *White Noise,* must come to terms with. The pervasive references to mortality reflect the characterization of death in the line from Saint Augustine that Warburton, the "Mad Memo-Writer," distributes: "And never can a man be more disastrously in death than when death itself shall be deathless" (23/21). Later, when Warburton glosses these words, he does not emphasize the spiritual imperative represented by death so much as the simple fact itself: "man shall remain forever in the state of death" because "death never dies" (108/101).

Bell's charm against death and social paresis may be his recurrent recollection of Akira Kurosawa's 1952 film *Ikiru,* especially the famous scene in
which its protagonist, an old man dying of cancer, sits swinging in a nocturnal
park amid drifting snowflakes.[4] Though he does not mention it, Bell must
know that *ikiru* is Japanese for "living." Certainly he understands in the image
something redemptive, something related to the fate of that other victim of
cancer, his mother. In his own film he includes a sequence in which Sullivan,
playing her, sits swinging like old Watanabe. In another, the amateur actor
representing his father recalls that during his captivity in the Philippines the
prisoners had filed by an old Japanese officer who sat in a swing and, moving
to and fro, seemed to bless them with a circular motion of his hand. This detail
may reflect only Bell's desire to graft certain intensely personal emblems onto
the imagined recollections of his father, but he seems in any event curiously
intent on weaving Kurosawa's parable into his own story of familial travail.

The submerged content of DeLillo's Kurosawa allusions suggests the
larger meanings here. Kurosawa's character struggles within an enormous,
implacable bureaucracy to drain a swamp (symbol of Japanese corruption and
of his own part in it) and build a children's park. David Bell speaks of "the
swamp of our own beings" (122), and, indeed, DeLillo's swamp and Kurosawa's represent the same discovery: that personal and national corruption
prove coextensive. Like Kurosawa, too (or for that matter Saint Augustine),
DeLillo understands that *ikiru,* living, can never be pursued outside the
process of dying. The power of Kurosawa's conclusion, in which, dying, the
protagonist sits in the swing, has to do with just how much his modest
achievement has come to signify: it is what one can do with the life that gives
the film its title. But this insight remains inchoate for Bell, who seems half-
fatalistically to relish the knowledge that his own culture clears swamps only
to achieve greater regularity—more straight lines, more utilitarian buildings—in a landscape progressively purged of graceful features that might
please children. As an American, he knows that the clearing of "what was
once a swamp" merely facilitates erection of some monument to transience
and sterility: the "motel in the heart of every man" (268/257).

The reification of this place, a motel near the Chicago airport, provides
the setting in which Bell and his ex-wife's cousin, Edwina, commit what she
refers to as "some medieval form of incest" (273/261). This jocular reference
contributes to a more substantial fantasy of incest at the heart of the book, a
fantasy or obsession that figures in other fictions of the period, notably Louis
Malle's witty and daring treatment of incestuous desire, *Un souffle au coeur*
(1971), and the starker meditations on the subject in Norman Mailer's *An
American Dream* (1965) and Roman Polanski's *Chinatown* (1974). If *Americana*
had been written a generation later, at the height of controversy over
repressed memory retrieval, it might, like Jane Smiley's *A Thousand Acres,*
involve the revelation of literal incest. Bell, however, seems guilty of trans-
gressing the most powerful of taboos only in spirit.

But he transgresses it over and over, nonetheless, for almost every woman he sleeps with turns out to be a version of his mother. In his relations with women he enacts an unconscious search for the one woman forbidden him, at once recapitulating and reversing the tragically imperfect oedipal model: as he was rejected, so will he reject successive candidates in what occasionally amounts to a literal orgy of philandering and promiscuity. Meanwhile he suffers the ancient oedipal betrayal at the hands of one surrogate mother after another. Thus when Carter Hemmings steals his date at a party, Bell spits in the ice cubes—a gesture that will make sense only later, when Bell describes his mother's similar (and perhaps similarly motivated) expression of disgust. Bell thinks Wendy, his college girlfriend, has slept with Simmons St. Jean, his teacher. Weede Denney, his boss, exercises a kind of seigneurial droit with Binky, Bell's secretary. And even Sullivan turns out to have been sleeping with Brand all along.

In Sullivan, at once mother and "mothercountry," Bell recognizes the most significant—and psychologically dangerous—of these surrogates. When she gives Brand a doll, she replicates a gesture made by Bell's mother on another occasion. To Bell himself she twice tells "a bedtime story" (332/320, 334/322). He characterizes three of her sculptures as "carefully handcrafted afterbirth" (114/106). Her studio, to which Bell retreats on the eve of his journey westward, was called the Cocoon by its former tenant; swathed in a "membranous chemical material" (116/108) that resembles sandwich wrap, it is the womb to which he craves a return. Here he curls up, goes to sleep, and awakens to the returning Sullivan: "A shape in the shape of my mother . . . forming in the doorway" (118/110), "my mother's ghost in the room" (242/230). Bell's attraction to this central and definitive mother figure is so interdicted that it can only be described in negative terms; indeed, the climactic sexual encounter with Sullivan, a "black wish fulfilled" (345/334), is remarkable for its sustained negative affect: "mothercountry. Optional spelling of third syllable" (345). "Abomination" (331/319, 344/333), he keeps repeating, for symbolically he is committing incest.

Sullivan's narratives, the bedtime stories she tells the filial Bell, represent the twin centers of this novel's public meanings—the heart of a book otherwise wedded to superficies and resistant to formulations of psychological, sociological, or semiotic depth (here the play of simulacra retreats to an attenuated reflexivity: one story is told *in* Maine, the other *about* Maine). Sullivan's first story concerns an encounter with Black Knife, aboriginal American and veteran of the campaign against Custer; the other concerns the discovery of her patrilineage. The subject of these stories, encountering the Father, complements the larger narrative's account of coming to terms with the Mother.

Black Knife, one-hundred-year-old master ironist, describes the strange asceticism that drives Americans to clear their world of annoying, wasteful clutter: "We have been redesigning our landscape all these years to cut out unneeded objects such as trees, mountains, and all those buildings which do not make practical use of every inch of space." The idea behind this asceticism, he says, is to get away from useless beauty, to reduce everything to "[s]traight lines and right angles" (126/118), to go over wholly to the "Megamerica" of "Neon, fiber glass, plexiglass, polyurethane, Mylar, Acrylite" (127/119). Black Knife hopes that we will "come to terms with the false anger we so often display at the increasing signs of sterility and violence in our culture" (127/119)—that instead we will "set forth on the world's longest march of vulgarity, evil and decadence" (128/120). These imagined excesses would reify a vision like that of the Histriones in Jorge Luis Borges's story "The Theologians" or the Dolcinians of Umberto Eco's *The Name of the Rose*—heretics who seek to hasten the Apocalypse by committing as many sins as possible. Black Knife looks to the day when, "having set one foot into the mud, one foot and three toes," we will—just maybe—decide against surrendering to the swamp and pull back from our dreadful course, "shedding the ascetic curse, letting the buffalo run free, knowing everything a nation can know about itself and proceeding with the benefit of this knowledge and the awareness that we have chosen not to die. It's worth the risk . . . for . . . we would become, finally, the America that fulfills all of its possibilities. The America that belongs to the world. The America we thought we lived in when we were children. Small children. Very small children indeed" (128–29/ 120–21). We would, that is, repudiate the swamp in favor of an environment friendly to children—a park like the one created by that Japanese Black Knife, the Watanabe of Kurosawa's *Ikiru*.

The second bedtime story, which parallels the interview with Black Knife, concerns Sullivan's misguided attempt to recover her patrimony. In a sailing vessel off the coast of Maine, Sullivan and her Uncle Malcolm contemplate "God's world" (336/324), the land the Puritans found when they crossed the sea: America in its primal, unspoiled beauty. The voyage, however, becomes Sullivan's own night-sea journey into profound self-knowledge—knowledge, that is, of the intersection of self and nation. The vessel is the *Marston Moor*, named for the battle in which the Puritans added a triumph in the Old World to complement the success of their brethren in the New. The vessel's master is himself an avatar of American Puritanism, with roots in Ulster and Scotland. What Sullivan learns from her Uncle Malcolm immerses her—like Oedipus or Stephen Dedalus or Jay Gatsby or Jesus Christ—in what Freud calls the family romance. The child of a mystery parent, she must be about her father's business. She dramatizes the revelation that Uncle Malcolm is her real father in language that evokes by turns Epiphany and Pentecost and Apocalypse—the full spectrum of divine mystery and revelation.

The imagery here hints further at Sullivan's identification with the American land, for the heritage she discovers coincides with that of the nation. Described originally as some exotic ethnic blend and called, on one occasion, a "[d]aughter of Black Knife" (347/336), Sullivan proves also to be solidly Scotch-Irish, like so many of the immigrants who would compose the dominant American ethnic group. In that her spiritual father is a native American, her real father a north country Protestant, she discovers in herself the same mixture of innate innocence and passionately eschatological Puritanism that figures so powerfully in the historical identity of her country.

The perfervid descriptions of the wild Maine coast and the travail of the seafarers recall nothing so much as the evocations of spiritualized landscape in Eliot's *Four Quartets* (Sullivan is not so many leagues distant from the Dry Salvages, off Cape Ann). In the present scene, as in Eliot, the reader encounters a meditation on the way eternity subsumes the specific history of a place, a meditation in which deeply felt religious imagery intimates meanings that strain the very seams of language. Yet the mystery proves ultimately secular, and the only direct allusion to Eliot is from "Gerontion," one of his poems of spiritual aridity. Sullivan's shipmate, appalled at the absence of "Christ the tiger" (342/330) in the apocalyptic scene into which he has steered, also sees into the heart of things, and an unquoted line from the same poem may encapsulate both their thoughts: "After such knowledge, what forgiveness?"

The allusion to "Gerontion," like the other Eliot allusions in *Americana*, recalls the reader to an awareness of the spiritual problem of contemporary America that the book addresses. The climax of the sailing expedition occurs when a boy with a lantern appears on the shore: he is a sign, a vision at once numinous and secular. He disappoints Uncle Malcolm, who seems to have expected a vision more palpably divine. As Sullivan explains him, his shining countenance reveals certain truths of the human bondage to entropy—yet he also embodies an idea of innocence and the generative principle: "the force of all in all, or light lighting light" (342/330). He is, in short, the child that America has long since betrayed, the principle of innocence that sibylline Sullivan, glossing Black Knife's parable, suggests America may yet rediscover—and with it salvation.

DeLillo conceived *Americana* on a visit to Mount Desert Island, a place that moved him unexpectedly with its air of American innocence preserved.[5] Sullivan and her companion are off the island when the boy with the lantern appears. Though the moment bulks very small in the overall narrative, it will prove seminal as DeLillo recurs in subsequent novels to an idea of the redemptive innocence that survives, a vestige of Eden, in children. The boy with the lantern, an almost inchoate symbol here, will turn up again as the linguistically atavistic Tap in *The Names* and as Wilder on his tricycle in *White Noise*.

When Sullivan, in her valedictory, calls Bell "innocent" and "sick" (348/336), she describes the American paradox that he represents, but DeLillo defines the canker that rots the larger American innocence in terms considerably stronger. Bell's sister Mary, as played by Carol Deming in the film, remarks that "there are good wombs and bad wombs" (324/312), and the phrase recurs to Bell as he contemplates the southwestern landscape from Clevenger's speeding Cadillac (363/353). In other words, the mother he

repeatedly violates is more than flesh and blood. DeLillo conflates and subverts a familiar icon of American nationalism: mother and country. In doing
so he augments and transforms the traditional symbolism of the American
land as the female victim of an ancient European violation. Fitzgerald, in *The
Great Gatsby,* reflects on Dutch sailors and "the fresh green breast of the New
World." Hart Crane, in *The Bridge,* and John Barth, in *The Sot-Weed Factor,*
imagine the land specifically as Pocahontas. But DeLillo suggests that the real
violation occurs in an oedipal drama of almost cosmic proportions: not in the
encounter of European man with the tender breast of the American land but
in the violation of that mother by their oedipal progeny. "We want to wallow," says Black Knife, "in the terrible gleaming mudcunt of Mother America" (127/119). Like Oedipus, then, Bell discovers in himself the source of the
pestilence that has ravaged what Beasley calls "mamaland" (243/231). The
American Oedipus, seeking to understand the malaise from which his country suffers, discovers its cause in his own manifold and hideous violations of
the mother, the land that nurtures and sustains. Physical and spiritual, these
violations take their place among the other *Americana* catalogued in DeLillo's
extraordinary first novel.

Works Cited

Champlin, Charles. "The Heart Is a Lonely Craftsman." *Los Angeles Times Calendar* 29 July
1984: 7.
DeLillo, Don. *Americana.* New York: Houghton Mifflin, 1971.
———. *Americana.* Rev. ed. New York: Penguin, 1989.
———. "Don DeLillo: The Art of Fiction CXXXV." Interview. With Adam Begley. *Paris
Review* 128 (1993): 274–306.
Keesey, Douglas. *Don DeLillo.* Twayne's United States Authors Ser. 625. New York: Twayne,
1993.
LeClair, Tom. *In the Loop: Don DeLillo and the Systems Novel.* Urbana: U of Illinois P, 1987.
Osteen, Mark. "Children of Godard and Coca-Cola: Cinema and Consumerism in Don
DeLillo's Early Fiction." *Contemporary Literature* 37 (1996): 439–70.
Pynchon, Thomas. *The Crying of Lot 49.* Philadelphia: Lippincott, 1966.
Rilke, Rainer Maria. *Gesammelte Gedichte.* Frankfurt: Insel-Verlag, 1962.

Notes

1. In preparing the 1989 Penguin edition of *Americana,* DeLillo made numerous small
cuts in the text, and, generally speaking, the gains in economy improve the novel. For the most
part, the author simply pares away minor instances of rhetorical overkill. For example, he
deletes a gratuitously obscene remark about the spelling of "mothercountry," and he reduces
the space devoted to the relationship of Bell and his ex-wife Meredith. Occasionally (as in the
former instance), the author cuts a detail one has underlined in the 1971 edition, thereby
affording the reader a glimpse into a gifted writer's maturing sense of decorum and understate-

ment. Thus a minor motif like that of the woman ironing (it contributes to the reader's grasp of Bell's oedipal obsession) becomes a little less extravagant in the longer of the two passages in which it appears. Elsewhere, one applauds the excision of the syntactically tortured and the merely pretentious—for example, unsuccessful descriptions of film's epistemological and onto-logical properties. At no point, however, does DeLillo add material or alter the novel's original emphases—and I have only occasionally found it necessary or desirable to quote material that does not appear in both versions of the text. Except in these instances, I give page numbers for both editions—the 1971 Houghton Mifflin version first, the 1989 Penguin version second.

2. Though *Americana* remains the least discussed of DeLillo's major novels, an oedipal dimension has been noted by both Tom LeClair and Douglas Keesey, authors of the first two single-authored books on DeLillo. Neither, however, foregrounds this element. LeClair, in his magisterial chapter on this novel (which he names, along with *Ratner's Star* and *The Names,* as one of DeLillo's "primary achievements" [33]), represents the oedipal theme as largely ancil-lary to the proliferating "personal, cultural, and aesthetic . . . schizophrenia" (34) that he sees as pervasive in the life of David Bell and in the culture of which he is a part. Thus LeClair explores the dynamics of what Gregory Bateson and R. D. Laing call "the double bind" in "the system of communications in Bell's family," which, "understood in Bateson's terms, establishes the ground of Bell's character and presents a microcosm of the larger cultural problems mani-fested in *Americana*" (35–36). Keesey, by contrast, takes a feminist view of Bell's personality and life problems. Keesey is especially interesting on the oedipal relationship between Bell and his father, and on the idea that Bell, in his film, is striving unsuccessfully to recover the mother's "way of seeing" the world—a way lost to him when he embraced the values expressed in his father's "ads for sex and violence" (23).

3. Rilke's "Der Panther," by the same token, may lie behind the desire Bell's fellow traveler Pike expresses to encounter a mountain lion face to face.

4. The only substantial discussion of the *Ikiru* allusions is that of Mark Osteen, who acutely suggests that Bell sees himself in the film's moribund main character, Watanabe, and "fears his own living death" (463). The recurrent references to the scene on the swing represent "David's attempt to generate the kind of retrospective epiphany that Watanabe undergoes" (462–63).

5. In a *Paris Review* interview, DeLillo describes the genesis of this novel in a positive evocation of *Americana:*

> I was sailing in Maine with two friends, and we put into a small harbor on Mt. Desert Island. And I was sitting on a railroad tie waiting to take a shower, and I had a glimpse of a street maybe fifty yards away and a sense of beautiful old houses and rows of elms and maples and a stillness and wistfulness—the street seemed to carry its own built-in longing. And I felt something, a pause, something opening up before me. It would be a month or two before I started writing the book and two or three years before I came up with the title Americana, but in fact it was all implicit in that moment—a moment in which nothing happened, nothing ostensi-bly changed, a moment in which I didn't see anything I hadn't seen before. But there was a pause in time, and I knew I had to write about a man who comes to a street like this or lives on a street like this. And whatever roads the novel eventually followed, I believe I maintained the idea of that quiet street if only as counterpoint, as lost innocence. (279)

This *recollection* dictates not only the scene off Mount Desert Island but also and more clearly the scene in picturesque Millsgate, the little town on Penobscot Bay where the travelers pick up Brand. Here, at the end of part 1, Bell conceives the idea for his film—just as DeLillo, in a similar setting, conceived the idea of *Americana.*

Deconstructing the Logos:
Don DeLillo's *End Zone*

The deconstructive ideas and operations of Jacques Derrida have found an amenable target in American experimental fiction of the last decade. Three recent books on postmodern fiction—Allen Thiher's *Words in Reflection,* Charles Caramello's *Silverless Mirrors,* and Jerome Klinkowitz's *The Self-Apparent Word*—provide Derrida-influenced readings of Barth, Barthelme, Coover, Gass, Pynchon, and those novelists, most of whom are associated with the Fiction Collective, that Klinkowitz introduced in his *Literary Disruptions:* Ron Sukenick, Raymond Federman, Walter Abish, Gilbert Sorrentino, and Steve Katz. Although the names of some new writers—Kenneth Gangemi, Frederick Tuten, Stephen Dixon, Guy Davenport—do surface in these three books, for the most part criticism repeats, covers the same texts with the same approach, a procedure at odds with Derrida's own methods. What I offer here is a Derridean analysis of a writer, Don DeLillo, and a novel, *End Zone,* that are unmentioned by Thiher, Caramello, and Klinkowitz. Several ironies surround DeLillo's absence from these and most other books on the contemporary American novel. Although his eight novels have been widely and well reviewed, and although several—*End Zone, Americana,* and *Ratner's Star*—are formally innovative, DeLillo has received comparatively little academic attention.[1] Although *End Zone* is a particularly explicit and perhaps Derrida-influenced deconstructive work, a novel in which DeLillo's intellectual and artistic sophistication is plainly evident, its subversions are largely ignored, whereas Coover's *Universal Baseball Association,* to which *End Zone* is similar, is explicated again and again. *End Zone* also has, as a "sports novel," readerly interests that the more academic or militantly theoretical novelists exclude, interests or expectations that, once denied, create a wider play of internal differences than more narrow, writerly texts can offer. "Midfiction" is the term Alan Wilde has coined for recent writers, such as Barthelme, Stanley Elkin, and Max Apple, who have synthesized or compromised experimental and realistic techniques. *End Zone* and the best of DeLillo's other books are, rather

Originally published in *Modern Fiction Studies* 33 (1987): 105–23. Copyright © 1987. Purdue Research Foundation. Reprinted by permission of the Johns Hopkins University Press.

than "midfictions," polarfictions, combinations of unusual extremes, popular subgenres such as the detective story, disaster book, or science fiction mixed with profound ideas and forms from extraliterary sources—linguistics, anthropology, cybernetics, mathematics, and neurophysiology. Polarization, says Derrida in *Of Grammatology,* is the structure of language. DeLillo's polarizations in *End Zone,* as well as in *Americana, Ratner's Star, The Names,* and *White Noise,* create a plurality of orientations—inward to the processes of language and fiction, outward to psychological, social, and ecological relations, and outward as well to the readers solicited and confuted by DeLillo's rhetoric. My analysis of these orientations will, I hope, draw academic attention to *End Zone* and, by extension, to DeLillo's other, equally substantial work.

Discussing the shift from his first novel, the film-influenced *Americana,* to *End Zone,* DeLillo has said that with this second book "I began to suspect that language was a subject as well as an instrument in my work" (LeClair and McCaffery 81). As one meaning of his title suggests, DeLillo pursues his linguistic investigation to its ends, its poles: the origins of delusion about language in 2500 years of philosophical usage and the final consequence of that delusion in nuclear holocaust. Set in a would-be football factory called Logos College, *End Zone* deconstructs a primary subject of Derrida's subversions— logocentrism, in the words of DeLillo's narrator, one of "the darker crimes of thought and language" (54). In more positive terms, *End Zone* illustrates what Wittgenstein, a figure referred to in the novel, asserted about language: "The language game is so to say something unpredictable. I mean, it is not based on grounds. It is not reasonable (or unreasonable). It is there—like our life." (73). The novel also directs us to see the similarity between the language game (appropriately played) and the ecology of living systems, an analogy that provides an alternative to self-destructive *End Zone*s of human behavior.

As a football novel, "the book as television set" (90), *End Zone* has a more conventional and wider initial appeal than any of the other subgenres DeLillo works within. It promises and furnishes the staples of sports fiction: "reveals" inside information about college football, its training camps, locker rooms, personnel dynamics, and terminologies; entertains with jock antics, both stupidity and misplaced intelligence; portrays a familiar protagonist, the outsider learning to play within the system, sorting out the differences between the game and life; supplies a lengthy description of the "big game," the clash of undefeated powers; and considers the popular notion that football is a "Microcosm of life" (16), especially American life in its qualities of competition, male testing and bonding, racial relations, and war. These genre elements dominate Part One, the first eighty-five pages. In Part Two, a thirty-page description of the "big game," and in Part Three, another eighty-five pages balancing Part One, *End Zone* departs from its popular satisfactions. Information is less about football, more about what desperations and aberrations fill the gap when the season ends. Comedy becomes increasingly ironic, turns toward violence and suffering. The gradually accommodating protagonist smokes marijuana before a game, walks off the field, and wanders in realms of ideas far from football simplicity. Even the "big game" is not what the sports reader probably expects: placed in the middle of the book instead of at a climactic end, it is described in fragments, fractured point of view, and "elegant gibberish" (90). The microcosm of the game proliferates beyond the cliches of American sociology to take in everything: science, religion, art, language, the novel *End Zone,* this commentary itself.

These differences between Part One and Parts Two and Three explode the centering, unifying, and "realistic" conventions of sports fiction. To reinforce this deconstructive effect, DeLillo imposes further discontinuities—of smaller structures, character, and irony—on the disoriented sports reader. There are thirty chapters, some of them no more than three or four pages long, in the 200 pages of *End Zone.* Spatial and temporal cutting within and between chapters is rapid and sharp, leaving rifts in the narration. Minor characters are thinly developed, fragmentary like the chapters, frequently only voices unmoored to naturalistic detail or identity. Without stable identities as sources of actual communication, the characters often seem, like one character's favorite cliche, "commissioned, as it were, by language itself" (41). They recite sports cliches, read aloud passages from textbooks, or, in a technique that illustrates shifting intertextuality and linguistic relativity, quote specialized definitions, usually from mathematics, of words used in common discourse. "Identity" itself offers a particularly illustrative example because of what is undercut by the shift: when one character says of his grandfather that "His whole identity was dominated by some tremendous vision," another character responds: "Identity. . . . An equality satisfied by all possible values of the variables for which the standardized expressions involved in the equality are quantitatively determined" (44–45). Oral discourse usually occupies one of two extremes, neither of which is mutual communication, a loop with information: redundancy or copying, in which characters repeat each other's words; and performance, in which a character speaks a monologue, sometimes irrelevant to the listener, sometimes authoritarian. When such voices lack a behavior that would locate and measure them or lack a recorder/narrator who will interpret them, the possibilities for irony expand, as in Barthelme's stories of drifting signifiers. Narrator and halfback Gary Harkness is himself a shifting, uncertain source, sometimes distanced and neutral, at other times mocking himself and others with understatement or hyperbole. When these discontinuities, which multiply ambiguity, are combined with techniques of reduction—an essentially single setting, a football season with very few flashbacks, an almost completely male cast— a fablelike quality results. Visibly fractured forms destroy formulaic expectations; bared concepts displace "realistic" surfaces.

The deconstructive fable of *End Zone* has as its focal subject "logos," "the word" and its cultural connotations from creation to gossip, as when charac-

ters ask one another, "What's the word?" Gary Harkness plays football at
Logos College in an unnamed place in West Texas. The college is surrounded
by desert, a silence so complete that it becomes a disturbing noise to Harkness. The founder of Logos, Tom Wade, "built it out of nothing. He had an
idea and he followed it through to the *end*. He believed in reason. He was a
man of reason. He cherished the very word" (6; my italics). Now dead, the
founder is succeeded as controlling presence by the football coach, Emmett
Creed, a man "famous for creating order out of chaos" (8) and brought to
Logos to reenact creation, to transform mediocrity into success. "To instill a
sense of unity" (8), he fences off the practice field and builds a tower from
which he watches and occasionally directs action. Space-definer, Creed is also
"the namegiver" (110): he changes the team's name "from the Cactus Wrens
to the Screaming Eagles" (9) and invents names for its plays, an activity
Harkness believes gives Creed his ultimate power. Creed's life fittingly doubles the founder's creation: a sickly youth, Creed has built himself up out of
nothing by force of idea and purpose: "the mind first and then the body"
(164), he tells Harkness. As Creed's name implies, he believes in returning to
the founder's original principles: "We're getting too far away from our own
beginnings" (164). His aim and method are single-minded: "We need to
renounce everything that turns us from the knowledge of ourselves" (164).
He lives "alone in a small room off the isometrics area—a landlocked Ahab
who paced and raged, who was unfolding his life toward a single moment"
(42). With Creed and in *End Zone,* though, Ahab's "monomania" takes on a
new, metameaning—not an obsession with one thing, but with oneness itself.
Many of the connotations here are, of course, Christian; one of the first statements Creed makes is, "Don't ever get too proud to pray" (9). But what
DeLillo sets up in the novel is a displaced monotheism, the absolutist, mono-
valent assumptions and rituals of Christianity now projected upon the logos
rather than flowing from the Logos. Earlier in his life and early in the novel,
Harkness has believed "Oneness" was "a good concept" but not "truly attractive unless it meant oneness with God or the universe or some equally
redoubtable super-phenomenon" (15). Now, in the novel's present, Harkness
says of God, "It's a concept that's incredibly outmoded" (77). "The Supreme
being of heaven and earth," absent even from Creed's harangues, is now only
"three letters" (7) in a crossword puzzle.

This displacement Derrida calls "logocentrism," a set of assumptions and
procedures based on a "metaphysics of presence," the awarding of priority and
primacy to terms of "presence" in logical oppositions: positive before negative,
simple before complex, pure before impure. "Absence" is not conceived as a
codeterminant of a system but as a later complication or fall. When philosophy is thus oriented "toward an order of meaning—thought, truth, reason,
logic, the Word—conceived of existing in itself, as foundation," the philosophical enterprise and method become the "returning 'strategically' in idealization, to an origin or to a 'priority' seen as simple, intact, normal, pure, stan-

dard, self-identical, in order *then* to conceive of derivation, complication, deterioration, accident" (Culler 92). In *End Zone* it is the founder's logos, a self-identical simplicity to be known and used "as foundation," to which Creed wants to return. However, when the assumptions of philosophical priority and their attendant procedures are tested on language, the means by which the return is to be effected, they are shown to be in error because any meaning that is present in language depends upon what is absent: a language event depends upon its context, sound on silence, print on spacing. Following Saussure, Derrida in *Positions* defines language as a circular "play of differences [that] involves syntheses and referrals that prevent there from being at any moment or in any way a simple element that is present in and of itself and refers only to itself. Whether in written or in spoken discourse, no element can function as a sign without relating to another element which itself is not simply present" (26). In *Of Grammatology* Derrida also goes beyond Saussure, deconstructing his hidden metaphysical assumptions that valorize speech over writing. "The logos can be infinite and self-present," Derrida writes, scornfully summing up Saussure's faith, "only through the *voice*" (98).

Because of the limits of language, a system of ideas that insists on the values of absolute presence and the possibility of finding what is "present in and of itself" will be self-contradictory, a rhetoric rather than a consistent system, a rhetoric protecting or asserting power and authority. In Derrida's terms, Creed's logocentric ideal of a return—to the founder's simple logos or to the full presence of the self to itself—is impossible because of the nature of language. This recognition of linguistic relativity Creed attempts to prevent when he says, "I've never seen a good football player who wanted to learn a foreign language" (163). Beyond its linguistic impossibility, Creed's ideal contradicts his life: the univocality he prizes would destroy the game he coaches and lives within. The contradictions of Creed's thinking are manifested in his hortatory formulation that football is "only a game . . . but it's the only game" (12). Football is, like other athletic games and what Derrida in *Of Grammatology* calls "*the game of the world*" (50), necessarily a "play of differences," oppositions and possibilities arising from those conflicts. Its end zones are not, in fact, origins or full terminations but punctuations of the constantly revolving play. Creed knows and tells Harkness that "Football is a complex of systems. . . . The individual. The small cluster he's part of. The large unit, the eleven" (163); but he chooses to stress what he calls the "Interlocking," the drive toward univocality of his team, and forgets the necessity of the other team as well as of the world outside the game. In effect, he attempts to create a closed system that protects his authority as single ruler and places him in a direct line of descent from the founder. Over most of his players Creed preserves his authority with his simple presence, which during the course of the novel becomes an enigmatic absence. On Gary Harkness, the skeptic, and Taft Robinson, the prize recruit, he uses the promise of knowing "the secrets," the "bottom of it" (195), a way back to the logos.

To the logocentric ideals and procedures comes the deconstructive activity, a shifting, doubling process that both works within a philosophical system's assumptions to show their inconsistency and stands outside it to show what it excludes. The difference between the logocentric and the deconstructionist is articulated in Derrida's *Writing and Difference,* where he defines two kinds of interpretation: "The one seeks to decipher, dreams of deciphering a truth or an origin which escapes play and the order of the sign, and which lives the necessity of interpretation as an exile. The other, which is no longer turned toward the origin, affirms play and tries to pass beyond man and humanism, the name of man being the name of that being who, throughout the history of metaphysics or of ontotheology—in other words, throughout his entire history—has dreamed of full presence, the reassuring foundation, the origin and the end of play" (292). Gary Harkness, who thinks of himself as an "exile" (5), oscillates between these two modes of interpretation, accepting and rebelling against logocentric values, playing games and searching for an end to them. Author DeLillo, fully conscious of how these two modes work, keeps a useful, illustrative tension between them, understanding, as a writer, that he cannot help but propose a deciphering, that his text has a first and last page, and that he cannot stand outside language. DeLillo's achievement in *End Zone* is not just speculatively turning language back upon itself but illustrating through the metaphor of football how logocentrism structures contemporary American culture, examining through Harkness and other characters the conditions, tropisms, and consequences of the logocentric ideal, creating both comedy and feeling out of its contradictions, and skillfully manipulating the framing, self-referring, and playful potentials of fiction for these deconstructive effects.

If fiction is by its nature a play of differences, a game against itself, both asserting and lying, then the writer can call attention to this fact and extend it by including self-referring, contradictory frames between himself and the world he stipulates. In *End Zone* both the narrator and the "author," who appears within the novel, perform this function. The narrative begins with statements of fact about an original event—"Taft Robinson was the first black student to be enrolled at Logos College in west Texas" (3; all page references in this paragraph are to this page) and statements of assured judgment—"They got him for his speed." After a sentence demonstrating that the narrative is composed from the perspective of a season now over, Harkness writes a series of subjunctive clauses about what Robinson's life might have been and what the account already begun might have been, the latter "A drowsy monograph . . . with foot notes." He then shifts—"But this doesn't happen to be it"—and says that his experience will be the narrative's focus, such matters as "words broken into brute sound." Apologizing that Robinson "no more than haunts this book," Harkness continues with a self-conscious literary allusion to Ralph Ellison's *Invisible Man:* "The mansion has long been haunted (double metaphor coming up) by the invisible man." If these first two paragraphs exhibit reversal—a shift of focus after discussion of alternative possibilities—the assertions in Harkness' next few sentences contradict the sophistication already exhibited: "But let's keep things simple," he says. "Football players are simple folk. Whatever complexities, whatever dark politics of the human mind, the heart—these are noted only within the chalked borders of the playing field." Gary Harkness, football player, is manifestly not simple: both the structure and the content of his previous assertions show complexity. From Harkness' reversals and contradictions numerous undecidable questions follow, undecidable because of the self-reference, the lack of any external corrective: is Gary Harkness unreliable in his narration? Unconsciously? Consciously? Reliable when describing events but unreliable when self-referring? Is he playing a game with the reader?

All of these questions are framed again and exfoliated at the beginning of Part Two. Like the first sentences of the novel, the first sentence (and paragraph) here describes historical fact—the beginning of the big game with Centrex: "The special teams collided" (89; further references in this paragraph are to 89–90)—and moves to the narrator's judgment: "quite pretty to watch." The next paragraph, like the second paragraph of Part One, shifts: enclosed within parentheses, it is spoken to "the spectator" by "the author." Is Gary Harkness the "author" speaking here? It is impossible to know. Like Harkness, the "author" provides misinformation, entertains alternatives, shifts focus, and shows literary sophistication through allusion. The "author" initially seems helpful, concerned with the spectator/reader's resistance to another "football game in print." But this "author" is also assertive, defining the "exemplary spectator," listing his desires, stating that this "game on paper" will fulfill those needs. Then comes the Harkness-like reversal: "But maybe not. It's possible there are deeper reasons to attempt a play-by-play," reasons the now elusive "author" doesn't explain. Instead, he warns against himself, raising to conscious explicitness Harkness' contradictions between doing and saying: because the author is "always somewhat corrupt in his inventions and vanities . . . grandmothers, sissies, lepidopterists and others are warned that the nomenclature that follows is often indecipherable." The allusion to Nabokov takes the reader beyond the doubling of Harkness' Ellison allusion to the possibility of many-layered and multiply false games, perhaps football as chess with its arcane vocabulary. Finally, says the "author," it is his "permanent duty to unbox the lexicon for all eyes to see—a cryptic ticking mechanism in search of a revolution."

This "author" who confesses to corruption, who asserts in orderly sentences that his aim is to reveal lexical disorder, is not just unreliable but the kind of self-undermining linguistic agent needed to work within the language to deconstruct logocentric delusions about authority and authorship that followed from theism. This deconstructive "author" is neither present nor absent but doubled and diffused. Instead of creating from nothing, as the founder did, he collects conventions, codes, rules, and names from literature and language. He does not impose a univocal pattern, following single-mind-edly like the founder from origin to end, but arranges a shifting play of differences. He explores fundamental assumptions but, unlike Creed, seeks no single originary idea or word; his text is multiple discourses grafted to one another, discontinuous, dialogic. Understanding that language has fictional qualities, this author produces fiction with linguistic qualities, a writing that circles, refers outward and inward, deciphers and encrypts simultaneously. These deconstructive qualities are exactly the compositional principles manifested in *End Zone,* the kinds of structures and selections that frame and express the characters' relationships with authority at Logos College. In the five or so months of the novel's time span, Gary Harkness struggles with and toward consciousness of these principles, perhaps succeeding and becoming the self-consciousness of these principles, perhaps succeeding and becoming the self-conscious "author"; perhaps succeeding and becoming an even more dangerous agent, the "naively" unreliable narrator of the first page; perhaps failing at consciousness but nevertheless manifesting a deconstructive behavior and account. Like his unreliability, these possibilities are undecidable. Only patterns of behavior, probabilities of motive, and conflicts in the logo-sphere can be adduced.

Logocentrism in *End Zone,* as in *Of Grammatology,* is very closely associated with paternal authority. If any details about minor characters' backgrounds are mentioned, they usually are facts about their fathers, powerful or successful men. Mothers are dead (Anatole Bloomberg's) or transparent (Harkness'). The three female students in the book, at odds about every other subject, agree on the vileness of their fathers. Creed is an "avenging patriarch" (5) without a son of his own. Even the founder's widow, known to everyone as "Mrs. Tom," is described as "Lincolnesque" (6). In the novel's only extended flashback, DeLillo shows how the founder's and Creed's values are replicated by Harkness' father, illustrating that logocentrism is not purely theoretical but complicated by early conditioning, Oedipal needs, and guilt. A fringe football player at Michigan State, Gary's father wants him to be a star. Like Creed, he believes in "the *simplest,* most pioneer of rhythms—the eternal work cycle. . . . Backbone, will, mental toughness" (13–14, my italics). Gary's problem is recognizing the double bind created by his father's ambition for him: again like Creed, the father essentially says "singlemind-edly play football" despite the fact that a game is double and requires a double or framing consciousness: the game and what is outside of it. This bind sets up several internal tensions: Gary enjoys football but resists a total commitment to it by withdrawing totally from it; he attacks his father's simplicities but attempts to inscribe them at a deeper level; he feels guilty when not playing football and guilty when he does. And in the terms I've been using, he early on deconstructs the language of authority and yet seeks it out at Logos. When Gary is fourteen, his father gives him a placard: "WHEN THE GOING GETS TOUGH THE TOUGH GET GOING" (13). Looking at this for three years, Gary finds that "Words can escape their meanings"; he sees "the words themselves, the letters, consonants swallowing vowels, aggression and tenderness, a semi-self-recreation from line to line, word to word, letter to letter. All meaning faded. The words became pictures" (13–14).

Despite this early deconstruction of the paternal message, an oral saying turned into the written word, Gary spends years enacting its possible meanings, either accepting or denying his father, unable to create a neutral or compromise space between these two responses. He first goes to Syracuse University, where he is dismissed after hiding out with a girl in a dormitory room where they read from an opaque economics text. This is an intuitive revolt, unanalyzed, but is, like his other leave-takings, one reading of the placard's "GET GOING": for Gary, going can be away from the tough situation. At Penn State, the repetition of plays and the coaches' demand for "Oneness," two qualities of the placard's message, bother Gary, so he returns home to an even more repetitious and enclosed existence. After seeing all over his neighborhood the new placard "MILITARIZE" (16), he goes to the University of Miami. Following this single order, he begins to read about thermonuclear war and thinks of Miami as "the beginnings of simplicity" (16); but when he finds himself fascinated with and made guilty by his readings about the military, he returns home again. Threatened then by the draft, the real military, he attends Michigan State, his father's school, and there accidentally contributes to the death of an opposition player, a source of further guilt. Again at home, he discovers "a very simple truth. My life meant nothing without football" (18) and decides to attend Logos. Though he frames in totalizing terms his attraction to football as a "simple truth," he still brings to Logos a saving ambivalence toward the singlemindedness demanded of him by his father and Creed.

For Harkness, playing a sport provides the simple pleasure of presence, the body operating without self-consciousness, "the sense of living an inner life right up against the external or tangible life. Of living close to your own skin" (192). Playing football at Logos also has other rewards: relief from the stillness, the motionlessness and silence, of the west Texas desert; relief from the guilt he brings with him; and, less obvious to him, integration within a logocentric system. Scanning the horizon in all directions, Harkness sees "a land silenced by its own beginnings in the roaring heat, born dead, flat stones burying the memory. I felt threatened by the silence" (25). He and his teammates have ways of dispelling that silence. They have drunken, noisy parties; exchange cliches and inconsequential news—all sound without significance beyond its time-filling, silence-banishing moment; and they play "Bang You're Dead," a game in which they shoot each other with childish imitations of the noise of guns. Significantly, "Nobody knew who had started the game or exactly when it had started" (25). But it is football that offers a verbal behavior that recalls a presumed originary discourse (the purpose of Logos College) and gathers many of DeLillo's linguistic themes. Before describing the Centrex game, the "author" discusses the "organic nature" of football, the "one sport guided by language, by the word signal, the snap number, the color code, the play name" (90). "All teams run the same plays," says Harkness, "but each team uses an entirely different system of naming. Coaches stay up well into the night in order to name plays" (95).

The naming theme is pervasive in the novel: characters Norgene Azamanian, Larry Nix, and Anatole Bloomberg discuss the origins and effects of their names; Harkness meditates on the relation between names and objects. Football offers the logocentric ideal. The names for plays that the coaches invent—

Twin deck left, ride series, white divide.
Gap-angle down, 17, dummy stitch.
Bone country special, double-D to right (115)

—are univocal. They have a numerical precision and separateness—one name, one play—for a very small, homogeneous speech community. Just as importantly, in Derrida's view, the words are *spoken,* recalling the Saussurian phonocentrism that supports the more general logocentrism. In the huddle, these spoken words are present in such a way, existing in themselves, simple and unambiguous, that they need not be placed in a context of explicit assertion. They are pronounced. In the text, DeLillo emphasizes the words' oral significance by setting them up and off as poetry. If in the game there remains a gap between signifier and signified, the gap between articulation and act is narrowed, in time at least. To say and to hear these words are to be close to doing, performing what they name. In an older linguistic distinction recalled by the author above, the names are signals rather than symbols. When the sounds are uttered by the single, present authority—the somewhat ironically named "quarterback"—the "words move the body into position" (35). The player's response to the message should be automatic; there is no debate, no communication loop in the signal language. There are, of course, errors, the opposition's counter signals, and interfering noise; but the play name has a univocal meaning and authoritarian effect, the qualities of logos, The Word before the Tower of Babel. This is why, for Creed in his new tower, football is the "only game." Looked at carefully, of course, the signal language is like natural language, as well as the game that it sets in motion. The names are not invented out of nothing; they depend on absence, difference, trace, and context; and at least one player, Chuck Deering, called a "fetuseater" (92) for his ignorance, doesn't know all the signals. But because the signal language is specialized, limited in context, spoken and authoritarian, it seems to drive back toward the purity of logos before what Derrida calls "fallen language."

Just outside the frame of signal language, there are several measuring ironies. After the game, Billy Mast and Harkness speak to each other in the jargon of astronauts carrying out essentially robotic activities, a parody of the automatism of signals. Shortly afterward, Harkness receives a letter from his father with primerlike, step-by-step instructions on how to return home, words that put the body in motion, a combination signal and ticket. Even more instructive than these parodies of signals are the sounds the players and coaches make before and during the game: "In the runway a few people made their private sounds, fierce alien noises having nothing to do with speech or communication of any kind" (83). On the field they make up words with purely personal meaning or speak only to themselves. One player does an imaginary play-by-play broadcast. Some strings of words are without context, full of contradictions or nonsequiturs. "Bed," Jerry Fallon says, "Pillow, sheet, blanket, mattress, spring, frame, headboard" (99). When the strings make some sense, they are frequently repeated, emptying out their meaning. By the end of the game, the reader understands the relevance of a detail intro- duced very early in the book: that the founder "was mute. . . . All he could do was grunt. He made disgusting sounds. Spit used to collect at both corners of his mouth" (6). Far from the "idea" with which Tom Wade founded Logos and distant from the precise ordering of Creed's signals, these actual linguistic events demonstrate what Wittgenstein recognized as the irrationality of the language game, mysterious in its origins, unpredictable in its mutations, rela- tive in its effects, an imperfect human attempt at ordering its own products and not the disorder left by a departure from some primal simplicity.

The logocentric quest for origin involves reductiveness, repetition, and self-contradiction. The death of Norgene Azamanian illustrates the first two effects: after his death in an auto accident, "State troopers stood on the road, writing in their little books, copying from each other" (56), turning an acci- dent into certainty by means of repetition and avoiding contradiction, which is the price more ambitious investigators pay. Billy Mast takes a course in "the untellable," inquiring "if any words exist beyond speech" (149), a linguistic paradox created by logocentric regression. In the desert, feeling threatened by both silence and his awareness of linguistic duplicity, Harkness desires to push even further than Mast—"in some form of void, freed from conscious- ness, the mind remakes itself" (70)—but, like Mast, engages in contradiction (between mind and consciousness). Earlier Harkness has said that exile in west Texas is "just an extension (a packaging) of the other exile, the state of being separated from whatever is left of the center of one's own history" (24). If any centrism, whether logocentrism or "Centrexism," is not an error (and for Derrida it is), then Harkness' desire to exist outside history, "the void," is yet another delusion offered by logocentrism, one that persuades him that "what we must know must be learned from blanked-out pages. To begin to reword the overflowing world. To subtract and disjoin. To re-recite the alpha- bet. To make elemental lists. To call something by its name and need no other sound" (70–71). These are the motives and methods of Creed, an attempt to recreate a creation, a logos, that never existed. Just before and just after this "revelation," Harkness recites an identical list of words: "The sun. The desert.

The sky. The silence. The flat stones. The insects. The wind and the clouds. The moon. The stars. The west and east. The song, the color, the smell of the earth" (69, 71). Creed's lists, his signals, had significance in his narrow context; Harkness' lists of elemental words from the huge possibilities of the lexicon and in his larger context of communication mean nothing without propositions. "A new way of life requires a new language" (193)—this statement by Taft Robinson may well be true, but "to reword the overflowing world" requires, precisely because it is overflowing, knowledge of all the discourses present in it: addition, not Harkness' subtraction. Some readers of *End Zone* have used Harkness' comments here to suggest that DeLillo is attacking science in the novel; but it is West Centrex Biotechnical Institute that handily defeats Logos College, and it is science professor Alan Zapalac who mocks logocentric reductionism. Indeed, scientific discoveries have produced the possibility of thermonuclear war, but nations' imitation of Creed's desire for the absolute, for total victory, is more threatening than science itself. Like Derrida in *Of Grammatology* (74–93) and like Pynchon and Gaddis in their novels, DeLillo in *End Zone* illustrates the misuse a logocentric humanism makes of scientific pluralism. In his interview, DeLillo clarifies his attitude, using language that recalls the language of Harkness' "revelation":

> Science in general has given us a new language to draw from. Some writers shrink from this. Science is guilty; the language of science is tainted by horror and destruction. To me, science is a source of new names, new connections between people and the world. Rilke said we had to rename the world. Renaming suggests an innocence and a rebirth. Some words adapt, and these are the ones we use in our new world. (LeClair and McCaffery 84)

If football combats the Texas stillness with a "pure" language, it also physically punishes its players for falling from a presumed state of purity and prepares them for a return. It is therefore appropriate for its setting, at least for Gary Harkness. He likes "that terrain so flat and bare, suggestive of the end of recorded time, a splendid sense of remoteness firing my soul. It was easy to feel that back up there, where men spoke the name civilization in wistful tones, I was wanted for some terrible crime" (24). A man for whom "arousals of guilt had considerable appeal" (58), Harkness enjoys the asceticism of training camp before knowing what Creed's final aims are: "There was even pleasure in the daily punishment on the field. I felt that I was better for it, reduced in complexity, a warrior" (24). During the Centrex game, Harkness is happy to be injured as are numerous other players who display their wounds as evidence of warriorship. Punishment for Harkness' part in an accidental death and for failing his father, the violence of football is also what one player calls "hyperatavistic" (50); another, playing on Gary's name, says football "harks back" (28) to human origins. When the organized violence of the season finishes, when "winter's purity and silence" arrive, "a chance for reason to prevail" (37), Harkness and others play a game in the snow, a game of tackle without equipment and with rules that increase violence. With its "simple physical warmth," "straightahead" play, and "grunting and panting" (161) rather than signals, this ad hoc game suggests that a single-minded pursuit of origin may overshoot the logos and language altogether, may return man to a simplicity that has little to do with the founder's reason.

If the desire for univocality conditioned by logocentrism unintentionally moves backward toward violent irrationality, it also moves forward to what Harkness terms "the rationality of irrationality" (17), the thermonuclear war he is guilty of being fascinated with. Although one might well see warfare in the novel as extending the competition of football—a sociological reading— Harkness' war games and meditations imply that this new kind of war is the product of a desire for the univocal, for an *End Zone* of meaning, a finality for the language game, what Derrida calls the dream of "an end to play." Harkness states that the language of thermonuclear war makes the language of other wars "laughable" (17) by comparison, but while language struggles to express or shield the nature of apocalypse, the weapons themselves obey the tropism of logocentrism—a movement toward ultimacy, finality. As Harkness' instructor in military science, Major Staley, says, "There's a kind of theology at work here. The bombs are a kind of god" (62), a new Logos. "We begin to capitulate," Staley goes on to say, "to the overwhelming *presence*" (62; my italics), just as the football players capitulate to the physically punishing power of Creed's system. As in signal-controlled football, in the war game Staley and Harkness play, the final move is automatic: "spasm response" (185).

How does contemporary man avoid "capitulation" and "spasm response"? DeLillo's arrangement of disparate but analogous materials offers large frames for seeing and, perhaps, preventing self-destruction. On one hand are analogies linking founder Tom Wade, Coach Creed, and superpower politicians; on the other, analogies linking the play of language, football as a game, and the ecology of living systems. In sum, the first group creates closed systems of entities and one-way cause/effect sequences obeying the principle of positive feedback, which can be expressed as "the more you have, the more you get of the same." The result is entropy. The second group represents open systems of relations and reciprocal communications obeying the principle of negative feedback, which is the self-correcting or balancing of the system from within. The result is possible regeneration. The founder fences out the desert, the coach fences out the rest of the college, and the superpowers exclude other countries from their polar competition. In these closed systems, words or ideas are reified, people are objectified, and nations are made equivalent to their technologies. These transformations reduce complex information loops to entities that then fit the mechanistic model of one-way causal sequences: bodies striking other bodies. Within each closed system are oppositions, but the tendency is toward uniformity or univocality, an obsession with simple presence, forgetting absence. What is excluded, if accepted, could become a "governor" on the positive feedback principle that rules. The eventual result of this kind of unbalanced "runaway" system is entropy, the running down or wasting away of the system. The worldwide entropic consequences of nuclear war are made explicit in lectures by Major Staley. DeLillo also shows the closed systems of Creed's brand of football and of Logos College in entropic decline. Football injuries are epidemic. Outside football, Norgene Azamanian dies in an auto accident, coach Tom Clark kills himself, Mrs. Tom dies in a plane crash, Major Staley begins to walk with a limp, and Creed is, in his last appearance, confined to a wheelchair. Motion is becoming stillness; even Taft Robinson gives up his speed to sit in his room.

The second group of analogies—language, football, and ecology—is less prominent, revealed through skirmishes with the dominating closed systems. Each of the three analogues is relational and contextual, a play of similarities and differences, sets of simultaneous frames. Their causal sequences are reciprocal, looping rather than one-way. Football may not, because of its strict boundaries and crashing bodies, seem to fit the set, but it too is shifting and balanced, a combination of communication and mechanics both in a single game and in its larger organization. In the closed systems, the repetition of positive feedback led to entropy. In language, football, and living systems, variation, increasing complexity, and mutation protect and preserve the system. Language grows with new scientific terms; football begins with the signal but becomes improvisational; ecological systems adapt and split. "Language and living systems," says Jeremy Campbell in *Grammatical Man,* "do not surrender to the randomizing effects decreed by the second law of thermodynamics, and they depend less than might have been expected on chance and accident. Their complexity is self-regulating" (99). Their open systems extend *End Zone*s. The new danger of thermonuclear war is its turning the whole world into a closed system; one can leave Logos College or Creed's football team, and one can speculate, as Harkness does, on "man-planet" after the holocaust—"I thought of men embedded in the ground, all killed, billions, flesh cauterized into the earth, bits of bone and hair and nails, man-planet, a fresh intelligence revolving through the system" (70)—but one cannot leave the planet. Although *End Zone* frightens with its details of absolute war, the novel does not so much warn against that specific event as use it to make apparent a logocentric way of thinking that everywhere destroys nature, whether biological, intellectual, or social.

Whether or not Gary Harkness understands the systems he occupies during the season, he does not finish it. Before the last game he smokes marijuana and then leaves the field after the first play. Some of his activities, ideas, and contacts outside the strict confines of the field also show him at odds with logocentric values. Using a figure—the circle—that opposes the straight lines of football and the centering of logocentrism, Harkness says he likes to "circle and watch, content enough to be outside the center and even sufficiently cunning to plan a minor raid or two" (166). He does expose cliches, how language is "used to cover silence" (57); does refuse involvement in the "evasive news" (123) of the sports information director's publicity; and critiques the power of traditional language: "The words were old and true, full of reassurance, comfort, consolation. Men followed such words to their death because other men before them had done the same . . ." (42). He is frequently ironic, engaging in double meanings, putting on his more simple teammates, a way to mock them and, as he confesses, a way to "undermine my sense of harmony. It's very complex. It has to do with the ambiguity of this whole business" (103). He increases ambiguity by lying, denying events that occur, taking the name "Robert Reynolds," itself a made-up name referring to no one. To Bing Jackmin—a player who sees the "double consciousness" of the football game (the "Old form superimposed on new. It's a breaking-down of reality" [105]) and who feels the football is "aware of its own footballness" (29)—Harkness puts what he calls the "ultimate test": "But was it aware of its own awareness?" (29). Although Harkness is often hyper-aware of himself, he does not seem to pass this test because much of what he does and thinks, even toward the end of the novel, demonstrates an unrecognized acceptance of logocentric values. He learns the name of an American president and a new word each day ("apotheosis" is fittingly the last one mentioned); he performs ascetic rituals not demanded by football training (partial fasting, the self-punishment of thinking each day of a city in flames); and he frequently voices a desire for "no tension" (138), either internal or with others. The scene that best summarizes his logocentric conditioning occurs in the desert, far from the football field. "It was important," he says, "to come upon something that could be defined in one sense only, something not probable or variable, a thing unalterably itself" (69), the logoslike object. What he finds is a "low mound of . . . simple shit, nothing more . . . perhaps the one thing that did not betray its definition" (69). But very quickly his emotional responses and the synonyms for shit—"defecation," "feces," "dung," "excrement"—multiply meaning, revealing shit's—if not language's—"infinite treachery," a revelation he hurries away from, back toward Logos.

The only woman to have major status in the novel, Myna Corbett, an obese and blotchy-faced figure to whom Harkness is attracted, effects a betrayal similar to that of the "simple mound" of excrement: she becomes complex. Like Harkness, she has an authoritarian father and dreams of flight; she is the character who suggests he smoke marijuana before the game. Harkness sees her as a "perfect circle" (51) and as "ultimate" (179). She initially confirms his view: "I feel like I'm consistently myself. . . . I'm the same, Gary, inside and out" (53). Their relationship, conducted mostly in a set of identical picnics, is without tension: "the simplest thing to say is that she made me feel comfortable" (51). When Harkness thinks of her in sexual terms, she becomes the "body of perfect knowledge, the flesh made word" (43). While reading the dictionary to each other in the library, searching for some "protomorphic spoor," they become sexually excited with Corbett "positing herself as the knowable word, the flesh made sigh and syllable" (179). Even in passion Harkness thinks logocentrically. Unfortunately for him, this "flesh made word," like simple shit becoming its synonyms, turns complex. Her face begins to clear, she loses weight, gives up her thoughtless consumption, refuses to comfort Harkness, and, as she puts it in terms that recall Jackmin's "double consciousness," begins "to catch my own reflection everywhere I go" (187).

If Myna Corbett begins as a partial double for Gary Harkness and becomes a threatening other, his more explicit doubles—his roommate Anatole Bloomberg and his running-mate Taft Robinson—increasingly reflect Creed's logocentric aims. Like Harkness, Bloomberg lacks speed, is not from Texas, is an "exile of the philosophic type" (12) who is trying to rid himself of past guilt, fasts to advance his cause, and seeks a new beginning in the desert. Although Bloomberg recognizes the connections between asceticism and violence, he nevertheless advances toward simplicity and single-mindedness. He wants to become the "superrational man" (177) by speaking straight and thinking straight. Harkness wonders if this cause-effect sequence might be "a little simplistic" (153) and during Bloomberg's last appearance if he might be crazy; but Harkness does not explicitly recognize how Bloomberg duplicates Creed's and some of Harkness' own desires. With Taft Robinson, the figure who haunts the book, Harkness does come to understand Creed's influence if not Robinson's hold on Harkness himself. Robinson is almost invisible until the very last pages of the book; until then we have mostly Harkness' responses to him. The other players see Robinson as a frightening "break with simplicity" (5), but Harkness welcomes his difference, "the legend, the beauty, the mystery of black speed" (156), and tries to ingratiate himself, protecting Robinson from other teammates' racism. During the "Bang You're Dead" game, Harkness wishes he could be shot by Robinson, evidence of reciprocal interest. But Robinson remains distant until Harkness visits him, for a second time, in his room. What Harkness finds, though he does not seem to recognize it, is that Robinson now plays a previous Harkness role, the mysterious drop-out, to the new, football-loving, co-captain Harkness. Like that earlier Harkness, Robinson is ironic and evasive with his questioner yet does reveal parallel interests: escape from the father, silence, space, language, and, most surprisingly to Harkness, fascination with mass death. Robinson also explains that Creed brought him to Logos with promises of self-denial and getting to "the bottom of it": "We would learn the secrets" (195). These are the reasons Robinson is quitting football: to spend more time in discipline and meditation, the kind of withdrawal Harkness has made before. Now, however, he tries to persuade Robinson that one can play football and pursue his studies, his investigations; he articulates multiple arguments for playing the game. Both the content and structure of these arguments differ from the logocentric single-mindedness of Creed as Gary Harkness argues for a double life with his other halfback.

Placed two pages before the novel's end, is this dialogue an optimistic closure for *End Zone,* evidence that Harkness has learned the perils of logocentrism, the totalizing of a game? In keeping with the deconstructive impulse to keep the play of differences circulating, DeLillo takes some pains to unmake a conclusive ending. Robinson's appearance in these last pages creates a structural circle of sorts because he was the subject of the novel's first sentences. Set against the optimistic reading is the possibility that Harkness may be functioning as an unwitting agent of Creed, wearing as co-captain what he calls "the deputy's badge . . . the law's small tin glitter" (166). After he leaves Robinson's room, he checks a "rumor concerning new uniforms" (199), a deputy's act. Then comes the last paragraph: "In my room at five o'clock the next morning I drank half a cup of lukewarm water. It was the last of food or drink I would take for many days. High fevers burned a thin straight channel through my brain. In the end they had to carry me to the infirmary and feed me through plastic tubes" (199–200). Harkness has fasted before; does the degree of this fast rival Robinson in self-denial, prove loyalty to Creed, take revenge on the dieting Corbett, comment on the obese Bloomberg, or fulfill some other motive? The intent is undecidable. So is the effect. What is the meaning of "thin straight channel"? Literal or metaphorical, like or unlike the other straight lines in the novel? "In the end," in Harkness' words, is there an end—to his life, to his career at Logos, to his account? In the second paragraph of the novel, Harkness says "by the end of that first season . . ." (3). With its "that first" rather than "that," this suggests that Harkness has returned to football at Logos, another cycle. And, returning to that first page, we remember that Harkness has written this account, that the narrative is full of inconsistent or crooked lines, and that the narrative itself may be the evidence that Harkness has recognized the punishing effects, as well as the deeply seductive needs, of logocentrism, that Harkness, as well as DeLillo, instructs us with circles in place of a center or end point, frames rather than a frame, words against the word, the deconstruction of the logos.

Notes

1.   Although *End Zone* was widely and positively reviewed, it has received full-scale academic attention only in Neil Berman's *Playful Fictions and Fictional Players.* I treat the relationship of *End Zone* to DeLillo's other novels in my *In the Loop: Don DeLillo and the Systems Novel,* forthcoming from the University of Illinois Press.

Works Cited

Berman, Neil. *Playful Fictions and Fictional Players: Game, Sport, and Survival in Contemporary American Fiction.* Port Washington: Kennikat, 1981.

Campbell, Jeremy. *Grammatical Man: Information, Entropy, Language, and Life.* New York: Simon, 1982.

Caramello, Charles. *Silverless Mirrors: Book, Self, and Postmodern American Fiction.* Tallahassee: UP of Florida, 1983.

Culler, Jonathan. *On Deconstruction.* London: Routledge, 1983.

DeLillo, Don. *End Zone.* New York: Pocket, 1973.

Derrida, Jacques. *Of Grammatology.* Trans. Gayatri Chakravorty Spivak. Baltimore: Johns Hopkins UP, 1976.

———. *Positions.* Trans. Alan Bass. Chicago: U of Chicago P, 1981.

———. *Writing and Difference.* Trans. Alan Bass. Chicago: U of Chicago P, 1978.

Klinkowitz, Jerome. *Literary Disruptions: The Making of a Post-Contemporary American Fiction.* Urbana: U of Illinois P, 1975.

———. *The Self-Apparent Word: Fiction as Language/Language as Fiction.* Carbondale: Southern Illinois UP, 1984.

LeClair, Tom, and Larry McCaffery. "An Interview with Don DeLillo." *Anything Can Happen: Interviews with Contemporary American Novelists.* Ed. Tom LeClair and Larry McCaffery. Urbana: U of Illinois P, 1983. 79–90.

Thiher, Allen. *Words in Reflection: Modern Language Theory and Postmodern Fiction.* Chicago: U of Chicago P, 1984.

Wilde, Alan. " 'Strange Displacements of the Ordinary': Apple, Elkin, Barthelme, and the Problem of the Excluded Middle." *Boundary 2* 10 (1982): 180–195.

Wittgenstein, Ludwig. *On Certainty.* Trans. Dennis Paul and G. E. M. Anscombe. Ed. G. E. M. Anscombe and G. H. von Wright. Oxford: Blackwell, 1969.

The End of Pynchon's Rainbow: Postmodern Terror and Paranoia in DeLillo's *Ratner's Star*

GLEN SCOTT ALLEN

Terror: from the Latin *terrere,* to frighten; intense fear; the quality of causing dread; terribleness; alarm, consternation, apprehension, dread, fear, fright.

Webster's New Twentieth Century Dictionary

Years ago I used to think it was possible for a novelist to alter the inner life of culture. Now, bomb-makers and gunmen have taken that territory. They make raids on human consciousness.

William Gray in *Mao II*

Terrorism has played an important part in nearly every novel Don DeLillo has written to date. While the terrorists of *Running Dog* (1978) are essentially cartoon figures in search of a hypothetical pornographic film made in Hitler's bunker, the more realistic terrorists in *Players* (1977) assassinate stockbrokers and attempt to convert (albeit apathetically) disillusioned upper-middle-class New Yorkers. Terrorism in *The Names* (1982) is more complex, positing a terrorist group—or perhaps cult is closer to the mark—whose assassinations are either random or based on an arcane understanding of a "pre-linguistic" language, depending on which philosophical justification for murder they espouse that day. *White Noise* (1985) presents, among other "natural" acts of terror, an "airborne toxic event," which elaborates on the theme in *The Names* of terrorism as something irrational, unpredictable, and ultimately unplotted, and which also points toward DeLillo's most controversial novel, *Libra* (1989). With its motif of terrorism as something that has progressed beyond the control and goals of any human agency at all, *Libra* suggests that terrorism of a myopic and fundamentally bureaucratic (but inherently ungovernable) nature lurks at the heart of the Kennedy assassination. And DeLillo's

This essay was adapted from "Raids on the Conscious: Pynchon's Legacy of Paranoia and the Terrorism of Uncertainty in DeLillo's *Ratner's Star,*" *Postmodern Culture* 4 (January 1994), 10 January 2000 <http://muse.jhu.edu/journals/postmodern_culture/v004/4.2allen.html>. Published by permission of the author.

115

Mao II (1991) provides the reader with an identifiable human terrorist, Abu Rashid, while suggesting a complex and almost hypnotic symmetry between his praxis and that of a famous but disillusioned writer in the novel, William Gray. This symmetry is of course not unique to *Mao II:* an extended meditation about "solitary plotters" in *Libra* posits that both the scheming terrorist and the struggling writer are basically "men in small rooms" who seek to reconnect with a society from which they feel alienated by "writing" themselves back into the world through the production of "plots."

Thus terrorism in DeLillo seems integrally linked with writing in that both are engendered by that cardinal symptom of the postmodern condition, alienation. In DeLillo's work, the ubiquitousness of terrorist events and their consequent anxieties aides and abets the construction of a postmodern subject who chooses almost randomly between a career of writing or one of weaponry. Paranoia for this subject is not so much a dysfunctional neurosis as an adaptive strategy necessary for survival in the postmodern world. This paranoia is represented as a proactive awareness of imminent danger and vulnerability and even perhaps powerlessness in the face of random disaster and ubiquitous toxicity, a sort of "sixth sense" that has evolved from the more primitive or "classical" paranoia associated with the counterculture fiction of the '60s and early '70s.

Certainly the works of Thomas Pynchon have become closely identified with themes of such classic paranoia, particularly his magnum opus, *Gravity's Rainbow* (1973). Terrorism in *GR* is represented as the result (and perhaps even the goal) of increasingly omniscient institutional surveillance over the increasingly impotent and isolated civilian, as exemplified by Tyrone Slothrop. While the agents of this surveillance are obscure, they nonetheless are distinguishable *as* agents; Blicero and Pointsman, among others, typify what Pynchon posits as an instinctual drive at the heart of any well-organized institution, regardless of its nationality or ideological justification, to surveil and control its members and to extend and perfect that surveillance ad infinitum. Thus the institutions that these characters head are conceptualized as coherent *sites* of surveillance and control; surveillance and control that, through their ubiquitous presence and Byzantine networks, create an atmosphere within which the average civilian feels terrorized. It is no mere coincidence that the object that looms over the entire novel, the V-2 rocket, was constructed by the Germans as a "terror weapon" meant to break the morale of the British civilian population, especially in that its targets were unpredictable and its destruction unpreventable.

However, in Don DeLillo's work terrorism seems to have developed beyond the need of pointsmen of any ideological stripe and to have seeped into the very texture of contemporary life. I will argue that not only is DeLillo's figuration of postmodern terrorism quite different from Pynchon's but that his response to this terrorism and consequent paranoia is quite different, too, in that it seems to argue for an almost romantic return to the sovereign powers of the individual—an entity considered essentially extinct in most theories of the postmodern subject. This resurgent individualism is in fact not only a rejection of the paranoid strategy for postmodern survival as formulated in Pynchon; it also represents a rejection of formulations of post-modern subjectivity as conceived in the works of contemporary critics such as Emile Benveniste, Fredric Jameson, and Jean Baudrillard (to name only a few), wherein the "individual" can no longer be written outside quotation marks and is something nearly inseparable from the semiotic "signal soup" of postmodern life.[1] For instance, Kaja Silverman singles out the writings of Benveniste as an example of the representation of this spectral postmodern subject: "[In Benveniste's writings], the subject has an even more provisional status. . . . it has no existence outside of the specific discursive moments in which it emerges. The subject must be constantly reconstructed through discourse . . ." (Silverman, 199). In contrast, I will argue that DeLillo seems to feel that our only hope for redemption from a self-perpetuating cycle of terrorism, repression, and paranoia is in moving away from constructions of the self that work to deny or subvert classical conceptions of the individual as the primary site of responsibility and authority.

Typically when we speak of terrorism we're referring to violence committed by a minority in demonstration of its status as victim: of political repression or geographic isolation or "cultural ghettoization." Thus terrorism is by definition an act meant to call attention to itself; like postmodern fiction, it is inherently self-conscious. And in order to disseminate its self-conscious image as victim, it must have recourse to the media. When DeLillo's character William Gray suggests that terrorists have usurped the role in the public consciousness that novelists once held, he is referring (on at least one level) to the fact that terrorist acts must be circulated to attain identity, and that such acts compete for the public's limited attention span with other circulating "texts."

As might be expected, much of the debate within the scholarship of terrorism does in fact center on whether mass media coverage encourages terrorist acts or is largely irrelevant to them. Two recent articles in the journal *Terrorism* are good examples of the extremes in this debate. In "Terrorism and the Mass Media: A Systemic Analysis of a Symbiotic Process," Russell Farnen argues that terrorism and TV have a fundamentally symbiotic relationship and that in fact terrorism is "made to order" for the specific requirements of the television media: "Terrorism is different, dramatic, and potentially violent. It frequently develops over a period of time, occurs in exotic locations, offers a clear confrontation, involves bizarre characters, and is politically noteworthy. Finally, it is of concern to the public" (Farnen, 111). Farnen cites what is apparently the majority opinion in terrorism studies by paraphrasing (unfortunately) Margaret Thatcher to the effect that TV coverage is the "oxygen" that allows terrorism to breathe. However, from the opposite camp, Ralph Dowling argues that TV coverage is utterly secondary to most terrorist aims and that putting limits on the coverage of terrorist acts by the media would have little or no effect on the actual practice of terrorism ("Victimage and Mortification: Terrorism and Its Coverage in the Media").

While the issue of whether media coverage is a contributing motivation for acts of terrorism seems very much an open question, a far more interesting point emerges from this debate when one begins to focus on asking exactly what a terrorist act *means,* both as and beyond an excuse for a mass media circus. By "means," I'm referring less to the struggle for a definition of terrorism than to the more challenging problem of how one goes about interpreting the "texts" through which terrorism communicates with the world. For instance, Dowling suggests that understanding terrorist acts ought to be no more—and certainly no less—difficult than understanding any human attempt at communication; and yet "understanding" terrorist acts is the one thing most authorities claim to be incapable of doing. By its very definition, terrorism, at least to modern Western democracies, is "mad." Farnen quotes the U.S. ambassador-at-large, L. Paul Bremer, who casts terrorism in its familiar Western role as mindless, lawless evil incarnate: "Terrorism's most significant characteristic is that it despises and seeks to destroy the fundamentals of Western democracy—respect for individual life and the rule of law" (Farnen, 104). When one remembers the words most often linked with terrorist acts in media coverage and government proclamations of outrage—words such as senseless, random, callous, mad, barbaric—one begins to understand the inherent difficulty of any true "hostage negotiations"; for while the powers that be consider themselves to be "keeping the terrorists talking," they are at the same time convinced that the terrorists are not saying anything worth listening to; that they are in essence "spouting nonsense." For them, the terrorist event is comprised entirely of medium and is devoid of message. Take for instance a quote from a member of Al Fatah on the purpose of their use of violence: "Violence will purify the individuals from venom, it will redeem the colonized from inferiority complex, it will return courage to the countryman" (quoted in Dowling, 52). Violence for this terrorist is not the medium, it *is* the message. Or put another way, in the language of this terrorist violence is the transcendental magnifier, the one term that cannot be reduced to any positive correlative within the discourse itself; violence is axiomatic, beyond justification or logical debate. Beyond logic. And that's exactly how his use of violence is "heard" by most authorities; that is, to the logocentric Western sensibility, the terrorists' use of violence is the most "senseless" of all terms he or she could possibly employ. It is, in terms of cultural linguistics, essentially impossible for most "First World" Western civilians to "read" the terrorist text, to see in it any expression worth interpreting.

Though ultimately these two authors disagree about the relationship between terrorism and the media, they do agree that terrorism serves a fundamental rhetorical purpose, like any form of human communication. The communicative act is, Dowling argues, the way humans "find a place in the world" through the process of identifying oneself and one's group as distinct from other selves and other groups. Thus terrorist acts signal to the terrorists *themselves* who they are. In Dowling's view, the cultural effect of mass media–broadcasted terrorist violence is quite secondary to the more fundamentally human need of terrorists to "speak" themselves: "The seemingly senseless killings by terrorists serve the same function for terrorist society that wars and punishment of criminals and dissidents perform for mainstream society" (Dowling, 51). Farnen, too, believes that terrorism is a form of expression, a text that all the parties involved seek to control.[2] He uses the example of the kidnapping of Aldo Moro in 1978 by the Brigate Rosse, which Farnen says was "played out" as a classic narrative of sacrifice and tragedy: "The saga was complete with 'Christians' (Moro and his martyred bodyguards), BR [Brigate Rosse] 'lions,' state 'Caesars,' media 'tribunes,' and the anxious Italian public . . ." (116). In fact, Farnen argues that the terrorists intentionally and specifically "wrote" various symbols into the drama through such acts as the "placement of [Moro's] dead body in the center of Rome, on a street linking the two major party headquarters . . ." (118). Even more interesting is Farnen's observation that, although the event was discussed at obsessive length in the Italian media for many months, very little was ever said about the terrorists' possible motivations or goals. In fact, he concludes that, like many such terrorist acts, the entire event was treated as though it occurred somewhere *outside* the normal course of human events: "The Moro affair was treated much like an *inexplicable natural disaster* or an act of God . . ." (118; italics added). Finally, Farnen points out terrorism's usefulness as a dramatic trope, which has made it a mainstay of TV shows and popular spy novels: "With the sudden demise of post-Gorbachev communism as the main enemy, terrorism has become 'public enemy number one' in American public discourse" (103). In other words, though terrorism au naturel remains an uninterpretable text, terrorism as trope has become well assimilated into the Western entertainment and social lexicons.

Even though these two articles represent polar views in the "terrorist studies" community, they do move the discourse about terrorist acts from reductive tactical debates focusing on airport security and diplomatic finger-pointing to more sophisticated analyses of terrorism as a means of *expression*. However, by downplaying and eventually denying the role the mass media audience plays in the formation of the "terrorist identity," Dowling (for one) skims over what is clearly for many postmodern writers, especially DeLillo, the most interesting, perhaps the most terrifying, aspect of modern terrorism; for if terrorists have truly become "players" in the contemporary social narrative, then, whatever the intent of their expressive acts, they contribute as much to the formation of *our* identity as to their own, and their acts of seemingly random and "meaningless" violence have become an integral component of what being a modern individual *means*. According to an authority on terrorism, its chief "objective . . . is to convey a pervasive sense of vulnerability . . ."; vulnerability that produces "consequent paranoia and guilt in the civilian"; guilt that arises "when terrorism proves that societal institutions cannot provide the peace and security they promise . . ." (quoted in Dowling, 52). Given that it has become a commonplace to say that being a postmodern subject entails a constant sense of anxiety and vulnerability, then terrorism's chief aim would seem to be perfectly consistent with that "meaning." Thus in a broad cultural context, terrorist acts are an all-too-material demonstration of the uncertainty principle, that is, that we cannot absolutely control our environments and destinies and that our ability to author the narrative of our own lives is limited and circumstantial.

In order to describe DeLillo's presentation of this dynamic of "socialized" terrorism, we first need to discuss what I named earlier as its precursor, that is, the more traditional or "classical" paranoia often considered Pynchon's chief theme, if not obsession. Pynchon's contribution to literature may already be considered a body of fiction where the legacy of a "paranoid" style—out of Orwell via Burroughs, Kerouac, and Mailer—comes to full fruition in an America that had witnessed in the span of less than a decade more assassinations and political upheavals than the country had known for the preceding century; a time that many now think of as (in the terms of a character in *Running Dog*) the "Age of Conspiracies." According to John McClure, the appeal of conspiracy theories stems from their essentially indisputable, self-justifying, self-referencing hermeneutics: "For conspiracy theory explains the world, as religion does, without elucidating it, by positing the existence of hidden forces which permeate and transcend the realm of ordinary life" (McClure, 103). Though McClure is writing here of Don DeLillo's works, particularly *Libra, Gravity's Rainbow* would serve as an even better example of this "conspiracy age" fiction. With its nearly infinite schemes crossing and crisscrossing national, continental, ideological, and even temporal boundaries, it represents perhaps the most thoroughly "paranoid" book of all American fiction. And as an icon of this paranoia we have forlorn Tyrone Slothrop, who sits at the center of all these intersecting plots like a target in a crosshairs.

But a target of what? Exactly which "them" is after Slothrop? Certainly the V-2 rocket is one possibility; by the end of the novel we have reason to believe that the rocket is in fact "pursuing" Slothrop, or that he is pursuing it, or that they are at least bound (due to the early experiments of Dr. Jamf with Imoplex-G) in some complicated dance of death. But this "chemical bond" is only conjectural, and certainly not the only candidate for some They out to get Slothrop. In fact, by the time Slothrop wanders into the Zone, They has become every postwar institution that has survived, regardless of its national or ideological boundaries. We might say that what pursues Slothrop is nothing less than the World, and what pursues the reader is the lasting image of a rocket, poised an infinitesimal inch above our heads, completing an arc that began with its vapor trail first witnessed by Pirate Prentice some 800 pages earlier.

In a purely physical sense, the greatest terror of the novel is the V-2, the German "terror weapon." By using the V-2 as a trope of paranoia arising concomitant with the end of the war, Pynchon categorically identifies the primary legacy of our victory in World War II as anxiety; anxiety fueled by a world armed with weapons that had transcended all classical theories and strategies of warfare. This fundamentally "material" terrorism is one easily recognized by anyone who lived through either World War II or the 25 years of intense Cold War that followed. As critic John Johnston has argued, the "They-system" of *GR* "is depicted as arising out of the new bureaucratic needs and technologies of World War Two . . ." ("Post-Cinematic Fiction," 91), bureaucratic needs and technologies that would come to identify Slothrop's "time" as the progenitor of this age of conspiracies:

> There is also the story about Tyrone Slothrop, who was sent into the Zone to be present at his own *assembly*—perhaps, heavily paranoid voices have whispered, *his time's assembly*—and there ought to be a punchline to it. But there isn't. The plan went wrong. (*GR,* 680)

Though Pynchon's Theys are depicted as beyond traditional national ideologies, Their politics are clearly identifiable as those of isolation, repression, and control. In the post–World War II world of Pynchon's fiction, the development of modern and efficient state surveillance is a form of terrorism that motivates the civilian to seek out patterns of information that may (or may not) reveal hidden agencies and concealed plots. Thus paranoia is an adaptive reaction to omniscient institutional surveillance. And the mass media portrayed in Pynchon—radio, TV, and print journalism, even the U.S. postal system—have been largely co-opted by these forces of surveillance and control until they have become little more than state-dominated networks for distributing disinformation. In short, Pynchon sees the Cold War as a period of superficial peace during which the surviving nation-states, unable to take to the battlefield against foreign enemies, would turn all their powers of surveillance upon their own citizens, projecting their institutionalized paranoia onto these civilians and thus constructing an international and domestic tension where peace in the world was purchased by sacrificing this very civilian as any sort of independent "subject." What Pynchon represents in *GR* is, for want of a better term, the ascendancy of State Terrorism; not the state terrorism claimed by the PLO et al. as an underlying reality in the foreign policy of the United States and other world powers, but rather an *intra* state terrorism— that is, the development of complex and interconnected domestic and international networks of surveillance that depend upon the acquisition and circulation of vast quantities of information.

While information management technologies are also central to the thematics of DeLillo's novels, one distinct difference is the absence of history. The characters in DeLillo's novels often "inhabit" identities whose connection to history—either personal or cultural—is purely theoretical. Compared to *GR,* DeLillo's fictions seem set in a time when World War II has become a distant influence, something of a rumor. In *Running Dog,* for instance, there is the pornographic film from Hitler's bunker, yet nothing else about World War II seeps into the novel, and even the Vietnam War seems to belong to an entirely other world. And while DeLillo's work shares many other elements with Pynchon's—conspiracies whose agencies are dispersed or uncertain, characters who disappear in ways that mirror the dispersal of those agencies, and endings that suggest imminent and perhaps apocalyptic revelation—all of these elements are "warped" by the sheer mass of information available in DeLillo's postmodern world, information that shapes or perhaps even *comprises* its postmodern subjects. In other words, many of DeLillo's characters seem to be in danger of becoming exactly the sort of postmodern "specter" who might be perfectly comfortable in a world theorized by Benveniste. In fact, critic Daniel Aaron has suggested that DeLillo's characters are less Cartesian individuals than "integers in a vast information network" (70). And Tom LeClair sees information and its various incarnations as the very essence of DeLillo's works: "The novels are all about communication exchanges, the relations between information and energy and forces, the methods of storing, retrieving, and using new kinds of information" ("Postmodern Mastery," 101).

How, then, is DeLillo arguing *against* the acceptance of the dissipated specter as the proper postmodern subject? This is a point I will return to in a moment. But first I want to pursue the ways in which DeLillo restructures Pynchon's legacy of paranoia, and the relationship in *Ratner's Star* between paranoia and what DeLillo presents as the "new, improved" version of postmodern terrorism.

To begin with, we might note that most of DeLillo's works remap Pynchon's legacy of global paranoia onto a distinctly American, largely urban posthistorical landscape. In novels of middle-class ennui like *Players, White Noise,* and even to a certain extent *Mao II,* DeLillo's America is not only a land existing completely within this "age of conspiracies," but its inhabitants seem incapable of defining themselves as anything other than victims *of* these conspiracies. Frank Lentricchia believes that DeLillo's works serve as cautionary tales about such conspiracy and media-bound identity, illustrating "how the expressive forces of blood and earth are in the process of being overtaken and largely replaced by the forces of contemporary textuality. Lives lived so wholly inside the media are lives expressed (in the passive mood) through voices dominated by the jargons of the media" (Lentricchia, 211). And while the terrorism in DeLillo's novels often begins as something familiar to us *as* terrorism—small bands of individuals plotting acts of violence against "innocent" civilians—this "prosaic" terrorism typically metamorphoses into something else: an independent, uncontrolled, mysterious, and perhaps even unfathomable force that disrupts the best-laid plans of terrorist and civilian alike. Again, the airborne toxic event in *White Noise* is one example. But the best sustained representation of this "agentless" terrorism is to be found in one of DeLillo's earliest novels, *Ratner's Star* (1976).

Certainly we recognize in *Ratner's Star* a distinctly "Pynchonian" mise-en-scène, complete with proliferating plots, daunting intertextual connections, hidden and potentially nonexistent agencies, dispersing narrative voices, and, at the center of the plots and counterplots, a lone and relatively naive protagonist, Billy Twillig, whose task it is to determine whether he is a perceptive victim or a delusional paranoid. It is one of my contentions that in *Ratner's Star* DeLillo rewrites the global plots of *Gravity's Rainbow* onto the larger stage of the Universe, which itself becomes both scheme and schemer as well as the chief resident "terrorist."

The premise of *RS* is that we have received a signal from outer space. Fourteen-year-old Billy Twillig, a mathematical prodigy, is summoned to a distant research complex, Field Experiment Number One (FENO), to help decode this message. From the beginning of the novel the ambiguity of Billy's task and the instability of the fictional world that surrounds him are everywhere emphasized: "Little Billy Twillig stepped aboard a Sony 747 bound for a distant land. This much is known for certain. . . . But ahead was the somnolent horizon, pulsing in the dust and fumes, a fiction whose limits were determined by one's perspective . . ." (*RS*, 3). From the moment Billy arrives at FENO, he is besieged by what any reader of Pynchon would recognize as an overabundance of signal that threatens to degenerate into mere noise; and the only scientist other than Billy capable of deciphering the alien message, the aged and venerable Henrik Endor, has run away from the complex and is out in the desert, digging a hole.

Billy's dilemma is thus not unlike that of Benny Profane or Oedipa Maas or Tyrone Slothrop: to sort signal from noise and determine whether there is an intelligent agent at the origin of the message, but to determine first of all if there *is* a message. And like Benny and Oedipa and Tyrone before him, Billy encounters a dizzying array of characters in his search, each with their own interpretation of the message, all with their entirely idiosyncratic agenda of signals and countersignals. But whereas in Pynchon the "terror" generated by mysterious plots is largely a result of the revealed size and complexity of those plots, in *RS* the terror arises from the randomness and potential irrelevance of the information with which Billy is bombarded; which is to say, in Pynchon what is learned contributes to the background of terror, while in DeLillo the acquisition of knowledge *itself* is problematized to the point where "learning" is experienced as an act of random, meaningless violence—a terrifying experience.

This epistemological terrorism is figured in the book as inescapably arising from the dynamics and limits of language itself. While the latter half of the novel is devoted to the revelation of many things Billy Twillig would rather not know (about adulthood and sex, trust and betrayal), the first half concentrates on reducing language to something sinister and mysterious. Dialogue between characters is not so much an exchange of information, but rather some subtle and deadly martial art. A conversation between Billy and a vaguely threatening man he meets on a plane (an entrepreneur who will turn out later to be the closest thing the novel has to an actual terrorist) goes like this:

> "How was the bathroom."
> "I liked it."
> "Mine was first-rate."
> "Pretty nice."
> "Some plane."
> "The size."
> "Exactly." (11)

Throughout the novel most of the characters play their conversational cards very close to the vest, and Billy's responses to questions particularly are more like stage directions for speech than speech itself: "My mouth says hello"; "I do not comment."; "I make no reply." And when Billy eventually reaches the secret complex FENO, he is literally assaulted by a blizzard of scientific jargon from a dozen different fields—biology, child "sexology," astrophysics, architecture—as well as the apparently secret agendas of everyone he meets. All of this secretive and gestural communication occurs in an atmosphere of instantaneous computer networks, portable communicators, superintelligent computers, and hyperbolic referentiality, all of which turns language into something violent, unrelenting, and unpredictable. No communication is simply referential, pointing to any unambiguous signified. In fact, signification in the world of FENO is (in Barthes's terms) all connotation, no denotation, rhetorical "slippages" alone accounting for what little coherent meaning can be derived. Language here is often so rote as to be almost all ritual, its meaning residing *entirely* in its formal context. For instance, when Billy reaches his room in FENO, certain "safety precautions" are read to him by his escort:

> "The exit to which your attention has been directed is the sole emergency exit point for this sector and is not to be used for any purpose except that contingent upon fire, man-made flooding, natural trauma or catastrophe, and international crisis situations of the type characterized by nuclear spasms or terminal-class subnuclear events. If you have understood this prepared statement, indicate by word or gesture."
> "I have understood."
> "Most people just nod," Ottum said. "It's more universal." (17)

And often language "attacks" occur without *any* context. In fact, individual words often take on a paranoiac aura that is completely independent of either their denotation or connotation. Billy feels certain words are threatening all by themselves; words such as gout, ohm, ergot, pulp; "organic" words that he refers to as "alien linguistic units." And Billy's paranoid reaction to this decontextualized language makes perfect sense, for in a world where all quotes are taken out of context, each utterance would indeed seem an "alien linguistic unit," something without precedent or sustainable reference and whose purpose is therefore always suspect and already threatening. Thus the material violence that is the transcendental signifier for terrorists like the member of Al Fatah becomes in *RS* the abstracted violence of decontextualized and (seemingly) nonsensical language; language without a logical referent, leaving it to point either to itself or nowhere, or both.

Of course, much postmodern fiction depends on some version of this technique of decontextualization for its disorienting effect. But typically accompanying this technique is the employment of intertextual references that signal to the reader exactly what sort of larger context—often ironic—is to be used to "ground" the otherwise ambiguous signification. Throughout *RS,* however, what we would typically refer to as the intertextual references are made not to individual texts at all, but rather to vague "sites" of cultural signification. These sites are in turn reduced to single tropes, what we might call "signature" tropes, the decoding of which depends on the reader's possession of a repertoire of contemporary cultural trivia: cliches from classic films, one-liners from TV shows, characters and quotes from comic books, popular novels, newspaper headlines, tabloids, the jargon of *Scientific American,* the newspeak of federal bureaucrats, the glib argot of tabloid journalists . . . all of these idiolects existing side-by-side as equally valid discourses. Thus "texts" in the world of FENO are less discrete and more continuous (terms that *RS* uses with considerable frequency), something like subatomic particles, which aren't really "particular" at all but rather fields whose density fades vaguely off into other fields. And very often these "fields" of reference merely deflect the reader to still other "tropic fields" (to coin a perfectly awful phrase) until the paths of reference become so intricate that any map of their referentiality would look like the tracings of subatomic collisions produced in particle accelerators.[3]

In such a miasmic communicative environment, traditional boundaries between "texts" are dissolved. The result is more chaotic tropic plasma than orderly intertextual network. In this new form of intertextuality, then, the process whereby texts make contributions to the intertextual langue is best thought of as something one measures with probabilities and approximations rather than certainties and units. And the characters of *RS* move through clouds of such tropes, charged with the reflexive urge to find some sort of order, to arrange these signals into "spectra" based not on the content of the original text from which the signature trope is derived, but rather on the degree to which each trope serves as a vector pointing toward a potential agency at the message's point of origin. For instance, even when Billy believes he has finally decoded the message from space, he is admonished for working toward an irrelevant goal: "Content is not the issue. So don't go around telling people you broke the code. There is no code worth breaking" (416). Robert Softly, the character who has conceived of the perfectly logical, perfectly useless language called Logicon (a language for which one of the key rules is "i. All language was innuendo"), speaks with every word—even articles and prepositions—in quotes: " 'It' 'is' 'time' 'for' 'me' 'to' 'get' 'out.' " Each word is thus partitioned by an ironic "valence" even from its immediate, syntagmatic context. Thus severed from all context global *and* local, much of the language in the book does indeed seem like the "alien linguistic units" that so terrorize Billy.

To what do such "alien linguistic units" finally refer? For Billy at least, that common direction, the principle that he uses in an attempt to bring shape to the tropic plasma, is the discourse of mathematics—the only discourse that he does *not* find threatening. Language that is not simply "alien" is "comforting" to the extent that it can be translated into mathematical equivalents. And what Billy finds comforting in mathematics is the distinct quality of its constituent components—at least its integer components: "Words and numbers, writing and calculating . . . Ever one more number, individual and distinct, fixed in place, absolutely whole" (7). Fractions, however, have always made Billy feel "slightly queasy."

The typical Pynchonian reaction to such a state of uncertainty would be a dispersal of agency. By dispersal of agency, I mean both the figurative way in which the plots in Pynchon's novels indicate multiple and indeterminate agency and are often self-perpetuating, and the literal manner in which Pynchon's protagonists have a tendency to disappear: we recall Benny in *V.* disappearing into the sunset of Malta, Oedipa in *The Crying of Lot 49* disappearing into the auction room, and most significantly, Slothrop in *Gravity's Rainbow,* who disperses into the plot itself, becoming a "pretext" and a concept that is "just too remote" to hold together. We might also remember the way in which Slothrop merges with the symbol of what's been pursuing him—the V-2 rocket—by becoming *Rocketmensch* just before he merges with the plot ever further and becomes only vaguely visible (at least to Pig Bodine) but insubstantial; before he becomes, that is, a specter. And such a move is, again, perfectly in keeping with the paranoid logos of the novel, as the other trademark of Pynchon's plots is their undecidability, their sense of *imminent but unrealized* revelation. And the imminence of revelation is absolutely key to our understanding of the dynamics of paranoia. While one might think that revelation would be the ultimate moment for the paranoid when the "truth" of his or her worldview is substantiated, made incarnate, on the other hand this ultimate moment is also the *final* moment. Which is to say, if paranoia is more the state of seeking agency than the moment of finding it, then *actual* revelation threatens the paranoid's very raison d'être. Thus the most canny paranoid would be the one forever able to defer this moment of revelation.

At this point I need to briefly digress and discuss the idea of tropes. The root of the word *trope* is the Greek *tropaion,* which was a marker left to indicate where an enemy had been turned back. We might ask, then, what "enemy" is it that tropes turn back? As tropic or figural language is, at least in a basic sense, considered the opposite of literal language, a first-order answer might be that tropes mark the place in language where literality is "turned back." What is literal is "made up" of letters; and literal reading is after all an effort to reduce the ambiguity of a term to a *single* meaning; to transform signifiers into signals whose interpretation is constant across all possible contexts. Tropes, on the other hand, tug language in the opposite direction, toward a multiplicity of meaning and an uncertainty of interpretation. With this (admittedly terse) understanding of the tension between literal and tropic reading in mind, I would suggest then that the paranoid reader is in fact a very *literal* reader, one who works to reduce the ambiguity of the signifiers about him or her to mere signals that can all be traced back to the same and central agent—the agent at the center of the "plot."

Who or what, then, would this agent be for Pynchon? To quote first from *Gravity's Rainbow:*

> "There never was a Dr. Jamf," opines world-renowned analyst Mickey Wuxtry-Wuxtry—"Jamf was only a fiction, to help him explain what [Slothrop] felt so terribly, so immediately in his genitals for those rockets each time exploding in the sky . . . to help him deny what he could not possibly admit: that he was in love, in sexual love, with his, and his race's, death." (861)

Is Death, then, the elusive agency at the heart of Pynchon's paranoid plots? After all, a paranoid's literal reading of Revelation—as in the revelation of agency—would necessarily dictate that it be followed by the completion of apocalypse, that is, annihilation. And here we might recall the ending of *Gravity's Rainbow,* with the tip of the rocket suspended above our heads and the words "All together now . . ." uniting us in the paranoid's penultimate embrace.

At first glance, *Ratner's Star* would seem to share this thematic of Death as the ultimate plotter and final secret revealed. By the end of the novel, Billy Twillig feels ". . . there was something between himself and the idea of himself . . . and what he knew about this thing was that it had the effect of imposing a silence" (*RS,* 361). But DeLillo raises the stakes of this imminent revelation by taking the global apocalypse of *GR* and making it "literally" universal. DeLillo does this by positing something called a "mohole," where all the recognized laws of physics cease to apply. " 'If I had to put what a mohole is into words' [asks the reporter, Jean, who is chronicling the development of Logicon] 'what would I say?' 'You'd have a problem,' Mainwaring said" (365). By the end of the novel, the earth seems to be in just such a place, to be "mohole intense," as it is cast into darkness by an "unscheduled" solar eclipse. Though the gathered scientists predict that life in a mohole will be radically different, they have no idea how to explain or describe this difference: "I don't feel any different," Softly said. "Rob, we don't know. That's it. We don't know what it means. This is space-time sylphed. We're dealing with Moholean relativity here. Possibly dimensions more numerous than we've ever before imagined" (410). Thus DeLillo gives Pynchon's formula of dispersed and uncertain agency a quantum boost by moving his imminent apocalypse into an area of potentially *absolute* dispersal and *infinite* uncertainty. Perhaps at the conclusion of *RS* we are on the verge of a literal apocalypse— an apocalypse of literality—and potentially the genesis of an entirely "figural" universe where there is absolutely no consistent, predictable relationship between one experience and the next, between cause and effect, between any word and any thing; in other words, an apocalypse of referentiality. At the very least, such a universe would mean, in Ambassador-at-Large Bremer's words, the definite end of "respect for individual life and the rule of law." That is, the final triumph of terrorism, but a triumph that robs the ultimate act of terror of any coherent meaning.

Perhaps Slothrop's disappearing act in *GR* could be considered a maneuver intended to outflank this revelation of universal uncertainty and thus omnipresent terrorism: a countering of the "reign of terror" engendered by the dispersal of agency by mirroring it and becoming the dispersed subject. And this dispersal of the subject is also found in *RS*—but again, with a twist. While Slothrop disperses *into* the narrative, still the narrating voice of *Gravity's Rainbow* remains relatively coherent. However, in *RS*, while Billy Twillig retains his coherence as a character, what had been the third-person omniscient narrating voice of the novel essentially disperses into the characters, moving in the same sentence between locales, even between thoughts:

> Softly stopped reading here, thinking I am old, I will die, no one cares, her upper body slumped forward on the desk and what an implausible object it is, she thought . . . the photoelectric command at the end of Bolin's hand, thinking I am old . . . Wu's middle ear conveying vibrations inward . . . the implausibility of my parts, she thought . . . (425)

In this final section of the novel, sentences intrude on one another like filaments of conversations overheard on cellular phones; as if the very atmosphere of the novel were filled with detached segments of dialogue drifting about, looking for a conversation to link up with. Thus it is the "voice" of *RS* that disperses, and that anticipates and evades the imminent revelation that its own end implies but does not quite reach.

As I mentioned earlier, for DeLillo terrorism and writing are integrally linked. DeLillo particularly seems interested in the link between death as the final paranoid revelation and the act of authoring itself. One of the entries quoted from Oswald's diary in *Libra* expresses Oswald's greatest longing, which is to cease being Oswald the individual and to merge into a spectral identity called "the struggle": "Happiness is taking part in the struggle, where there is no borderline between one's own personal world, and the world in general" (quoted in Lentricchia, 197). Lentricchia sees in Oswald's banal desire something other than merely a soldier of the revolution wishing to *become* the revolution. Rather, he suggests that Oswald wishes to exchange places with Win Everett (the former CIA agent who is "plotting" Kennedy's fake assassination), to become the author of the plot in which he is only a character—or perhaps to become an author, period: "Oswald, in his desire for a perfectly distilled, scripted self—propelled by itself as its own novelist/ prime mover—is a figure of the assassin as writer, a man isolated by his passion, room-bound, a plot schemer." Lentricchia suggests that in his feelings of impotence, victimhood, and insubstantiality Oswald is the perfect representation of the spectral and manipulated postmodern subject: "Self-constructed, constantly revised, Oswald's narrative is a search for the very thing—a well-motivated, shapely existence—whose absence is a mark of the negative libran . . . Oswald's patched voice produces the presiding tone of the postmodern absence of substantial and autonomous self-hood . . ." (209).

And DeLillo's most recent novel, *Mao II,* centers on another "room-bound" plotter, a writer whose infrequent books are considered vastly intricate and dauntingly knowledgeable (only one of several attributes that link this figure to Thomas Pynchon). The writer's name is William Gray—a fine name for blending into the background.[4] Gray is a recluse, and has become something of a cultural "trope," whose usefulness to his culture resides in the very insubstantiality of his celebrity. However, Gray feels his best work is behind him; or rather, that the best role of the author in society is behind him, and that authors as enactors of literature no longer have any effect on society. "Years ago I used to think it was possible for a novelist to alter the inner life of culture. Now, bomb-makers and gunmen have taken that territory. They make raids on human consciousness" (*Mao II,* 87). Yet the "plot" Gray eventually becomes involved with is one authored by terrorists, not novelists; a plot that leads him to the realization of what seems to be his ultimate desire, which is not so much a merging into the struggle, as Oswald wanted, but a disappearing altogether into an anonymous death. There is the suggestion that Gray trumps the terrorist Abu Rashid's plans for him by dying before he can be victimized, by making his sacrifice his own statement rather than allowing it to be shaped to Rashid's purposes. But of course this is a statement no one reads, which we can think of either as an act of supreme idealization or supreme futility.

For *Mao II* hardly endorses Gray's self-willed abdication of self, his "devout" wish "to be forgotten," as any sort of positive solution to the problem of postmodern terrorism and paranoia. For one thing, Gray's anonymous death does not end the novel; we see the various characters adjusting to Gray's disappearance, using it, shaping his absence to their own ends: his friend Scott settles into Gray's house, becoming a simulacrum of the absent author; the photographer Brita who sought to "reproduce" Gray shifts her aim easily to the terrorist instead, in a move both opportunistic and smoothly adaptive (and one that models the very sort of symbiotic interdependence Farnen suggests between those who "write" violence into the text of everyday life and those who disseminate it). Gray's dispersal leaves only a vacuum that others rush in to fill, without giving a second thought to the "message" intended by his disappearance. Thus the novel poses a subtle, even tragic question: what are the limits of dispersed subjecthood? If one seeks to evade the terror of random violence by blending into the background and denying the terrorist—whether individual or Universe—a coherent, identifiable target, what is sacrificed? To what extent is Gray's preemptive vanishing a death not only of potential victimhood, but also of personal identity, of responsibility, and thus of self. How thoroughly can the author disown author-ity before also surrendering integrity; the ability, in the words of *Gravity's Rainbow,* to appear as any sort of "integral creature"?

Lentricchia suggests that, in the traditional American novel, the author provides a stable point of reference from which the reader can take society's "critical measure," that the reader can find relative detachment

> within the value of the "omniscient" author who displays the workings of the dynamic but is not himself subject to them. The author, then, is a transcendent figure, someone the reader is implicitly asked to identify with . . . that constantly throws us forward into some other, some imagined, existence. (Lentricchia, 210)

Lentricchia goes on to say that this "exit" is "sealed off" in *Libra.* Johnston makes essentially the same observation about *RS,* which he sees as refusing to grant authority to any univocal narrator or point of view:

> [*RS*] refuses to privilege any single "authoritative" version or to subordinate its varied stories and discourses to a higher or more englobing authorial narrative discourse, which would amount to yielding to precisely those powers and functions that it wants to lay bare. Instead, it inscribes an uncertainty and indeterminacy in its own narrative structure, and plays with how we might know certain connections between events. ("Postcinematic Fiction," 91)

As an example, I would point again to the novel's last section, when what has previously been a coherent and recognizable narrating voice disperses into the "text." Thus *RS* robs the reader of the comfort of any transcendental authorial figure who might otherwise serve to "make sense" of the random violence of decontextualized language; who might, that is, provide relief from the terrorism of meaninglessness. And this absence further denies the reader any detached platform from which he or she might, with impunity, take his or her society's "critical measure." Thus, in the absence of the narrator *and* author, the reader is forced to construct some central embodying principle to grant overall context to the otherwise terrifying uncertainty; to build upon an interpretive principle that is secretive, elusive, coded, with a potentially totalizing or "universal" agenda, and capable of explaining vast and obscure connections. In other words, the reader must construct a plot. He or she must actively engage the terrorism of meaninglessness that seeks to overwhelm the novel, to assert, that is, his or her individual strategies of sense-making in order to resist the dissolution into apocalypse and chaos suggested by the end of the novel.

And yet, however ambiguous the endings of DeLillo's novels, there is almost always at least one character who "models" this sort of adaptive strategy for the reader. One thinks of Pammy in *Players,* moving away from the violent ennui of her husband-become-terrorist toward an alternative she can't quite articulate; or Bucky Wunderlick in *Great Jones Street* (who, like Bill Gray, has been fascinated with rumors of his own "kidnap, exile, torture, self-mutilation and death") coming to terms with his newly found obscurity and accepting that "[w]hen the season is right I'll return to whatever is out there"; or the "tongue-tied" boy at the end of *The Names,* running (like Billy Twillig) into a violent landscape, looking "in vain for familiar signs and safe places." Time and again DeLillo's novels end with his characters feeling a strange serenity in the face of near-apocalyptic Nature that has become unintelligible, chaotic, terrifying; yet a Nature that inspires even as it diminishes. Certainly the most evocative such scene closes *White Noise,* with Jack Gladney and his neighbors climbing to a freeway overpass to witness the technicolor sunsets that are a byproduct of the airborne toxic event:

> What else do we feel? Certainly there is awe, it is all awe, it transcends previous categories of awe, but we don't know whether we are watching in wonder or in dread, we don't know what we are watching or what it means, we don't know whether it is permanent, a level of experience to which we will gradually adjust, into which our uncertainty will eventually be absorbed, or just some atmospheric weirdness, soon to pass. (*WN,* 324–25)

And as with so many of the other novels, Gladney makes an explicit connection between this moment of contemplative awe (if awe it is) and an undercurrent of terror generated by the loss of traditional ordering systems—in this case of the local supermarket shelves: "It happened one day without warning. There is agitation and panic in the aisles, dismay in the faces of older shoppers. They walk in a fragmented trance, stop and go, clusters of well-dressed figures frozen in the aisles, trying to figure out the pattern, discern the underlying logic . . ." (325). Gladney thinks all this even as he dispassionately muses over his own mortality, and there is something in this multilayered experience of wonder and dread that both unites him with his community and reminds him of his individuality: "It is not until some time after dark has fallen . . . that we slowly begin to disperse . . . restored to our separate and defensible selves" (325).

Then there is the final image in *Ratner's Star,* which is not the ascendancy of the dispersion of the protagonist (as in *Gravity's Rainbow*), but rather the exuberant image of Billy Twillig—who has spent the last half of the novel almost paralyzed with terror—furiously pedaling a tricycle straight into the "reproductive dust of existence" (120). This is a supremely suggestive figure, however brief or ambiguous; for while Billy's two mentors—Endor and Softly—respond to the near-advent of the new Universe of Nonsense by disappearing into a hole (much like Slothrop disappearing into the text), there is no reason to believe that Billy is following their lead. Rather, he seems headed for some sort of revitalization, perhaps rebirth amidst the "reproductive dust of existence."

DeLillo's representation of postmodern terror—a terror residing in the toxified landscape and perhaps fundamental to the very nature of the universe—seems finally even more insidious and hegemonic than Pynchon's in *Gravity's Rainbow;* yet his work does not endorse Pynchon's solution, that is, an abandonment of the field to the ablest postmodern paranoids. DeLillo's characters often embrace the plots that surround them, that perhaps construct them, and work—against all reasonable odds—to adapt to such a statement of existence so that they might in turn alter the statements of that existence. They seek some alternate way of existing within a world admittedly filled with random violence and meaningless communication, to resist both the role of surveilled, terrorized subject and paranoid, dispersed specter. Though there is certainly an overlay of despair and futility in DeLillo's work, there often seems too an indefatigable energy, a belief just as strong that the production of plots we call novels might *not* be completely futile or always already culpable. DeLillo himself has expressed a willingness to embrace rather than resist what other writers see as the terrorism of technology and technological modes of existence in postmodern society: "Science in general has given us a new language to draw from. Some writers shrink from this . . . To me, science is a source of new names. . . . Rilke said we had to rename the world. Renaming suggests an innocence and a rebirth" (LeClair, "Interview," 84).

Thus I would argue that much of DeLillo's work points toward a strategy of adaptation and rebirth, particularly of our sense of individual identity and responsibility as, perhaps, the only alternative to becoming dispersed and irresponsible postmodern specters. But his work also recognizes that such a rebirth of our sense of self and community involves a considerable struggle; a struggle Jacques Derrida seems to have had in mind when, writing about the importance of a new formation of European cultural identity in response to terrorism—whether it be religious, political, or ethnic—he calls for a postmodern subject that is informed by rather than frightened of our increasing and inescapable connectedness; a cultural identity "constituted in responsibility" and shaped by, in a quite traditional way, the anticipation of one's cultural legacy. "For perhaps responsibility consists in making of the name recalled, of the memory of the name, of the idiomatic limit, a chance, that is, an opening of identity to its very future" (Derrida, 35). Admittedly, perhaps such an interpretation reads DeLillo (and Derrida) as more neoexistentialists than postmodernists; perhaps it even suggests that DeLillo's work needs to be reexamined for its links to modernism, even romanticism, in its representation of the theoretically obsolete individual as the only viable site of resistance to the ubiquitous terror of postmodern life.

Bibliography

Aaron, Daniel. "How to Read Don DeLillo." In *Introducing Don DeLillo,* ed. Frank Lentricchia, 67–81. Durham, N.C.: Duke University Press, 1991.

DeLillo, Don. *Great Jones Street.* New York: Vintage Books, 1973; *Ratner's Star.* New York: Vintage Books, 1980 (1976); *Players.* New York: Vintage Books, 1977; *Running Dog.* New York: Vintage Books, 1978; *The Names.* New York: Vintage Books, 1982; *White Noise.* New York: Penguin Books, 1985; *Libra.* New York: Penguin Books, 1989. *Mao II.* New York: Penguin Books, 1991.

Derrida, Jacques. *The Other Heading: Reflections on Today's Europe.* Trans. Pascale-Anne Brault and Michael B. Naas. Bloomington: Indiana University Press, 1992.

Dowling, Ralph E. "Victimage and Mortification: Terrorism and Its Coverage in the Media." *Terrorism* 12, no. 1 (1989): 47–59.

Farnen, Russell F. "Terrorism and the Mass Media: A Systemic Analysis of a Symbiotic Process." *Terrorism* 13, no. 2 (1990): 99–123.

Harris, Robert R. "A Talk with Don DeLillo." *New York Times Book Review,* 10 Oct. 1982, F26.

Johnston, John. "Generic Difficulties in the Novels of Don DeLillo." *Critique* 30, no. 4 (1989): 261–75.

———. "Post-Cinematic Fiction: Film in the Novels of Pynchon, McElroy, and DeLillo." *New Orleans Review* 17, no. 2 (1990): 90–97.

LeClair, Tom. "Interview with Don DeLillo." In *Anything Can Happen: Interviews with Contemporary American Novelists,* ed. Tom LeClair and Larry McCaffery, 79–90. Urbana: University of Illinois Press, 1983.

———. "Postmodern Mastery." In *Representation and Performance in Postmodern Fiction,* ed. Maurice Couturier, 99–111. Nice: Delta Press, 1983.

———. *In the Loop: Don DeLillo and the Systems Novel.* Chicago: University of Illinois Press, 1987.

Lentricchia, Frank, ed. "Libra as Postmodern Critique." In *Introducing Don DeLillo,* ed. Frank Lentricchia, 193–215. Durham: Duke University Press, 1991.

McClure, John A. "Postmodern Romance: Don DeLillo and the Age of Conspiracy." In *Introducing Don DeLillo,* ed. Frank Lentricchia, 99–115. Durham, N.C.: Duke University Press, 1991.

Price, Andrew Jude. "The Entropic Imagination in 20th Century American Fiction: A Case for Don DeLillo." *Dissertation Abstracts International* 49, no. 5 (1988): 1143A.

Pynchon, Thomas. *Gravity's Rainbow.* New York: Viking, 1976.

Silverman, Kaja. *The Subject of Semiotics.* New York: Oxford University Press, 1983.

Notes

1. See, for instance, Emile Benveniste's *Problems in General Linguistics* (1971), Fredric Jameson's *Postmodernism or, the Cultural Logic of Late Capitalism* (1992), and Jean Baudrillard's *In the Shadow of the Silent Majorities, or The End of the Social* (1983).

2. Farnen also has a second and more interesting point to make, which is that the portrayal of terrorism in the media has created a false trope. He quotes at length statistics that show that, especially in the last five years, terrorist acts have become so rare that "[i]n the United States, a person is more likely to die as a victim of an asthma attack than as a victim of a terrorist attack" (101).

3. See John Johnston's discussion of the heavy use of cinema in the works of both Pynchon and DeLillo, where he suggests that "the interest in cinema revealed in these novels seems to respond to a sense of the cinema as an apparatus for producing and disseminating images which both construct and control a new kind of subject." A subject, I would add, that is a product not of the accumulated content of interrelated texts but rather the transient acontextual moment of intersecting tropes.

4. In fact, it is rumored that Bill Gray is the name Don DeLillo often used when traveling incognito.

Marketing Obsession:
The Fascinations of *Running Dog*

Mark Osteen

Don DeLillo has stated that the pared-down prose, flat characters, and rapid pace of his novel *Running Dog* reflect his intention to write "a thriller," and the novel indeed displays the violent actions and suspenseful structure of that genre.[1] Like many thrillers, it is a quest tale in which a character or group competes for a valuable object. But *Running Dog* subverts the form: whereas classical quest tales—exemplified by medieval Grail stories—depict a protagonist's search for identity through a series of ordeals that educates both hero and reader about morality or proper conduct, the quest of Glen Selvy, this novel's ascetic soldier/monk and nominal protagonist, brings no purification or transcendence, but rather exposes him as the machine and trained animal of his masters. Moreover, while the Holy Grail inspires righteous behavior in those who seek it, *Running Dog*'s desired object—an allegedly pornographic home movie of Hitler and his minions filmed in the Führerbunker in April 1945—seems to contaminate all the characters and remake them in its image.

That the desired object is a film is appropriate to the screenplay-like style of *Running Dog,* which depicts a world where the ubiquity of the camera eye has created a superpanopticon that blurs the distinction between behavior and performance. DeLillo suggests that this phenomenon of omnipresent cinematic surveillance not only replays the Nazis' staging of history as cinema, but also induces a similarly fascistic ideology. Propelled by what DeLillo has elsewhere called a "terrible acquisitiveness,"[2] the novel's questers serve an amoral, fetishistic, fascistic capitalism that turns humans into objects or "running dogs." In this postmodern pastiche of the Grail quest in which the sacred icon is "the century's ultimate piece of decadence,"[3] DeLillo mounts a complex consideration of the enduring appeal of the fascist mentality, of the power of film to shape and record human subjectivity and history, and of the convergence of fascism and film in pornographic representation. The novel simultaneously investigates the fascinations of fascism and examines how such fascistic fascinations become marketable commodities. In sum, *Running*

This essay was written especially for this volume and appears here by permission of the author.

Dog explores both the obsession with marketing and what DeLillo calls "the marketing of obsession."[4]

THE UNHOLY

The novel's prologue offers its sole instance of a character's direct narration: "You won't find ordinary people here. . . . Of course you know this. This is the point" (3). The use of second-person narration here adumbrates the novel's depiction of postmodern subjectivity as a condition at once singular and plural, both self- and other-directed, one in which the subject simultaneously acts and comments upon his or her performance.[5] The narrator, Christoph Ludecke, possessor of the Hitler film, is costumed in his wife's clothing while making his way toward a transaction, an exchange of flesh in the service of "the God of Body. The God of Lipstick and Silk. The God of Nylon, Scent and Shadow" (4). Similar exchanges, both commercial and narratorial, dominate the novel. An intertextual exchange also appears here: as his name indicates, Christoph is a parodic Christ-figure dying for his God; like Christ, he is the source of the Grail, and the abandoned building where he is killed serves as the Wasteland of the Fisher King (although Ludecke is dressed as a "queen" [8]).[6] As in the Grail legends, his death comes by stabbing. At this point, however, the reader doesn't know Ludecke's identity, and both he and the cops who discover his body immediately vanish from the novel. Although Ludecke quickly loses his narrative voice (just as he has lost what he believes to be his patrimony in Germany), his spectral presence haunts the novel, and his nostalgia, self-consciousness, and dedication to a pseudospiritual ideal are repeated in several other characters.

The cop who finds his body laments that today "[e]verybody's in disguise" (8). His description certainly fits Senator Lloyd Percival, whose surname suggests his role as seeker of the Grail. But unlike the youthful Percival of medieval Grail legends, this Percival is an expert dissembler. Although allegedly investigating PAC/ORD, a funding mechanism for U.S. covert operations that later plays a major role in the novel, he is actually following his own agenda, which mostly involves adding pornographic artifacts to his vast collection. No "righteous type" (25), Percival is merely a skilled actor, as indicated by the orange TV makeup he is wearing when he first encounters journalist Moll Robbins, *Running Dog*'s second protagonist (30). Like the TV actor he resembles, Percival is "all image" (31), and virtually disappears in the second half of the novel, just as Sir Percival vanishes from the second half of Chrétien's Grail story.[7] Still, Percival is the only character who understands the allusions in the name *Running Dog*, the magazine for which Moll writes; perhaps this is appropriate, since he is one of the many "[c]apitalist lackeys and running dogs" who populate the novel (30).

Moll also plays roles, using costumes to "safeguard . . . her true self" (29). As a journalist for a magazine that survives (barely) by trafficking in conspiracy stories, Moll too is involved in marketing obsession. As her first name indicates, she is fascinated by violent men such as her ex-lover, terrorist Gary Penner, perhaps because they possess an element of mystery that appeals to her bloodhound curiosity about "whatever I don't see clearly" (110). Like Pammy Wynant of *Players,* she values "[t]ransience and flash" over commitments and attachments (109). Ironically, Moll's attraction to men "without a history" (63) such as Glen Selvy makes her complicit with the clandestine power structures that her magazine claims to expose. Tacitly accepting Selvy's obsessive behavior and secretly drawn to Percival, she has become the running dog of a capitalism that consumes its own opposition. Nevertheless, Moll's combination of curiosity and self-awareness permits her to observe the others' quests from a slight distance.

Selvy—in his long underwear resembling an English lancer (36)—is a late-twentieth-century version of the knight in quest romances.[8] Although his first name suggests that he is playing Sir Gawain, he is actually performing as a postmodernist Sir Percival. Like that knight, whose love for singing birds is emphasized in several Grail stories,[9] Selvy is constantly associated with avians, including Robbins: he appears early in the novel surrounded by birds (26), and near the end identifies with the birds of prey that presage his death. Initially involved in the quest for the Hitler film, Selvy eventually departs to pursue his own private quest for identity. Displaying that "element of resolve and fixed purpose" (35) so typical of DeLillo's many pseudo-ascetic characters, Selvy maintains an elaborate set of rituals that preserve a "fine edge to be maintained in preparation for—he didn't know what" (54). A soldier without a war, Selvy is as transient as Moll, eschewing emotional attachments (one of his rules is to have sex only with married women) to protect "the severity of the double life" (81). If his refusal to consider consequences ultimately paralyzes him, nonetheless his mental blinders recall Sir Percival, whose failure to ask the right questions in the Fisher King's castle prevents the King's full recovery.[10] Like *Libra*'s Lee Oswald, Selvy is a monkish devotee of a "theology of secrets"[11] who aims to "build . . . a second self" through a fetishistic identification with guns, his "inventory of personal worth" (83, 92). But like Ludecke he refers to himself in second person, thereby betraying a deep self-alienation: a mechanism nearly as mindless as his weapons, Selvy has no self beyond his scripted rituals.

Consequently he is not a believable actor, and Moll notices that when he plays the "junior tycoon" his reactions are "just the tiniest bit mechanical" (15, 17). In fact, Selvy is under double cover, pretending to be Percival's porn buyer while actually working for Radial Matrix, a secret arm of PAC/ORD, and reporting to Arthur Lomax, a man identified by his black limousine and running dogs (see 29, 54, 108). Ironically, Selvy's expertise in dismantling surveillance devices (he "squashes the bug" that Earl Mudger, former head of

Radial Matrix, uses to eavesdrop on Ludecke's widow) prompts his employers to target him for assassination by Augie the Mouse, who, like all killers in *Running Dog,* dons a costume (ear protection and shooting glasses) as he fires at Selvy (65). But the sources of Selvy's rituals are not political. At one point, he and Percival contemplate an erotic statue of St. Teresa, and Percival comments, "her ecstasy always was sexual" (46). So is Selvy's. Springing from "sexual sources and coordinates" (111), his routine allows him to become the star of his own private erotic film, as well as an object for detached observation and manipulation by people like Mudger.

NAZIS IN MOTION

The unholy Grail itself—that allegedly pornographic film of Hitler and company—embodies the complex relationships among fascism, film, and subjectivity. All those who pursue the film must approach it through a man named Lightborne, who runs a "worldwide network, buying and selling and bartering" (16) fake erotica. The vain, dapper Lightborne is a movie-mad figure who tries to project an image of refinement and erudition; but his chronically flapping sole unmasks him as the novel's pseudo–Charlie Chaplin. An avatar of Hermes in his role as "amoral connecting deity,"[12] Lightborne, as his name implies, is a faux-divine messenger who sets things in motion and caters to the others' acquisitive obsessions. If Lightborne symbolizes the spirit of capitalist exchange, his counterpart, Richie Armbrister, 22-year-old "smut king" and "master of distribution and marketing" (49), exemplifies its material flux. Armbrister is entirely a creature of his appetites; he himself admits that he doesn't "exist as a person" (50). Capitalists of lust, Lightborne and Armbrister are little more than matrixes of the profit motive.

Still, it is Lightborne who delineates the fundamental aesthetic of twentieth-century erotica: it must have "[m]ovement, action, frames per second. . . . [A] thing isn't fully erotic unless it has the capacity to move" (15). Indeed, everything in *Running Dog* seems to be in motion, as the novel exploits film as both plot device and narrative paradigm. Like *Libra* and *Players, Running Dog* is structured as a series of cinematic crosscuts from character to character and scene to scene in which meaning is generated through montage-like juxtapositions. Moreover, just as the plot revolves around a competition to possess the Hitler film, so the narrative stages a battle for the possession of voice, as though the text were also a commodity that the characters are vying to control. Thus the novel's focus rapidly shifts among its large cast before finally settling on a dual plot depicting the parallel quests of Selvy and the would-be film buyers. These narrative movements—the type that Ian Reid calls "dispossessions"[13]—reflect not only the novel's plot, in which each actor maneuvers for advantage over other prospective purchasers, but also the deeper, spiritual dispossessions wrought by capitalism and cinema: everything is a commodity, everything is a surface.

As the novel's chief "student of the [Nazi] period" (19), Lightborne speculates about the Hitler film: "Unedited footage. One copy. The camera original. Shot in Berlin, April, the year 1945" (18). The film would be a historical document without precedent; as such it would possess the "aura" that Walter Benjamin famously describes as the source of classical aesthetic value.[14] Benjamin cites film as the most destructive agent of that aura: infinitely reproducible, cinematic images act like money, transposing use-value to exchange-value, and wrenching beauty from tradition.[15] Indeed, when the film is finally found, it turns out to destroy the "aura" of originality in a multitude of ways, not least because Hitler, the lead "actor," is imitating a movie star who parodied him. Of course, Hitler was in some respects himself an actor who introduced "aesthetics into political life" through the manipulation of mass images.[16] By commissioning such propaganda films as Leni Riefenstahl's *Triumph of the Will* and *Olympia,* and by carefully staging his appearances, Hitler incited the adulation and "collective frenzy" now characteristic of a "pop hero" (147). Using cinema and simple icons, the Nazis trained the masses in an uncritical obedience in which "thoughts [were] replaced by moving images."[17]

As Lightborne puts it, "Those Nazis had a thing for movies. They put everything on film. . . . Film was essential to the Nazi era. Myth, dreams, memory" (52). At the original headquarters in East Prussia, in fact, the Nazi elite showed a movie every night at 8 P.M.[18] Having once "worked for a photographer," Eva Braun made 8 mm home movies of Nazi leaders and arranged screenings of popular films.[19] She claimed that "cinema is an art, it isn't just entertainment," and fancied herself an actress; her ultimate desire was to die and leave a beautiful corpse.[20] The Nazis were inordinately concerned about the cinematic images they would pass down to posterity. During a conference at the Propaganda Ministry on April 17, 1945, Goebbels reportedly predicted that "in a hundred years' time they will be showing a fine color film describing the terrible days we are living through. Don't you want to play a part in that film?. . . Hold out now, so that a hundred years hence the audience does not hoot and whistle when you appear on the screen."[21] Thus, as Susan Sontag asserts, the Nazi myth represents a "radical transformation of reality: history become theater."[22] Of course this desire to turn themselves into filmed historical fetishes backfired, since we now have inarguable proof of their atrocities. Ironically, then, by obsessively filming themselves the Nazis convicted themselves through the same process that brought them to power. As Hannah Arendt argues, "the perpetual-motion mania of totalitarian movements which can remain in power only so long as they keep moving and set everything around them in motion" generates the very fragmentation and restlessness that led to their demise.[23] By filming themselves the Nazis became flickering images on the screen of history.

Nevertheless, the fascist phenomenon fulfills Lloyd Percival's assessment of the "history of reform," in which "there's always a counteraction built in. A low-lying surly passion. Always people ready to invent new secrets, new bureaucracies of terror" (74). *Running Dog* resurrects this broader history through individual characters' attempts to revise it. Ludecke's wife, Klara, for example, believes that owning the film will bring her husband back to life and lend her some of the Third Reich's lost power (97). Lightborne exploits a similar urge, telling prospective collectors that "[h]istory is so comforting. . . . Isn't this why people collect? To own a fragment of the tangible past. Life is fleeting, and we seek consolation in durable things" (104). But collectors do not really recapture history; rather, they detach artifacts from the past and create a separate order that is both an elision and an emblem of history. That, at least, seems to be Percival's aim: he sees the Hitler film as a trophy, a way of enhancing his personal worth. In this regard, film plays a special role, because, as John Frow comments, "film seems to guarantee the solidity of history, to ensure a special access to historical truth."[24] Yet as Riefenstahl's films brilliantly proved, filmed history is always staged history: cinematic images are constructed out of fragments, and thus can be made to "say" anything the filmmakers wish. A film therefore occupies a paradoxical temporal position: it is a solid object in time but comes into being only when moving through a projector; while presenting itself as verifiable reality, a film is always an aesthetic construct.

Running Dog's characters are motivated largely by nostalgia, by a yearning to recapture a lost simplicity or origin. Thus Selvy journeys back to Marathon Mines, the site of his training and the closest thing he has had to a home; Moll repeatedly tries to relive the thrill she got from consorting with a terrorist; Percival wants to own the past as a pornographic object. Even Mudger's fetish for surveillance and secrecy is, as Patrick O'Donnell has observed, a "form of nostalgia" for the Vietnam War.[25] Nostalgia transforms historical artifacts into souvenirs, into embodiments of personal emotions; and filmed nostalgia turns history into a "museum" or "supermarket . . . where people are free to shop around for their values and identities."[26] As he does throughout his oeuvre, in *Running Dog* DeLillo exposes the symbiotic relationship between nostalgia and fascistic ideologies like Nazism.

For the characters in *Running Dog*, however, history is useful only if they can market it; thus Mudger, Lightborne, and the mob figures who later enter the chase want the film because they believe it will make money. And that exchange-value depends upon both its historical veracity and its alleged pornographic content, which in turn derives from a well-established association between SS regalia and SM pornography. As Lightborne notes, Nazis are "automatically erotic. The violence, the rituals, the leather, the jackboots.

The whole thing for uniforms and paraphernalia" seems "endlessly fascinating" (52). Why? In part because both fascism and sadomasochism stage power relationships in overtly theatrical form. Indeed, according to Susan Sontag, both Nazi ideology and the aesthetics of sadomasochistic pornography "flow from (and justify) a preoccupation with situations of control, submissive behavior, extravagant effort, and the endurance of pain; they endorse two seemingly opposite states, egomania and servitude."[27] In this regard SM pornography merely enacts more plainly the ontology of most pornography, which, as Douglas Keesey observes, generates an imaginary world where the viewer may be safely totalitarian.[28] In short, just as fascism produces a pornography of power, so pornography, in *Running Dog,* is a form of fascist representation.[29]

More generally, any transformation of bodies into instruments or sites of detached observation is fascistic. A prime example of this condition is Glen Selvy who, as Tom LeClair notes, "treats his body as a pornographic object,"[30] as a fungible medium of exchange. Seeking visionary experience or pseudo-religious self-transcendence, Selvy can find it only in bodily mortification and violence. He thus fulfills the fascist ideal in which "everyday reality is transcended through ecstatic self-control and submission."[31] His zeal also couples pornographic and fascist aesthetics: just as fascist art "glamorizes death," so Selvy's pursuit of extreme states reduces subjectivity to a vehicle for a linear movement toward self-annihilation and the "gratifications of death, succeeding and surpassing those of eros."[32]

While Selvy's fanatical rituals weave together the novel's Grail plot with its anatomy of pornography and its analysis of fascism, these links are even more explicitly established in a conversation between Lightborne and Moll. As Lightborne outlines Armbrister's career, Moll comments, "Fascinating." Lightborne replies: "Fascinating, yes. An interesting word. From the Latin *fascinus.* An amulet shaped like a phallus. A word progressing from the same root as the word 'fascism' " (151). Lightborne's etymology, though fanciful, synthesizes the novel's themes.[33] That phallic amulet embodies the relationship between fascism and sadomasochistic eroticism, while also figuring the way that Mudger, Lomax, and Selvy reenact the Nazis' reduction of human possibility to relations of dominance and submission. Perhaps most significantly, the connection between fascination and fascism implies that the marketing of obsession—in different ways the shared business of Armbrister, Mudger, Percival, and Moll Robbins—resembles the Nazis' mass marketing of communal identity. In other words, the fascination with fascism, with observing obsession in action, makes the observer complicit with the behavior, and engenders a similarly objectifying relationship between audience and actors: such fascination is itself fascistic. If so, we readers of *Running Dog,* engaged as we are in observing the observers, are also implicated in the ideology of exploitation. Fascinated by fascists, we play Nazi by proxy.

BUREAUCRACIES OF TERROR

Running Dog further characterizes fascism, capitalism, and pornography as forms of power linked and amplified by technology. The figure who best embodies this connection is Earl Mudger, whose organization, Radial Matrix, a secret arm of PAC/ORD, operates as a "centralized funding mechanism for covert operations" against foreign governments (74). Ostensibly serving liberty, Radial Matrix imitates the methods of antidemocratic governments, thereby fulfilling Percival's "historical counterfunction" that requires new bureaucracies of terror. But as it looks out for the interests of corporations while earning its own profits, Radial Matrix really serves capitalism itself. Mudger's greatest achievement is the way he combines "business drives and lusts and impulses with police techniques, with ultrasophisticated skills of detection, surveillance, extortion, terror and the rest of it" (76). As Lomax later declares, in Mudger's domain business and spying don't merely support each other—rather "[o]ne *is* the other" (156). It is thus only fitting that Mudger becomes interested in the pornography industry: where better to blend surveillance and surplus value?

Porn both depicts and embodies capitalist commodification by depicting human behavior as nothing but a series of "sexual *exchanges.*"[34] We buy not only the bodies on screen and their sex interactions, but also an ideology that renders the erotic into consumable products. *Running Dog* suggests that pornography is, as LeClair suggests, the purest expression of American consumerism.[35] As a man who views persons as objects, Mudger has always been a pornographer; likewise, his military tactics are "just a slam-bang corporate adventure" for which he needs "product" (139). Mudger's organization thus mirrors the porn industry: both are bureaucracies devoted to the arrangement, manipulation, reorganization, regulation, and management of bodies by means of social categories.[36] That is, Mudger exercises power by controlling representations of selfhood. In this regard the apparently meaningless name Radial Matrix—a geometric figure describing sets of numbers in rows that branch out from a common center—accurately captures the way Mudger's paramilitary program imposes, as Robert Nadeau writes, "categorical definitions or functions upon that which is subsumed under [his] control."[37]

Mudger's power is also pornographic in that it relies upon a network of surveillance devices that transforms everyone into actors in his private movie. Yet Mudger himself claims to worry about technological snooping: "You can't escape investigation. The facts about you and your whole existence have been collected. . . . Devices make us pliant. If *they* issue a print-out saying we're guilty, then we're guilty" (93; emphasis in original). Not surprisingly, then, Mudger is "close to religious" (105) in his devotion to listening devices— which is why he targets Selvy for assassination when he dismantles his bug. Lightborne later expands upon Mudger's description, adding the visual component that Mudger omits: "Go into a bank, you're filmed. . . . Go into a department store, you're filmed. . . . They're looking into the uterus, taking pictures. Everywhere. . . . Putting the whole world on film. . . . Everybody's on camera" (149–50). Although *Running Dog* satirizes such paranoid philosophies even as it voices them, nonetheless it depicts the profound consequences of this condition—or the belief in it.

One consequence, as I have been arguing, is that all the characters in *Running Dog* exist in a cinematic world that conflates behavior and performance so that nobody lives in the first person. Yet these performances do not produce a consistent sense of subjectivity. Instead, like film actors, these subjects create their personae by bits and pieces. As Luigi Pirandello argues, because the film actor's persona becomes continuous only through editing, he or she always "feels as if in exile—exiled not only from the stage but from himself. With a vague sense of discomfort he feels inexplicable emptiness: the body loses its corporeality, it is deprived of reality, life, voice . . . in order to be changed into a mute image."[38] Their lives in the movies prevent *Running Dog*'s characters from grasping their own motives. Not only is everyone an actor; everyone acts in a vacuum, alienated from both other persons and from any interior life. The characters exist, notes John Frow, as "stylizations" of self to whom the world appears *après-coup,* as after-effect or preview or déjà vu.[39] As in Baudrillard's famous description of simulacra, subjectivity becomes an endless series of imitations without originals. The characters have no existence outside of their cinematic surfaces; all they can do is reshuffle the frames. This condition also makes them prone to easy manipulation by those who control the means of representation, those for whom, in Michel Foucault's description, "our society is not one of spectacle, but of surveillance; under the surface of images, one invests bodies in depth; behind the great abstraction of exchange, there continues the meticulous, concrete training of useful forces." Thus in *Running Dog* "we are neither in the amphitheatre, nor on the stage, but in the panoptic machine."[40]

As in the penitentiary panopticon, so in *Running Dog* the collective has been "abolished and replaced by a collection of separate individualities" in discrete cells.[41] Subjects are unsettled by the awareness that they are being looked at, but even more by their inability to tell when they are being observed and when they aren't. If the initial result of panoptic observation is for creatures like Selvy the "penetration of regulation into even the smallest details of everyday life . . . [and] the assignment to each individual of his 'true' name, his 'true' place, his 'true' body, his 'true' disease," the ultimate consequence is the dissemination of self outward toward the camera eye, so that the observed identifies with the observer and becomes "the principle of his own subjection."[42] *Running Dog* depicts the world from inside the panopticon—an "inside" that is empty in a world "thoroughly exteriorized."[43] No longer can one say that everybody is in costume; since subjectivity is indistinguishable from performance, disguise is no more possible than authenticity.

Hence, although I have been treating the novel's named personages as characters, in a sense *Running Dog* really has no characters, but only bundles of gestures, voices, and desires, radial matrixes of conflicting motives and forces.

The clearest embodiment of these effects is again Glen Selvy, who is simultaneously discipliner and disciplined subject.[44] The prize creature of Mudger's royal menagerie, Selvy is the running dog of the title, as he himself tells Nadine, the young woman he rescues (in proper knightly fashion) from a nude storytelling parlor (160). He brandishes this mock-Indian name as an emblem of autonomy, but the economic nature of his clandestine activities—making undercover payments to clients, paying secret commissions to foreign agents, financing terrorist bombings—demonstrates that he runs in service of an anonymous and dehumanizing capitalism. Indeed, Mudger, his master, doesn't even know his name. The true nature of their relationship is dramatized in chapter 4 of the Radial Matrix section, where DeLillo intercuts Mudger's work on his knives with Selvy's encounter and escape with Nadine. The satisfactions of precision machine work and the names of the tools constitute for Mudger a "near-secret knowledge" (119), a religion with its own litany—the knives lovingly catalogued at the end of the chapter (129–30). Mudger's meticulous labor reassures him of his power and reflects his ability to shape himself as a violent instrument, like his invention the "Mudger tip" (92).[45] But his greatest weapon is Selvy, whom Lomax calls the "[b]est I've ever run" (141); both dog and machine, Selvy is merely a thing that "runs." This juxtaposition of Selvy and Mudger identifies the former as the latter's magic blade and alter ego: they are knight and sword, Hitler and his prize Alsatian, Blondi.[46] Selvy's final journey back to Marathon Mines, the site of his paramilitary and espionage training by Mudger, is thus at once a linear quest for termination and a loop backward toward his origins. Ironically, although Selvy views his life in the clandestine service as "a narrative of flight *from* women" (135), his flight back home sends him to Mudger, who is no less than his surrogate mother.[47]

True Believers

Eventually Mudger withdraws from the pursuit of the Hitler film, choosing instead to cultivate his private zoo. Lloyd Percival likewise backs off, finding his Grail at the Medical Museum of the Armed Forces Institute of Pathology (a "Fascinating" place [196]), which enables him to pursue the "cosmic" potential of erotica through ancient artifacts (221). Like the Fisher King, Percival feels "reborn, revitalized" by DeDe Baker, who enables him to abandon *"Nazis in motion"* for "the art of mystics and nomads" (222). Nonetheless, Percival remains, in his devotion to the power of celebrity and the mystical force of erotic images, a true believer.

So are the organized crime "families" who eventually take the Hitler film. As Lomax says, they are "the only ones who believe in what they're doing. . . . They're totally committed" (220). Their chief representative, Vinny (the Eye) Talerico, acquired his sobriquet because of partial facial paralysis that has rendered his sagging right side numb and expressionless. Like Mudger with his zoo and Lomax with his dogs, Vinny cares for living things—in his case, house plants (perhaps the only creatures lower on the evolutionary scale than he). If Mudger is all ears, his "bugs" permitting him to extend aural surveillance across hundreds of miles, Vinny's power is embodied by his right eye, which resembles that of a "hawk, a snake, a shark," and evinces his simultaneously bestial and mechanical mentality (175). Resembling an allegorical figure in a medieval romance or mystery play, Vinny the Eye is a pure embodiment of the most brutal aspects of postmodern capitalism. Not surprisingly, this incarnation of avarice models himself after film actor Richard Conte (who played numerous gangster roles in such films as *The Big Combo*). Like the others, then, Talerico is a creature of images, a deadly caricature of movie gangsters.

He travels to Dallas and accompanies one Sherman Kantrowitz (a.k.a. Kidder) to Richie Armbrister's warehouse, which is guarded by silent, deadly dogs (202). They believe Richie has the film, because Lightborne has given Richie a decoy—a tin of Danish cookies. Self-consciously appearing outside the warehouse like a film star in a cameo, Richie hopes to prove that he isn't just a set of accounting ledgers (205). But he remains mostly a ghost or dark angel interested only in "the higher issues. Demography. Patterns of distribution" (194), and thereafter withdraws from the chase in order to avoid having to materialize more often. Kidder and Talerico's attempt to take the film from Richie is portrayed in a strange scene narrated as a movie sequence, first from close up, with "[o]verlapping dialogue. Volume increasing all the time" (204), and then from the point of view of Lomax, who watches from a nearby car. After Kidder is shot by Richie's bodyguard, Lomax goes to him, but offers no help; from Lomax's perspective, this violent encounter seems as silent as a Chaplin film, and as Kidder expires, Lomax imagines himself "playing eighteen holes a day" on a faraway golf course (211).

But even these obsessives pale next to the truest believer, Selvy, whose terminal journey alternates with the screening of the Hitler film in the novel's final scenes. As Lomax had earlier pointed out, Selvy is the one who truly "[b]elieves. . . . in the life" (141), in that fascist faith that, according to Susan Sontag, "transform[s] sexual energy into a 'spiritual' force."[48] Through Selvy's journey toward ritual suicide, the novel resumes its character as a metaromance, but now the aim of the quest, as John McClure has observed, "is to find a viable romance form, a script that will enable Selvy, and perhaps the reader, to begin pursuing redemption."[49] As Selvy travels toward an origin that is also an end, the barren terrain surrounding Marathon Mines is refigured as the Fisher King's wasted domain, with Nadine's fishing-obsessed father, Jack, in the regal role (182). Just as Chrétien's Percival first knows and speaks his true name only after his encounter with the Fisher King,[50] here Selvy awakens to his true identity and purpose:

> All those weeks at the Mines. . . . The routine. The double life. . . . The narrowing of choices. . . . It was clear, finally. The whole point. Everything. All this time he'd been preparing to die. It was a course in dying. In how to die violently. In how to be killed by your own side, in secret, no hard feelings. . . . It was a ritual preparation. (183)

Selvy experiences that mystical transcendence sought by so many of DeLillo's protagonists, that endland of purity and simplicity in which "[v]alues, bias, predilection" are all behind him, whereby he is freed from choice, that "subtle form of disease" (192).

The conclusion of his quest is surrounded by symbolic trappings appropriate for an allegorical romance. As Mudger observes, the scene has the "preordained character of some classical epic, modernized to include a helicopter," that modern, mechanical bird of prey (209). Similarly, as Mudger's men, former ARVN soldiers Van and Cao (Portuguese for "dog") pursue Selvy, he sees birds—a hawk (184), a buzzard (190), and a raven (222)—that signify his condition as quarry. Selvy seems to accept his destiny, buying a Filipino guerrilla bolo knife because he finds the name "romantic" (191), as if aware of its condition as twentieth-century substitute for the magic sword of the Grail romances. Selvy also seems to know that this blade—one of those weapons of hard metal—will be used against him.

DeLillo even provides the stereotypical mystic sage in Levi Blackwater, a man who, having survived torture to "the machine of self," "had things to pass on, knowledge to impart" (231). But Levi's wisdom seems dubious, since his torture made him identify with his captors (223), just as Selvy has devoted himself to a surrogate parent who aims to kill him. Levi thus exemplifies Foucault's "disciplined subject" who has internalized the punitive codes of his captors.[51] Although DeLillo presents Levi's mysticism somewhat satirically, his pseudo-Indian creed of self-narrowing and purification through pain still seems preferable to the brutal lust for power and possession—the marketing obsession—that typifies the novel's other running dogs. Levi himself knows that Selvy believes too "easily and indiscriminately, taking to things with a quick and secret fervor" (245), and cautions him that if "you think you're about to arrive at some final truth. . . . You'll only be disappointed" (233). But as Van and Cao approach, Selvy imagines himself in a movie Western (186), and feels a "[s]trong sense of something being played out. Memory, a film. Rush of adolescent daydreams. He'd been through it in his mind a hundred times . . ." (239). Even death, that moment of utter solitude and private meaning, reels out as a movie in the postmodern panopticon.

The complex symbolic strands in Selvy's final encounter converge in his choice of apparel. As Selvy readies himself for his meeting with Van and Cao,

Levi places a hood over his head. This combination of cowl and executioner's hood suits Selvy, a would-be monk whose death comes by an execution that is also a suicide. It also fits the avian symbology in the scene: Selvy resembles a falcon rehooded for return to his falconer. Most significantly, the hood again places him in a disguise that, ironically, betrays his true identity: as Johnson comments, Selvy "becomes 'himself' by being executed."[52] But his death isn't merely personal; as Mudger might wish, Selvy's final struggle with Van and Cao allegorically replays the Vietnam War. Thus when Selvy thrusts his blade into Cao, he stabs him too deeply, disabling himself from pulling out the blade and protecting himself. "He was attached, in effect, to the man he'd stabbed" (239), just as the American military became suicidally attached to the war and to the South Vietnamese government that sucked them into the quagmire. Two dogs of war, Glen and Cao die in an ironic embrace.

After Van finishes off the paralyzed Glen, he uses Selvy's chosen weapon to cut off his head as a trophy for Mudger. Selvy's maiming is ironically appropriate: a man who has closed off the possibility of choice and made himself into a subject for observation and manipulation, his final destiny is to become a pornographic artifact, an emblem of *Running Dog*'s other fractured subjects. Indeed, as Johnson points out, Selvy was effectively decapitated long ago.[53] Levi finds him, hoping to leave the body for "the large soaring birds" (245) after consecrating it in a Native American ritual that will free Selvy's spirit. Alas, one must begin the ceremony by "plucking a few strands of hair from the top of the dead man's head" (246). Thus even in death the luckless Selvy remains denatured, anonymous, denied both the body he has trained so rigorously and the solace of the spiritual ideology he has tried to cultivate. With this sardonic conclusion, the novel abjures a thriller's resolution: Selvy's quest seems absurd, his death meaningless, and the conclusion a grim jest on all concerned. DeLillo's violation of expectations thus not only subverts the genre's conventions and exposes its ideology, as John Frow argues;[54] it also reveals how the clandestine operations that inspire thrillers are themselves influenced by filmic representations. Thrillers are not so much modeled after real behavior as "real" behavior is modeled on thrillers.

AN ACCURATE REPRODUCTION

The conclusion of the other plot defeats our expectations as well. I am treating them separately, but DeLillo dramatizes their parallel qualities by cross-cutting back and forth from Selvy's quest to the preparations for screening the Hitler film: in effect, Selvy's performance in Mudger's "film" enacts the fascistic mentality also displayed in the Hitler home movie; both events are attempts to relive and revise history; both blend tragedy and macabre farce; both involve "radial matrixes," as illustrated when the helicopter blades "dissolve" to the sound of the film in the projector (234), as if Lightborne and the others are watching Selvy's movie. Both plots are also Grail quests in which the desired object is first found and then found wanting. And both quests disappoint Moll Robbins who, by resisting Mudger's sexual blandishments, has been left out of the loop of observation and performance: "No one watched or listened any longer. . . . Why did it feel so disappointing?" (213). Her detachment, however, allows her to furnish the novel's sole sliver of potential redemption, because she is forced to confront her own complicity in the exploitation she documents. Lightborne asks Moll to screen the film with him as a "disinterested intelligence" who can help him explain his fear that "[i]t was all so real. It had such weight. . . . History was true" (188). But although the film disappoints Lightborne, it nonetheless offers a complex instance of the convergence of the artificial and the real, of history and theater, of "acting" and behaving.

These convergences also characterize the first film "shown" in the novel, Charlie Chaplin's 1940 satire of Nazism, *The Great Dictator,* which Moll and Selvy watch just before the gun battle in part 1. Moll tells Selvy that he and Chaplin are now "forever linked" in her mind (61), a pairing less strange than it might first appear: like Chaplin and his neotramp character, Selvy is attempting to play a "great dictator," devoting himself to a cause that consumes his life. But the primary pairing is that of Hitler and Chaplin. *The Great Dictator,* like *Running Dog,* juxtaposes two plots that comment upon each other. Chaplin portrays a Jewish barber and veteran of World War I who is finally released from the hospital on the eve of the next war, just in time to be subjected to the Nazis' anti-Semitic atrocities. Chaplin also portrays Adenoid Hynkel, the Hitleresque dictator. The film implies that the infantile, self-absorbed, and stupid Hynkel—who can't control his own underlings, engages in a hilariously idiotic struggle for authority with a competing dictator, and generally attempts to fulfill an image of magnificence beyond his powers—is merely impersonating a "great dictator." It thus suggests what Lightborne earlier stated: that Hitler modeled himself after cinematic versions of greatness, that he too was impersonating a great dictator. In the film's most *"celebrated scene,"* Hynkel performs an *"eerie ballet"* with a balloon globe, a performance suggesting that his *"great romance of acquisition and conquest"*—the same kind enacted by DeLillo's running dogs—is really a form of child's play (60; emphasis in original). Later in Chaplin's film, when the dictator falls out of his boat while duck hunting, the barber who looks just like Hynkel replaces him and addresses the multitude. In this famous and much-maligned speech,[55] Chaplin addresses the movie audience in his own persona, exhorting us to replace hatred with laughter and hope. That the barber can stand in for the dictator suggests again that Hynkel and Hitler are no more worthy of dictatorial powers than anyone else, and, moreover, that anyone, given the proper circumstances, can use images to manipulate the masses.

Some critics of *The Great Dictator* have claimed that Hitler is not a proper subject for satire, and Chaplin himself later said that he would never have made the film if he had known the horrors of which the Nazis were capable. But DeLillo's gloss on the film reveals another facet of Chaplin and the tramp. His narrator notes that even the humble barber *"studies his image"* in a bald man's head, as if fascinated by his own appearance. And the barber's standing in for Hynkel may imply that he, too, possesses the potential for megalomania. More significant, Hitler and Chaplin also shared features other than the *"world's most famous mustache"* (60): they were born the same week, rose to fame through the global dissemination of cinematic images, and combined commonness with colossal ambition. Charles Maland notes that both Hitler and Chaplin "at times demanded strict control over subordinates when . . . they achieved positions of power."[56] Just as the dictator was in some sense a comedian (61), so the comedian was also a dictator. Indeed, Chaplin's Little Tramp was probably the most recognizable figure in the world—aside from Hitler—and so when Chaplin addresses the multitudes, he is using the power of his image to sway audiences as Hitler did, albeit for diametrically opposed aims.[57] In *The Great Dictator* even Charlie Chaplin exploited the growing fascination with Nazism: he too marketed obsession.

Chaplin's film foreshadows the highly ironic multilayered impersonation that appears in the Hitler home movie. Obviously, to imagine such a movie DeLillo is adjusting history—but not as much as one might think. Certainly the atmosphere in the bunker was scarcely conducive to shooting cute home movies. In fact, the bunker's remaining denizens—Hitler and Eva, the Goebbels family, their servants and aides, and a few remaining military advisers—were traumatized, frightened, desperate. In the final days of the bombing of Berlin, electrical power was intermittent, and thus it would have been extremely difficult to operate a movie camera. But there were two occasions when making such a film would have been possible: April 20 and April 23, 1945. The first date is that of Hitler's 56th birthday; the second marks the point when, finally recognizing that the German army was defeated, Hitler reportedly assumed an "unnatural state of calm,"[58] and thus could have been ready to engage in some frivolity.

But regardless of its historical plausibility, the film brilliantly consummates the novel's multiple themes. In its first segment, the stationary camera observes people behaving as themselves; in the second, the camera moves, and a subject performs; in the third segment, the subjects pretend to be an audience, thereby becoming, like the novel's characters, performers and at the same time observers of themselves and their own observers. In the initial sequence, amid flickering light caused by the bombing overhead, a room fills with children and a couple of adults setting up chairs for a performance. There is a cut to another room in which a woman, probably Eva Braun, sits reading a magazine and talking to someone offscreen. Moll Robbins finds this banal material fascinating: "it was primitive and blunt, yet hypnotic, not without an element of mystery" (227). Mystery—a word frequently invoked in DeLillo's texts to suggest pseudoreligious possibilities—is precisely what makes the film "hypnotic." The viewers wonder who these people are, who else will appear, what will happen, why it was filmed. At the same time its primitiveness convinces Lightborne that "it's true. It's happening" (229): the film is simultaneously an authentic document and an elusive artifact that refuses to yield to inspection. When the five children and four adults gaze at the camera,[59] they place themselves in the panopticon like the Nazis' own subjects, as if submitting themselves to the verdict of history while at the same time staring down those future observers as if to say, "Judge us if you can claim yourself free of sin."

Likewise, in the next sequence, the audience of 11 seems to watch their audience watching them, as they prepare for the entrance of the leading man. The camera slowly pans toward him and then up from his shoes: it is the Führer, playing Chaplin's Little Tramp. He shuffles toward the camera, flooded in light, and *"produces an expression, finally—a sweet, epicene, guilty little smile. Charlie's smile. An accurate reproduction"* (236). This "ultimate postmodern moment," as Paul Cantor dubs it,[60] is not just Hitler playing Chaplin; it is Hitler impersonating Chaplin as the barber impersonating Hynkel, himself an "accurate reproduction" of Hitler. The tragedy of history is reenacted as farce, with Hitler as clown or pretender.[61] This, along with the dictator's other human frailties—his *"trembling arm, nodding head {and the} . . . stagger in his gait"* (235)—renders him ineffectual, even pathetic.[62] Hitler now becomes the aged Fisher King unable to restore his wasted kingdom. But the question arises: for whom is Hitler performing? For the children? For the adults? Or is he making a final appeal to posterity, as if to say, "I'm no monster, just a humble soul like Chaplin's clown"? The pitiful Hitler represents Nazism as a tired joke, a bad movie, a simulacrum of greatness. But if Hitler resembles an "accurate reproduction" of himself, this is a function not only of his impersonation, but of the nature of cinema: any filmed event, even if "true," can be no more than an "accurate reproduction" of reality. Thus while DeLillo is certainly depicting Nazism as a "derivative imitation" of greatness and power,[63] he is also demonstrating the difficulty of escaping from the radial matrix of representations that do not distinguish between the Little Tramp and the Great Dictator.

Although undisturbed by earlier speculation that the movie would show these figures in sexual intercourse, Lightborne finds "Hitler humanized" to be "disgusting" (237). Perhaps this reduced Hitler repels him because it asks us to identify with him as "the subject of surveillance."[64] Or perhaps, believing that this film will have no commercial value, Lightborne is disgusted by his own wasted effort: "I expected something hard-edged. Something dark and potent. . . . The perversions, the sex" (237). If truth be told, so did we. The film both disappoints and intrigues for a number of reasons. First, it depicts

Hitler not as he "really" was, but in disguise, as if he could simply replace one persona—say, dictator—with another. And if Hitler was himself an imitation, then was he really evil, or just a melodrama villain with a silly mustache? Indeed, because the impersonation works only if we know who is behind it, in portraying Chaplin/Hynkel/the barber, Hitler is playing himself, playing. Hence it becomes impossible to separate the real from the representation, and we seem no closer to understanding the fascinations of fascism—at least not if we insist upon looking outside of ourselves. But the film's final segment hints at a more complex relationship between audience and performer. In this final setup, the *"sole attempt at 'art' "* (237), the filmed spectators silently *"applaud the masquerade"* (238) taking place offscreen. In turn, we readers of the novel watch the audience of the Hitler film watch another audience (the viewers within the film) "watch": we view a mirror image of ourselves, riveted to the screen while history passes in front of them but remains beyond either their or our possession. We cannot own it; we cannot even own our own observation of it, because the film has appropriated it from us in advance. The newsreel of history turns out to be merely another looking glass: events are staged so as to be observed by actors.

DeLillo's hall of mirrors contains another figure who stands for us: Lightborne, who has admitted to his fascistic fascinations throughout the novel. As the film travels through the projector, Lightborne acknowledges that, like the Nazis, he has "put powerful forces to work" (238). Not only, then, is he another of the novel's running dogs, but in collaborating to rewrite history as Ludecke (and Hitler) would have liked, he has also colluded with contemporary authoritarian programs. And if we have read this far, we have probably shared Lightborne's fascinations. Thus DeLillo implies that we readers and viewers, fascinated by these lightborne images, are ourselves "Lightborne." This is not the same as saying, as Bruce Bawer claims, that "we are all Hitler."[65] It means, rather, that Hitler and the little Hitlers who populate the novel express not only our fascination with, and even nostalgia for, larger-than-life figures who epitomize grand abstractions such as Good and Evil, but means also that fascism continues to manifest itself in late capitalism's seemingly neutral obsession with marketing. It also means that we are inextricably imbricated in the matrix of images that exists inside, outside, and between history as event and history as representation, because a novel or a film can exist only if we choose to "set it in motion." Hence the neutrality with which the camera presents its material implies that such observation ineluctably accedes to a nihilism that cannot differentiate between hilarity and horror, altruism and atrocity.

If the conclusion of the film plot at first seems as anticlimactic as Selvy's quest, it does satisfactorily synthesize most of the novel's themes. But Moll remains disappointed: after watching the first reel, she departs, leaving Lightborne to meet Augie the Mouse (even less appealing than a running dog) on the fire escape. Augie too makes clownish gestures (wiping his nose on his lapel) and speaks of himself as if he were a film image in slow fade-in: "There's nobody here. . . . I'm beginning to hear. . . . I'm taking form. . . . You're beginning to see me" (242). His words, echoing those of the cop in the prologue, bring the novel full circle. Although Augie's lines seem to have been learned from movie gangsters, they also prove again that the "families," those true believers, do not need to "audition" (243) for their part, because they have played it for centuries. For them, Hitler and the unholy Grail are only commodities like any other. Augie himself is merely a middleman, a facilitator of exchange—like Lightborne, who readily switches gears to contemplate marketing outlets for the film. What else can he do? "Could he tell them people like to dress up? Could he tell them history is true?" (244).

Both quests, then, end in ironic irresolution. Just before she watches the Hitler film, Moll contemplates quests in a passage that seems to describe DeLillo's own standpoint:

> At the bottom of most long and obsessive searches, in her view, was some vital deficiency on the part of the individual in pursuit, a meagerness of spirit. . . . Whether people searched for an object of some kind, or inner occasion, or answer, or state of being, it was almost always disappointing. People came up against themselves in the end. Nothing but themselves. Of course there were those who believed the search itself was all that mattered. The search itself is the reward. (224)

In *Running Dog* the outcome is sardonic. All of this novel's questers seek the film as a way of extending power and ownership, and hence ego, into the world: Percival wants to complete his collection, and thus to extend his body through objects; Lightborne wishes to serve the idea of commerce and make a name for himself; Mudger, conceiving capitalism as an outgrowth of guerrilla warfare, craves the thrill of the hunt; Talerico and Armbrister want to expand their empires. In each, the desire for the film reveals an absence that can be filled only by a commodity that reaches across time; even Selvy searches for a fullness of being that, despite his routine, he senses he lacks. Moll's words mark a confrontation with her own "life in the movies" (224). She is self-aware enough to recognize her complicity with the running dogs of capitalism and their nihilistic machinations. But it is not clear whether she gains anything from it: her fictional existence ends indeterminately as, accompanied by a flock of pigeons (242), she leaves Lightborne's gallery dissatisfied that nobody is watching her, that nothing remains but the bare ugliness of reality, "the blatant flesh of things" (244). On the one hand, this seems a victory: Moll has awakened from the nightmare of history-as-commodity and has checked out of the panopticon. She is free to become somebody other than a "moll." On the other hand, even the "blatant flesh of things" now looks like another bad movie in which all things are pornographic commodities.

Moll's thoughts about quests also turn the camera back at readers to challenge our expectations about plots, novels, and genre. As McClure notes, the novel "reminds us that we are, as a culture, addicted to fantasies of quest, conspiracy, and illumination."[66] Why are we? Moll provides a partial answer when, awaiting the screening, she muses, "[T]he anticipation was apart from what followed. It was permanently renewable, a sense of freedom from all the duties and conditions of the nonmovie world" (225). We pursue quests for the same reason that we watch movies: because through them we inhabit narratives that lead to clearly defined goals. In reading about or observing quests, we come to share the questers' fascinations, to possess them like a Grail— which now becomes anything that permits us to authorize our own destinies. As he does in *End Zone, Players,* and *The Names,* DeLillo here interrogates the value of plots, and scrutinizes his and our participation in the games of novel reading and film watching. He does so by withholding satisfaction: like Selvy, we are denied the vicarious self-renewal of the completed quest. Instead he indicates that the desire to read and write quest plots may itself be fascistic, presupposing a yearning to master, dominate, and dictate material and form; a longing to compress history into objects and own them; a need to turn others into artifacts. Moreover, by depicting how obsession and marketing converge in postmodern capitalism, he interrogates his own activity—for isn't he too marketing obsession, fascinated with fascism?

It may seem, then, that DeLillo exposes the marketing of obsession and the obsession with marketing but then shrugs his shoulders, as if admitting that one can do nothing but yield to the radial matrices of late capitalism and panoptic observation. Likewise, his thriller may not transcend its reductive treatment of character and structure. But while it is true that the novel's relentless motion and apparent nihilism render it a touch facile, Moll's incremental growth—she does resist Mudger's seduction and thereby escapes her previous role as a "Mafia wi[fe]" (131)—and her self-aware comments about quests and plots self-critically articulate how narratives can be liberating as well as ensnaring. Precisely because the characters in *Running Dog* are so two-dimensional, the reader strives to give them depth, instinctively understanding that the mysteries of subjectivity extend beneath and beyond the tentacles of capitalist representations. Indeed, because we live in the cinematic panopticon and perceive ourselves as filmed images, we require at least the illusion of freedom and autonomy. If films and novels furnish that, they enable us to imagine ourselves as other, to be free from our daily obsessions, and even, perhaps, to recapture a sense of mystery in transfiguring "the blatant flesh of things" into an accurate reproduction.

Notes

1. Don DeLillo, "An Interview with Don DeLillo," interview by Thomas LeClair, *Contemporary Literature* 23 (1982): 23. For discussions of how *Running Dog* both fulfills and violates generic expectations, see John Frow, *Marxism and Literary History* (Cambridge, Mass.: Harvard University Press, 1986), 147; John Johnston, "Generic Difficulties in the Novels of Don

DeLillo," *Critique* 30 (1989): 271–72; and Tom LeClair, *In the Loop: Don DeLillo and the Systems Novel* (Urbana: University of Illinois Press, 1987), 174.

2. Don DeLillo, " 'An Outsider in This Society': An Interview with Don DeLillo," interview by Anthony DeCurtis, *South Atlantic Quarterly* 89 (1990): 302.

3. Don DeLillo, *Running Dog* (New York: Alfred A. Knopf, 1978), 20. Future references to this novel are hereafter cited by page number in the body of the text.

4. Don DeLillo, "The Art of Fiction CXXXV," interview by Adam Begley, *Paris Review* 128 (1993): 302.

5. DeLillo uses second person for similar thematic ends in the "Texas Highway Killer" section of *Underworld*. See Don DeLillo, *Underworld* (New York: Scribner, 1997), 155–60.

6. In Wolfram von Eschenbach's *Parsival,* the hero is forced to wear the queen's mantle when entering the Fisher King's castle. See Arthur C. L. Brown, *The Origin of the Grail Legend* (Cambridge, Mass.: Harvard University Press, 1943), 181. According to Jessie L. Weston (*The Quest of the Holy Grail* [New York: Haskell, 1965], 33), in the earliest extant Grail story, an unknown knight is met on his quest by Guinevere and Sir Gawain; they agree to accompany him, but before they reach camp, he is killed by a dart cast from an invisible hand. Thus in the figure of Ludecke, DeLillo conflates Christ, Sir Percival, and the anonymous knight who inspires the Grail quest.

7. See Weston, 18.

8. See John A. McClure, "Postmodern Romance: Don DeLillo and the Age of Conspiracy," *South Atlantic Quarterly* 89 (1990): 345.

9. Weston, 40.

10. Chrétien de Troyes, *Perceval, or, The Story of the Grail,* trans. Ruth Harwood Cline (New York: Pergamon Press, 1983), 99, lines 3582–900.

11. Don DeLillo, *Libra* (New York: Viking, 1988), 442.

12. Lewis Hyde, *The Gift: Imagination and the Erotic Life of Property* (New York: Random House, 1983), 247.

13. Narrative "dispossession" is a "textual strategy for pre-empting or usurping interest as to whose side of the story will be heard," carried out through a "wresting or arresting of control over the relative positions of the parties." See Ian Reid, *Narrative Exchanges* (New York and London: Routledge, 1992), 27.

14. Walter Benjamin, "The Work of Art in the Age of Mechanical Reproduction," in *Illuminations,* trans. Harry Zohn (New York: Schocken, 1968), 221.

15. Benjamin, 221.

16. Benjamin, 241.

17. Benjamin, 238.

18. Pierre Galante and Eugene Silianoff, *Voices from the Bunker: Hitler's Personal Staff Tells the Story of the Führer's Last Days,* trans. Jan Dalley (New York: Anchor, 1990), 41. Ironically, the only person who never attended was Hitler.

19. Galante and Silianoff, 52, 64, 71.

20. Galante and Silianoff, 4, 63.

21. Alan Bullock, *Hitler: A Study in Tyranny* (London: Odhams, 1952), 728.

22. Susan Sontag, "Fascinating Fascism," in *A Susan Sontag Reader* (New York: Vintage, 1983), 311.

23. Hannah Arendt, *Totalitarianism: Part Three of The Origins of Totalitarianism* (New York: Harcourt, Brace, World, 1966), 4.

24. Frow, 145.

25. Patrick O'Donnell, "Obvious Paranoia: The Politics of Don DeLillo's *Running Dog,*" *Centennial Review* 34, no. 1 (1990): 67.

26. Paul A. Cantor, " 'Adolf, We Hardly Knew You,' " in *New Essays on* White Noise, ed. Frank Lentricchia (Cambridge: Cambridge University Press, 1991), 41.

27. Sontag, "Fascism," 316. In an essay originally published in 1989, DeLillo similarly remarks on how "Nazi lore and notation represent a rich source of material to be consulted in the service of fantasy and self-fulfillment. For your sub-erotic side, there are bondage hoods and tooled black leather." He goes on to note how Nazism addresses us as individuals, because "each of us spins on a life-axis of power and submission." See Don DeLillo, "Silhouette City: Hitler, Manson and the Millennium," in *White Noise: Text and Criticism,* ed. Mark Osteen (New York: Viking, 1998), 345.

28. Douglas Keesey, *Don DeLillo* (New York: Twayne, 1993), 101–2.

29. Sontag describes the SS as the "ideal incarnation of fascism's overt assertion of the righteousness of violence, the right to have total power over others and to treat them as absolutely inferior" ("Fascism," 321). In a similar vein, Eddie Fenig, the hack writer in DeLillo's earlier novel, *Great Jones Street* (Boston: Houghton Mifflin, 1973), claims that "[e]very pornographic work brings us closer to fascism" (224).

30. LeClair, 174.

31. Sontag, "Fascism," 313. Selvy exemplifies Sontag's argument elsewhere that the rise of commercial pornography is related to "the traumatic failure of modern capitalistic society to provide authentic outlets for the perennial human . . . need for exalted self-transcending modes of concentration and seriousness." See Susan Sontag, "The Pornographic Imagination," in *A Susan Sontag Reader* (New York: Vintage, 1983), 231.

32. Sontag, "Pornographic," 224.

33. Actually, "fascism" derives from the Latin *fasces,* referring to a bundle of rods with a projecting blade used by ancient Roman magistrates as a symbol of authority. Thus fascism seeks to unite the many under a single dictatorial authority that relies upon the everpresent possibility of violence—hence the projecting blade.

34. Sontag, "Pornographic," 229; emphasis in original.

35. LeClair, 173. Susan Stewart observes that pornography is "the simulacral 'sex itself' of consumer culture": porn presents actual sex on film through a process that alters its continuity and thereby makes it seem idealized, perfect—artificial. See *Crimes of Writing: Problems in the Containment of Representation* (New York: Oxford University Press, 1991), 256.

36. Stewart, 241.

37. Robert Nadeau, *Readings from the New Book on Nature: Physics and Metaphysics in the Modern Novel* (Amherst: University of Massachusetts Press, 1981), 179.

38. Quoted in Benjamin, 229.

39. Frow, 144.

40. Michel Foucault, *Discipline and Punish: The Birth of the Prison,* trans. Alan Sheridan (New York: Vintage Books, 1979), 217.

41. Foucault, 201.

42. Foucault, 198, 203.

43. O'Donnell, 62. Perhaps for this reason several critics have commented that the novel is largely " 'about' representation" (Frow, 145). See also Stuart Johnson, "Extraphilosophical Instigations in Don DeLillo's *Running Dog," Contemporary Literature* 26 (1985): 75. O'Donnell even describes the novel as a "parody of representation" (70–71).

44. As Johnson notes, Selvy is merely an "extreme example of what DeLillo often gives us: a site at which various lines and pressures converge, rather than a 'character' " (76).

45. His bladework also harks back to classical Grail legends, which usually feature an enchanted sword that must either be pieced together or pulled out. For example, one of the strange sights that Sir Percival (in some versions, Sir Gawain) encounters is a Bleeding Lance, a sword from which blood flows (Chrétien, 88, line 3197; cf. Weston, 35). Mudger approximates such a blade when he nicks his thumb to test his weapon's sharpness (120).

46. Numerous observers remarked upon Hitler's devotion to dogs, particularly Blondi (see Bullock, 717). One of the dictator's final acts was to euthanize his pet.

47.   This pattern again fits Grail romance tales. For example, the conclusion of the early English quest romance *Sir Percyvelle* finds Percival reunited with his mother (Weston, 46).

48.   Sontag, "Fascism," 317.

49.   McClure, 346.

50.   Chrétien, 98; lines 3570–76.

51.   Whereas Selvy is a dog or bird, and his pursuers are birds of prey who act like bloodhounds, Levi is identified with his cats—domesticated predators who possess an aura of mystery.

52.   Johnson, 78.

53.   Johnson, 79. This gruesome fate also has a medieval intertext. In one early Grail legend, the thirteenth-century Welsh romance *Peredur,* the young knight is presented, along with the Grail, a "platter containing a severed head swimming in blood" (Cline, "Introduction" to Chrétien, xx).

54.   Frow, 146.

55.   Many critics have found this final peroration jarring, because it abruptly shifts the film's tone, and fails even to provide closure for the Hynkel/Barber mistaken identity plot. For several years afterward, nonetheless, Chaplin delivered the speech to public audiences. For a summary of the critical reception of the film and speech, see Charles J. Maland, *Chaplin and American Culture: The Evolution of a Star Image* (Princeton: Princeton University Press, 1989), 176–86.

56.   Maland, 164.

57.   Chaplin became very active in the Second Front movement during the war, and his antifascism later shaded into a pro-Soviet position that eventually got him into a great deal of trouble with Cold Warriors during the late '40s and early '50s.

58.   Hugh R. Trevor-Roper, *The Last Days of Hitler* (New York: Macmillan, 1947), 136–37.

59.   Goebbels did indeed have six children whose names all began with "H." As Lightborne notes, all six were poisoned after Hitler's death and died along with their parents.

60.   Cantor, 56.

61.   Frow, 145; Cantor, 53.

62.   Hitler's medical conditions—probably Parkinson's disease or a small stroke—have been amply documented. See, for example, Galante and Silianoff, 7, or Trevor-Roper, 127.

63.   Cantor, 58.

64.   O'Donnell, 60.

65.   Bruce Bawer, "Don DeLillo's America," *New Criterion* 3 (April 1985): 40.

66.   McClure, 345.

Discussing the Untellable:
Don DeLillo's *The Names*

PAULA BRYANT

Writer and editor Gordon Lish once affectionately called Don DeLillo "as various and private" as his books. Winner of the American Book Award for *White Noise* (1985) and author of the recent play *The Day Room,* DeLillo has yet to receive widespread commercial success. Yet the steadily increasing number of reviews and criticism of his novels since *Americana* (1971) attest to his burgeoning reputation as an author of unique stylistic power, whose incantatory recreations of American mores have been compared to that of Kurt Vonnegut, Jr., and Thomas Pynchon.

Like Pynchon's Stencil, Jim Axton, the protagonist of Don DeLillo's *The Names* (1982), is an expatriate adrift in the world of words, an authoritarian world constructed from language which has become reductive and coercive, a doxa under which everything has ostensibly been said. Most postmodern fiction presents modern humanity as lost in a verbal funhouse whose center is empty. Like Michel Foucault, DeLillo advocates that we fill up that absence at the heart of language with pure—and not so pure—invention. In his previous novels, DeLillo has played variations on the modern dilemma of the limitations of discourse in diverse arenas: sports, science, rock music, politics. In *The Names,* his most complex novel to date, DeLillo lures the reader on a labyrinthine trek through language itself, culminating in a radical final chapter, offered as a reaffirmative metafictional response to the serious questions about language the novel itself raises.

The solution of this last chapter, a rebuttal to the typical modernist ending DeLillo has embedded within his narrative, serves to shake both Axton and reader by an exuberant, unsettling demonstration of the potential for human freedom inherent in the deliberate disordering and recreation of language. The chapter's eccentric content and form argue for illogical expression in an illogical universe through words that satisfy expression of feeling through intuition rather than reason. However, before Axton can appreciate

Originally published in *Critique* 29, no. 1 (1987): 16–29. Reprinted with permission of the Helen Dwight Reid Educational Foundation. Published by Heldref Publications, 1319 Eighteenth St., N.W., Washington, D.C. 20036–1802. Copyright © 1987.

the reanimating force of renaming demonstrated in the manuscript chapter he reads, he must explore the appeal of the various naming systems already extant. He confronts them skeptically in his global wanderings as a perpetual tourist under fire. Ultimately, his direct experience with the artifice of language allows him to recognize the message of his son's "mangled" words: "Neither life nor language is fixed; therefore, we must have the courage to recreate both, by freely playing the never-ending game of naming."

The Names is language obsessed. Jim's estranged wife, an archaeologist's assistant, shuts down communication by resorting to an exclusive childhood jargon; their erudite friend Owen Brademas is a compulsive language collector; a spate of cult killings prove to be reactions against the tyranny of the alphabet. The limitations of dialogue are a frequent subject of conversation. Yet much of the novel is dialogue, philosophical in content and painstakingly rendered. The characters discuss language and its failure to order for them situations that seem increasingly disordered. Language is the net they seize upon in order to pull their experience neatly together, yet reality keeps escaping through the warp and weft—words no longer contain meaning, and no one speaker can contain all language. In the first pages of *The Names,* the reader is quickly frustrated by the aimless, apparently inconsequential dialogue as the characters, seeming as anonymous to us as their words appear empty, banter sleepily in the back of a Greek taxi after one of a series of high-powered business dinners:

> "I didn't know you were so deep," she said.
> "I'm not normally."
> "You've clearly studied the matter. . . . We need a Japanese monk." (5)

Yet, as Budge remarks gleefully in *The Day Room,* "Things come out in casual talk." In keeping with Mikhail Bakhtin's notion of polyphony, voices speak meaningfully only when placed in context with, or set in opposition to, other voices. Cumulatively, and in relation to one another, the silly speakers talk larger sense, "You don't want to climb it because it's there," she said. "Lindsay cuts to the heart of things."

Yet, Jim must explore language more intimately before he can sift out the "heart" of language even amid such brittle, often desperate chatter. This intimate exploration takes place through direct, participatory encounters, more sustained conversational interactions than these elliptical fragments that begin the novel. Neither the reader nor Axton is yet prepared to make connections between these fragments. Yet, somewhat grudgingly, we are intrigued.

Interestingly, one character tells Jim Axton that his first name is also the name of an Arabic letter (144). DeLillo's characters themselves are, in fact, literal characters, hieroglyphs within the larger text of the novel. If DeLillo's characters can be considered letters whose synchronic combinings form words or utterances within a larger discourse whose subject, language itself, is self-reflexive, then Axton's own verbal encounters with other characters who are counterparts of himself can be seen as part of that ongoing dialectical inquiry whose subject, medium, and ultimate answer is language.

Like the rest of the characters, then, Jim Axton is subsumed by language. As his last name suggests, he perceives himself to be "acted upon," even "axed on," by a language system which refuses to fulfill its implied promise to define reality, let alone allow him to communicate with others to his satisfaction. Jim's job mirrors his situation—he is a "risk analyst" for a nameless multi-national corporation that insures governments against terrorist attacks, terrorism probably sanctioned by the self-same corporate empire. The corporation is itself an oppressive construction that mutates words to suit its purposes—Jim soon realizes that the term "risk analyst" is every bit as oxymoronic as "military intelligence." (He realizes he has been "engaged in a back-channel dialogue with the CIA" and resigns.) Jim seeks expression, connection, and satisfaction through language, not repression of individuality in exchange for false security. His willingness to play government pawn co-opts not only his humanity, but his language as well: once a freelance writer, he now sends telexes.

At the beginning of *The Names,* it is apparent from his hyper-awareness of words that Jim has already realized that the system under which he operates is made of language. He then attempts, like a double agent, to work within the very system he hopes to overturn, by examining the workings of its grammar. His progress through the novel is thus a movement away from an entrapment within language, toward a realization that words, despite their ancient origins, can be regenerated within himself. He can recombine the elements of discourse into new utterances that satisfy rather than oppress. Language is a mutable medium, not a monument, a manmade offering rather than the temple itself. "This is what we bring to the temple, not prayer or chant or slaughtered rams. Our offering is language" (331). However, before he can make that offering, he must acknowledge its artifice. Through his examination of language, in the form of a series of increasingly direct conversational encounters with characters we perceive as the "Others" of Foucault's discourse, he sees not only language's artifice, but how people have forced it to function as a protective construction to shield them from doubt, and thus from direct experience as well. The option for freedom, Jim discovers, likewise comes from language.

The danger of demanding that language recreate a single, arbitrary reality is brought home to Jim in emphatic terms during a disturbing interchange with a member of a cult responsible for a series of random killings. Andahl, who wears women's fleecy synthetic boots, belongs to an arcane sect of nomads bent on obeying the "letter" of their own grim law. They murder according to the initials of their victim's names, which in turn must match those of the murder locale—this schema in order to attempt the binding of symbol and object into one-to-one correspondence through a terminal act of

connection. "It had to be this one thing, done with our hands, in direct contact" (209). Threatened by the chaotic flux of existence, the killers superim-
pose uncertainty with pattern, however arbitrary and destructive, in an
attempt to relieve their frustration over their own indeterminate destinies.
Like the slogans they chisel on stone, their murders are chiseled expletives of
defiance.

In a perverse version of Wittgenstein's logical positivist search for one
ideal language that will redeem confusion by establishing an inexorable
equivalence between word and world, Andahl's gang becomes enraged with
the old language and spawns a new logic of violence. As he explains to Jim,
who is a calm interlocutor despite his repulsion, the group terms themselves
"abecedarians. . . . Learners of the alphabet. Beginners" (210). Their new
speech denounces that which is inconsistent or aberrant—victims are the
crippled or infirm, precisely because these individuals deviate from the reassuring human norm. As Andahl insists, "We are here to carry out the pattern," not to create a new one. Their language is thus reactionary rather than
revisionist; the murders are obscenities protesting furiously the way "numbers
behave, words do not" (208). Andahl's cult feels nostalgia for a language system that never was and never will be, a language of stasis and order. Theirs is
an apocalyptic vision in which all men must speak one tongue, or not speak
at all. Their murders freeze time by precipitating death, but the moment of
violent contact remains fleeting and unsatisfactory. For example, Andahl
admits that there was never as much blood as they expected, and the sound of
the blows themselves became repetitive. As if trying a new idiom, one of the
murderers switched to the "cleft end" of his hammerhead and began to gouge
rather than bludgeon—"anything to change the sound" (211) of the already
limited vocabulary. In other words, even the perverse thrill of murder escapes
them because the pattern they enforce refuses to remain consistent with their
intent.

Therefore, Andahl's desire that a document be written about the murders is a desire to freeze things as they are, to reify the act of murder into an
ultimate artifact of fury against the inconsistency of the unknown. By killing
history through murder, Andahl (whose name sounds like "end all") hopes to
stop time's headlong rush toward decay. However, in order to create a new
history, he realizes he needs the help of the written word, through Jim, a
writer. "What do you think, Axstone?" he asks Axton, implying again that
his wordsmith will be a weapon.

While Jim has no intention of documenting Andahl's horror stories, he
listens in fascination, identifying with both victims and murderers. He has
already noted that his own initials match the name of a projected murder site,
Jebel Amman (158). He also identifies with Andahl's dismay at language's
refusal to replicate experience reassuringly. So, by acting as Andahl's gentle
interlocutor, Jim tries to interpret the horror, to lend meaning to Andahl's
perverted logic by putting himself inside it. By now, Jim is beginning to real-

ize the danger of a fanatically logical stance such as Andahl's: "It made me think of the night I'd vomited pigeon swill in that alley in Jerusalem, an episode I now saw as a clear separation, a space between ways of existing" (211). Yet Jim still identifies, in a less extreme way, with Andahl's exacerbated position regarding language. ("We are trying to define things," Andahl says modestly [212].) Jim's complicity is reflected in his inadvertent adoption of Andahl's speech pattern. "Through the rest of the conversation I found myself eliminating contractions from my speech. Not to ridicule or mimic Andahl. It was something of a surrender to the dominance these complete words seemed to possess, their stronger formulation, spoken aloud" (210). Axton, like Andahl, is smothering under an oppressive blanket of words that has never provided security. Violence is one way of crying out against the stifling sensation caused by a recognition of language's potentially stultifying limitations; sexuality is another. Shortly after his interview with Andahl, Jim interviews Janet Ruffing on an even more intimate basis. Again, the self-conscious medium is words, but this time the subject is the immediate communication of physical union, rather than the abstract commentary of idealized murder.

Jim meets Janet Ruffing among a group of his American acquaintances in a Greek nightclub. She is a banker's wife, masquerading as a belly dancer. Jim is attracted by what he perceives as the sincerity of her dancing, a nonverbal communication of innocence and hope which proves more direct than her subsequent evasive and hypocritical retorts to his seductive remarks when she joins them at the table, covered by a cardigan, the traces of her exotic makeup poeticizing a face that is "a clear work of household prose" (221). The passage functions as a step toward a more direct and emotional language for Axton. By encouraging Janet to use language directly, he is urging himself to do the same. Their dialectic serves to renew his own faith in language's ability to evoke the inexpressible. He perceives that theirs is "an exchange of misunderstood remarks" (222), yet their conversation, however elliptical, is nevertheless for Jim the beginning of "the party," a celebration of the sense-beyond-logic of language: "I like the noise, the need to talk loud, to lean into people's faces and enunciate. This was the true party, just beginning, a shouted dialogue lacking sense and purpose. . . . I huddled next to Janet, asking questions about her life . . ." (222). From the "party," Jim learns that not only can communication be physical and nonverbal, but that the body can speak one language, the analytical mind another.

Janet admits to the group that her dancing was not spontaneous but performed "by rote" (222). She proceeds to analyze her body's actions as though it were a piece of machinery. Throughout her flirtatious dialogue with Jim, she continually denies that she is flirting: "No, honest, I don't do this" (222). In order to feel secure, she'd prefer to know exactly where things stand: "I'm not even sure who you are. I don't think I have it quite straight, who belongs to what at this table" (222). Yet it is this very ambiguity of the unexpected and undefined that attracts both Jim and Janet to the situation and to each other. Jim suggests they acknowledge their experience of shared attraction by naming it, and feels instinctively that naming should arise directly from the situation. "Say belly. I want to watch your lips. . . . Say thighs. I want to watch your tongue curl up in your painted mouth. . . . Say breasts. Say tongue" (222–23). But Janet reacts as if she is being addressed, or undressed, in a foreign language. "How can I talk? This isn't real to me. . . . It's just so foreign to me. I don't know the responses" (228).

Part of the problem is that Jim must use conventional words with which to reach out to his verbal opponent, words whose familiarity confuses Janet, because their directness is at variance with the customary double entendre phraseology of stock pick-up lines. The words are everyday ones, but their blunt raunchiness serves as a counterpoint to her refined denial of their shared experience. Jim's unorthodox flirtation is an attempt to unite the double tracks (physical and verbal) of Janet's discourse into one harmony, this by directing her attention to the workings of their own dialogue, the nature of their shared language.

But the real education is not Janet's, but Jim's. He recognizes that not only do Janet's makeup and gauzy costume constitute a mask that separates her body from his, even while pointing to it. So, too, does the self-reflexive language they must use—conventional language itself is a mask, the old words molded into place by the press of connotation. After exhorting her to use names, and failing, Jim resorts to communicating with his body. They leave the club and couple against a ruined wall, using the logic of the body as if trying to render the word flesh. "I paused, then used my knees to move her legs apart. I worked in stages, trying to reason it, to maneuver things correctly. . . . I worked at her clothes, my mind racing blankly" (230). Action has been substituted for verbalization, both as a medium of connection and as a means for making sense of the world. As he performs the full act of physical union, he pronounces her full name. However, Janet's discourse remains, in parallel, one of denial: "I don't do this. I don't" (230), even as she does. The passage ends in an echo of the language of cult violence, transmuted into positive personal connection. Again, place name is linked with event: "We stood under an iron balcony, in the upper sector of the old town, beneath the rock mass of the north slope of the Acropolis" (230).

Having thus far encountered two methods of discourse, which struggled through language to break the conventional boundaries of its own medium, Jim next confronts Owen Brademas's method of coping with language—intellectual abstraction. Owen is Jim's wife's friend and mentor (but apparently not, because he represents the power of mind only, her lover). Jim himself often refers to an intuited connection between himself and Brademas: "So we talked, so we argued, the anthropologist, the storyteller, the mad logician" (173). Both the "we" and the three epithets are indeterminate, seeming to refer to both men at once. "Maybe all the talking had brought us closer to an understanding, a complicity, than we wanted to be" (175). Owen, like Jim, is drawn to the mystery of the cult killings, and he and Jim meet again in the desert to discuss the implications, and unavoidably, language itself.

In this meeting it is minds, rather than bodies, that overlap. But this time, unlike his connections with Andahl and Janet, Jim resists his "other," struggling instead for autonomy even as Owen insistently points out the similarities between himself and his friend. Jim resists Owen's measured analysis, leaning instead toward ambiguity: "Was this true? Was he right? I would never completely understand Owen, know his reasons, know the inner shapes and themes. This only made the likeliness more plausible" (294). Owen is Jim Axton's double in that they both wish to rationally account for not only their personal situations, but all situations. Unlike Janet, they are even attracted to the indeterminacy inherent in language, but Owen still hankers after an illusory belief in language's capacity to explain all. If only he knew enough obscure dialects, he seems to feel, then life would fall into place around him. As things stand, however, he is doomed to detachment, while Jim's will is to move toward connections, using language for what it is, rather than categorizing it according to what it is not.

Andahl says of Owen: "He is not hurried. He is not grasping for satisfaction. This is what it means to know languages" (207). However, Andahl's character endorsement implies stasis and detachment. Jim does wish to achieve satisfaction through language, but not through abstractions—he seeks a language which connects directly with the changeability of life, thus with growth. We learn from listening to Owen, as does Jim, that Owen uses language, including the language of memory, as a means of safely distancing himself from experience. When he calls up in literate monologue the scene from his childhood that will be reconstituted by Jim's son Tap in the last chapter, he speaks of separation and distance through words that provide a sterile refuge: "These early memories were a fiction in the sense that he could separate himself from the character, maintain the distance that lent a pureness to his affection" (305). This is in contrast to the later "muddiness" and vitality of Tap's fictional rendering.

DeLillo reveals Owen's thoughts through Jim, his "mouthpiece." This is more evidence that the two are linked through Jim's increasing willingness to connect with others through words. Again we enter Owen's mind unexpectedly: "Owen was afraid of him [Singh]. He was too clearly on the maniacal edge. . . . Not a true games-player, not an observer of the rules, Owen thought, astonished at the stupidity of this reflection" (294). Singh, a member of Andahl's cult, is "mercurial and deft" (294). Owen, unwillingly yet knowingly bound to rigid patterns, is not. Again, while Owen is drawn to ambiguity as much as Jim is, he is concerned by its presence, both in life and language. He can neither accept uncertainty nor progress from it; he is stuck. Like Janet Ruffing, he feels he must know the correct responses when faced with the unexpected. Owen discusses his considered reaction to Singh's off-hand remark: ". . . Hell is the place we don't know we're in. I wasn't sure how to take the remark. . . . Is hell a lack of awareness? Once you know you're there, is this your escape? Or is hell the one place in the world we don't see for what it is, the one place we can never know? Is that what he meant? Is hell what we say to each other or what we can't say, what is beyond our reach? The sentence defeated me. I was afraid of the desert but drawn to it, drawn to the contradiction" (215).

It is clear that Owen, the "mad logician," is obsessed with wresting meaning from language, and Jim sees traces of his own needs in Owen's impossible struggle. Owen explains, "It's important to get it right, to tell it correctly. Being precise is all that's left. But I don't think I can manage it now" (299). Jim, still in search of evidence about the cult but also feeling his way through this encounter toward what language can be for him, responds, "You were with them. Did you learn their name?" (249). For Jim, names have become symbolic containers holding more than their capacity; rather than Owen's series of neatly interlocking verbal compartments, they are the proverbial Chinese box, opening onto further mystery, a sign that signifies multiple texts. To discover names, to pronounce names, to rename—all acts of naming have acquired a significance for Jim. To him, naming implies the innocence of reseeing, revision of meaning. "How do you connect things? Learn their names" (328). Owen, like Jim, seeks a language of continual renewal and innocence, reminiscent of the language of the parishioners in his boyhood Pentecostal church: "Is it the language of innocence those people spoke, words flying out of them like spat stones? The deep past of men, the transparent words. . . . It is not quite there. It passes over and through" (360). To Owen, the speaking in tongues he witnesses as a boy and refused to participate in, a phenomenon that still haunts his memory and conversation, is "absent" because it expresses neither the literal nor the abstract, but something with which he fears to connect beyond both. This spontaneous language Owen speaks warily of, however, may represent "the whole language of the spirit" (338) that Jim seeks, but Jim does not fully realize this language through Owen's distracted musings.

Thus, Jim Axton's encounter with his son Tap's writing is timely. After each successive conversational encounter, Axton has become more aware of his need for a language that celebrates, rather than denies, its own ambiguity. The manuscript pages written by his precocious nine-year-old embody in form and content this direct participation in the flux of existence. The last chapter in which they are excerpted offers Jim the option for the renewed faith in language that he needs.

In the last chapter of *The Names,* then, Tap retells Owen's story of his dismayed encounter with the Pentecostal practice of glossolalia, or the gift of tongues, a form of worship in which believers spontaneously pray, each in his own way, in a language said to be divine. However, Tap rechristens (revises) Owen Brademas into "Orville Benton" and proceeds to transmute Owen's tale in the telling. In a makeshift church, Orville struggles to orient himself in the midst of a revival meeting in full swing. ("The strange language burst out of them, like people out of breath and breathing words instead of air" [335].) The youth is urged to join in the prayer, and longs to do so, but is dumbfounded. ("His tongue was a rock, his ears were rocks" [333].) His inchoate feelings surge from confusion and envy to despair that he cannot speak as his family and neighbors do. He longs for a return to the safe routines of childhood, when self-expression was unnecessary because all wants are met without effort. The tension of this compact scene builds to an explosive climax when the boy bolts out the door into the rain, headlong across the muddy prairie. "Familiar signs and safe places" (339) are not forthcoming, within the church or without. "Nowhere did he see what he expected. . . . He ran into the rainy distance, smaller and smaller. This was worse than a retched nightmare. It was the nightmare of real things, the fallen wonder of the world" (339).

This chapter functions as a thematic microcosm for the rest of the novel, not only because of its concentrated intensity and symbolic content, but because of its unusual structural placement. In the penultimate chapter 13, we are told that Jim has found Tap's manuscript inspiring, "freedom seeking" (313). DeLillo then ends the novel, so we think, in a traditional modernist manner. Jim Axton returns to an image, the Parthenon, which held negative connotations for him at the novel's opening, and which now holds positive ones in the light of his new experiences. Thus the book appears to culminate in a neat, circular return to its own beginning, the protagonist infused with new insight into old dilemmas. And yet, we turn the page and find this closed system reopened by the addition of an openended, exuberant, unorthodox coda, an ostensible epilogue that functions more like a prologue, because it implies continuance and reaffirmation rather than stasis and closure. Tap's words are the revitalizing element introduced into the closed system of the text, shattering its structure in order to jar the reader in the same way that its eccentric language formations shatter words themselves. Its radically distinct form contains familiar elements culled from the body of the novel, imitating thematic refrains like a jazzy canon, recombining previous imagery with the twisted potential of DNA. Because the last chapter doesn't present a single traditional ending, it instead implies multiple new beginnings.

The idea of perpetual regeneration (Pentecostal implies "second coming") is further affirmed by DeLillo's device of a child serving as the chapter's author and protagonist. In fact, some of the unusual constructions in the chapter are transcribed verbatim from the writing of a real child, Atticus Lish, son of editor and Columbia professor Gordon Lish, a friend of DeLillo's. (DeLillo thanks Atticus with a "printed shout from the housetops" in his acknowledgements.) The viewpoint of child-author attests to the necessity for a sense of childlike wonder when approaching the world through language. Orville, the preadolescent protagonist, is on the brink of transition. Thus his situation is similar to Jim Axton's. At the passage's end, Orville remains a "still pool" (338) of perplexity, his words still waiting to flow forth, just as Jim Axton has yet to embark upon his renewed love affair with language, "some kind of higher typing, a return to the freelance life" (318). Thus, instead of a tidy, hence crippling conclusion, the reader is allowed to share the characters' mingled relish and trepidation as they anticipate and move toward a new, perhaps satisfying personal contact with language. It is significant that this liberating message should come in the form of a message from child to father. By writing, Tap is parenting his father by showing him new inspiration through words. His name suggests his role—he has "tapped" an explosive fountain of expression his father can revel in. It is not an accident that the chapter is presented as a rough draft "novel-in-progress." The implication is that language is a process without conclusion, one denouement opening out onto another prologue. Writing itself is reaffirmative for DeLillo, representing the willingness to piece together the universe, no matter how fragmented, into a new pattern, no matter how idiosyncratic, no matter if the strands of warp and woof are ancient ones.

In furtherance of the notion that the last chapter represents an escape from stasis, it is significant to note that its form is reflexive. Because it is a rewrite, from a different perspective, of a previous scene in the novel, the reader is urged into a back-and-forth motion between the chapter and the previous episode. We compare versions, enjoying differences. Instead of enforcing linear progression, then, the novel encourages free movement within its text, liberating both DeLillo and his reader from convention. (On a different scale, the chapter performs a function similar to the notes in *Pale Fire*.) That the chapter is a revision from another angle argues for the possibility of rewriting realities. We all author our own realities, DeLillo's form suggests. We write on top of other writing, because an individual's life in language begins not as a *tabula rasa*, but as a palimpsest, already scored over and smudged by prior contact. We are inspired by DeLillo's use of form to delight in the movement of our words and to decide, like Jim Axton, to add our own lines to the scroll.

In addition to its placement, the chapter's quirky style is liberating as well. Tap's personal fictional style, while unusual in its bizarre phonetic spellings and strange phraseology, is not a private, insular language like the childhood jargon, "ob," used by Tap's mother. (Note, by the way, that the initials of both Orville Benson and Owen Brademas spell "ob," a root syllable meaning "against," which could be read as short for "obscurity" or "obfuscation.") There are no questions in ob, leaving it a language of exclusion and stasis rather than interchange and discovery. By contrast, Tap's own language is filled with agonized questions and flagrant expressions of feeling bursting out at the reader, a continuing dialectic written to be shared. Tap's passion transmits itself from his writing to his metafictional first reader, his father, who is enthralled by Tap's "spirited mispellings. I found these mangled words exhilarating. He'd made them new again, made me see how they worked, what they really were. They were ancient things, secret, reshapable" (313).

Thus, the unusual look of the words on the page draws attention to the aesthetic, malleable nature of all words. DeLillo purposely foregrounds style as if concurring with Michel Foucault: "By means of the spontaneous redoublings of language/we/discover a rare and unsuspected space . . . recover therein things never yet said" (Sturrock 87). To use DeLillo's recurrent metaphors, words are not fixed but fluid, not rocks but air. Tap's language burgeons, exfoliates, looses itself upon the wind over the prairie it conjures. More akin to the broken-down and restructured words of the future created, or precreated, by Russell Hoban in *Riddley Walker* than an attempt at imitation of actual child-like scribblings fraught with "mistakes," the method draws attention to its own medium. The reader slows to ponder the individual implications and connotations of each word—each syllable becomes a sacred offering, an artifact held up to the light. Conversely, however, the reader, once captivated by the wit and weirdness of the familiar words made strange, begins to gather momentum as the events rush forward, as if both characters and reader gain strength from the vitality of the words. The style is not static, but galvanizing.

Specifically, the second sentence of the text catapults us into Tap's world of reshaped vocabulary. "There was a man in a *daise* like a *drunkerds skuffling* lurch, *realing* in a corner" (335). Of the four odd, Joycean punning spellings (not to mention a blithe omission of an apostrophe) it is the word "realing" that especially intrigues and jars us. How does one *real*? Is this a reference to making one's own reality? The spelling nudges us toward profundity but teasingly stops short: being drunkenly real in a corner. We almost know what that means.

Such wordplay trips multiple connotations and thus corroborates rather than resists ambiguity. "*White* words. . . . Pure as the *drivelin* snow" (336), the circuit-riding preacher exclaims. "White," as in Melville's whale, hints not only at right or rite, but at the color that contains all colors. "To drivel" is to let flow from the mouth, to speak the language of fools and newborns. The uncouth word becomes the essence of the preacher's injunction throughout: "Do whatever your tongue finds to do! Seal the old language and loose the new" (336). It's "child's play" (335). Puns such as "worldwind" and "the whurl of his ignorant tongue" (a "whorl," among other things, is a flywheel) are more evocative than directly translatable—they engage the reader's sensibility through their paradox and playfulness. Like the words of the ecstatic worshippers, Tap's words are "upside down and inside out" (337).

When Orville hurtles across the "sogging turf" of the prairie, he longs to be taken in by his grown-up friend Lonnie Wright (write?) who "would have opened his door to any young wafe, even a bad one" (339). Spelled this way, "waif" could be short for wayfarer, transforming an image of helplessness into one of bold errantry. Earlier, Tap's young hero reminds himself, "True there is always a creature out there that will be happy to lick and saver the curious wandrer" (337). "Lick" and "saver" carry plural meanings of both danger and satisfaction, while the last word plays on its qualifying adjective: "wandrer" can be transformed by the reader into "wonderer," rendering both words synonymous and underscoring the theme of the passage—that we must become wondering wanderers, wayfarers (even wayward ones) through language, before our tongues will loosen and speak of what we find on our journey.

If the coined orthography causes us to stumble, thus tripping circuits that spark unique connections, then the structure of sentences containing traditionally spelled words can create a participatory language of ambiguity as well, through juxtaposition and connotation. The unwarranted use of the word "or" in the first paragraph implies multiplicity and uncertainty merely from the sense of the conjunction: "*Or* someone said. . . ." (335). The communion of the congregation linked through language is implied by the mismatched subject and referent in this observation: "People threw *an arm* up with figitty fingers to shake around" (336). And the worshippers are compared to texts by dint of the ambiguity created by sentence placement here: "*People* burst out in sudden *streams. They* were like long dolerous *tales.* . . ." (336). This vagueness provides the reader freedom of choice through words themselves. We may reshape them as we will and reconnect them to remake meanings. These contradictory possible readings create a proliferation of interpretation—no single fiction, then, is true.

Again, the message of the last chapter, supplied through its medium, is an optional one. The character Orville Benton, thrust within the upheaval and chaos depicted, is overwhelmed. In the first version of the event, as it is remembered and foreshadowed by Owen Brademas, Owen describes himself as "growing toward the world unwillingly" (305). Tap's Orville, too, ultimately resists taking the leap forward toward engagement and fulfillment through a personal, even perverse, revision of language. Instead, he imagines himself taking refuge "like a shortlegged dwarf hidden in the tall grass" (338), a homunculous, still fetal. However, we and Jim both come to the chapter infused by the previous chapters of exploration with an awareness of language's artifice. Thus, we are receptive to the chapter's suggested solution. Both Jim and reader accept the option afforded by the chapter's example, the option to transform the words we use, "poor, clattery English" though they may be, and thereby transform the realities they create.

A return to the modernist ending of chapter 13 underscores this reading of the last chapter. The Parthenon image expresses the way Jim's reading of Tap's manuscript (he has already reread it once before the end of chapter 13) has transformed his approach to language. We see, by his revisiting/revision/revised-reading of the Parthenon symbol that Jim has gone from despising language as timeless, pure, abstract, and thus limited and limiting, to seeing its potential as a dynamic medium, irrational, immediate, expressive, although impure (because reworked and reworkable). Jim was loathe to visit the Parthenon while in Greece because of the forbidding mystery he believed it contained, remarking, "What ambiguity there is in exalted things. We despise them a little" (3). However, after reading Tap's audacious manuscript and becoming inspired by its casual juggling of alphabetical stones, Jim is able to see the Parthenon as another human construction, like language itself: ". . . the Parthenon was not a thing to study but to feel. It wasn't aloof, rational, timeless, pure. . . . I hadn't expected a human feeling to come from the stones but this is what I found, deeper than the art and mathematics embodied in the structure, the optical exactitudes. I found a cry for pity. This is what remains to the mauled stones in their blue surrounding, this open cry, this voice we know as our own" (330). Therefore, it is the voice, transpiring language in individual utterance, which matters now to Jim, rather than the monumental abstractions that language, unshaken by feeling, can construct. (He tells Janet, "I want to put your voice back inside your body, where it belongs" [228].) When Orville Benton longs for the comforting illusion of control he experienced when words were, he thought, familiar and immutable as marble, he is reacting against what Jim is now ready to recognize and embrace. This view is embodied in the voices he hears rising from the steps of the Parthenon: "one language after another, rich, harsh, mysterious, strong. . . . Our offering is language" (331).

Thus, the implication is that Jim has been inspired, by his reading, to rewrite reality with the only medium available, evidenced not only by his return to the Parthenon, but to writing. Because it required the reading of Tap's writing to reach this ultimate renewal of faith in language, DeLillo seems thereby to emphasize that it is writer and reader together who create the alchemy of vital language. In other words, language should be a medium, not of coercion nor self-protection, but of direct interchange between self and other. From this interchange, the world is created from the word. The individual becomes his own dialect: signifier and signified unite. It takes a willingness to entertain all of language's infinite possibilities to attain this fleeting, satisfying exchange. This willingness is best expressed in the phrase Don DeLillo uses to conclude his novel, a conclusion which can be read as an injunction to celebrate and begin again: "fallen wonder of the world." The reader has a choice of readings. From the timeless world of fiction, where patterns are created, we can "fall into the world" (339). Yet, we are already falling—and are fallen—far away from the ideal and statically pure language of Eden. Therefore, we might do well to fall "in wonder," not only of the world, but of the word.

Works Cited

DeLillo, Don. *The Names*. New York: Vintage Books, 1982.

Dreyfus, Hubert L., and Paul Rabinow. *Michel Foucault: Beyond Structuralism and Hermeneutics*. Chicago: Univ. of Chicago Press, 1982.

Federman, Raymond. *Surfiction: Fiction Now and Tomorrow*. Second Edition. Chicago: Swallow Press Books, 1975.

Foucault, Michel. *Language, Counter-Memory, Practice*. Ithaca, NY: Cornell Univ. Press, 1977.

Foucault, Michel. *Madness and Civilization: A History of Insanity in the Age of Reason*. New York: Random House, Inc., 1965.

Fraser, Russell. *The Language of Adam: On the Limits and Systems of Discourse*. New York: Columbia Univ. Press, 1977.

Harris, Robert R. "New York Times Book Review Interview with Don DeLillo," *New York Times*, 10 October 1982.

Hoag, David. "Los Angeles Reader Review of White Noise by Don DeLillo," *Los Angeles Reader*, 31 May, 1985.

LeClair, Thomas, and McCaffery, Lawrence. *Anything Can Happen: Interviews with Contemporary American Novelists*. Urbana: Univ. of Illinois Press, 1982.

Sturrock, John, editor. *Structuralism and Since: From Levi-Strauss to Derrida*. Oxford: Oxford Univ. Press, 1979.

"Who are you, literally?":
Fantasies of the White Self in Don DeLillo's
White Noise

T IM E NGLES

D on DeLillo's *White Noise* can be read as a novel about the noise that white people make. As in many whitened communities in America, unless one pays strict attention, the brief presences of racialized others can be difficult to detect. Isolated for the most part from daily contact with people who are not "like" themselves, people like Jack Gladney who live in such communities tend to experience a certain unease when encountering unfamiliar "types" of people.[1] Appearing as sporadically and momentarily as they do, the differences that such people represent have yet to intrude much on the presumptions of middle-class whiteness to universality. However, as DeLillo's novel prophetically indicates, these presumptions have increasingly come under fire with the new immigration patterns that are reconfiguring American demographics. Thus Jack notes of his German tutor, for example, that "his complexion was of a tone I want to call flesh-colored," without pondering further why he hesitates to go ahead and call it "flesh-colored" (DeLillo, *White* 32). A person such as Jack would most likely hesitate because he dimly realizes that such a term has been rendered problematic by the gradual encroachment of people who have flesh of different hues, different from that of the "flesh-colored" ("white") people. In many ways, while DeLillo depicts the unmarked details of "ordinary" (white, middle-class) American life, he also suggests that in an increasingly diverse society, the white self's troubles of this sort are just beginning. White people are becoming increasingly marked *as* white, and their status as exemplars of ordinary American subjecthood threatened.[2]

Missing from almost all critiques of DeLillo's portrayals of postmodern identity formation is analysis of the persistent whiteness of his protagonists.[3] Given the relative unimportance to most white Americans of their racial status, as well as their relative ignorance about the significance of race in their daily lives, critical disinterest in such aspects of DeLillo's work is not surprising. Nevertheless, as DeLillo's main characters consistently demonstrate,

Originally published in *Modern Fiction Studies* 45 (Fall 1999): 755–87. © 1999. Purdue Research Foundation. Reprinted by permission of the Johns Hopkins University Press.

being racialized as white plays a tremendous part in how one responds to the environment. As anthropologist Ruth Frankenberg points out in her wonderfully nuanced account of the influences race has on the lives of white American women, "White people are 'raced,' just as men are 'gendered' " (1). She argues that "there *is* a cultural/racial specificity to white people, at times more obvious to people who are not white than to white individuals" (5).[4] In regards to literature, while most contemporary authors who describe ordinary white characters display little direct interest in the influences of race on their characters, American racial formations still affect their literary creations in an array of traceable ways. In DeLillo's case, his considerable interest in contemporary threats to autonomous selfhood is inextricably tied to the whiteness of his protagonists. In *White Noise,* DeLillo illustrates the forces in ordinary life that threaten individual autonomy, but he also develops a subtextual portrait of white American modes of racialized perception. In particular, DeLillo demonstrates with the case of Jack Gladney that the notion of individual autonomy is itself a fantasy, and that middle-class white men are especially apt to harbor this particularly American form of self-delusion.

(White) American Individualism

Explicating this racialized subtext in *White Noise* calls for discussion first of a particular result of America's continued reliance on race as a primary method for categorizing people. Such middle-class whites as the characters in this novel usually live in a social environment in which whites constitute the numerical majority. As a result, white people within such a setting tend to be regarded by others not in terms of their racialized group membership, but rather on an individual, "case by case" basis. Their membership in the "white race" seems to them to have little impact on their daily lives, and indeed, the fact of their racial whiteness rarely occurs to them.[5] As DeLillo's depiction in *White Noise* of an identity quest undertaken by the highly self-reflective Jack Gladney suggests, white individuals tend to conceive of themselves in more individualized terms than do people "of color." On the other hand, the racialized difference signified by "non-white" people is often immediately registered within predominantly white settings, rendering these individuals representative members of their racial groups.[6] Ross Chambers describes this phenomenon:

> Whereas nonwhites are perceived first and foremost as a function of their group belongingness, that is, as black or Latino or Asian (and then as individuals), whites are perceived first as individual people (and only secondarily, if at all, as whites). Their essential identity is thus their individual self-identity, to which whiteness as such is a secondary, and so a negligible factor. (192)

Consequently, as Chambers adds, "whiteness itself is [. . .] atomized into invisibility through the individualization of white subjects" (192). As a white American author, DeLillo might be inclined to create works that join a lengthy tradition of literary paeans to American individualism by describing the efforts of protagonists who eventually achieve a hard-won sense of personal autonomy. However, in each of his novels he has opted to do otherwise. In *White Noise,* DeLillo works to expose as a fantasy the notion of independent selfhood, a notion particularly encouraged by covertly racialized whiteness. He does so by depicting in Jack Gladney the irony of both the white self's ontological dependence on its reception by others, and of its reliance on conceptions of others as a way of simultaneously conceiving of itself. After establishing early on the novel's interest in the ironically dialogic nature of white identity-construction, DeLillo goes on to depict contemporary difficulties faced by the white self. As a series of closely described encounters between Jack Gladney and various "non-white" characters suggest, the increasing presence of racialized others challenges certain racial and cultural presumptions commonly held by middle-class white Americans.

DON DELILLO, (WHITE) AMERICAN AUTHOR

The American emphasis on the individual's inherent freedom and autonomy has, of course, a lengthy history grounded in particularly Western notions of the individual as an independent entity. Renowned American individualists who still resonate as such in the mainstream cultural imagination include Benjamin Franklin, who constructed a thoroughly practical self in his *Autobiography;* Huckleberry Finn, who decides to stand apart from the culture of his upbringing (and ultimately to "light out for the territory" [281] alone); and Hemingway's protagonists, who stoically construct their own ways to live. The celebrity status accorded contemporary examples of "self-made" individualists—Ross Perot, Steve Jobs, Donald Trump, Bill Gates—demonstrates the persistent appeal of the rags-to-riches mythology, promulgated perhaps most famously in Horatio Alger's novels, that such wealth is potentially available to any American. One could list innumerable manifestations of mainstream America's fantasy of itself as a meritocracy, in which any individual who works hard will succeed as much as his or her talents allow. I want to focus, though, on the largely unremarked whiteness at the root of this myth, and then go on to show that, as DeLillo's depictions of whiteness in *White Noise* illustrate, this conception of the autonomous self *is* a myth, as well as one to which whites are particularly susceptible.

Crucial to the iconographic resonance of the figures just listed is their commonly unremarked race and gender. When their status as "white males" is highlighted, their stature as representatives of an "all-American" notion of ideal selfhood becomes problematic: the exemplary significance of such "self-made" individuals, even those of today, is entirely contingent upon their being both white and male. The American myth of unfettered individuality, both at the level of upliftingly representative figurehood and at the level of everyday life, requires that for those white males who do attain notable success, these two forms of group membership remain unremarked. On the other hand, those heroic individuals who are differently racialized and/or gendered tend to become *representatively* heroic, their group membership firmly affixed to them, largely because they are perceived as having fought against forces that oppress their particular group.

On the level of everyday social interaction, as DeLillo's depiction of Jack Gladney illustrates, middle-class white Americans are also rarely confronted with their own racialized status. This fact contributes to their tendency to think of themselves as individuals largely responsible for their own actions, and for having achieved whatever gains they have made largely on their own. Members of racialized minorities in America who live within a dominant culture that encourages the subordination of communal interest to self-interest may also think of themselves in these terms. However, as minority writers often suggest, daily life tends to impress upon people "of color" a continual awareness of their supposed membership in a racial and cultural group. On the other hand, since representative American normality remains largely white and middle class and unremarked as such, most middle-class whites are by and large taken as autonomous individuals, discouraging inclusion of the privileges afforded by their classed and racialized group membership as conscious components of their identities.

In regards to literary authorship, the ramifications of this phenomenon are traceable in DeLillo's case, particularly in terms of race and ethnicity. Born in the Bronx to Italian immigrant parents, DeLillo faced at the beginning of his writing career the choice of identifying himself as an Italian American author by writing about markedly Italian American characters and themes. In some of his earliest stories, published in the 1960s, DeLillo did describe such characters within the setting of his childhood. Like such writers as Phillip Roth and Mario Puzo, who are ethnically marked because most of their fiction contains explicitly ethnic characters and issues, DeLillo could have become marked as an Italian American writer if he had chosen to focus on Italian American characters, as he finally does at various points in *Underworld*. Two of his first stories do contain markedly ethnic protagonists, complete with broken English and strong accents. In "Take the 'A' Train," for instance, his second published story, one man in a "garlic-and-oil Bronx tenement" shouts to another, " 'Hey, Caval [. . .] Ima joost on my way to calla the cops. Noomber one, eighty-five dollar I gotta comin' from you. [. . .] You pay me now, or I calla the cops' " (22–23). Another early story concerns the efforts of two men, speaking "mainly in Italian," to decide what they would eat if they could "only have one thing to eat" for the rest of their lives

("Spaghetti" 244); one settles on a dish that is also the title of the story, "spaghetti and meatballs" (248). By going on to write instead about ethnically unmarked protagonists, DeLillo has in effect become an unremarkably white writer, exercising in the process an ethnic option far less available, and perhaps not available at all, to American writers "of color."[7]

As Daniel Aaron has observed, nothing in DeLillo's novels prior to *Underworld* "suggests [even] a suppressed 'Italian foundation'; hardly a vibration betrays an ethnic consciousness. His name could just as well be Don Smith or Don Brown" (68). DeLillo's own consequent, generally unremarked whiteness has contributed to the widespread reception of his work as that of an individualist who goes against the crowd, an impression that DeLillo has repeatedly fostered by declaring himself "an outsider in this society" ("Outsider" 50).[8] Unlike explicitly racialized writers, who tend to write about racially marked characters and are usually read as representative spokespeople for their racial group, DeLillo tends to write in opposition to conceptions of group membership. In *Mao II,* for instance, perhaps his most extended meditation on this topic, DeLillo characterizes the highly individualistic writer Bill Gray (clearly modeled after such literary recluses as J. D. Salinger and Thomas Pynchon) as having worked in carefully guarded isolation for decades. After realizing that writers have lost the influence they once had on "mass consciousness," Gray emerges from his seclusion, only to die a grim, symbolically anonymous death (significantly, a pickpocket steals from his corpse the wallet containing his identification papers). As the narrator of *Mao II* intones in a statement that many critics have since read as representative of DeLillo's persistent concern about contemporary threats to individuality, "The future belongs to crowds" (16).

DeLillo's assumed status as a white writer might be expected, then, to foster in his work an expressed faith in the possibility of individual autonomy. However, as *White Noise* in particular demonstrates, he counters the white male authorial tendency to create autonomous, individualistic protagonists.[9] Beginning with the novel's opening scene, DeLillo complicates white identity by foregrounding recognition of the countervailing, fundamental relationality of identity-formation, thereby countering the particularly white fantasy of autonomous individualism. He does so by carefully detailing the tendency of his characters to place others into various reliable categories, a process by which they simultaneously place and define themselves as well.

THE IRONICALLY RELATIONAL FOUNDATIONS OF WHITE IDENTITY

As the novel begins, narrator and protagonist Jack Gladney describes an annual "spectacle" at the college where he works as a professor, "the day of the station wagons" (DeLillo, *White* 3). As he closely observes a long line of cars driven by parents dropping off their children, Jack detects among these people a sense of community grounded not in common values or interests, but rather in mutual recognition of familiar attitudes and poses: "The students greet each other with comic cries and gestures of sodden collapse. [. . .] Their parents stand sun-dazed near their automobiles, seeing images of themselves in every direction. The conscientious suntans. The well-made faces and wry looks. They feel a sense of renewal, of communal recognition" (3). DeLillo immediately highlights here the narcissistic nature of the connections the people in this novel tend to register between each other. The people in this scene would seem content merely because they are among others who are like themselves, but Jack recognizes more precisely the foundations of their sense of community. These parents and their children actually appreciate the presence of others who are like themselves because, in looking at these familiar others, they see themselves. As Jack recognizes, they also base their "sense [. . .] of communal recognition" on a flood of products, including the "bicycles, skis, rucksacks, English and Western saddles, inflated rafts, [. . .] the stereo sets, radios and personal computers; small refrigerators and table ranges, [. . .] the junk food still in shopping bags—onion-and-garlic-chips, nacho thins, peanut creme patties, Waffelos and Kabooms, fruit chews and toffee popcorn; the Dum-Dum pops, the Mystic mints" (3). Jack's use of the definite article here signals his weary familiarity with these objects, and with this "spectacle," which he has "witnessed [. . .] every September for twenty-one years" (3).[10] But the familiarity of these items is crucial to the communal bond among these people, for, in seeing others who also own them, they can categorize such people as like themselves, thereby categorizing themselves as well. Indeed, as Jack notes, because so much is on display here, this "assembly of station wagons, as much as anything they might do in the course of the year, more than formal liturgies or laws, tells the parents they are a collection of the like-minded and the spiritually akin, a people, a nation" (4).

DeLillo thus establishes immediately the novel's interest in the relational, dialogic nature of identity formation, showing that our perception of others necessarily relies on categorical placement in relation to categorical placement of oneself. Subsequent examples of this phenomenon include the implicit assertion of the white self via the explicit recognition of "non-white" others; such moments show that in order to assert themselves, implicitly white individuals, like members of other, more marked categories, rely symbiotically for their conceptions of self on the categories of people that have developed in this country. DeLillo eventually demonstrates that in racial terms, members of the "white race" tend to rely on racialized categories for "non-whites" when regarding them, but not when regarding other whites. They thus seem to escape such categorization themselves when regarded by the dominant (that is, white) gaze (and certainly not, much to their probable surprise, when regarded by the gaze of an overtly racialized other).[11]

Of course, as time goes by and American racial formations continue to mutate, generational differences in habitual deployment of racial categories evince themselves. DeLillo's portraits in *White Noise* of variously aged characters periodically reflect such changes. At one point, Jack and his fourteen-year-old son Heinrich demonstrate such a difference in their perceptions of an apparently "non-white" other, Heinrich's friend Orest Mercator. As the three of them chat together on the front steps of the Gladney home, Jack is befuddled by Orest's plans to enter the record books by sitting for sixty-seven days in a cage full of poisonous snakes. Heinrich is struck with admiration, and he seems not to mind that his friend's skin is distinctly darker than his, nor that his race is difficult to discern. Jack, on the other hand, tries to get a fix on this "older boy [. . .] of uncertain pigmentation" by attempting to insert him into familiar racial categories (DeLillo, *White* 206). "What kind of name is Orest?" Jack wonders, studying his features: "He might have been Hispanic, Middle Eastern, Central Asian, a dark-skinned Eastern European, a light-skinned black. Did he have an accent? I wasn't sure. Was he a Samoan, a native North American, a Sephardic Jew? It was getting hard to know what you couldn't say to people" (208). Jack's colloquial usage of an indefinite "you" here refers implicitly to a white audience. His complaint acknowledges that white people accustomed to easily categorizable others are often at a loss in the face of the contemporary influx of immigrants, who could be from almost anywhere. As part of a gradual awakening to his habitual reliance on perceptual categories, Jack becomes vaguely aware, as he is here with Orest Mercator (whose cartographically resonant name evokes "the rest of the world"), of the eroding reliability of traditional American racial categories. Nevertheless, Jack has been raised as an implicitly white person in a culture bolstered by iconographic celebrations of heroic white men acting out their individualized roles against a backdrop of "inferior," racialized others. Thus, he eventually reverts to habitual uses of racialized others, casting them as bit players within his own similar enactments of a received, white male fantasy of selfhood. Prior to portraying Jack doing so, DeLillo establishes his protagonist's more general reliance on habitual categories to conceive of others, thereby implicitly registering a relational, falsely individualistic conception of himself.

FORMATIONS OF THE WHITE SELF

In Jack's opening description of "the day of the station wagons," his wry observations demonstrate not only his insight into the narcissistic nature of materialistic display, but also his own unconscious, reflexive tendency to categorize others. That is, he believes he knows the people populating this scene, not because he knows any of them personally, but rather because he has decided what type of people they are. Thus he assumes, for example, that as fathers who can afford to send their children to a private college, the men in this crowd are "content to measure the time, distant but ungrudging, accomplished in parenthood, something about them suggesting massive insurance coverage" (DeLillo, *White* 3). Significantly, however, Jack subtly indicates as he describes these people, and as he discusses them later with his wife, Babette, that in identifying them in certain ways, he simultaneously registers a conception of himself.

As Jack wearily views this "spectacle," the identificatory distance he feels from its participants is signaled by the physical space between them and himself (he watches, apparently unseen, from his office window), and by the mildly derisive tone with which he assesses the scene's elements. Jack then returns home and reminds Babette that she's missed the show. Babette says,

> "It's not the station wagons I wanted to see. What are the people like? Did the women wear plaid skirts, cable-knit sweaters? Are the men in hacking jackets? What's a hacking jacket?"
> "They've grown comfortable with their money [. . .]. They genuinely believe they're entitled to it. This conviction gives them a kind of rude health. They glow a little."
> "I have trouble imagining death at that income level," she said.
> "Maybe there is no death as we know it. Just documents changing hands."
> "Not that we don't have a station wagon ourselves."
> "It's small, it's metallic gray, it has one rusted door." (DeLillo, *White* 6)

It might seem that Jack and Babette are merely comparing notes in an off-hand manner here, but DeLillo carefully portrays as well the Gladneys' simultaneous recognition of themselves as they consider these others. As Babette wonders what the people are wearing, for instance, she registers her own unfamiliarity with "their" clothing; Jack's response vaguely marks his own income level by noting "their" higher level of income, a difference Babette then acknowledges as well with her mention of "death at that income level." Babette's eventual reminder that the Gladneys also have a station wagon indicates her polite awareness that their mutual assessment of this group of people has gone too far toward marking a separation between "them" and the Gladneys. Jack, however, is finally quick to note sardonically the *relative* shabbiness of the Gladney station wagon, thereby solidifying the difference between his family and these other families that he has been perceiving since the book's opening sentence.

While Jack and Babette enact here a common tendency to register mundane features of their self-conceptions while ostensibly assessing others, Jack's inclinations toward asserting his individual difference are particularly markable in both racial and socioeconomic terms. If pushed a bit further, he would probably identify the categorical difference he detects here as a difference in class. Jack does not explicitly identify himself as a member of the middle class, a class whose relative lack of wealth separates its members from the sort of people who send their children to such places as "the College-on-the-Hill," where Jack works. Yet Jack's inclination toward declaring his individual difference rather than his group membership is largely due to his membership in both the "white race" and the "middle class." Because the white middle class constitutes the representative majority, particularly in the media, its members tend not to foreground either of these group affiliations within their self-awareness. As a consequence, and as Jack repeatedly demonstrates, they are apt to adopt the mainstream American emphasis on individuality by thinking of themselves in individualistic terms. Ironically, however, when regarding others they must do so in categorical terms, registering them as this or that type (friend, co-worker, man or woman, "black" or "white"). As they do so, whites, like everyone else, categorize others as either like or unlike themselves, thereby asserting in the process who and what they themselves "are." Accordingly, Jack continually resists being pigeonholed as this or that type, but he does so himself by identifying other people as members of a category to which he does not belong, thereby, inadvertently and unavoidably, placing himself into an *opposite* category.

Later in the novel, as the "Airborne Toxic Event" threatens the Gladneys after a train wreck releases a cloud of pesticide by-products, Jack again enacts what amounts to a class-based mode of self-assertion. When it becomes evident that the chemical cloud is approaching his family, Jack is reluctant to leave town. He explains his reluctance to his increasingly restless family, enacting once more his tendency to assert who he is by marking his difference from those in another apparent category: "These things happen to poor people who live in exposed areas. Society is set up in such a way that it's the poor and uneducated who suffer the main impact of natural and man-made disasters" (DeLillo, *White* 114). Later he continues, "I'm not just a college professor. I'm the head of a department. I don't see myself fleeing an airborne toxic event. That's for people who live in mobile homes out in the scrubby parts of the county, where the fish hatcheries are" (117). Jack has no doubt seen televised news footage of flood victims who live in mobile homes. He has trouble imagining himself as the victim of a similar disaster because, like his children, he often relies habitually on categories of others supplied by the media, his conceptions of whom implicitly define who he is by defining who he is not. In this case, Jack's conception of himself as different from the members of a lower class does not result in his *overt* placement of himself into another group, the middle class. His placement in this class is implied rather than stated because the middle class is another default category rendered invisible by its supposed ubiquity, and by the media's implicit positing of it as the norm.[12]

Aside from asserting his own identity by perceiving the nonracialized differences of other (white) people, Jack also demonstrates the relational nature of identity-formation when he briefly encounters various racialized others. As he does so, he demonstrates that, as Frankenberg puts it, "whites are the nondefined definers of other people" (197). That is, while he never explicitly relies on the category of "white" to conceptualize other white people, nor himself, he relies immediately on racial categories in his conceptions of apparently racial others. One such incident occurs after the Gladneys are evacuated to a campground outside of Blacksmith during the "Airborne Toxic Event." As they mill about among the others there, Jack and Babette encounter a family of Jehovah's Witnesses "handing out tracts to people nearby" (DeLillo, *White* 132). This family also has differently colored skin, and Jack immediately categorizes them in terms of this difference: "We were next to a family of black Jehovah's Witnesses" (132). Of course, Jack does not mention as well that his own family is "white," but he has nevertheless implicitly done so by identifying these people as "black." Again, as Jack repeatedly demonstrates, while whites tend to use race as a means for defining others as different from themselves, they tend not to use it for defining other whites as similar to themselves. When white individuals encounter either white or "non-white" people, they tend in both cases not to register racial whiteness. When confronted with people of indeterminate ethnicity, as Jack demonstrates during his first encounter with Orest Mercator, the white self can become frustrated and vaguely anxious, unable to insert them immediately into familiar racial categories. Jack most fully enacts this frustration when he confronts the visibly "foreign" Willie Mink.[13]

All of this is not to say that ordinary white people like Jack are overt racists, but they nevertheless demonstrate the common American tendency to foreground race in their conceptions of other people by immediately conceiving of racialized others in racial terms. People such as Jack and Murray would no doubt reject immediately the suggestion that they themselves are racists. Indeed, at one point, as Jack discusses with Murray whether or not the latter's landlord is a "bigot," they simultaneously distance themselves from overt racism. Murray tells Jack,

"He fixes things eventually [. . .] . Too bad he's such a bigot."
"How do you know he's a bigot?"
"People who fix things are usually bigots."
"What do you mean?"
"Think of all the people who've ever come to your house to fix things. They were all bigots, weren't they?"
"I don't know."
"They drove panel trucks, didn't they, with an extension ladder on the roof and some kind of plastic charm dangling from the rearview mirror?"
"I don't know, Murray."
"It's obvious," he said. (DeLillo, *White* 33)

As is often the case, Murray reveals nothing "obvious" here, aside from his own classist bigotry regarding "people who fix things." More significantly, however, in positing in someone else the presence of extreme racism, Murray implicitly defines himself as distanced from it. Nevertheless, in a fundamentally racialized society, as Jack often demonstrates, it is often tempting for whites who would resist being labeled as racists to fall back on supposedly reliable racial categories when confronted with darker-skinned people, thereby habitually employing racist patterns of thought.

By thus illustrating in several instances the white self's tendency to resort to categorical habits when regarding other people, DeLillo establishes in *White Noise* a subtextual interest in the submerged racial dimensions of middle-class white American lives. He also deepens this portrait by suggesting the historical underpinnings of the general white American disinterest in racial issues. By interspersing racially inflected moments throughout his portrait of a professor of Hitler Studies who teaches his subject without ever mentioning what most people now consider the most memorable result of Nazism, "the Holocaust," DeLillo prompts consideration of a similar severance of contemporary America from its own racialized past. Murray and Jack are both satiric depictions of narrow, overly professionalized academics, but their glaring neglect of "the Holocaust" invites certain questions. How could it be, for instance, that a Jewish American like Murray could find entirely unobjectionable his colleague's blithe indifference to Hitler's treatment of Jews? Further consideration of their relationship could also raise the question of how it came to be that a white professor like Jack could unblinkingly welcome a Jewish colleague like Murray, something virtually unthinkable until fairly recent times.[14] Jack and Murray display no historical awareness that could prompt discussion of these issues between them. Also, within the novel's setting of relatively isolated whiteness, none of the characters seems to wonder how it is that an environment saturated with white people ever came about. Indeed, in a social landscape where the only object of monumental significance is a barn that memorializes nothing more than its own fame, an awareness of the past as in any way significant to the present is entirely absent. The novel eventually suggests that such phenomena are logical results of the initial establishment of a superior "white race," whose contemporary members must repress the genocidal tendencies of its racialized past in order to believe in the fiction of a racially harmonious, equitable present.

THE PRESENT ABSENCE OF THE HISTORY OF WHITENESS

DeLillo prompts consideration of the lost history that has led to current racial configurations by inserting into Jack's seemingly aimless narrative a visit to a place conspicuously labeled "THE OLD BURYING GROUND." Upon entering the graveyard, Jack sees that the headstones are "small, tilted, pockmarked, spotted with fungus or moss" (DeLillo, *White* 97). As he struggles to read the "barely legible" names and dates on the neglected grave markers, Jack begins to feel isolated, listening in vain for something that could assuage his growing fear of death. In the silence that fills this one place in Blacksmith that is not infused with the circumambient buzz of white noise, Jack's isolation signals the severed connections of the white self from a historical narrative that could account for its formation. In coming to live in Blacksmith, Jack has moved away from any direct familial connections he may have once had to the past. None of his own ancestors are buried in this cemetery, and his psychic distance from them is suggested by his neglecting even to mention them. As a result of his ancestors having become "white," Jack also finds himself cut off from their ethnic origins. DeLillo suggests here this bleaching out of ethnic affiliations and of the past by emphasizing the whitest thing in nature, snow: "I stood there listening. The wind blew snow from the branches. Snow blew out of the woods in eddies and sweeping gusts. [. . .] I stood and listened" (97–98). Jack finds no comfort here, and a certain uneasiness prompts him to utter what amounts to a contemporary, middle-class, white American prayer: "May the days be aimless. Let the seasons drift. Do not advance the action according to a plan" (98). Having achieved a comfortable, self-gratifying material success, and encouraged by absorption into the "white race" to cast off its ancestral and cultural past, the middle-class white self finds honoring its ancestors less important. Of course, subsequent "Americanized" generations of explicitly racialized people tend to lose cultural ties as well. However, the process is particularly exacerbated for whites by the emphasis implicitly placed on the seemingly autonomous, unmarkedly white self, shorn of racial affiliations.

Another significant, howling absence in this scene, of course, is religion. As a thoroughly secularized American, Jack formulates his own prayers and seeks no solace from higher authority. Death itself thus takes on an emptiness, a quality contemplated by Jack and Babette after they admit to each other their mutual fear of dying. Babette asks,

> "What if death is nothing but sound?"
> "Electrical noise."
> "You hear it forever. Sound all around. How awful."
> "Uniform, white." (DeLillo, *White* 198)

In *White Noise*, which DeLillo has described as a novel "about death on a personal level" (qtd. in Moses 86), whiteness is repeatedly intertwined with the notion of death. At another point, for instance, Jack is awakened just before dawn by his son Wilder, who gestures for him to look out a window. When Jack does so, he notices "a white-haired man" sitting in their backyard. Having been exposed to Nyodene-D, Jack has become increasingly superstitious; he wonders, for instance, if he's been awakened at an "odd-numbered hour," odd numbers having come to remind him of death. Half-awake and in a dream-like state, Jack is gripped by the chilling thought that he has died, and that this mysterious apparition has come to get him:

Was he as old as I'd first thought—or was that hair purely emblematic, part of his allegorical force? That was it, of course. He would be Death, or Death's errand-runner, a hollow-eyed technician from the plague era, from the era of inquisitions, endless wars, of bedlams and leprosariums. He would be an aphorist of last things, giving me the barest glance—civilized, ironic—as he spoke his deft and stylish line about my journey out. [. . .] I was scared to the marrow. (243)

Eventually, Jack manages to shake off the sense that his last moment has arrived. Before he does so, he repeatedly describes himself as "white" for the only time in the novel: "I felt myself getting whiter by the second. What does it mean to become white? How does it feel to see Death in the flesh, come to gather you in? [. . .] I moved quickly through [the children's] rooms on bare white feet" (244–45). Teetering on the edge of the void, Jack returns from intimations of an empty, white death into ordinary life; after hiding for a while in the bathroom and clutching his copy of *Mein Kampf,* he steps outside and discovers that this specter is only his father-in-law, Vernon Dickey.

As DeLillo's repeated conflation of whiteness and death suggest, one cause of the white self's lack of self-awareness *as* white may be a certain emptiness in whiteness itself, a blankness unable to support sustained consideration, not unlike that brought to mind by the idea that death itself may be nothing more than nothing. In its dramatization of Jack's representative tendency to recoil from the emptiness of whiteness, *White Noise* recalls another, more direct literary contemplation of the topic. In a chapter entitled "The Whiteness of the Whale," Herman Melville's Ishmael ponders the associations that have gathered around this hue. After offering a compendium of examples of the positive connotations whiteness has had in many cultures, Ishmael wonders (enacting with a pun his own tendency to intertwine the comic with the horrific) why "it was the whiteness of the whale that above all things appalled me" (Melville, *Moby-Dick* 163). In DeLillo's slightly eerie conflations of "white noise," a bleached-out, "white" American existence led by unspokenly white people, and a series of associations between death and whiteness, he creates the same sense Ishmael describes, a sense that "for all [the] accumulated associations, with whatever is sweet, and honorable, and sublime, there yet lurks an elusive something in the innermost idea of this hue, which strikes more of panic to the soul than that redness which affrights in blood" (Melville, *Moby-Dick* 164).

Moby-Dick and *White Noise* both suggest that to turn away from whiteness because its very emptiness strikes a "panic to the soul" is a natural, even primitive response. In addition, both texts are also readable as meditations not merely on the color itself, but on what has been *made* of the color, particularly the racial deployment of it.[15] A specific terror both novels evoke is that of the construction of the "white race" and of the driving forces that led to its construction. In these terms, the blankness of racial whiteness signals the absence from white consciousness of a historical awareness that would account for its formation *as* "white." Facing up to this past and its connections to one's own whiteness is indeed discomfiting, so much so that generations of whites have repressed it to virtual irrecoverability. Thus, when Jack hears only silence in the deathly white cemetery, evoking nothing from the past, he suggests the contemporary white severance from history itself. As in his contented conception of Blacksmith as a place that is "not smack in the path of history and its contaminations," Jack enacts the white self's separation from a history that is lost because, when the white self looks at it for long, it tends to feel a "contaminating" culpability (DeLillo, *White* 85). History no longer speaks to the white self because to contemplate the historical results of the establishment of a "white race" would require acknowledgment of the part that one's own whiteness has played in America's own versions of "the Holocaust." As several historians have recently noted in their efforts to re-envision history from this perspective, conceptions of the "white race" necessarily included conceptions of other racial categories.[16] The result of the white establishment of Other, "inferior races" was the eventual ruthless exploitation of those races. Subsequent formations of white cultural identity have included a gradual repression of these ugly facts because closely attending to America's past would reveal the heart of darkness at the heart of whiteness.

Like Melville, then, DeLillo evokes the white tendency to turn away from the sense of horror that this history of whiteness can inspire. In addition, DeLillo subtly portrays some of the innumerable ways that this history still shapes the conception of the white self, even as the white self denies its affiliations with whiteness in a continual conception of itself as merely an autonomous individual. At one point in his account, for instance, Jack reflexively reaches back into the historical underpinnings of whiteness to reassert himself when he faces exposure as an ordinary, undistinguished face in the crowd. While shopping with his family in "a huge hardware store at the mall," Jack is recognized by a university colleague, Eric Massingale (DeLillo, *White* 82). Having never encountered Jack off-campus, Massingale is struck by how different Jack looks when unadorned by sunglasses and a gown, his symbolic projections of a professorial self. Asking twice for Jack's promise that he " 'won't take offense,' " Massingale tells him, " 'You look harmless, Jack. A big, harmless, aging, indistinct sort of guy' " (83). As one "average" guy to another—meaning one white, middle-class male to another—Massingale hesitates to make this observation because, being such a man himself, he intuitively senses that being subsumed into the homogenous, unvariegated ordinary counters the white self's conception of its own individual autonomy. " 'Why would I take offense?' " Jack asks, "hurrying out the door" (83). He obviously is offended by having his membership in the ordinary pointed out, and his response is to assert himself in a distinctly contemporary way, by shopping.

Jack conceives of himself while shopping in a particularly white, male way, by selectively reaching back into history to retrieve narrative elements for the construction of a setting that is especially suited to a white man's assertion of self. Jack has laid some of the groundwork for this setting by describing the enormous hardware store, in which he notes a "great echoing din, as of the extinction of a species of beast" (DeLillo, *White* 82). This peculiar sense he has of something wild about this space continues to guide his description, prompting him to note "power saws that could fell trees," "sacks of peat and dung," rope that "hung like tropical fruit"; in addition, flickering at the margins like the "colored spots" he repeatedly glimpses at the peripheries of his vision, are people who speak "Hindi, Vietnamese, related tongues" (82). As a character observes in DeLillo's first novel, *Americana,* "To consume in America is not to buy; it is to dream" (270). By depicting Jack's search here for a way to assert himself against the facts of his membership in the unremarked, white, American ordinary, DeLillo portrays in him a white tendency to resist categorical inclusion and to assert instead a fantasized version of autonomous selfhood.

As Jack and his family move out into the mall's "waterfalls, promenades, and gardens" after his demeaning encounter with Massingale, Jack inserts himself into the role of an aggressive, plundering white adventurer, sampling and grabbing from an international array of exotic "goods," paternalistically directing his family members like underlings on an expedition:

> When I said I was hungry, they fed me pretzels, beer, souvlaki. The two girls scouted ahead, spotting things I might want or need. [. . .] I shopped with reckless abandon. [. . .] I traded money for goods. The more money I spent, the less important it seemed [. . .] I was the benefactor, the one who dispenses gifts, bonuses, bribes, *baksheesh.* (DeLillo, *White* 83–84)

Jack does describe the excited participation of his family members here, but mainly in reference to himself. His primary focus is his own satisfying sense of self-enlargement: "I began to grow in value and self-regard. I filled myself out, found new aspects of myself, located a person I'd forgotten existed. [. . .] I felt expansive" (84). The irony here is that while Jack seeks in his empowering conception of a shopping self a distinguishing difference from his membership in "the ordinary," he unwittingly marks himself *as* white by enacting the particularly white habit of asserting one's individuality, and by inserting himself into a role that relies on the conception of an exotic, racialized environment.[17]

Hovering at the margins of this scene, as throughout the book, are the absences of death and history. The various racialized peoples evoked by Jack's description of foreign "tongues" recall the subjugated others forced to make way for colonizing whites. After establishing in several scenes this connection between Jack's white reliance on racialized others in order to conceive of himself, DeLillo more fully evokes in another hushed scene the repressed presence of these peoples buried deep within the white psyche. Having become increasingly desperate to quell his anxiety over his impending demise, Jack searches for his wife's supply of Dylar, the white pills supposedly designed to "speed relief" to the part of the brain that harbors the fear of death. When Jack's daughter tells him that she threw the pills away, Jack goes to the kitchen compactor and braces himself, then pulls out an "oozing cube of semi-mangled cans, clothes, hangers, animal bones and other refuse" (DeLillo, *White* 258). In a scene that prefigures DeLillo's extensive deployment of garbage imagery and motifs in *Underworld,* Jack takes this cube out to the garage, then gingerly pokes it apart with the handle of a rake.

Jack soon realizes that the garbage contains no Dylar, but he keeps poking through it anyway, feeling like a "household spy" as he does so. In depicting at length Jack's careful consideration of what he finds here, DeLillo gradually builds on the subtle connections he has established between racial whiteness and its forgotten past. Unable to find the symbolic "white" pill that would suppress his awareness of death, Jack confronts instead "product colors [that are] undiminished in color and intensity" (DeLillo, *White* 258). In a novel so infused with aural, visual, and cultural whiteness, the moments of vivid color are highlighted by contrast, and thus rendered suggestive. As part of a racial subtext, DeLillo's account of the predominantly white setting of this novel continually registers the presence of racialized Others flickering at the margins, including the occasional "foreign tongues" at the shopping mall, Orest Mercator, the "Iranian" who delivers Jack's newspapers, and finally, Willie Mink.

When considered within the novel's constellation of racialized colors, the product colors here become racially encoded as well. Jack invokes the sense of a search for lost human remnants when he notes that he "felt like an archeologist about to sift through a finding of tool fragments and assorted cave trash" (DeLillo, *White* 258). As Jack confronts this brightly colored "cube" of garbage, he describes it as sitting "there like an ironic modern sculpture, massive, squat, mocking," and inviting interpretation (259). Reluctant at first to confront the "full stench" that has hit him "with shocking force," Jack eventually does just that: "I picked through it item by item, mass by shapeless mass, wondering why I felt guilty, a violator of privacy, uncovering intimate and perhaps shameful secrets" (259). Prying into any unpleasant subject that is habitually ignored is bound to inspire this sensation that one "shouldn't" be doing so, be it the family garbage or the "white" past. Indeed, in light of the color-encoded connections made here to the novel's subtextual interest in American racial formations, Jack's actions suggest the response of the contemporary white person who would attempt to face the buried, repressed history of whiteness.

So fully has mainstream American culture repressed the unpleasant aspects of its past that to look back at it would be like being hit with the "full stench" of the garbage that assaults Jack. For most whites, acknowledgment of the white past is particularly unpleasant, to say the least, so middle-class whites often regard bringing up this past as something like an invasion, and a particularly impolite one at that. Most white people asked to consider the connections of their own whiteness to such a past are likely to *feel* as Jack does here, as if they are being confronted with "shameful secrets." In addition, if generations of whites habituate themselves to avoiding such subjects for long enough, and to dissociating themselves from their own racial status by thinking of themselves instead in individualized terms, they eventually forget how to "read" such aspects of the American past. Jack's own avoidance of even glaringly evident racial atrocities in the past has already been indicated by his position as a professor of Hitler Studies who studiously avoids the "white" Nazi decimation of the racialized Jewish other. Unsurprisingly, then, he is finally mystified by the "signs" and "clues" that he suspects are here. Similarly, a full account of America's fundamentally racialized past is virtually beyond recovery for most whites, leaving them with a sense of history no fuller than the broad reveries of populist patriotism. As the novel progresses, Jack's enactment in this scene of the white self's turning away from the collective past of whiteness finally coalesces with brief portrayals of the ironic white tendency to rely on others to assert a supposedly unique self. Eventually, in the novel's climactic anti-climax, Jack makes a last-ditch, racially charged effort to assert himself by shooting Willie Mink.

THE DEATHLINESS AND THE DEATH OF THE WHITE SELF

In Jack's typically wayward manner, he opens one chapter with a veiled description of a suppressed white anxiety: "Our newspaper is delivered by a middle-aged Iranian man driving a Nissan Sentra. Something about the car makes me uneasy—the car waiting with its headlights on, at dawn, as the man places the newspaper on the front steps. I tell myself I have reached an age, the age of unreliable menace. The world is full of abandoned meanings" (DeLillo, *White* 184). In another attempt here to parse out his feelings in a world he often has trouble recognizing, Jack experiences a characteristic drift into abstraction, unable to say just why this sight troubles him. It seems to me that what prompts this insecurity in Jack is not only this markedly foreign car, but also the driver's apparent ethnic status as an "Iranian." Jack can hardly admit, even to himself, the racist underpinnings of such fears, having adopted the polite middle-class reluctance to consider an overtly racialized individual in overtly racist terms. Thus he transfers his anxiety to the Iranian man's car, finding himself as a result unable to explicate his uneasiness. Writing in the early 1980s, DeLillo clearly evokes here the media-generated associations of Iranian men and Japanese cars with threats to American security.

The "Iranian Hostage Crisis" had recently occupied much of America's attention, as had the media's focus on a series of incidents that contributed to the
general stereotype of Middle Eastern men as potential terrorists. Also alluded
to here by Jack's discomfort with the "Nissan Sentra" is the gradual incursion
into American markets of Japanese products, an incursion marked most
explicitly as an invasion by the attention the media paid to Japanese sales of
that most American of products, the automobile.[18] Again, Jack would be
unlikely to consider himself a racist. Thus, the negative associations swirling
auratically around this man may be too clearly racist for Jack to acknowledge
them fully, so he registers instead a vague unease inspired by the generally
threatening "age" in which he lives.

Severed as he is from the realities of the history leading to his own racial
invisibility, Jack has nevertheless inherited that history's legacy, including a
predisposition toward making potentially threatening Others a more reliable
"menace" by placing them into pre-established, predictable categories. As
Jack says here, "the world is full of abandoned meanings," and these include
the old, reliable categories of race, ethnicity, and nationality (184). As American demographic patterns continue to decrease the majority status of whites,
and as people of innumerable apparent types continue to intermingle, the
reliability of the traditional categories will continue to erode. DeLillo subtly
prophesizes as well that the increasingly frequent presence of other people
who look, talk, behave, and think differently from "normal" (middle-class
white) ways will gradually expose middle-class whites and culture as but one
group of racialized people and one culture among many others.[19]

Jack most fully enacts his habitual use of racialized others to establish his
own, unmarkedly white autonomy when he inserts himself into a revenge
plot against Willie Mink, another man of markedly "foreign" ethnicity. As
Jack heads for Iron City after learning where to find Mink, he has constructed
a carefully arranged, cinematically inflected revenge plot in which he means
to play a role. As many critics have noted, DeLillo's satiric depiction of abject,
postmodern suggestibility culminates in this scene, particularly in the bizarre
characterization of Willie Mink. For Dylar-addled Mink, the difference
between reality and media-generated representation has virtually collapsed,
as evinced by his tendency to intersperse his scattered, spoken thoughts with
snatches of TV-speak: "Dylar failed, reluctantly. But it will definitely come.
Maybe now, maybe never. The heat from your hand will actually make the
gold-leafing stick to the wax paper" (DeLillo, *White* 308). Mink also takes
words themselves for the real thing; when Jack says, for instance, "hail of bullets" or "plunging aircraft," Mink cringes and cowers in terror, as if the words
themselves are real. As his revenge plot progresses, Jack also demonstrates his
dependence on the simulacrum-like categories of perception encoded in
words, including racial ones.

As Jack enters the motel where Mink resides, he believes that he sees
"things anew. [. . .] I was moving closer to things in their actual state as I

approached a violence, a shattering intensity" (DeLillo, *White* 304–05). Ironically, though, Jack again resorts to reliable categories in which he inserts a perceived Other in order to construct an appropriate backdrop for his assertion of an individualized self. DeLillo emphasizes Jack's particularly white reaction to racialized others by again depicting him as frustrated by the poor fit of his old racial categories with a new figure, Willie Mink: "Did he speak with an accent? His face was odd, concave. [. . . W]as he Melanesian, Polynesian, Indonesian, Nepalese, Surinamese, Dutch-Chinese? Was he a composite?" (307). Jack's white American maps for a handsome, male appearance also do not apply to such a figure, so he feels sorry for Babette because in order to get Dylar, she had to "kiss a scooped-out face" (310). DeLillo confirms that the jutting features of a white male still constitute mainstream American standards of attractiveness by having Mink admit that when Babette visited him incognito, she kept a ski mask on " 'so as not to kiss my face, which she said was un-American' " (310). The logical outcome of this persistent, paradoxical need of the white self that Jack demonstrates here— the need to mark others as "Other" so that it can implicitly define itself—is tyranny, the present absence in Jack's teachings of "Hitler Studies." Just as the Nazi notion of Aryan whiteness depended on a contrasting notion of racialized Others, so the white self needs to establish definitions of Others in order to define itself.

Jack has hunted down Mink for entirely tyrannous, "selfish" reasons, and he carries out his meticulous plan in a particularly white way. Jack has long been obsessed with his own death, bolstering his sense of himself by appropriating the aura of whatever strikes him as "death-defying," including Hitler, the German language, and things Germanic in general. His exposure to the "Airborne Toxic Event" has accelerated this self-interest, leading up to this absurd effort to affirm his life by taking that of another. By continuing to intermingle images of whiteness and death in this scene, DeLillo suggests that a gnawing fear of death is the logical outcome of the American obsession with self, and that this obsession is especially encouraged in white individuals by their lack of conscious racial affiliation. In addition, DeLillo emphasizes a blind spot in this sense of self by showing that in order to *have* a sense of self, the white self must nevertheless rely on a conception of how the presentations of that self are perceived by others.

Jack's whiteness is repeatedly challenged here in two ways: its invisibility begins to dissipate as Mink verbally marks Jack's racial whiteness, and Jack's habitual efforts to get a fix on this apparent racial "composite" by resorting to familiar categorical templates are again frustrated. Mink, on the other hand, has no trouble pigeonholing Jack in racialized terms, noting upon first seeing him, "I see you as a heavyset white man about fifty" (DeLillo, *White* 308). The white colonial past, when the white man was visibly marked as such by contact with the racialized others he sought to exploit, is more concretely evoked by Mink when he asks, "Why are you here, white man?

[. . .] You are very white, you know that?" (310). When Jack finally chases Mink into cowering behind a toilet, he describes himself moving forward, "seeking to loom. [. . .] I loomed in the doorway, conscious of looming, seeing myself from Mink's viewpoint, magnified, threatening" (311–12). Jack also notes that Mink's "face appeared at the end of the white room, a white buzz. [. . .] He sat wedged between the toilet bowl and wall, one sandal missing, eyes totally white" (312). By thus highlighting whiteness as Jack shoots Mink, DeLillo dramatizes the ultimate outcome of the white fetishization of self, its denial of its particularly parasitic dependence on others for the establishment of itself. If the white self can only establish itself in individualistic terms by establishing what others supposedly are (thereby establishing what it itself is not), then the white self has no answer to Willie Mink's sudden, odd question: "Who are you, literally?" As historian David Roediger sums up this central insight in regards to the broader context of American history, "Whiteness describes, from Little Big Horn to Simi Valley, not a culture but precisely the absence of culture. It is the empty and therefore terrifying attempt to build an identity based on what one isn't and on whom one can hold back" (13). In this sense, aside from the symbols the white self adopts to project and represent itself on the basis of how others are expected to interpret those symbols, white racial identity, the white conception of itself, is "literally" nothing.

To note this fact, however, is not to say that the hyperreal notion of the autonomous, unmarkedly white self is any more absolutely inescapable than those generated by the media. We can turn away from the radio and the television and become more aware of the influences of the media-generated simulacrum, and whites can become aware of the dependence of their self-conceptions on categorized conceptions of others (racialized and otherwise). Doing so would also constitute a step toward an awareness of the constitutive facts of white communal membership. DeLillo finally suggests as much, a conversion from self-interest to an interest in others, when Jack's willfully selfish conception of himself dissolves as he realizes what this self-centeredness has led him to do. When he sees after shooting Mink that his victim's focus has changed from fear of a gun-wielding white man into self-absorbed pain, Jack's engorged self-conception begins to deflate, dependent as it is on Mink's fear of that self: "I tried to see myself from Mink's viewpoint. Looming, dominant, gaining life-power, storing up life-credit. But he was too far gone to have a viewpoint" (DeLillo, *White* 312). Jack's racialized fantasy completely dissipates after he attempts to set up a suicide scene by putting the gun in Mink's hand. Mink shoots Jack in the wrist, and Jack finally learns what he "literally" is, after all—just another human body, not unlike Willie Mink: "The world collapsed inward. [. . .] What had happened to the higher plane of energy in which I'd carried out my scheme?" (313). Jolted by the sight of his own blood out of conceiving of himself and Mink as players in a staged, racialized plot, Jack is moved to conceive of Mink as more like than unlike himself.

Suddenly infused with the "old human muddle and quirks [. . . like c]ompassion, remorse, mercy," and feeling that he is "seeing [Mink] for the first time as a person," Jack turns from a killer to a rescuer, doing what he can after shooting Mink to keep him alive (DeLillo, *White* 313). As he turns to his own wound first, Jack explains that "[b]efore I could help Mink, I had to do some basic repair work on myself" (313). Unfortunately, this turn back inward continues. Aside from literally stanching the flow of his own blood, Jack also halts the flow of his selfless sympathy toward Mink by again focusing on himself as he carries out another pre-scripted set of actions. While Jack would seem to have broken free from his fantasized focus on himself, his self-conscious habits are finally too entrenched for his newfound sympathy to remain truly centered in another person. As he drags Mink out into the street in search of help, Jack soon constructs another scenario in which he again acts out a media-induced, life-affirming sense of himself:

> I felt virtuous, I felt blood-stained and stately, dragging the badly wounded man through the dark and empty street. [. . .] There was a spaciousness to this moment, an epic pity and compassion. [. . .] Having shot him, having led him to believe he'd shot himself, I felt I did honor to both of us, to all of us, by merging our fortunes, physically leading him to safety. (314–15)

As a member of a race whose middle-class, male members are particularly discouraged from constructing their identities in raced, classed, and gendered terms, Jack finds himself unable to break out of the resultant habit of focusing single-mindedly on himself, even when ostensibly focusing on others. Such may not seem to be the case as he drops Mink off at a hospital and closes his account by describing the people and scenery of Blacksmith.

Jack's wider perspective in this final section frames his account by recalling in its cinematic sweep his initial, distanced observation of "the day of the station wagons." He describes in careful detail the near-death experience on the highway of his son Wilder, the awe-struck gatherers before the "postmodern sunset," and the befuddled older shoppers trying to find their ways amidst the rearranged supermarket shelves. But while this sudden outward orientation might suggest that Jack has reintegrated himself into a community, DeLillo indicates that it is anything but the traditional, interconnected notion of such a collective entity. Instead, Jack's description highlights how the traditional connections between various representative members have been severed. The shouts of an elderly pair of women trying to call attention to Wilder's dash across the highway go unheard, suggesting a lack of generational contact depicted throughout the novel, most particularly during Jack's visit to the Blacksmith cemetery. In addition, the people who have gathered for the "stunning" sunsets, which have become more breathtaking since the "Airborne Toxic Event," turn away from each other to absorb the spectacle on their own. As the anxiety-ridden older shoppers fumble about in the re-

arranged supermarket, the unmoved, unnamed centrality of whiteness is suggested by the location and appearance of the unmarked food: "Only the
generic food is where it was, white packages plainly labeled" (326). The
novel's racial subtext is completed in the image of suggestive, "brightly colored packages" that swirl around generic whiteness. The people "of color"
evoked by these colors will continue to challenge the universalizing presumptions of whiteness, befuddling those who insist on trying to label them with
outmoded racial categories. In his depiction of Jack Gladney's inability to
wrest himself from his white modes of self-assertion, DeLillo finally suggests
that if the notion of a "white race" is ever to loosen its obdurate grip on cultural centrality, people labeled (yet not labeled) as "white" will have to look at
themselves *as* supposedly "white" people, thereby attaining a truer sense of
cultural identity, and coming a step closer to relinquishing the fantasy of
autonomous selfhood.

Notes

1. The absent, excluded other from middle-class white communities is usually conceived as a racialized Other, race being the major marker of difference in the U.S., but the category also includes members of other economic classes, such as those often labeled "white
trash" or "the homeless."

2. For a discussion of these demographic changes as depicted in *White Noise* within a
broader context of "globalization," see Thomas Peyser.

3. In *Underworld,* DeLillo carefully explores, for the first time, the racial and/or ethnic
identities of several African American and Italian American characters.

4. Feminist critique in general has long argued that the cultural centrality of men has
resulted in the apparent universalization of unspoken male standards and norms, and thus in the
common assumption that such a topic as "gender studies," and indeed any interest in gender
issues, is by and large concerned with women. Such assumptions are homologous, of course, to
the common white assumption that race and racial problems are something that people "of
color" have. For further discussion of this analogy, see Peggy McIntosh and Mike Hill.

5. As McIntosh writes, while describing her own upbringing in which she was rarely
encouraged to think of herself *as* a white person, "I was taught [instead] to see myself as an
individual whose moral state depended on her individual will" (78).

6. Dean MacCannell notes, in his illuminating discussion of the "nouvelle racism"
faced by racialized others living within a contemporary, predominantly white community,

> The minority individual begins to feel that the reputation of the entire ethnicity is
> riding on every detail of his or her behavior, diction, attire, condition of the lawn,
> appearance of the car and the living room, comportment of the children, the dog,
> and so on. [. . . A] black professional learns to accept that her white neighbors con-
> sistently call her by the name of the other black woman on the block. (103–04)

7. DeLillo has thus exercised what Mary Waters usefully delineates as a choice particularly available to those who can be taken as "white." Waters writes in summary of her extensive study of this option:

> Census data and my interviews suggest that [for middle-class whites] ethnicity is
> increasingly a personal choice of whether to be ethnic at all, and, for an increasing

majority of people, of which ethnicity to be. An ethnic identity is something that does not affect much in everyday life. It does not, for the most part, limit choice of marriage partner (except in almost all cases to exclude non-whites). It does not determine where you will live, who your friends will be, what jobs you will have, or whether you will be subject to discrimination. It matters only in voluntary ways. (147)

8.   DeLillo has also said regarding the writer as an individualist: "We need the writer in opposition, the novelist who writes against power, who writes against the corporation or the state or the whole apparatus of assimilation. We're all one beat away from becoming elevator music" (qtd. in Begley 290).

9.   The unmarkedness of DeLillo's racialized, authorial status as a writer is vigorously contested by John Kucich, who argues that DeLillo does not write "strenuously engaged political fiction" because he accepts as a given outcome of recent debates over identity politics the contention that a marginalized social status is necessary if one is to challenge authority, because the white male position is always already an authoritative position (329). Thus, Kucich claims, DeLillo's fictional portrayals of protagonists who are perpetually frustrated in their attempts to challenge authority express his agreement that "in aesthetic practice [. . .] the marginal or aggrieved social position of the speaker [. . .] guarantee its political legitimacy" (333). As this chapter will in part indicate, I would argue that while DeLillo does depict in Jack Gladney an effort to resist larger social forces that ultimately he is rendered impotent. This depiction need not be read as DeLillo's own authorial declaration of impotence, and particularly not as a declaration grounded in recognition of the political illegitimacy of his own position as a white male. For an excellent discussion of John Updike's depictions of white American masculinity in his *Rabbit* novels, see Sally Robinson.

10.   Frank Lentricchia also notes, "The key cultural marker in [Jack's] list [. . .] is the innocent little definite article: He says the stereo sets, the hairdryers, and the junk food ('The station wagons arrived at noon' is the way the book begins) because he's evoking generic objects and events, things seen everywhere and all the time" ("Tales" 95).

11.   As Frankenberg writes, "Whiteness, as a set of normative cultural practices, is visible most clearly to those it definitively excludes and those to whom it does violence. Those who are securely housed within its borders usually do not examine it" (229). In her discussion of "Representations of Whiteness in the Black Imagination," bell hooks has noted of her white students:

> Usually, white students respond with naive amazement that black people critically assess white people from a standpoint where "whiteness" is the privileged signifier. Their amazement that black people watch white people with a critical "ethnographic" gaze is itself an expression of racism. Often their rage erupts because they believe that all ways of looking that highlight difference subvert the liberal belief in a universal subjectivity (we are all just people) that they think will make racism disappear. They have a deep emotional investment in the myth of "sameness," even as their actions reflect the primacy of whiteness as a sign informing who they are and how they think. (168)

12.   As Barbara Ehrenreich remarks, mainstream culture has a "tendency to see the middle class as a universal class, a class which is everywhere represented as representing everyone" (4). She elaborates, "[I]n our culture, the professional, and largely white, middle class is taken as a social norm—a bland and neutral mainstream—from which every other group or class is ultimately a kind of deviation" (3).

13.   As Jack speaks to the father of this "black" family over the course of several pages, the novel's racial subtext briefly rises to the surface, suggesting connections to other themes in the novel. For instance, as this man speaks to Jack, DeLillo renders him as vaguely "black" in his use of English ("He doesn't have showy ways is how you know a saved person" [DeLillo,

White 136]), and in his bodily movements ("He squatted easily, seemed loose-jointed and comfortable" [135]). These slight differences from the discourse and bodily hexis of Jack bring to mind for DeLillo's protagonist, and perhaps for his readers, vaguely primitivist associations; indeed, Jack cements such associations in his sudden question, "Why are we talking to each other from this aboriginal crouch?" (137). DeLillo thus ties this scene to many other moments in which Jack makes a connection between such technological advances as the chemical death that threatens the Gladneys and a human response of primitive fear to them. Jack explicitly states this connection in response to a rumor sweeping the campground that synthetic organisms have been deployed to consume the toxic cloud: " 'The greater the scientific advance, the more primitive the fear' " (161). DeLillo has made virtually verbatim comments in interviews, and he may be working to enhance this connection in this scene by suggesting associations that linger within the white imagination between blackness and the primitive. At the very least, this scene recalls in such ways the more explicit statement regarding such associations made by David Bell, the narrator and protagonist of DeLillo's first novel, *Americana,* as he listens to jazz: "I felt this music had been in me all along, the smoky blue smell of it. [. . .] I pleased myself by thinking, as white men will do, that some Afro-instinct burned in an early part of my being" (*Americana* 144–45).

14.   For further discussion of the systematic, pre–World War II efforts of American universities to exclude Jews, see Karen Brodkin Sacks, who writes, "The Protestant elite [at major American universities] complained that Jews were unwashed, uncouth, unrefined, loud, and pushy" (82). See also Takaki, 304–07.

15.   For further discussion of Melville's meditations on racial whiteness, see Valerie Babb and Toni Morrison.

16.   See in particular David R. Roediger, Alexander Saxton, Theodore W. Allen, and Noel Ignatiev.

17.   Members of an explicitly racialized category could no doubt seek self-assertion through shopping in such a space as well, but if they were to describe themselves doing so, they would be likely to construct the setting and describe their experiences in entirely different ways. Many African Americans, for example, might tell of the suspicious, watchful stares of clerks and managers, or of being repeatedly asked for further identification while using a credit card, or of entering an elevator and watching white shoppers protectively clutch their bags and purses. While Jack's whiteness leads him to conceive of a shopping mall as an exotic backdrop for individualized action, such a place can be an unpleasant and even distinctly hostile environment for an explicitly racialized American. For further discussion of black experiences while shopping, see Austin. For discussion of the privileges she enjoys as a white woman while shopping, see McIntosh.

18.   As MacCannell writes, "While negative ethnic stereotyping is guarded against in European and American public life, and seems to be on the decline, it recurs more or less automatically, even in public settings, whenever an 'ethnic' group stands as a barrier to the unfettered economic pursuits of whites. 'Ethnicity' was invented in the first place for use on such occasions" (138).

19.   See Waters and Alba, who both note a resurgence since *White Noise* was published in white reclamations of ethnic identity, largely as a response to the increasing presence and claims of racialized others.

Works Cited

Aaron, Daniel. "How to Read Don DeLillo." Lentricchia, *Introducing* 67–81.

Alba, Richard. *Ethnic Identity: The Transformation of White America.* New Haven: Yale UP, 1990.

Allen, Theodore W. *The Invention of the White Race.* Vol. 1. London: Verso, 1994.

Austin, Regina. " 'A Nation of Thieves': Securing Black People's Right to Shop and Sell in America." *Utah Law Review* 1994 (1994): 147–77.

Begley, Adam. "The Art of Fiction CXXXV: Don DeLillo." *Paris Review* 35.128 (1993): 274–306.

Babb, Valerie. *Whiteness Visible: The Meaning of Whiteness in American Literature and Culture.* New York: New York UP, 1998.

Chambers, Ross. "The Unexamined." Hill, *Whiteness* 187–203.

DeCurtis, Anthony. " 'An Outsider in This Society': An Interview with Don DeLillo." Lentricchia, *Introducing* 43–66.

DeLillo, Don. *Americana.* 1971. New York: Penguin, 1989.

———. *Mao II.* New York: Viking, 1991.

———. "Spaghetti and Meatballs." *Epoch* 14.3 (1965): 244–50.

———. "Take the 'A' Train." *Epoch* 12.1 (1962): 9–25.

———. *White Noise.* New York: Viking, 1985.

Ehrenreich, Barbara. *Fear of Falling: The Inner Life of the Middle Class.* New York: Pantheon, 1989.

Frankenberg, Ruth. *White Women, Race Matters: The Social Construction of Whiteness.* Minneapolis: U of Minnesota P, 1993.

Franklin, Benjamin. *The Autobiography and Other Writings.* New York: Bantam, 1982.

Hill, Mike. "Introduction: Vipers in Shangri-La: Whiteness, Writing, and Other Ordinary Terrors." Hill, *Whiteness* 1–18.

Hill, Mike, ed. *Whiteness: A Critical Reader.* New York: New York UP, 1997.

hooks, bell. *Black Looks: Race and Representation.* Boston: South End, 1992.

Ignatiev, Noel. *How the Irish Became White.* New York: Routledge, 1995.

Kucich, John. "Postmodern Politics: Don DeLillo and the Plight of the White Male Author." *Michigan Quarterly Review* 27.2 (1988): 328–41.

Lentricchia, Frank. "Tales of the Electronic Tribe." Lentricchia, *New* 87–113.

Lentricchia, Frank, ed. *Introducing Don DeLillo.* Durham: Duke UP, 1991.

———. *New Essays on White Noise.* Cambridge: Cambridge UP, 1991.

MacCannell, Dean. *Empty Meeting Grounds: The Tourist Papers.* New York: Routledge, 1992.

McIntosh, Peggy. "White Privilege and Male Privilege: A Personal Account of Coming to See Correspondences through Work in Women's Studies." *Race, Class, and Gender: An Anthology.* Ed. M. L. Anderson and P. H. Collins. Belmont, CA: Wadsworth, 1995. 76–87.

Melville, Herman. *Moby-Dick; or, The Whale.* 1851. New York: Norton, 1967.

Morrison, Toni. *Playing in the Dark: Whiteness and the Literary Imagination.* Cambridge: Harvard UP, 1992.

Moses, Michael Valdez. "Lust Removed From Nature." Lentricchia, New 63–86.

Peyser, Thomas. "Globalization in America: The Case of Don DeLillo's *White Noise.*" *Clio* 25.3 (1996): 255–71.

Robinson, Sally. " 'Unyoung, Unpoor, Unblack': John Updike and the Construction of Middle American Masculinity." *Modern Fiction Studies* 44.2 (1998): 331–63.

Roediger, David R. *Towards the Abolition of Whiteness: Essays on Race, Politics, and Working Class History.* London: Verso, 1994.

Sacks, Karen Brodkin. "How Did Jews Become White Folks?" *Race.* Ed. Steven Gregory and Roger Sanjek. New Brunswick: Rutgers UP, 1994. 78–102.

Saxton, Alexander. *The Rise and Fall of the White Republic: Class Politics and Mass Culture in Nineteenth Century America.* New York: Verso, 1990.

Takaki, Ronald. *A Different Mirror: A History of Multicultural America.* Boston: Little, 1993.

Twain, Mark [Samuel Clemens]. *The Adventures of Huckleberry Finn.* 1884. New York: Bantam, 1981.

Waters, Mary. *Ethnic Options: Choosing Identities in America.* Berkeley: U of California P, 1990.

Baudrillard, DeLillo's *White Noise,*
and the End of Heroic Narrative

Leonard Wilcox

From *Americana,* through *Great Jones Street, White Noise,* and *Libra,* Don DeLillo's novels have been concerned with the relationship between American identity and the mediascapes. If the two earlier works were preoccupied with the way in which the American dream is manipulated by the media, the later two chart a world that is mediated by and constituted in the techno-logico-semiotic regime. In *White Noise* DeLillo's protagonist Jack Gladney confronts a new order in which life is increasingly lived in a world of simulacra, where images and electronic representations replace direct experience. In *Libra,* Lee Oswald is a product of that order; a figure devoted to media self-fashioning, he constructs his life—and indeed his death—from the proliferation of charismatic images and spectacles of a postmodern society.[1]

White Noise and *Libra* particularly, with their interest in electronic mediation and representation, present a view of life in contemporary America that is uncannily similar to that depicted by Jean Baudrillard. They indicate that the transformations of contemporary society that Baudrillard describes in his theoretical writings on information and media have also gripped the mind and shaped the novels of Don DeLillo. For *White Noise* especially—because it most specifically explores the realm of information and mediascape—Baudrillard's works provide an interesting, valuable, and even crucial perspective. The informational world Baudrillard delineates bears a striking resemblance to the world of *White Noise:* one characterized by the collapse of the real and the flow of signifiers emanating from an information society, by a "loss of the real" in a black hole of simulation and the play and exchange of signs. In this world common to both Baudrillard and DeLillo, images, signs, and codes engulf objective reality; signs become more real than reality and stand in for the world they erase. Baudrillard's notion that this radical semiurgy results in the collapse of difference, firm structures, and finalities (the "fixities" by which stable meaning is produced) markedly resembles DeLillo's vision of an entropic breakdown of basic rituals and concepts in the informational flow of

Originally published in *Contemporary Literature* 32, no. 3 (1991): 346–65. Copyright © 1991. Reprinted by permission of the University of Wisconsin Press.

electronic communication. Moreover, for both Baudrillard and DeLillo a media-saturated consciousness threatens the concept of meaning itself. For Baudrillard, "information devours its own contents; it devours communication," resulting in "a sort of nebulous state leading not at all to a surfeit of innovation but to the very contrary, to total entropy" (*In the Shadow* 97, 100). Similarly for DeLillo, the flow of electronic information obliterates coherent meaning. The very notion of "white noise" that is so central to the novel implies a neutral and reified mediaspeech, but also a surplus of data and an entropic blanket of information glut which flows from a media-saturated society.

But the similarities between Baudrillard and DeLillo do not end here. For both, this increasingly simulational and nonreferential world brings about radical changes in the very shape of subjectivity. For Baudrillard an older modernist order—with its dialectic of alienation and inner authenticity—is eclipsed by new forms of experiencing the self. Lured and locked into the "uninterrupted interfaces" of video screen and mediascape, the subject experiences an undifferentiated flux of pure signifiers, an "ecstasy of communication" in which conventional structures of meaning dissolve and the ability to imagine an alternative reality disappears. A new experience of euphoria, an ungrounded "delirium" replaces the anxiety and alienation of an earlier period. Unlike the earlier experience of alienation, which attested to a coherent private sphere, an interiority of self, this new delirium, a vertiginous fascination with the "instantaneity" and "obscene" visibility of media events, attests to the "extermination of interstitial and protective spaces" ("Ecstasy" 127). Indeed the "communicational promiscuity" of the omnipresent and ubiquitous mass media strips society of its secrets, inhibitions, repressions, and depths and leads inexorably to the hollowing out of the self—or better to say, the dispersal of self, the generalized destabilization of the subject in the era of networks and electronic transmission of symbols ("Ecstasy" 130–31).[2]

Similarly DeLillo sees a new form of subjectivity emerging as the modernist order is eclipsed by the postmodern world. Indeed, an older modernist subjectivity is in a state of siege in the information society. Jack Gladney, the narrator of *White Noise,* is a modernist displaced in a postmodern world. He exhibits a Kierkegaardian "fear and trembling" regarding death and attempts to preserve earlier notions of an authentic and coherent identity by observing the tribalistic rituals of family life. Gladney attempts to "shore up the ruins" of an older order, ironically by chanting advertising slogans as if they were sacred formulas. Yet he often succumbs to the Baudrillardian condition, floating "ecstatically" in a delirium of networks, hyperreal surfaces, and fetishized consumer objects. Gladney's narrative is interspersed with the entropic chatter and snippets of talk shows that emerge from a television that "migrates" around the Gladney household, moving from room to room, filling the air with jingles and consumer advice ("The TV said: 'And other trends that could dramatically impact your portfolio' " [61]). His narrative is interpenetrated by brand names and advertising slogans as he chants, "Mastercard, Visa, American Express . . . Leaded, unleaded, superunleaded . . . Dristan Ultra, Dristan Ultra . . . Clorets, Velamints, Freedent" (100, 199, 167, 229). These "eruptions" in the narrative imply the emergence of a new form of subjectivity colonized by the media and decentered by its polyglot discourses and electronic networks. They imply the evacuation of the private spheres of self, in Baudrillardian terms "the end of interiority" ("Ecstasy" 133).

Moreover, for Baudrillard and DeLillo the dissolution of a modernist subjectivity in the mire of contemporary media and technology is integrally connected to another issue: the passing of the great modernist notions of artistic impulse and representation, the demise of notions of a "heroic" search for alternative, creative forms of consciousness, and the idea of art as specially endowed revelation. Such a heroic modernism struggled through extraordinary artistic and intellectual effort to create meaning from the flux and fragments of an atomized contemporary world, to pierce the veil, to reveal underlying truth. But for Baudrillard, the very impulses that gave impetus to this project have dissipated in the contemporary world: "Something has changed, and the Faustian, Promethean, (perhaps Oedipal) period of production and consumption gives way to the 'proteinic' era of networks, to the narcissistic and protean era of connections, contact, contiguity, feedback and generalized interface that goes with the universe of communication" ("Ecstasy" 127). For Baudrillard these heroic Faustian, Promethean, and oedipal impulses to struggle, to illuminate, and to unveil a (repressed) truth give way to "the smooth operational surface of communication" ("Ecstasy" 127); they have all but dissolved in the pure, empty seriality and the decentering forces of a "proteinic" information society.

Similarly, for DeLillo, such heroic striving for meaning has been radically thrown into question in the contemporary world. For at the core of the modernist version of the heroic is the notion of the constitutive power of the imagination, the idea of an autonomous and authentic subjectivity out of which springs vision and illumination. Such is the modernist "epiphany": a moment of profound imaginative perception in which fragments are organized and essence revealed, and (on the level of narrative) in which a hermeneutical core of meaning is contained within a constellation of luminescent images. But *White Noise* suggests such moments of authentic and unfettered subjectivity are being supplanted by a Baudrillardian euphoria or "schizophrenia" which characterizes the experience of the self in the space of the simulacrum. By rendering moments of "heroic" vision and imaginative epiphany as parody and pastiche—as he does in the climactic "show-down" between Gladney and Gray (a.k.a. Willie Mink)—DeLillo implies the exhaustion of late modernist, existentialist notions of heroism. As well, DeLillo's parody and "terrific comedy" (Lentricchia 1) underscore a crisis of representation relating directly to the collapse of patriarchal authority and to the breakup of the oedipal configurations that underpin the heroic narrative itself.

The passing of a heroic modernist "Faustian and Promethean era" and the emergence of a "proteinic" postmodern order is registered in *White Noise* through the narrative voice of Jack Gladney. Gladney sifts through the layers of white noise—electronic media, printed information, traffic sounds, computer read-outs—listening for significance, for a grasp of essence in the flux. In modernist fashion, he struggles in an almost Sisyphean way to glean meaning from the surrounding noise of culture and is drawn toward occasions of existential self-fashioning, heroic moments of vision in a commodified world. When he shops with his family he notes that "I began to grow in value and self-regard. I filled myself out, found new aspects of myself, located a person I'd forgotten existed" (84). And when he hears his daughter Steffie uttering the words "Toyota Corolla, Toyota Celica, Toyota Cressida" in her sleep, his response is "whatever its source, the utterance struck me with the impact of a moment of splendid transcendence" (155).

Yet Gladney's modernist impulse toward authentic selfhood and his quest for transcendental meaning seem oddly out of place in the postmodern world. Gladney's colleague Murray Siskind, a visiting lecturer in "living icons" who lives in a one-room apartment with a television set and stacks of comic books, and who teaches popular culture courses in "Elvis" and "The Cinema of Car Crashes," insists that looking for a realm of meaning beyond surfaces, networks, and commodities is unnecessary; the information society provides its own sort of epiphanies, and watching television, an experience he describes as "close to mystical," is one of them. For Murray television proffers the Baudrillardian "ecstasy of communication," a "peak experience" of postmodern culture. Television, he says,

> welcomes us into the grid, the network of little buzzing dots that make up the picture pattern. There is light, there is sound. I ask my students, "What more do you want?" Look at the wealth of data concealed in the grid, in the bright packaging, the jingles, the slice-of-life commercials, the products hurtling out of darkness, the coded messages and endless repetitions, like chants, like mantras. "*Coke is it, Coke is it, Coke is it.*" (51)

For Murray the Postmodernist, the euphoric forms of electronic data and informational flow are to be enthusiastically embraced, and Murray takes it upon himself to be Gladney's tutor in the new semiotic regime. When Murray and Gladney drive into the country to see "The Most Photographed Barn in America," for example, Murray explains the significance of the tourist attraction within the new order of image and simulacrum. Rather than conjuring up associations with a pioneering past or an authentic rural life, the barn has been subsumed into the process of image replication; it is surrounded by tour buses, roadside signs, venders selling post cards of the barn, people taking pictures of the barn, people photographing other photographers photographing the barn. Observing the tourists, Murray points to the postmodern experience of proliferating images without ground: "they are taking pictures of taking pictures" (13). Murray expounds solemnly on the unfolding of a new order where the distinction between reality and representation, sign and referent, collapses: "Once you've seen the signs about the barn, it becomes impossible to see the barn" (12). He explains to the reluctant Gladney the logic of a simulational world where signs triumph over reality, where experience is constructed by and in service of the image, and the ephemeral image takes on its own resplendent, mystical "aura": "We're not here to capture an image, we're here to maintain one. Every photograph reinforces the aura. Can you feel it, Jack? An accumulation of nameless energies" (12).[3]

Yet if Murray savors the flux of images and signs, Gladney is increasingly nonplused by a world without referents, where the responses of an authentic interior self vanish in the undertow of the simulacrum and where media images and spectacles proliferate, terrorize, and fascinate. The "Airborne Toxic Event" (besides registering the postmodern preoccupation with toxic poisoning) depicts a condition where subjective responses are both constructed and validated by radio and television: initially the "toxic event" is reported as a "feathery plume," which induces curiosity and mild alarm; later it is described as a catastrophic "black billowing cloud," evoking fear "accompanied by a sense of awe that bordered on the religious" (127). Increasingly it becomes impossible to distinguish between the spectacle and the real. Even the natural world—the ultimate ground of the "real"—succumbs to a hyperreal condition of multiple regress without origin. Spectacular sunsets (which Gladney refers to as "postmodern sunsets") appear after the release of toxins into the atmosphere, but it is never certain whether the sunsets are caused by toxic chemicals or by the residue of microorganisms subsequently discharged by scientists into the atmosphere to "eat" the airborne chemicals. Exposure to the toxic materials released by the "event" causes déjà vu in the Gladney children (déjà vu itself being a "recollection" without origin), but it is unclear whether this is a "real" symptom or a psychosomatic one resulting from suggestion, since they get the symptoms only after they hear them reported on the radio.

Gladney's encounter with the SIMUVAC (simulated evacuation) underscores most profoundly the simulated or hyperreal world depicted in *White Noise*. SIMUVAC regularly stages efficient rehearsals for coping with real disasters—volunteers play dead and videotapes are sent for prompt analysis. Yet at the evacuation site during the toxic event, Gladney discovers that the SIMUVAC personnel are using the real event to rehearse and perfect a simulation. The world has been turned inside out; simulation has become the ground of the real: "You have to make allowances for the fact that everything we see tonight is real," the SIMUVAC man complains to Gladney; "we don't have our victims laid out where we'd want them if this was an actual simulation. . . . There's a lot of polishing we still have to do" (139).

Finally the world of *White Noise*—one based on the abstract circulation of information—follows the logic of the utter commutability of signs. Any semiological network can become a hermetic system into which the individual subject can be inserted and which constructs the self. Gladney's German teacher, for example, tells Jack how after his loss of faith in God he "turned to meteorology for comfort" and soon had created a universe of significance from the weather: "It brought me a sense of peace and security I'd never experienced. Dew, frost, and fog. Snow flurries. The jet stream. . . . I began to come out of my shell, talk to people on the street. 'Nice day.' 'Looks like rain.' 'Hot enough for you?' " (55).

Indeed, Gladney finds himself unwittingly drawn into this order in which the subject is assembled in signs. Gladney is chairman of "Hitler studies" (which in itself suggests a grim nostalgic impulse to recuperate the "real" in an age of simulation) but is nevertheless warned by the chancellor of the university about his tendency to make "a feeble presentation of self" (17). Gladney begins to wear heavy-rimmed sunglasses to bolster his credibility and changes his name from Jack Gladney to the more distinguished J. A. K. Gladney. Later, when his wife Babette expresses her irritation at the imposing, mirrored sunglasses and asks Gladney to stop wearing them, he retorts, "I can't teach Hitler without them" (221). Any notion of an essential identity is all but erased in this realm of free-floating signifiers and simulation. Yet Gladney is unable, like his friend Murray, to submit himself happily to surface and simulacrum; rather he is plagued by a nagging late modernist, existential sense that he is in "bad faith": "I am the false character that follows the name around" (17).

This crisis of subjectivity that Gladney faces in this hermetic universe of afterimages, ghosts, floating signifiers, and simulacra is compounded by another—his impending death after exposure to the deadly gas "Nyodene D." during the evacuation. Gladney exhibits a modernist angst about death, ruminating about its significance, visiting graveyards, and talking about it with his friend Murray. Yet Gladney's existential crisis is obsolete in the new postmodern order. Gladney's anguished confession, "I want to live," merely evokes from Murray a flight of free association along the intertextual surfaces of popular culture: "From the Robert Wise film of the same name, with Susan Hayward as Barbara Graham, a convicted murderess. Aggressive jazz score by Johnny Mandel" (283). Moreover, even death is not exempt from the world of simulation: the experience of dying is utterly mediated by technology and eclipsed by a world of symbols. The body becomes simulacrum, and death loses its personal and existential resonances. When Gladney is subjected to a computer scan to obtain a "data profile" on his condition, he notes that "it is when death is rendered graphically, is televised so to speak, that you sense an eerie separation between your condition and yourself. A network of symbols has been introduced, an entire awesome technology wrested from the gods. It makes you feel like a stranger in your own dying" (142). And as

Gladney later tells Murray, "there's something artificial about my death. It's shallow, unfulfilling. I don't belong to the earth or sky. They ought to carve an aerosol can on my tombstone" (283).

Thus media and technology transform death into a sign spectacle, and its reality is experienced as the body doubled in technified forms: death by "print-out."[4] But if death, the last vestige of the real, the final border of the self, becomes part of the precession of simulacra, what possibilities exist for meaning, value, for the autonomous self's endeavor to create meaning against death's limits and finality? In an order given over to simulation, such heroic impulses can only be rendered as parody and pastiche—the "blank parody" of exhausted or dead forms, the postmodern response to the disappearance of narrative norms that previously figured heroic action.

When Gladney discovers that Babette has contrived to obtain Dylar (a high tech chemical "cure" for the fear of death) by sleeping with the project manager of the group working on the drug's research and development, he resolves to hunt out the project manager—identified by Babette as "Mr. Gray"—and kill him. Such a confrontation has all the makings of a heroic showdown. Yet from the outset Gladney's role of hero in the showdown is undermined in a variety of ways. A note of literary parody is struck even before Gladney meets Gray. After his exposure to Nyodene D. during the airborne toxic event, Gladney is diagnosed by the computerized scanner as harboring a fatal "nebulous mass" in his body. His comments on his own predicament constitute an overt parody of the existential hero contemplating radical freedom against the knowledge of the inevitability of death: "How literary, I thought peevishly. Streets thick with the details of impulsive life as the hero ponders the latest phase in his dying" (281).

When Gladney confronts Gray (identified as Willie Mink), the "residential organizational genius" of the Dylar research group, now a shabby, demented recluse, the scene becomes a pastiche of the existentialist epiphany— a "negative" epiphany which involves a lucid recognition of the absurd and contingent nature of reality, a moment of heroic self-fashioning based on the sudden perception that existence is grounded in nothingness and the individual is utterly free. When he goes to the seedy motel where Mink is living, there is a strong sense of the utter provisionality and freedom which characterizes Gladney's actions: he proceeds by instinct, continually updating his plans. Like Meursault in *L'Étranger,* who experiences a sensory epiphany—an amplified awareness of the play of sunlight and the sounds of water just before he commits his act of violence, Gladney experiences an intensity of sensation as he enters Mink's room: "I stood inside the room, sensing things, noting the room tone, the dense air. Information rushed toward me, rushed slowly, incrementally" (305). Like Roquentin, who has a visionary moment in *La Nausée,* Gladney experiences with almost hallucinatory intensity the essential pulsating "thusness" of reality, and in so doing believes himself to be experiencing an unmediated vision of pure existence: "I knew the precise nature of events. I was moving closer to things in their actual state as I approached a violence, a smashing intensity. Water fell in drops, surfaces gleamed" (305).

Yet these perceptions are related in a dry, toneless fashion appropriate to pastiche, which Fredric Jameson describes as "the wearing of a stylistic mask, speech in a dead language . . . without parody's ulterior motive, without the satirical impulse, without that still latent feeling that there exists something normal compared to which what is being imitated is rather comic" ("Consumer Society" 114). Pastiche implies a world where fragmented or heterogeneous linguistic islands supplant centered, heroic narrative positions, a world where the possibility of unique vision and style has been lost. Thus rather than the parodic imitation of a peculiar and unique style, DeLillo's pastiche involves a play of stylistic mannerisms, from the high modernist heroics of the existential hero to the B-movie heroics of the hard-boiled detective. Even as he approaches the motel, Gladney assumes the voice-over style of the Raymond Chandler hero: "It occurred to me that I did not have to knock. The door would be open" (305). This B-movie quality is furthered by Gladney's insistence upon inflating the narrative as he dwells repetitively on his sensory apocalypse: "Surfaces gleamed. Water struck the roof in spherical masses, globules, splashing drams" (307); "The precise nature of events. Things in their actual state" (310). But these observations of an intensified reality rapidly descend into ludicrous banality, and rather than an epiphany of identity, Gladney undergoes a farcical loss of self:

> I continued to advance in consciousness. Things glowed, a secret life rising out of them. Water struck the roof in elongated orbs, splashing drams. I knew for the first time what rain really was. I knew what wet was. I understood the neurochemistry of my brain, the meaning of dreams (the waste material of premonitions). Great stuff everywhere, racing through the room, racing slowly. A richness, a density. I believed everything. I was a Buddhist, a Jain, a Duck River Baptist. (310)

Moreover, just as the secure narrative position required by the heroic figure is destabilized by pastiche, the revelations of the heroic transcendental ego are ultimately transformed into a postmodern decentering of self, an "ecstatic" Baudrillardian dispersal of consciousness in the world of screens and networks. As Gladney enters Gray's motel room he observes that "I sensed I was part of a network of structures and channels" (305). As the narrative continues, metaphors of the experience of Dasein through which Being coalesces in an existential moment of recognition startlingly shift to metaphors of the world of networks, information, and white noise: "The intensity of the noise in the room was the same at all frequencies. Sound all around. . . . I knew who I was in the network of meanings" (312). The whole atmosphere, so charged with unusual vitality, now becomes bathed in the eerie glow of television: "auditory scraps, tatters, whirling specks. A heightened reality. A dense-ness that was also a transparency. Surfaces gleamed" (307).

For Gladney's confrontation with Mink is an allegorical confrontation with postmodern culture itself. Mink is the personification of a new order; a composite man of undecidable ethnicity, he suggests a world where national and ethnic differences have been eradicated in an increasing internationaliza-tion of American popular culture. Mink wears Bermuda shorts with a Bud-weiser pattern on them; he sprawls on his couch "in the attitude of a stranded air traveler, someone long since defeated by the stale waiting, the airport bab-ble" (307). "I had American sex the first time in Port-O-San, Texas," Mink announces; "American sex, let me tell you, this is how I learned my English" (308–9). A repository of Lyotardian "linguistic clouds" of splintered and frac-tured discourse, Mink repeats phrases, from television weather reports ("And this could represent the leading edge of some warmer air" [313]) to popular geography merged with popular nutrition hints ("This is the point, as opposed to emerging coastlines, continental plates. Or you can eat natural grains, vegetables, eggs, no fish, no fruit" [311]). Mink voices the drone of the mediascapes; more than that he physically resembles a television set. Gladney notes that "his face was odd, concave, forehead and chin jutting" (305–6). Mink is the embodiment of white noise ("His face appeared at the end of the white room, a white buzz" [312]) and of a system in a state of entropic decay: he is exhausted and depleted; he shows "a senile grin" (309). Moreover he is obsessed with his own deterioration, quelling his fear of death by consuming Dylar tablets one after another.

Gladney's existential epiphany now begins to resemble the "peak experi-ence" typifying the postmodern condition—one similar to Baudrillard's description of schizophrenia—the ultimate outcome of an "obscenity of com-munication" in which the self succumbs utterly to "networks of influence." Baudrillard describes schizophrenia as "the absolute proximity, the total instantaneity of things . . . the overexposure and transparence of the world which traverses [the schizoid] without obstacle" ("Ecstasy" 133). In this "delirium" of communication, the schizophrenic exists only as a nodal point or "switching center"; his mental and physical boundaries dissolve in the flow of information as he experiences the cognitive equivalent of white noise.

Alarmingly, Gladney's peak experience rapidly metamorphoses into this Baudrillardian nightmare. Indeed, it becomes similar to Fredric Jame-son's description (elaborating on Baudrillard) of the transformation of the expressive energies of modernism into the fragmentation of emotions in the diffuse and discontinuous schizoid world of postmodernism. For Jameson, this schizophrenic experience is one in which the world takes on a "hallu-cinogenic intensity" ("Cultural Logic" 73). Gladney's experience has this hal-lucinatory quality, yet if it initially resembles the Sartrean visionary moment in its intensity, its sense of depth, of unmediated reality and pure existence, is ultimately a chimera. Rather than an epiphany of identity, it constitutes a dissolution of self, a lifeworld reduced, in Jameson's terms, "to an experience of pure material Signifiers, or in other words of a series of pure and unrelated presents in time" ("Cultural Logic" 72). Gladney is temporally suspended as he continues to revise his plans to kill Mink in a toneless, chantlike fashion, perpetually rewriting a present which seems without link to past and future. And as temporal continuities break down, his experience of the present becomes overwhelmingly vivid: when he shoots Mink he marvels at Mink's blood, sees its color "in terms of dominant wavelength, luminance, purity" (312). Yet in spite of this heightened intensity, the encounter suggests not the existentialist sense that pure existence looms up as artificial words and constructs drop away, but rather the postmodern awareness that words themselves construct reality. The dominant impression of Gladney's account, in fact, is wordiness, a proliferation of words. Words themselves loom up in hyperpresent materiality; when he shoots Mink, not sound so much as words echo around the room: "I fired the gun, the weapon, the pistol, the firearm, the automatic" (312).

But it is Mink himself who most completely suggests the postmodern "schizophrenic" experience in an instantaneous world of discrete and discontinuous moments in which signifiers fail to add up, to produce the "meaning-effect" of an interlocking syntagmatic series. One of the side effects of the Dylar that Mink ingests to eradicate the fear of death (and coextensively the sense of time) is the sort of literalizing attention to words that results from the isolation of signifiers in pure and unrelated presents and the consequent breakdown of the play of meaning along the temporal manifold of the signifying chain. In their condition as jumbled and isolated signifiers, words are ultimately reduced to mere signals which form a mechanical one-to-one relationship with their referent.[5] Thus Gladney, stalking Mink, says "hail of bullets" and Mink runs for cover; when he says "plunging aircraft" Mink folds himself into the recommended crash position.

Gladney ultimately botches his plan to kill Mink and steal the Dylar: Mink devours the Dylar, and Gladney, after wounding Mink, takes him to the hospital. More significantly, the encounter with Mink suggests the untenability of heroic self-fashioning, as Gladney's epiphany collapses into postmodern schizophrenia. Rather than a moment of pure, unfettered subjectivity, Gladney's experience implies the evacuation of the self, as the deep structures of modern experience—as well as modern narrative—succumb to a postmodern crisis of the sign and representation, to "networks of influence," to a discontinuous schizoid world, and to white noise.

But there is yet another way in which *White Noise* figures the impossibility of heroism and the demise of the heroic narrative. Baudrillard's suggestion that the "proteinic" era of networks has replaced not only Faustian and Promethean but oedipal strivings is relevant here. For DeLillo's postmodern world is one of free-floating and endless simulacra, a meaning cut off from all bases. This is a world in which in Lacanian terms the stability of the *nom du père* is subject to doubt, indeed where notions of a centered authority are mere residues from an earlier period. Even religious belief is swallowed in the order of the simulacrum. When Gladney drags Mink to a Catholic hospital after the bungled murder attempt, he asks the resident nun about the Church's thinking on heaven, God, angels, and the saving of souls. Her response is "saved? What is saved? This is a dumb head, who would come in here to talk about angels. Show me an angel. Please. I want to see" (317). The nun informs him that church officials have long since ceased to believe in the "devil, the angels, heaven, hell"; they merely pretend to. "Our pretense is a dedication," she says. "Someone must appear to believe" (319).

This world in which the ultimate, transcendent "name of the father" is simulational implies a crisis in the deeply patriarchal structures of late capitalism, a world in which there is a troubling of the phallus, in which masculinity slips from its sure position. Initially this insufficiency of masculine authority is suggested by Gladney's position as head of a family of five children, most of whom are brought from earlier marriages. This postmodern family is no longer organized around the *nom du père;* rather it is utterly decentered and globally dispersed. Gladney's string of ex-spouses and his collection of children from previous marriages are connected through time and global space by electronic networks. When one of Jack's ex-wives telephones, he comments that "her tiny piping voice bounced down to me from a hollow ball in geosynchronous orbit" (273).

Gladney's attempts to recover patriarchal authority by wearing sunglasses and teaching courses in Hitler notwithstanding, his narrative is hardly authoritative, nor does it carry a sense of mastery. It is a decentered and toneless montage of voices, ranging from outcroppings of media slogans to metaphysical meditations on the meaning of death. But if Gladney's narrative registers the decline of patriarchal authority, the breakup of the order of phallic power is suggested most strongly by the figure of Gray/Mink and the dynamic of Gladney's confrontation with him. Gray seems initially to represent patriarchal privilege and power. He is a scientist, the "project manager" of the research work on Dylar. And he is the man who has usurped Gladney's wife Babette, lured her into bed in a seedy motel room in exchange for the drug. Stung by Babette's confessed adultery, Gladney imagines Gray and his wife in the motel. The figure of Gray initially suggests phallic mastery, a dominance which affirms the masculine gaze and its power of appropriation: "Bedward, plotward. I saw my wife reclining on her side, voluptuously rounded, the eternal waiting nude. I saw her as he did. Dependent, submissive, emotionally captive. I felt his mastery and control. The dominance of his position" (241).

The "bedward, plotward" trajectory suggests the oedipal narrative itself, with Gray representing the corporate father (or "project manager") who has usurped Gladney's "motherly" wife (Babette exhibits "an honesty inherent in bulkiness" [7]). This trajectory also implies the need to bring the narrative logic to its fruition by Gladney's killing Gray and reclaiming his love object. Yet Gray is finally not a figure of centered authority; he is a "composite man," as Babette informs Gladney, and "Gray" is a convenient name she uses to refer to several scientists with whom she had transactions in the research group. Further, Gladney imagines Gray as "four or more grayish figures," vague organization men without potency or phallic power, technocrats devoted to eradicating human emotion, especially the fear of death: "selfless, sexless, determined to engineer us out of our fear" (241). Moreover, oedipal logic gives way to the "proteinic" world of information as Gray appears in Gladney's fantasy as a televised image, a representative and embodiment of a postmodern informational world of networks and circuits: "I sat up late thinking of Mr. Gray. Graybodied, staticky, unfinished. The picture wobbled and rolled, the edges of his body flared with random distortion" (241). Finally the "bedward, plotward" trajectory of the oedipal narrative, culminating in the primal scene itself—the moment of consummation between Gray and Babette—is dissipated by the echoes of brand names and a ubiquitous "panasonic" white noise: "[I] heard them in their purling foreplay, the love babble and buzzing flesh. Heard the sloppings and smackings, the swash of wet mouths, bedsprings sinking in. An interval of mumbled adjustments. Then gloom moved in around the gray-sheeted bed, a circle slowly closing. Panasonic" (241).

Similarly Willie Mink (incarnation of the spectral Gray) is associated with the flow of information and with white noise. But as the one-time project manager of the Dylar research group, which is "supported by a multinational giant," he is also connected with a global economy. The Mink/Gray composite in fact is associated both with informational flow and transnational monopoly, a new world of multinational capitalism whose channels of control are so widespread and dispersed that no single authoritative father figure is necessary for its operation. Rather than figuring the power of a centered, authoritative, symbolic father, Mink/Gray represents the "flow of desire" of postindustrial society, a society of services and information in which desire tends less and less to be sublimated and organized within the patriarchal oedipalized family.[6] The figure of Mink/Gray is as amorphous and diffused as the relays and networks of the social desiring machine in the desublimated and postoedipal space of late capitalism. Mink/Gray provides no focal point for an oedipal dynamic that might otherwise underpin the sort of heroic confrontation Gladney undertakes. "This is the grayish figure of my torment, the man who took my wife" (308–9), Gladney resolutely tells himself when he sees Mink. Yet Mink is less a usurper than a repository for the rambling, metonymic discourses of a consumer culture, and Gladney, even if he could carry off a heroic encounter, has nothing substantial to fight. The battle on the heroic terrain of oedipal rivalry and phallic power is abortive: if Gladney symbolically castrates Mink, shooting him in the "midsection" and "hipbone" ("his lap a puddle of blood"), he carelessly allows Mink to do the same to him

(Mink shoots him in the "wrist"). Finally Gladney's antagonism toward his opponent collapses; he begins to identify with Mink and regard him as a brother in adversity: "I felt I did honor to both of us . . . by merging our fortunes, physically leading him to safety" (315). Both are now figures of the powerless male, and Gladney finds himself, on the way to the hospital, "growing fond" of Mink.

In DeLillo's world, where the *nom du père* is simulational or dispersed in the networks and channels of a multinational capitalism, the crisis of phallic power also suggests a crisis of representation. Roland Barthes observes that narrative provides an "Oedipal pleasure (to denude, to know, to learn the origin and the end)" and that it may be true that "every narrative . . . is a staging of the (absent, hidden, or hypostatized) father" (10). But if all narrative has traces or residues of this oedipal dynamic, in DeLillo's postmodern landscape the oedipal configuration lingers as an impossible memory forever closed off to the errant hero. The very basis of the oedipal logic of the heroic narrative is thrown into question, leading to a breakdown in the economy of representation and the collapse of heroic narrative itself.

After the debacle with Mink, Gladney finds himself back where he started—in a world where experience is so technologically mediated and processed that televised courses are offered on basic bodily functions such as "Eating and Drinking: Basic Parameters." Gladney is left in the "ambient roar" of white noise in the shopping center, in the realm of the simulacrum where signs are constantly mutating and reorganizing the consumers' cognitive world: the supermarket shelves having been rearranged, shoppers wander aimlessly, "trying to figure out the pattern, discern the underlying logic, trying to remember where they'd seen the Cream of Wheat" (325).

Thus ends DeLillo's grimly satiric allegory of the crisis of the sign in the order of the simulacrum, the dissolution of phallic power, and the exhaustion of heroic narratives of late modernity. These processes of postmodern culture, the novel suggests, are finally tied up with the issue of death. For the existential "fear and trembling" in the face of death represents that last vestige of subjectivity, that deep alterity which both threatens and delineates the self. Dylar promises to erase the awareness of death—the last absolute truth in a world of simulation, the last traces of the deep structures of a modernist consciousness. Yet as the lab technician Winnie Richards tells Gladney: "I think it's a mistake to lose one's sense of death, even one's fear of death. Isn't death the boundary we need? Doesn't it give a precious texture to life, a sense of definition? You have to ask yourself whether anything you do in this life would have beauty and meaning without the knowledge you carry of a final line, a border or limit" (228–29). Moreover, Gladney himself concurs that death provides an essential boundary that gives shape and meaning to life; "dying," he notes, "cures us of our innocence of the future" (15). And he adds: "All plots tend to move deathward. This is the nature of plots. Political plots, terrorist plots, lovers' plots, narrative plots, plots that are part of children's games" (26).

Gladney's comments imply an awareness that life or narrative "plots" presuppose an end (death), and that it is in the light of an ending that narrative (or life) takes on meaning. The passion for meaning that animates readers is the desire for an end; to eradicate a sense of ending in life or narrative is to extinguish meaning.[7] Yet the sense of boundaries and endings that define the self and give life or narrative meaning (or "heroic" possibilities, moments of self-knowledge, moments of vision) are erased in postmodern society. In a sense the processes under way in DeLillo's contemporary America—the loss of significant existential moments such as angst and the fear of death that register a space of interiority and authenticity—resemble the effects of Dylar. The "delirium" of communication, the arbitrary sign's rapturous loss of referent, and the flow of desire in late capitalism erode a sense of temporal continuity, history, limits, and endings—death included. As Murray Siskind observes, "here we don't die, we shop" (38).

In its concern with the importance of plots and narrative, therefore, *White Noise* suggests that the breakdown of grand narratives (such as the heroic narrative) does not mean a diminished reliance on plotting. Rather the novel implies that we still rely on plots and have recourse to narrative representations of some kind, that narratives still function to construct and criticize our world, that storytelling is ultimately a historical and political act.[8]

Indeed, DeLillo's novels engage historical and political issues; they do not exhibit the ahistoricism and pastiched depthlessness often associated with postmodernism. If his works exhibit the postmodern concern with the unstable nature of subjectivity and textuality, with representation and narrative process, his postmodernism retains the legacy of the modernist impulse to explore consciousness and selfhood and to create an imaginative vision that probes and criticizes its subject matter. If DeLillo uses postmodern devices like parody, pastiche, and parodic intertextual echoes, if he exhibits an interest in the play of language in the postmodern text (exhibited especially in a novel like *The Names*), these devices are deployed with a commitment to interrogate culture in America, to connect the transformations of narrative and subjectivity to cultural and historical processes.[9] Thus his depiction of postmodern culture in *White Noise* is no celebration of the ephemerality of *jouissance*. His vision of the dissolution of an older modernist subjectivity in a "mediated" world is not one of "nomadic" and flexible selves that find liberation in the play of style and image, selves that find release of primary desire from oppressive structures in a ludic postmodern "schizophrenia."[10] Nor is his parodic treatment of the patriarchal structures that underpin heroic-narrative paradigms yet another "deconstruction" that serves to remind us once again of their artifice and to expose naturalized myth, embedded ideology. Rather his novel connects the postmodern delirious and decentered subjectivity to a decentered capitalism and to the array of technological and representational apparatuses in the contemporary world—to the flood of media which disarticulates the subject and which dissolves the Faustian, Promethean, and oedipal impulses, replacing them with a new ecstasy of ever-shifting bricolage, with intersubjectivity as schizophrenic seriality.

In his depiction of a Baudrillardian landscape, therefore, DeLillo differs from Baudrillard in one important respect. Baudrillard's position toward the postmodern world is ultimately one of radical skepticism: finally there is nothing outside the play of simulations, no real in which a radical critique of the simulational society might be grounded.[11] DeLillo's writing, on the other hand, reveals a belief that fictional narrative can provide critical distance from and a critical perspective on the processes it depicts.

Given a world such as that which *White Noise* depicts, a culture based on the mode of information, there seems little chance of returning unproblematically to a modernist sensibility, with its heroic strivings for imaginative unity and an "unmediated" vision. In fact the novel suggests that to go back would be a form of nostalgia, could in fact lead in the direction of "Hitler studies" and a grim recuperation of a mythic unity and an "authenticity" of blood and soil ("the more powerful the nostalgia, the closer you come to violence," says Murray [258]). Yet the final image of Gladney suggests that DeLillo would wish to retain some aspects of the legacy of modernism (as he has done in his writing) in a postmodern world—such as the ideal of a rational, autonomous subjectivity—and that he is highly critical of a commodified, fast-image culture that threatens to bring about "the end of interiority." Gladney's modernist "last stand" is his refusal to submit to the "imaging block," in which the body is irradiated with the information of "ecstatic communication" and in which his impending death is consigned to a technologico-semiological hyperreality:

> Dr. Chakravarty wants to talk to me but I am making it a point to stay away. He is eager to see how my death is progressing. . . . He wants to insert me once more in the imaging block, where charged particles collide, high winds blow. But I am afraid of the imaging block. Afraid of its magnetic fields, its computerized nuclear pulse. (325)

A failure at heroism, Gladney shops at the supermarket and contemplates his "fear and trembling" about death, an indication that his subjectivity has yet to be completely swallowed up in the hyperreal. DeLillo's sympathies surely must be with his protagonist as Gladney holds tight to his fear of death in a society where the fear of death, like other aspects of the deep structures of subjectivity, is being transformed into images, codes, simulations, and charismatic spectacle; standing in the supermarket checkout line, Gladney ominously notes the "tabloids in the racks" and their tales of the "cults of the famous and the dead" (326).

Works Cited

Barthes, Roland. *The Pleasure of the Text*. Trans. Richard Miller. New York: Hill, 1975.

Baudrillard, Jean. "The Ecstasy of Communication." *The Anti-Aesthetic: Essays on Postmodern Culture*. Ed. Hal Foster. Port Townsend, WA: Bay, 1983. 126–34.

———. *In the Shadow of the Silent Majorities . . . or the End of the Social: And Other Essays*. Trans. Paul Foss, Paul Patton, John Johnston. New York: Semiotext(e), 1983.

———. *Jean Baudrillard: Selected Writings*. Ed. Mark Poster. Stanford: Polity, 1988.

———. *Simulations*. Trans. Paul Foss, Paul Patton, Philip Beitchman. New York: Semiotext(e), 1983.

Brooks, Peter. "Freud's Masterplot: Questions of Narrative." *Literature and Psychoanalysis: The Question of Reading Otherwise*. Ed. Shoshana Felman. Baltimore: Johns Hopkins, 1982. 280–300.

Crary, Jonathan. "Eclipse of the Spectacle." *Art after Modernism: Rethinking Representation*. Ed. Brian Wallis. New York: New Museum of Contemporary Art, 1984. 282–94.

DeLillo, Don. *White Noise*. London: Picador, 1986.

Hutcheon, Linda. *The Politics of Postmodernism*. London: Routledge, 1989.

Jameson, Fredric. "Postmodernism and Consumer Society." *The Anti-Aesthetic: Essays on Postmodern Culture*. Ed. Hal Foster. Port Townsend, WA: Bay, 1983. 111–25.

———. "Postmodernism, or the Cultural Logic of Late Capitalism." *New Left Review* 146 (1984): 53–92.

Kellner, Douglas. "Baudrillard, Semiurgy, and Death." *Theory, Culture, and Society* 4 (1987): 125–46.

———. Jean Baudrillard: *From Marxism to Postmodernism and Beyond*. Stanford: Stanford UP, 1989.

Kroker, Arthur, and Marilouise Kroker. "Thesis on the Disappearing Body and the Hyper-Modern Condition." *Body Invaders: Panic Sex in America*. Ed. Arthur Kroker and Marilouise Kroker. New York: St. Martin's, 1987. 20–34.

Lentricchia, Frank. "Don DeLillo." *Raritan* 8.4 (1989): 1–29.

Lyotard, Jean-François. *The Postmodern Condition: A Report on Knowledge*. Trans. Geoff Bennington and Brian Massumi. Minneapolis: U of Minnesota P, 1983.

Morris, Matthew J. "Murdering Words: Language in Action in Don DeLillo's *The Names*." *Contemporary Literature* 30 (1989): 113–27.

Polan, Dana. "Brief Encounters: Mass Culture and the Evacuation of Sense." *Studies in Entertainment: Critical Approaches to Mass Culture*. Ed. Tania Modleski. Bloomington: Indiana UP, 1986. 167–87.

Poster, Mark. *Foucault, Marxism, and History: Mode of Production versus Mode of Information*. New York: Cambridge UP, 1984.

Notes

I wish to thank David C. Harlan for his helpful comments on this essay.

    1.   For a discussion of *Libra* and DeLillo's mediascapes, see Lentricchia 10–29.

    2.   In this formulation of Baudrillard's position, I am indebted to Crary 285–86 and Kellner, "Baudrillard" 126–27.

    3.   Here I am indebted to a considerable extent to Lentricchia 7–10.

    4.   The issue of death provides another comparison between Baudrillard and DeLillo. For both, death is the ultimate signified, the single natural event which ultimately cannot be subsumed into simulacra, models, and codes. As Baudrillard conjectures in *Symbolic Exchanges*

and Death, "Perhaps only death, the reversibility of death is of a higher order than the code. Only symbolic disorder can breach the code" (*Jean Baudrillard* 122). And for both Baudrillard and DeLillo the symbolic mediations of contemporary society deprive the individual of an intimate relation with death, with the result that society is haunted by the fear of mortality (Kellner, *Jean Baudrillard* 104).

     5.   Baudrillard similarly notes the collapse of signification into mere "signals" in postmodern society. For a discussion of Baudrillard and the "signal," see Poster 29.

     6.   I am indebted here to Dana Polan's discussion of the father figure and transnational capitalism; see Polan 178. For another discussion of the same issue, see Kroker and Kroker 27.

     7.   For a discussion of the relationship between narrative and death (to which I am indebted here), see Brooks 283–84.

     8.   Linda Hutcheon argues that much postmodern diction reflects the view that we are still reliant on narrative representations in our verbal discourses in spite of the demise of grand narratives; see Hutcheon 49. Jean-François Lyotard, of course, argues that "little narratives"— among which are literary texts devoted to a flexible "narrative pragmatics"—operate in the absence of master narratives and are in fact antagonistic to any grand totalizing narrative (20).

     9.   In an article on *The Names,* Matthew J. Morris similarly argues for a political effectiveness and commitment for DeLillo's postmodernism, despite its interest in language play (121).

     10.   Here DeLillo differs from Baudrillard. Baudrillard may decry the "obscene delirium of communication," but as Douglas Kellner points out, his more recent works speculate that even though the disappearance of the subject "might create dizziness or even panic," there may nevertheless be "new pleasures and new modes of being awaiting us as we de-subjectify and progressively objectify ourselves" (*Jean Baudrillard* 175).

     11.   See Kellner, *Baudrillard* 90.

The Fable of the Ants:
Myopic Interactions in DeLillo's *Libra*

BILL MILLARD

There are only two things in the world. Things that are true. And things that are truer than true.

— Weird Beard (Russell Lee Moore, a.k.a. Russ Knight),
KLIF disk jockey in *Libra*

I. PARANOIAS AND PARADIGMS: WHO'S AFRAID OF DON DELILLO?

One of the most challenging qualities that Frank Lentricchia finds in Don DeLillo is that he "offers us no myth of political virginity preserved, no 'individuals' who are not expressions of—and responses to—specific historical processes" ("Introducing" 241). While most mainstream fiction of the Reagan era is marked by regionalisms and privatisms that bespeak an alarming poverty of imagination, DeLillo dares to project a world in its full political complexity and to grapple with ideas that might make some sense of events observed in the public sphere. Working within a culture that was both postmodern and nostalgic, a culture that longed for the pieties of laissez-faire economics and Euro-American bourgeois individualism while its socioeconomic institutions were busily breaking down any remaining space for individuals or individuality, DeLillo recognized that the 1980s could not be understood without attention to the problem of individual behavior in a social sphere hypersaturated with the products of signifying systems. The "seven seconds that broke the back of the American century" (*Libra* 181) is a superb symbolic moment on which to focus such attention, since it is obviously much more than a symbol.

To publish a historical novel that posited a plausible chain of events leading to the assassination of John Kennedy was more than an act of defiant

Originally published in *Postmodern Culture* 4, no. 2 (1994), 12 January 2000 <http://muse.jhu.edu/journals/postmodern_culture/v004/4.2allen.html>. Copyright © 1994 Bill Millard. Reprinted by permission.

imagination or political chutzpah; it raised the stakes for the enterprise of fiction within a culture rapidly losing its allegiance to written language as a practical means of organizing experience. *Libra* makes the implicit claim that no matter what one might believe of the lone-gunman theory or the Warren Commission's report—in CIA master-researcher Nicholas Branch's view, "the megaton novel James Joyce would have written if he'd moved to Iowa City and lived to be a hundred" (181)—the assembly of explanatory narratives from the available evidence surrounding the events at Dealey Plaza is as legitimate a concern for a novelist as for any journalist, historian, or member of an investigative body. Given the evidentiary problems surrounding this assassination, the unexplained (or unsatisfyingly explained) deaths of participants in these events and witnesses to them, and the proliferation of conspiracy theories of varying degrees of credibility, the novelist may in fact be on stronger ground than members of these other fields in asserting truth claims about Kennedy's death.

This position depends on a precise characterization of the nature of a historical truth claim. *Libra* achieves its disruptive force by offering a fresh paradigm by which an event like the Kennedicide may be understood. This paradigm[1] is post-individualist, while accounting for individual actions and decisions within social signifying systems; it refuses both the easy gambit of universal skepticism toward the possibility of explaining such an event and the equally easy temptation of overreaching causal conjecture. It is immune to charges that might be lodged from opposite directions: the accusation of credulity, involving the sense of universal connectivity associated with conspiracy theory (regarded as paranoid in both the vernacular and the Pynchonian senses), and that of ahistorical nihilism, involving the disjunctivity of explanations that lodge sole culpability with Oswald (and thus reduce an incident with massive social causes and consequences to private motivation, mere inexplicable insanity). DeLillo's text implies an interpretive paradigm that neither overplays nor underplays its hand, connecting events with participants' intentions while eschewing any model of those intentions as deliberate, purposeful, or necessarily connected with their outcomes.

Libra's reception among the guardians of a conceptual border between fiction and the presumably nonfictional discourses of history, politics, and journalism was venomous to an astonishing but hardly inexplicable degree. Like Lentricchia, journalist Hal Crowther assesses the vituperation directed at DeLillo by George F. Will and Jonathan Yardley of the *Washington Post* as a significant barometer of the book's power, an indication of the authoritarian paranoia that it arouses—a deeper and truer paranoia than the accounts Oliver Stone, James Garrison, the aficionado of the Austin bookstore's "Conspiracy" section in *Slacker,* or any caller to a WBAI-FM talk show might conjure. Crowther posits a credible reason why the paranoia in corporate journalism's higher circles might mirror or exceed the paranoia in the lower: "At the *Post* they love to talk about Watergate, but they don't want to talk about

Dallas. Establishment journalists know in their guts that they chickened out on the biggest story of their time and left it to fringe players and exhumers of Elvis" (330).[2]

Both of the *Post* commentators are sniffishly dismissive of the political implications of *Libra,* but Will also makes an explicit case for historical disjunctivism: "It takes a steady adult nerve to stare unblinkingly at the fact that history can be jarred sideways by an act that signifies nothing but an addled individual's inner turmoil" (qtd. in Crowther 323). Characteristically, Will takes a reasonable-sounding position in favor of willfully limiting the reach of historical reasoning. One may safely presume that any historian, journalist, congressional investigator, or novelist does desire "a steady adult nerve," but Will's argument fails to consider why causal inquiry must stop with the observation of individual pathology.

Oswald, as DeLillo represents him in *Libra,* is indeed addled—afflicted, apparently congenitally, with a moderately severe combination of dyslexia and dysgraphia—and in constant personal turmoil. Will's criticism thus seems not only disproportionate but misapplied to this novel. In depicting a clueless gunman who bases his actions on romantic adolescent notions of political destiny, plays into the hands of nearly every conspirator or would-be conspirator around him, and even carries the requisite familial baggage for the privatistic banalities of Freudian interpretation (absent father, domineering mother, and largely repressed but recurrent gay desires), doesn't DeLillo provide individual-pathology theorists with all the evidence they need? But the crucial distinction here is between a reading that incorporates individual pathology and an individualist, disjunctivist reading. DeLillo's offense, beyond merely "exhibit[ing] the same skepticism that was almost universal at the time the Warren Report was released" (Crowther 323), is continuing the investigation into and through the pathological individual. Oswald is pathological without being particularly distinct from his surroundings.

Will and Yardley's wagon-circling responses to *Libra* also resemble Tom Wolfe's comments about Noam Chomsky's theories of the structural imperatives of the news media within the corporate state, included in the documentary *Manufacturing Consent* (1992). Wolfe derisively dismisses Chomsky's argument about control over the limits of permissible public debate on the grounds that it would require the manipulation of the media by a cabal of plotters, presumably gathered in a single room—a laughably cinematic image of organized malignity, mirrored from the right by Gen. Edwin Walker's rant about the "Real Control Apparatus":

> The Apparatus is precisely what we can't see or name. We can't measure it, gentlemen, or take its photograph. It is the mystery we can't get hold of, the plot we can't uncover. This doesn't mean there are no plotters. They are elected officials of our government, Cabinet members, philanthropists, men who know each other by secret signs, who work in the shadows to control our lives. (*Libra* 283)

Because his account of the Chomskyist critique adheres to the same individual-intentionalist paradigm, Wolfe cannot imagine a controlled discourse without conscious and practically omnipotent controllers; because they refuse to entertain possibilities beyond Warren Report orthodoxy and rational intentionalism, Will and Yardley conflate DeLillo with the "fringe players and exhumers of Elvis." To posit mechanisms by which fringe players operate is hardly to embrace the fringe oneself. Like Chomsky elucidating the hard-wired requirements of the information industry, DeLillo outlines certain inevitable tendencies of organized sub rosa actions, aware that those tendencies go into effect no matter who does the organizing or why.

Cluelessness is indeed central to the actions of this novel, but it is crucial to recognize that cluelessness in this political atmosphere is by no means limited to Oswald. From Win Everett's private mixture of motivations (only belatedly incorporating the recognition that "the idea of death is woven into the nature of every plot" [221]) to David Ferrie's sexual desires and religious mysticism, private perceptions with distinct limits shape the actions of each participant in the action of Libra. A plot against JFK arises, but without the conscious guidance of its master plotters. It is a conspiracy that Wolfe, Will, and Yardley would not recognize, an overarching "deathward logic" (221) that encompasses clever players like George de Mohrenschildt, whose loathing for Gen. Walker elicits his only expressions of strong emotion (55–56), and the CIA's Laurence Parmenter ("part of the Groton-Yale-OSS network of so-called gentlemen spies . . . the pure line, a natural extension of schoolboy societies, secret oaths and initiations" [30]) along with willfully delusional Birchers like Guy Banister, who spends late-night hours poring masturbatorily over his "final nightmare file" purporting to document "Red Chinese troops . . . being dropped into the Baja by the fucking tens of thousands," and who "wanted to believe it was true. He did believe it was true. But he also knew it wasn't" (351–52). Each conspirator, seeing no further than his own interests, fears, or desires for revenge, moves in a private direction; the resultant vector of all these individual movements is something no individualist interpreter dares call conspiracy.

II. INSECTS AND INSUBORDINATIONS: A MYOPIC-INTERACTION MODEL

An interdisciplinary model of collective behavior that develops its own directionality, regardless of any single participant's agenda, comes from the improbable intersection of two fields of study: entomology (as practiced on an amateur basis by a budding physicist) and computer science. Richard Feynman, recalling his home experiments with ants' navigational behavior, finds that the insects either move randomly or follow each other's trails, and that the repetition of small deviations when they follow each other results in a composite trail that gives the illusory appearance of order.

> One question that I wondered about was why the anttrails look so straight and nice. The ants look as if they know what they're doing, as if they have a good sense of geometry. Yet the experiments that I did to try to demonstrate their sense of geometry didn't work. . . . At first glance it looks like efficient, marvelous, brilliant cooperation. But if you look at it carefully, you'll see that it's nothing of the kind. (95–96)

None of Feynman's ants moves individually in a straight line, but the collective movement nevertheless produces a straight line, simulating purposeful effort.

Transylvanian computer scientist Alfred Bruckstein, working with mathematical pursuit problems at the Technion in Haifa, Israel, has formalized Feynman's conjecture, proving the theorem that an initially disorderly series of pursuit paths will converge to the straight segment connecting the initial point of departure, e.g., an anthill, and the destination of the original "pioneer ant," e.g., a recently discovered food source (Bruckstein 60–61). His model of "global behavior that results from simple and local interaction rules" (62) has implications for robotics as well as for the behavior of animal colonies. It also has implications for the behavior of human organizations, at least metaphorically—and perhaps, if one notes its resemblance to the "political resultant" theory used in the field of geopolitical decision analysis (Allison 7–8), literally as well.[3] If "globally optimal solutions for navigation problems can be obtained as a result of myopic cooperation between simple agents or processors" (Bruckstein 62), can any form of multiple myopia—perhaps the combined myopias of a disgraced, "buried," and resentful CIA agent; a soldier of fortune with no fixed address and undiscernible loyalties; a disease-obsessed and mystically inclined pilot, sacked from an airline job because of institutional homophobia, who contemplates developing hypnotism as a weapon and claims to "believe in everything" (*Libra* 314–15); and a dyslexic political naif who daydreams of merging with the flow of history—also give the appearance of directed movement?

In the national security state as depicted by DeLillo, myopic interaction is not a human imperfection in an otherwise efficient system; it is built into the system from the outset. During the planning that resulted in the Bay of Pigs invasion, Everett and Parmenter were part of a layered and deliberately fragmented bureaucracy, described by DeLillo in parodically numbing detail:

> The first stage, the Senior Study Effort, consisted of fourteen high officials, including presidential advisers, ranking military men, special assistants, undersecretaries, heads of intelligence. They met for an hour and a half. Then eleven men left the room, six men entered. The resulting group, called SE Aug-

mented, met for two hours. Then seven men left, four men entered, including Everett and Parmenter. This was SE Detailed, a group that developed specific covert operations and then decided which members of SE Augmented ought to know about these plans. Those members in turn wondered whether the Senior Study Effort wanted to know what was going on in stage three.

Chances are they didn't. When the meeting in stage three was over, five men left the room and three paramilitary officers entered to form Leader 4. Win Everett was the only man present at both the third and fourth stages. (20)

The point of all this Beckettish enumeration is not simply that antlike bureaucrats come and go, talking of Guantanamo, but that the form of rationality peculiar to such organizations depends precisely on minimizing the possibility that anyone might know enough to comprehend the full narrative:

> Knowledge was a danger, ignorance a cherished asset. In many cases the DCI, the Director of Central Intelligence, was not to know important things. The less he knew, the more decisively he could function. It would impair his ability to tell the truth at an inquiry or a hearing, or in an Oval Office chat with the President, if he knew what they were doing in Leader 4, or even what they were talking about, or muttering in their sleep. . . .
>
> It was the President, of course, who was the final object of their protective instincts. They all knew that JFK wanted Castro cooling on a slab, but they weren't allowed to let on to him that his guilty yearning was the business they'd charged themselves to carry out. The White House was to be the summit of unknowing. (21–22)

Resemblances to the Reagan-Bush White House, the unpenetrating Tower hearings into the Iran-*contra* phase of covert national security operations, and the doctrine of "plausible deniability" are perfectly coincidental, of course. But the plot against Castro, taking grimly comic turns at first (poisoned or exploding cigars, "a poison pen in the works . . . testing a botulin toxin on monkeys . . . fungus spores in his scuba suit" [21]), then culminating in the botched invasion at the Bay of Pigs, serves as a kind of prologue-plot, prefiguring the myopically planned spectacle of Dealey Plaza. When the control of public events requires the diffusion of awareness and dispersal of control, it is unsurprising that Everett's initial idea of a theatrically managed, well-controlled near miss—as executed, or functionally interpreted, by black-ops technician T-Jay Mackey and his team of shooters, including "Leon" Oswald—goes out of control, its multiple shades of signification simplified to the brutality of an actual hit.

The tendency toward myopic interactions pervades the official and unofficial national security apparatus, not only in the Bay of Pigs fiasco but in the meetings that continue after the official dispersal of groups such as Leader 4 and SE Detailed. "True believers" like the men of Leader 4 may be too "overresponsive to policy shifts, light-sensitive, unpredictable" (22) to continue in covert operations, but they carry on meeting obsessionally out of sheer momentum, a shadow-cabal without real powers (and a caricature of Tom Wolfe's vision of conspirators). Everett, the one agent who knew enough details of the anti-Castro operations to serve as the Agency equivalent of a pioneer ant, is relegated to the emasculated existence of a planted fake professor at Texas Woman's University, repeating pointless movements:

> Mary Frances watched him butter the toast. He held the edges of the slice in his left hand, moved the knife in systematic strokes, over and over. Was he trying to distribute the butter evenly? Or were there other, deeper requirements? It was sad to see him lost in small business, eternally buttering, turning routine into empty compulsion, without meaning or need. (16)

He imagines a painting commemorating the confrontation of Leader 4 with agents of the CIA's Office of Security, titling this canvas "Light Entering the Cave of the Ungodly" (24)—implying religiosity and the Fall, not instrumental rationality, which they have tried for a time and found inoperative.

III. CINEMA AND SIMULACRA: THE FALLACY OF FORENSIC ROMANCE

Everett and his fellow ex-"clandestines" are drawn to pointless activity as lapsing believers are drawn to ritual, no longer convinced that their actions have political content, but compelled to continue them nonetheless. They are not so much a conspiracy as the simulacrum of a conspiracy, performing according to a script whose composition is ongoing and is not under their control. They have effects on history, but hardly the "personal contribution to an informed public. . . . the major subtext and moral lesson" (53) that Everett hopes will ensue, redeeming him in the eyes of history. He fails to see that this romantic vision (the truth seeing the light of day!) is incompatible with the simulacral nature of postmodern political activity—that his plan's complex elegance is unlikely to survive its implementation by field operatives such as Mackey and Wayne Elko, who have consumed too many images of themselves as Seven Samurai (145) to be reliable executors of subtle instructions (much as follower ants simplify the intricate paths of a pioneer ant).[4] Once Everett has embraced the politics of the public image, hoping to manipulate the media and the Agency through the perception of a vengeful Castro—publicly raising the question of just what actions Castro is seeking to avenge—he reveals his myopia: he forgets that the politics of the public image tends to embrace you back.

It is practically inevitable that a consideration of *Libra,* with its displacements of agency and its recurrent coincidences between engineered events and happenstance ("It was no longer possible to hide from the fact that Lee

Oswald existed independent of the plot" [178]), will lead to a Baudrillardian vision of social processes. The use of Oswald, Boy Marxist, as the instrument of the anti-Castroite conspiracy (a "negative Libran" [315] whom Ferrie believes might flip in either direction) is a clear example of Baudrillard's "Moebius-spiralling negativity" whereby

> [a]ll the hypotheses of manipulation are reversible in an endless whirli-
> gig. . . . Is any given bombing . . . the work of leftist extremists, or of extreme
> right-wing provocation, or staged by centrists to bring every terrorist extreme
> into disrepute and to shore up its own failing power . . . ? All this is equally
> true, and the search for proof, indeed the objectivity of the fact does not check
> this vertigo of interpretation. (30–31)

Even the *Post*'s pet conspiracy Watergate was a nonscandal to Baudrillard, a show trial designed to create a "moral superstructure" (27) behind which the amoral capitalist state can function. To interpret such events as struggles of right and left over rationally expressible questions of public interest—rather than structural fictions obscuring the fact that the Watergate break-in and cover-up, or whatever plot culminated in Dealey Plaza, were closer to normative than exceptional state behavior[5]—is to mistake vertigo for orientation.

Power, in Baudrillard's vision, both uses and fears simulacra. It strives for a monopoly on simulation, punishing acts such as a theatrical "fake hold-up" (39); it fears unsanctioned simulation more than it fears violent transgression, precisely because simulation "always suggests, over and above its object, that *law and order themselves might really be nothing more than a simulation*" (38, emphasis Baudrillard's). The Everett/Parmenter/Banister/Mackey/ Elko/Raymo/Ferrie/Oswald mechanism converts the near-miss, a simulation that might have publicized sensitive covert operations, into a hit on Kennedy, a shock that the state apparatus can ultimately absorb. Sociopolitical structures could tolerate actual violence against this president, but not symbolic violence against the system of signs that functions as protective coloration for the operations of capital. "Power can stage its own murder to rediscover a glimmer of existence and legitimacy. Thus with American presidents: the Kennedys are murdered because they still have a political dimension. Others . . . only had a right to puppet attempts, to simulated murders" (37).

Discourses of truth come in for rough treatment in Baudrillard's world, and the figures in *Libra* who try to enact discourses of truth are likewise disoriented and defeated. At the opposite end of the plot from the hapless Everett, who thought he could induce media hyperreality to do the work of the real, sits Nicholas Branch, performing historical reconstruction from the masses of evidence supplied to him by the Curator. Branch, the would-be panoptical reader who can synthesize the entire mass of materials into a credible historical truth claim, is at first driven to complete his history whether or not anyone will ever read it. It steadily becomes apparent to him, however, that he is performing a simulacrum of research. His position is both a scholar's heaven, with apparently infinite research materials provided instantly on request, and a scholar's hell of overabundance and nonintegration; his papery environment is hallucinatorily Borgesian, part Library of Babel and part Garden of Forking Paths. Branch is *Homo documentarius,* linear-thinking Gutenbergian Man, with his logical and recombinatory faculties underscored in his surname,[6] but his attempt at a definitive reconstruction of the Kennedicide peters out as miserably as Everett's attempt to send true information to the public.

For his naive belief in the possibility of a realist discourse about Dealey Plaza, Branch receives a different form of knowledge, which he comes to interpret as a form of punishment, from the sources he depends on. He is damned to an eternal investigation, drowned in information that is sensory as well as documentary, including the contradictory, the irrelevant, and the gruesome. The primary texts that the Curator continues to send him include not only the obligatory Zapruder film (that most exhaustively scrutinized of cinematic texts) but autopsy photos, "the results of ballistics tests carried out on human skulls and goat carcasses, on blocks of gelatin mixed with horsemeat. . . . an actual warped bullet that has been fired for test purposes through the wrist of a seated cadaver. We are on another level here, Branch thinks. Beyond documents now. They want me to touch and smell. . . . The bloody goat heads seem to mock him. He begins to think this is the point" (299). In place of the coherence of an explainable conspiracy, he comes to see the plot as "a rambling affair that succeeded in the short term due mainly to chance. Deft men and fools, ambivalence and fixed will and what the weather was like"—yet "[t]he stuff keeps coming" (441), defying comprehension at Branch's end of the plot just as events defied control at Everett's. Instead of attaining the closure one expects from a narrative syntagm, the successful completion of his forensic romance, Branch becomes the Sisyphus of mediated information. He is still reading signs at the close of the novel; he has still written little; he has accepted a grim role as the goatherd of historical hell, keeper of the unintelligible secrets of the state.

IV. INFOCIDE

DeLillo's plot is a nightmarish parable of the transmission of any type of consequential information through the public sphere under late capitalism. The sender, mediators, and receiver of the message (Everett, the other conspirators, and Branch, respectively) are all maintained in a state of myopia throughout the process; the initial message is replaced by an antithetical counter-message and never reaches its true intended receiver, the politically responsible public. This is precisely as ruling-class apologists of George Will's ilk would have it, of course, with forensic interpretation forestalled and political accountability rendered risible. Useful communication is stultified under such conditions; the state's literal control apparatus (from police to spies) becomes redundant, if not vestigial, when much of the citizenry is occupied with information-games that lack real referents and consequences. In Baudrillard's glum description of daily life in the realm of infinite simulation, there is "[n]o more violence or surveillance; only 'information,' secret virulence, chain reaction, slow implosion and simulacra of spaces where the real-effect again comes into play. We are witnessing the end of perspective and panoptic space" (54).

The capitalist polity, of course, has always had its own defensive mythologies to characterize its processes as positively benign. The theory of myopic interactions is by no means the only case of insect behavior offering a metaphoric explanation of human behavior. If, under this paradigm, a series of antlike actions in pursuit of private interests combine to result in public calamity, one formative myth of the early capitalist era uses another arthropod collective to extol the processes that Adam Smith would anthropomorphize and anatomize some 70 years later as capitalism's benevolent Invisible Hand. Bernard Mandeville's *The Fable of the Bees: or, Private Vices, Publick Benefits,* first appearing in 1705, offers a conceptual structure remarkably similar to Bruckstein's. His beehive prospers as long as it tolerates a rich array of interlocking iniquities, but it loses both its wealth and its power relative to other hives when it gives in to the impulses of reform, economic leveling, and anti-imperialism. A critical difference between these two images of human-society-as-insect-colony is that Mandeville, while applauding the system that transmutes private vices into public benefits, also inverts the equation and identifies public-spiritedness itself, on an individual scale, with disaster on the social scale. Throughout the period of capital's social dominance, it seems, one encounters a form of consciousness that willfully refuses to form a lucid and integrative social vision.

Mandeville's account of apian society is founded on the same sort of macro/micro disjunction by which Feynman and Bruckstein explain formic navigation: behavior that looks like error or disorder at the individual level combines with other such behavior to produce order for the collective. Like any capitalist utilitarian, pre-Marxian or post-, Mandeville rationalized the glaring class distinctions among his bees with the observation that "Industry / Had carry'd Life's Conveniences, / It's real Pleasures, Comforts, Ease, / To such a Height, the very Poor / Lived better than the Rich before" (ll. 198–202). This is the classical rationalization of inequities and iniquities under capitalism; it would recur in the Reaganite trope of a rising tide lifting all boats. And Mandeville's identification of social reform as counterproductive, removing the incentives that drive the invisible hand, would recur nearly three centuries later in Margaret Thatcher's denouncements of any public policy based on compassion or economic justice as tearfully sentimental, or "wet."

The same contempt for social interaction reaches a peak of comic exaggeration in *Libra* when David Ferrie, joking with Mafioso Carmine Latta (who will later manipulate Jack Ruby into taking his role in the script) about the Cold War apocalypse that might ensue if the U.S. tried to bomb Cuba to retrieve it from the Communists for the mob, asserts a positive preference for postnuclear Hobbesianism:

> . . . I like the idea of living in shelters. You go in the woods and dig your personal latrine. The sewer system is a form of welfare state. It's a government funnel to the sea. I like to think of people being independent, digging latrines in the woods, in a million backyards. Each person is responsible for his own shit. (173)

How clearly can one distinguish this parodic hyperindividualism from the attitude expressed in the *Impeach Earl Warren* signs[7] and swastika graffiti that sends Weird Beard into nervous premonitory improvisations? (381–82).

On a fundamental level, communication itself is at odds with the belief system shared by Mandeville, Will, Reagan (the "Great Communicator"!), Ferrie, Latta, Gen. Walker, and the looming Bircher population of 1963 Dallas. This is a community that has been immunized against community, unified in acceptance of fragmentation. Much has been written about the proliferation of signifiers from commercial culture in DeLillo's works, and about how these intersecting messages shred the idea of an individual consciousness: "a whole network of popular mythology, allowing DeLillo to show how the possibilities of meaning and action are shaped by the contemporary *ethos* of simultaneity and indeterminacy. . . . Character, the transformation and realization of the novelistic subject's depth through narrative time, is replaced by the notion of character as a function of the frequently self-canceling languages of representation in which the novelistic self is situated" (Wacker 70–71).

These environments are so oversaturated with disconnected messages that they pose a risk of what one might call "death by information"—a particular hazard for someone like Oswald, who lacks (probably for hereditary neurologic reasons) the integrative capacity that makes purposeful linguistic behavior possible. For all his protestations about economic injustice, Oswald's image of Communism is a consumer item, a boy's perverse fantasy of becoming the Other the whole culture fears; the roles of Stalin and Trotsky are natural outgrowths of teenage idol-worship, exotic alternatives to John Wayne, in whose screen-sanctified presence he also bathes while on mess duty at Corregidor (93–94). He forgets to visit Trotsky's house in Mexico City, and "[t]he sense of regret makes him feel breathless, physically weak, but he shifts out of it quickly, saying so what" (358), like a visitor to Hollywood missing part of a

Universal Studios tour. Writing his Historic Diary while in Russia, he is "[s]tateless, word-blind":

> Always the pain, the chaos of composition. He could not find order in the field of little symbols. They were in the hazy distance. He could not clearly see the picture that is called a word. A word is also a picture of a word. He saw spaces, incomplete features, and tried to guess the rest.
>
> He made wild tries at phonetic spelling. But the language tricked him with its inconsistencies. He watched sentences deteriorate, powerless to make them right. The nature of things was to be elusive. Things slipped through his perceptions. He could not get a grip on the runaway world. (211)

Word-blindness is not the same thing as ignorance: "He knew things. It wasn't that he didn't know" (211). Spymaster Marion Collings gives Oswald a recruiting speech about the interpretive importance of context—"A fact is innocent until someone wants it. Then it becomes intelligence. . . . An old man eating a peach is intelligence if it's August and the place is the Ukraine and you're a tourist with a camera. . . . There's still a place for human intelligence" (247)—but Oswald is unsuited for this type of cognitive work. He incorporates within his own cranium the perspectivelessness and disconnection of the whole culture; he is a living representative of a myopically interactive informational realm.

Death by information goes hand in hand with the death of information. In a hyperreal environment where messages are infinitely reproducible and convertible, Collings' elision of the two meanings of "intelligence" (the raw informational material itself and the human skill at making sense of it) metastasizes throughout the culture, and the former overcomes the latter. As William Cain observes after discussing this passage, "in American culture, there are always more facts, more intelligence. . . . The irony is that the spread of information fails to lead to clearer meaning and more finely focused intelligence. People assemble knowledge, and its transmission from person to person and place to place does signify, yet the import of it all stays mysterious" (281). Such a quantity of information ensures that little or no actual informing ever occurs.

Is the dominance of the myopic-interaction paradigm absolute? Does *Libra* reinforce "what we darkly suspect about the postmodern alteration of the mind" (Cain 281)? The bathetic but intensely imagined monologue by Marguerite Oswald (448–456), patching together incoherent cliches and insights until they achieve a desperate coherence, concludes *Libra* in a minor key, but it is hardly the same fatalistic minor key in which Baudrillard composes. Implicitly, at least on a metafictional level, passages like this imply that it is still possible to select information from the ceaseless media Babel and combine it in ways that generate power (at least if one has Don DeLillo's ear for the spoken American language). The question remains whether the borders between art-language and world-language are permeable.

For one alternative to communicative myopia, one can do worse than return to the empiricist intelligence of Richard Feynman. The ant-navigation paradigm is opposed in his text by a recurrent behavioral model that equates global awareness of purpose with problem-solving effectiveness. The most explicit description of this informed-interaction model occurs in the long chapter "Los Alamos from Below," where he recounts his experiences working on the Bomb. Security interests have mandated the fragmentation of knowledge—with a level of control and surveillance that can properly be called paranoid, however justifiable under wartime conditions—but Feynman intuits that disseminating more knowledge about the project among technical workers will improve the quality and efficiency of their work. Experience proves him right:

> The real trouble was that no one had ever told these fellows anything. The army had selected them from all over the country for a thing called Special Engineer Detachment—clever boys from high school who had engineering ability. They sent them up to Los Alamos. They put them in barracks. And they would tell them nothing.
> Then they came to work, and what they had to do was work on IBM machines—punching holes, numbers that they didn't understand. Nobody told them what it was. The thing was going very slowly. I said that the first thing there has to be is that these technical guys know what we're doing. Oppenheimer went and talked to the security and got special permission. . . .
> Complete transformation! They began to invent ways of doing it better. They improved the scheme. They worked at night. . . . [A]ll that had to be done was to tell them what it was. (127–128)

The bureaucrats who set up Special Engineer Detachment counted on the efficacy of myopic interactions, under the assumption that only a small coterie (analogous to the pioneer ant that knows the location of the food) could be trusted with information about the direction of the collective endeavor, but Feynman explicitly demonstrates the superiority of informed interactions for certain types of operations. What works for ants and assassins does not necessarily improve results for engineers, and DeLillo's account of the information-structures that produced the Kennedicide—regardless of whether the specific events he imagines to occupy that structural framework are veridical, a proposition unlikely ever to be confirmed or disproved—qualifies him as something like a conceptual engineer. This status adds weight to his works' implicit claim to have influence in the public sphere.

In *Mao II,* DeLillo extends and deepens the intimation that the Gutenberg/Branch paradigm cannot make sense of the postmodern era's public events. The transition from the world of *Libra* to that of *Mao II*—perhaps a paradigm shift within DeLillo's work to mirror the one he sees occurring in the political world—becomes clear toward the conclusion of the latter book as Bill Gray approaches death, sensing that his form of information is in eclipse during the days of Moon and Khomeini (" 'What terrorists gain, novelists lose' " [157]). The literary world where he once enjoyed ferocious debate with his friend and editor Everson is in decline, eroded by the perks of capital (" 'Who owns this company?' 'You don't want to know.' 'Give me the whole big story in one quick burst.' 'It's all about limousines' " [101–02]). His belief that his actions have public consequences is also in decline; his agreeing to meet with Abu Rashid's hostage-holders represents the beginning of a prolonged suicide for both Gray and his mode of thought. Moving eastward toward the rendezvous and the grave, Gray sustains an inner monologue that retreats from public observation into the myopic realm of personal and familial nostalgia.

The individual artist in language, this plot implies, is obsolete because he has always been bounded by, and bound to, his privacy—an artifact of a social order that no longer exists. Yet Gray's language is succeeded by a different language, that of Brita Nilsson's camera. She does not refuse to participate in history; her gesture to unmask the armed youth at the end of her meeting with Abu Rashid dramatizes her willingness to be an active participant in events, not a passive recorder (236). She, like DeLillo, is still a public citizen and an artist who can surprise the public; her visual language produces factual texts that are indeed selected—hardly the panoptical god's-eye view of a would-be master historian like Branch, or of the illusory "objective" news media—but selected with the informed, receptive eye of a new kind of informational engineer. Myopia, after all, is easily corrected with lenses.

Notes

1. I will designate this paradigm the "theory of myopic interactions," borrowing the term from Alfred Bruckstein. Bruckstein does not use the term "myopic interactions" in his *Mathematical Intelligencer* article, but the phrase is attributed to him in a brief description of this article in *Science* (April 23, 1993). It is broader in scope than the phrase he originally uses, "myopic cooperation," since it allows for noncooperative or actively antagonistic interactions such as those involving governmental operatives and Oswald or Ruby.

2. Whether they would still love to talk about Watergate after talking about it with Baudrillard, however, is an open question.

3. Graham Allison offers competing explanatory models for a particularly intricate geopolitical test case, the installation of Soviet missiles in Cuba. According to the "Rational Actor" or "classical" model, the one most foreign policy analysts and laymen have implicitly embraced, governments make decisions monolithically as individual chess players do, referring to specific defined objectives and calculating the rational means of attaining them. However, the "Organizational Process" and "Governmental (Bureaucratic) Politics" models better explain the "intra-national mechanisms" (6) that determine international behavior: each apparent monolith or chess player is in fact a black box containing competing organizations, interests, and individuals, each of whom pursues distinct and only partially compatible objectives. Analysis of the organization, routines, and relative bargaining power of these components

yields an understanding of how participants come to make irrational decisions. I am indebted to Katie Burke, MD, FACEP, for calling my attention to Allison's work and its applications to medical and governmental decision analysis, as well as to the argument presented here.

4.   Elko's identification of his paramilitary role with cinematic models is made explicit, as is his own form of myopia, when he muffs his task of killing Oswald at the arranged rendezvous site, the Texas Theater, by waiting through the feature (*Cry of Battle*) to "let the tension build. Because that's the way they do it in the movies" (412), allowing police to apprehend him instead. Staying for the second feature (*War Is Hell*) after "Leon" is removed confirms Elko's priorities.

5.   "In fact, the charges against Nixon were for behavior not too far out of the ordinary, though he erred in choosing his victims among the powerful, a significant deviation from established practice. He was never charged with the serious crimes of his Administration: the 'secret bombing' of Cambodia, for example. The issue was indeed raised, but it was the secrecy of the bombing, not the bombing itself, that was held to be the crime. . . . We might ask, incidentally, in what sense the bombing was 'secret.' Actually, the bombing was 'secret' because the press refused to expose it" (Chomsky 81–82).

6.   Branch is among the first characters introduced in the book, appearing within six pages of another Nicholas: one of young Oswald's taunting truant companions in the Bronx, Nicky Black, who "know[s] where to get these books where you spin the pages fast, you see people screwing" (8). Referring to himself in the third person as "the kid," collapsing the distinction between written language and cinema with his primitive porn, bearing the Devil's conventional given name (though "the name was always used in full, never just Nicky or Black" [8]), and vanishing from the book after a single scene, Nicky Black is the sort of background character whose very irrelevance to the narrative charges him with symbolism. When a second Nicholas B. then appears among larger, more important masses of paper, does the inference that DeLillo is setting up early subtextual linkages between an obsession with textual forms and Auld Nickie-Ben constitute interpretive overaggression?

7.   The irony of rightists calling for the impeachment of the very man who would head the commission that performed a simulacral investigation, thus protecting the plotters (in yet another Moebius-spiral), is unlikely to be lost on many readers of *Libra* but is probably lost on quite a few of the rightists.

Works Cited

Allison, Graham T. *Essence of Decision: Explaining the Cuban Missile Crisis.* Boston: Little, Brown, 1971.

Baudrillard, Jean. "The Precession of Simulacra," in *Simulations.* Trans. Paul Foss, Paul Patton, and Philip Beitchman. New York: Semiotext(e), 1983. 1–79.

Bruckstein, Alfred M. "Why the Ant Trails Look So Straight and Nice." *Mathematical Intelligencer* 15.2 (1993): 59–62.

Cain, William E. "Making Meaningful World: Self and History in *Libra.*" Rev. of DeLillo, Don, *Libra. Michigan Quarterly Review* 29.2 (1990): 275–287.

Chomsky, Noam. *Towards a New Cold War: Essays on the Current Crisis and How We Got There.* New York: Pantheon, 1982.

Crowther, Hal. "Clinging to the Rock: A Novelist's Choices in the New Mediocracy." *South Atlantic Quarterly* 89.2 (1990): 321–336.

DeLillo, Don. *Libra.* New York: Viking Penguin, 1988.

———. *Mao II.* New York: Viking, 1991.

Feynman, Richard. "Surely You're Joking, Mr. Feynman!" *Adventures of a Curious Character.* Ed. Edward Hutchings. New York: Norton, 1985.

"Follow-the-Leader Math." (News report on Bruckstein's paper, with quote from Bruckstein.) *Science* 260 (April 23, 1993): 495.

Lentricchia, Frank. "The American Writer as Bad Citizen—Introducing Don DeLillo." *South Atlantic Quarterly* 89.2 (1990): 239–244.

————. *"Libra* as Postmodern Critique." *South Atlantic Quarterly* 89.2 (1990): 431–453. Originally published in *Raritan* 8.4 (1989): 1.

Mandeville, Bernard. The Fable of the Bees: or, Private Vices, Publick Benefits. *Eighteenth-Century English Literature.* Ed. Geoffrey Tillotson, Paul Fussell, Jr., Marshall Waingrow, and Brewster Rogerson. New York: Harcourt, 1969: 267–277.

Manufacturing Consent: Noam Chomsky and the Media. Dir. Peter Wintonick and Mark Achbar. 1992.

Slacker. Dir. Richard Linklater. 1991.

Wacker, Norman. "Mass Culture/Mass Novel: The Representational Politics of Don DeLillo's *Libra.*" *Works and Days* 8.1 (1990): 67–87.

Libra and the Subject of History

CHRISTOPHER M. MOTT

Most accounts of John F. Kennedy's assassination propose and rationalize various "theories" that trace the causes of the incident; Don DeLillo's *Libra* asserts that only effects can be traced from the event. However, in DeLillo's work these effects move into the past and into the future as the ways that we represent the assassination to ourselves. These forms of representation, the questions we ask about the episode and how we ask them, the things we look for and how we describe them, can best be described in terms of the discourse of a pervasive ideology that dominated the United States and linked it to the Soviet Union during the Cold War. More than any conspiracy theory, DeLillo's study of our ways and means for understanding ourselves reveals the problems and possibilities of recent American history.

In 1983, DeLillo wrote an article for *Rolling Stone* magazine entitled "American Blood," in which he describes the events and consequences of the assassination of President Kennedy. DeLillo believes that the assassination gave rise to or brought into focus a whole new way of perceiving reality. "What has become unraveled since that afternoon in Dallas," he tells us, "is not the plot, of course, not the dense mass of characters and events, but the sense of a coherent reality most of us shared. We seem from that moment to have entered a world of randomness and ambiguity." Furthermore, "the lines that extend from that compressed event have shown such elaborate twists and convolutions that we are almost forced to question the basic suppositions we make about our world of light and shadow, solid objects and ordinary sounds, and to wonder further about our ability to measure such things, to determine weight, mass and direction, to see things as they are, recall them clearly" (22).

In one sense, then, *Libra* is a chronicle of our time, an investigation of the episteme born in the slow-motion bloodspray of the Zapruder film and nurtured to maturity by the library of testimony, speculation, intrigue, evidence about the assassination, and, of course, the Warren Report. In another sense, however, the novel is intended as a "refuge," a "way of thinking about

Originally published in *Critique: Studies in Contemporary Fiction* 35 (1994): 131–45. Reprinted with permission of the Helen Dwight Reid Educational Foundation. Published by Heldref Publications, 1319 Eighteenth St., N.W., Washington, D.C. 20036-1802. Copyright © 1994.

the assassination without being constrained by half-facts or overwhelmed by possibilities, by the tide of speculation that widens with the years" (*Libra* "Author's Note"). On the one hand, then, *Libra* is a Foucauldian impossibility, an investigation of our own episteme, carried out much in the spirit, though nowhere near the letter, of Foucauldian historiography. On the other hand, *Libra* is a narrative, an attempt to give meaningful structure to an event that admittedly defies coherence and clarity.

Libra is both a continuation and a culmination of DeLillo's work up to 1988. The themes he found in the assassination, as well as his fictional orientation to those themes, inform each of the novels. In a recent interview, DeLillo admits to his preoccupation with the Kennedy assassination, revealing what a careful reader already knows: "A lot of tendencies in my first eight novels seemed to be collecting around the dark center of the assassination" (286). The theme of a secret or cult history that runs through *Libra* also underpins his approach to history in *Ratner's Star* and describes the activities of the Happy Valley Farm Commune in *Great Jones Street*. In addition, DeLillo's treatment of the main characters in *Libra* seems to grow out of his earlier explorations of character and subjectivity, especially as subjectivity comes to mean a subject position within an interpellative ideology. In *Running Dog* and *The Names*, DeLillo investigated the government institutions that carry out such interpellations and maintain the ideologies that position subjects. In all his novels, he has examined the danger and the necessity of structuring the flow of our lives; in *Libra* we find this necessity both at the level of the stories that the characters create to give order to their lives and at the level of the novel itself—the text that suggests relationships that link the stories and gives some coherence and structure to the narrative. However, the "dark center of the assassination" around which his novels orbit has more to do with the change in our way of perceiving the world as he described in "American Blood." All his novels explore what DeLillo characterizes as a time of uncertainty.

In *Libra*, DeLillo's attempt to describe the epistemology of our time epitomizes the other novels and diverges from them. In this novel, DeLillo is caught in a postmodern dilemma: he seems quite suspicious of structures and the effort to construct and impose "perfect structures" onto experience. At the same time his novels, *Ratner's Star* in particular, are very carefully crafted structures. *Libra* is a prime example of this dilemma. He finds himself facing a chaotic mass of data on the Kennedy assassination, a mass of data that he believes represents our time of information overload. To reduce the mind-numbing effects of such a chaotic blizzard of information, DeLillo creates sheltering structures. But are these structures also strictures? In addition to the question of narrative structure, DeLillo faces the problem of character and subjectivity. He seems uncomfortable with the notion that individuals possess a unique self to which they can retreat from the world. Yet he also vilifies the material processes (such as language and discourse) that constitute human consciousness. More accurately, *Libra* encompasses the divergence arising among the rest of the novels. This divergence parallels the divergence in postmodern historiography. On the one hand, the historiography of Hayden White foregrounds the narrativization of history. White emphasizes the structures, especially the linguistic structures such as rhetorical tropes by which we organize and give meaning (retroactively) to the flow of human events. On the other hand, Michel Foucault, although very much aware of the linguistic structures used to give coherence to human events and to create history, focuses more on the construction of subject positions initiated and maintained through the power of ideological imposition and manifested in discursive practices.

In *Libra,* DeLillo performs a historical investigation the two guiding concerns of which parallel the two principal orientations of postmodern historiography. Following the influential work of Hayden White, postmodern historiographers approach history as a cultural construct, or, more precisely, as a narrative. Moreover, this concern with narrative reflects recent narratological developments that grew out of work in semiotics and rhetoric. Both the tropological content and the structure of narrative reveal a particular set of values and beliefs held for a limited period of history. Thus, the narratological or tropological study of history is more interested in how the story is told than the story itself. By the same token, the second major orientation in postmodern historiography, the archaeological and genealogical projects of Michel Foucault, are more interested in establishing how events are perceived than in chasing the phantom of the "raw events" themselves. Foucault is interested mainly in exposing the rules that govern the dominant discourses of a particular time, the rules that determine what we can see and what we can say. These matters become epistemological in Foucault's work—and in the work of postmodern historiographers who follow his ideas—because the "reality" that we know consists of the discourses that condition our perceptions. In *Libra,* DeLillo interweaves a thread of narratological duplicity with a thread of epistemological skepticism. His depiction of the characters emphasizes their "stories" as the means by which they understand the swirl of events that surround them. In addition, the characters relate their stories not as some expression of their true nature, or the true nature of the events, or even of the true nature of their understanding of the events and themselves, but more as the documented evidence of the various versions of the world that collided in Dallas on November 22. To incorporate these stories into his text, DeLillo employs what we might call a dialogic narrative, a narrative expressed in the "voices" of the characters, themselves figures representative of specific ideologies in our recent history. Indeed, many of these voices will seem quite familiar to those acquainted with DeLillo's work.

DeLillo winds his way out of the chaotic vortex of the assassination by following a theme and its variations. In this case he has focused on an issue that remains unresolved in unspoken public debate but that he feels is obvious. The most disturbing question that haunts the American psyche about the assassination is whether or not this was the work of a "lone gunman." However, in *Libra,* this question is merely the manifestation of a contradiction at the heart of the way we perceive ourselves as a national culture. The possibility of a conspiracy unsettles our traditional notions about ourselves. Conspiracies happen in other countries: "Europeans and Middle Easterners are notoriously prone to believe in conspiracies. We were willing to grant them that quaint persuasion. They have a rich history, after all, of craft and deceit. Intricate maneuverings for advantage, cunning pursuits of power— these are Byzantine, they are Machiavellian" ("Blood" 22). The Europeans are different. We can define ourselves against them; they are our other. Their governments are based on clever schemes and alliances. Our government is based on the worth of the individual.

"American Blood" and *Libra* make clear that what is at stake here is the ideology of American government, or the American myth of America. This ideology is based on the idea(l) of the individual. Our economy is based on free competition between individuals; it depends for its success on individual "initiative." Our Constitution and Bill of Rights ostensibly protect the rights of the individual—indeed, this becomes something of a litany for Oswald throughout *Libra:* "I know my rights." DeLillo recognizes that this idea(l) informs our cultural narratives as well: "A stranger walks out of the shadows, a disaffected man, a drifter with three first names, and an Oakie look about him, tight-lipped and squinting. We think we know exactly who he is" ("Blood" 22). We have seen this man in a thousand films. The silent man. Even the epithet of the "lone gunman" has the ring of a Hollywood western. Of course the epitome of this silent, powerful stranger is John Wayne. DeLillo inserts Wayne into the narrative precisely in the capacity of the strong indiidual' as he has come to us in the cultural icon of the lonesome cowboy. Oswald sees Wayne and thinks of him in "the cattle drive in *Red River,* . . . the deep, sure voice of aging John Wayne. . . . the honest stubbled faces (men he feels he knows)" (94). Just as Oswald is a lone gunman that we think we know. Indeed, DeLillo is so intent on making his point here that immediately after describing the scene with John Wayne he tells about Oswald reading Walt Whitman. What at first seems a clash of opposites, the free-spirited Whitman and the serious and imposing Wayne, becomes resolved in light of the American myth of the individual: Walt Whitman singing his song of the self and John Wayne cutting a lonely and wide path across the prairie. *Libra* foregrounds this myth as the pervasive assumption behind the American interpretation of the assassination as the work of a loner. In other words, the myth at work here can be understood in terms of the rules that govern what we say and see about ourselves. These rules prohibit us from saying that we are a wily and conniving nation (as the Europeans are); therefore we cannot see a conspiracy at work in Kennedy's assassination.

Even Oswald himself believes in the myth of the lone individual. Early on we find out that he felt "as if there is a veil between him and other people through which they cannot reach him, but he prefers this veil to remain intact" (12). This social worker's report simply extends the informing myth in American governmental ideology. The social worker represents an institution of the government and so his or her perceptions are conditioned by this myth. The myth takes on the role of an ideology when it determines what these institutions (and the people in them) see and say. The only governmental institution that attracts Oswald is the Marine Corps. Here again we find the embodiment of this mythos. As a Marine guard beats Oswald, he recites the Marine litany based on the Marine Corps manual:

> "In the final assault," said the guard, "it is the individual Marine, with his rifle and his what, who closes with the enemy and destroys him."
> "Bayonet," the prisoner said.
> "A vigorous bayonet assault, executed by Marines eager to drive home cold steel, can do what, what, what." (104)

This passage, besides presenting vivid evidence to corroborate Malcolm X's statement that violence is as American as cherry pie, a quotation to which DeLillo refers in an interview, illustrates the mythos of the individual as it becomes a subject position in American culture. DeLillo exposes this position in the same way that Foucault analyzes a discursive formation—he reveals its site, its material manifestation, and its distinct set of rules that determine the appearance of "objects" in its field (*Archaeology* 27, 33, 38). As Foucault might appreciate, what we have here is the irony of a system based on the free individual (in battle, American soldiers are, according to our own mythology, supposed to have an edge over the numerically superior forces of the Soviet bloc because our troops act independently; they show initiative—just as the good American businessman does), the irony of a system that distinguishes itself through its promotion of individual self-determination imprisoning a man for having spoken his mind. Oswald is jailed for the "wrongful use of provoking words," but as he sees it he is in jail for demanding his "military rights." However, through ideology, forms of incarceration, even more potent than physical ones, are available. As Foucault has shown in *Discipline and Punish,* the more effective means of control uses people to police themselves. The material manifestation of this ideology, its "testament," is the Marine Corps manual. Oswald read the manual as a teenager when his brother was a Marine. However, "read" does not capture the experience. As Althusser might put it, Oswald recognized himself in the Marine Corps manual. He read "deeply in the rules, impressed by the strictness and precision, by the stream of awesome details, weird, niggling, perfect" (42). Throughout the novel, Oswald strives to perfect himself according to the Marine he imagines in himself, as revealed in his "reverie . . . [of] the powerful world of Oswald-hero, guns flashing in the dark. The reverie of control, perfection of rage, perfection of desire, the fantasy of night, rain-slick streets, the heightened shadows of men in dark coats, like men on movie posters." Once again the irony arises from the fact that Oswald considers this reverie "the true life inside him" (46).

Oswald's interpellation in the Marine Corps's version of the world, one that represents its highest value in the form of the disciplined and self-reliant individual, recalls the interpellation of Gary Harkness in *End Zone*. Both Harkness and Oswald are drawn to the apparent empowerment of perfect structures—that is, the possibility of perfectly structuring themselves. In both cases, the myth of the perfectible individual is a delusion; and in both cases, this delusion is linked to death. Harkness reduces himself to a nearly perfect state; his reduction of himself to the essential leads him close to an uncluttered state, free from distraction and error—and so free from signs of life that he must be taken to the infirmary. Perhaps Glen Selvy of *Running Dog* more closely resembles Oswald's interpellation. Selvy also reduces distractions, perfects his rage and his discipline, and ends up a headless corpse in the Texas desert. The clearest link here is with the assassination, the death in Texas. This discipline has one main purpose—to prepare the individual to kill or be killed. According to John Wayne and the ideology of American government this discipline protects individual freedom. *Libra* indicates how this ideology actually exists to cover up a powerful contradiction (see also *Archaeology* 150–51). This is the contradiction between the image of the free and self-determining individual from whose success America grows stronger and the interpellation of the individual into a regimented position in which she or he will be ordered to give up his or her life. This is the contradiction between the autonomous and unique person and the culturally determined subject position, both of which exist, though at different levels, of course, in the ideology of American government.

The ideology of American government exploits the power of myth to cover its contradictions. A myth resembles language in its need to establish difference in order to assert identity. American culture represents the individual as free and self-determining by contrasting this person to the enslaved populations of totalitarian countries. Indeed, we might take a further step, as DeLillo seems to do, by noting that myth suppresses contradiction not only by establishing difference but by projecting difference. The contradiction that threatens to become an aporia in the discourse is projected onto an other. As we have seen, in "American Blood," Americans project the evil and unmanly behavior of conspiracies onto a European other. In *Libra* this projection becomes obvious in the way that the ideology of American government maintains the myth of individual liberty by positing the "tyranny" of communist or dictatorial regimes. We all know by now that this is a mythical, if not rhetorical, construct; that in fact, the United States has backed dictators and tyrants for almost as long as we have had dictators and tyrants to back. *Libra* foregrounds this mythic construction of an opposite in two ways. First by alluding to the Cold War—the embodiment (supposedly) of the difference between our system in which the individual is prized for his self-determination and the Soviet system in which the individual is flushed into the tide of the "collective." The novel also emphasizes the Cuban revolution as a historical unfolding of another mythic opposite. The text abounds with allusions to Batista. Yet, however much American myths tried to establish Batista as a democratic leader by focusing on his Communist opposition, the novel indicates that this identity was never completely established or believed by Cubans. The exiles who took up arms against Castro were not for Batista; *Libra* shows, through the character of Raymo, that the exiles felt that Castro had betrayed the revolution. Ironically, Communism is supposed to free individuals by forcing them to take part in the collective. Ironically, too, the United States–backed group attempting to overthrow Castro would have implemented an even stricter communistic rule. The novel indicates the confusions that abound when ideologies (the ideologies of capitalism and communism) attempt to overcome contradictions. With a base no firmer than language and rhetoric, the attempt to wrestle contradictions into order ends up in a swirling mass of figures and ironies.

Perhaps these contradictions are best embodied in Oswald himself. DeLillo sees Oswald as a person characterized by "self-contradiction" ("Interview" 289). This is most evident early on in the novel when Oswald decides to read some Marxist texts. These books advocating that the individual lose himself to the sweep of history first attracted Oswald because they set him apart as an individual; they indicated his uniqueness among his classmates. These were books that "put him at a distance from his classmates, closed the world around him" (33). Ironically, Oswald enters the world of Marxism through the mythic door of American individuality and the loner. He believed that these books "contain[ed] the secret of who you are" (41). At the same time that Oswald revels in the fact that these books create a distance between him and his classmates he feels that "the books made him part of something. . . . He would join a cell" (41). DeLillo cleverly puns on "cell" throughout the novel. Of course a cell is an organizational unit that is connected to the larger Communist movement. But a cell is also a small room, a room that houses cloistered monks or prison inmates. Thus, it is an image of connection and of isolation, the contradiction that besets Oswald and the systems of government he tries to live in. He is a loner seeking connection in the United States, and he is a "comrade" seeking individuality in the Soviet Union.

Another profound irony occurs in the book when Oswald's position within American ideology is juxtaposed to "the promise" of Soviet Communism. He believes that somehow Communism will give him the individual opportunities—for education, personal growth, and economic prosperity—

denied him in the United States. What he discovers is that the USSR, the nation on the side of history, also treats him as an object. Ironically, he gets just what he sought. He thinks that "the only end to isolation was to reach the point where he was no longer separated from the true struggles that went on around him. The name we give this point is history" (248). In Moscow, Oswald believes, "he was a man in history now" (149). At the same time that Oswald entertains thoughts of himself in history he complains that "no one could distinguish him from anyone else" (151). When he becomes a worker, when he becomes connected to the great sweep of Soviet history, he feels ashamed of the dirt on his clothes and "did not like thinking of himself as a factory hand, a manual laborer, slotted to do a certain eternal task" (202). Oswald does indeed become a part of history, but not the grand history of the "struggle"; he does not become part of the mythic march into eternity that he fantasizes. What he becomes is exactly what the KGB agents refer to him as: a subject. He becomes a subject, an object of a historically determined ideology. In this case, he is the object of the Cold War ideology with all its myths and narratives. He realizes that because this ideology permeates both sides of the Iron Curtain, he has the same status in the East and in the West; he is "a zero in the system" (151).

Thus, *Libra* reveals that the Cold War ideology that dominates the contemporary episteme leads not to an Oswald but to a subject position filled by "Oswald." The ideologies that define the East and the West and their opposites create a place for the subject. They allow the subject to be perceived only according to the rules that govern the ideological practices. Here those practices are political and governmental. In the discourse of collectivity, Oswald "recognizes" himself, but he also identifies with the myth of the strong individual. He identifies with Trotsky throughout the novel, but not for Trotsky's achievements as a socialist. Oswald finds in Trotsky a man who struggled against oppression, who bettered himself through suffering and long hours of study in the small room of a prison cell, and who, most significantly for Oswald, lives on in history. Although Oswald fantasizes about being like Trotsky, being a powerful individual who suffers for the "true struggle," he never becomes more than a figure to be fitted into a preconceived role. He will become, in the assassination plot, simply a physical body to play a part scripted for him by Win Everett: "His role was to provide artifacts of historical interest, a traceable weapon, all the cuttings and hoardings of his Cuban career" (386). Of course, we soon realize that Oswald's role is not really the creation of a single man, nor a specific group of men. Oswald's role is a position created by the confluence of ideologies that define his/our episteme.

In an important reading of *Libra*, Frank Lentricchia argues that Oswald's role is best understood as that of a "negative Libran," a term borrowed from the novel emphasizing the "nonidentity of sheer possibility—of the American who might play any part" (14). Oswald is a figure of all contemporary Americans who are "so enthralled by the fantasy selves projected in the media as our possible third person, and, more insidiously, an everyday life so utterly enthralled by the charisma of the media, that it makes little useful sense to speak of sociopathology or of a lone gunman" (17–18). Lentricchia believes that contemporary life is "lived totally inside the representations generated in the print and visual media" (19–20). There is no escape from such representation because "film . . . is the culturally inevitable form of our self-consciousness" (21). Thus, Oswald's, and our, goal is to achieve a life lived in the third person, that third person wholly defined by media representations. Lentricchia is absolutely right to read *Libra* as an exploration of the historical forces that determine contemporary subjectivity. In addition, his suggestion that *Libra* gives a postmodern twist to the naturalistic novels that emphasized the social forces that determined the self seems consistent with DeLillo's work. However, to place the whole burden of contemporary representation onto the media drastically narrows DeLillo's field of investigation. We might look to the media as purveyors of dominant discourses at work in society, but we do not follow the full range of DeLillo's exploration if we stop there.

Oswald clearly stands as an example of postmodern subjectivity, a subjectivity without a transcendent self beneath the "false" layers of social conditioning. He is his culture's ideologies, not simply the discourse of the media— though this, too, is a part of him. Oswald exists in the third person; he exists in a subject position that precedes and lives beyond him. We can be more specific and more general in defining this position: this position entails more than simply wanting to be the person (no one in particular) on the TV screen. As I have argued, this position consists of two myths engendered by the same basic contradiction, the contradiction of the collective individual. Although this contradiction and the myths that attempt to conceal it have a long history, the idea that the individual is no longer the locus of power that recuperates contradiction and resists ideology is recent. The idea that consciousness exists separately from and more genuinely than the social forces impinging upon it has given way to speech—the utterance that is merely a manifestation of ideology. In naturalistic fiction, the individual and the social forces that oppressed him or her were given faces and souls; in *Libra* ideology can be known only through discursive practice, the "body of anonymous, historical rules, always determined in the time and space that have defined a given period, and for a given social, economic, geographical or linguistic area, the conditions of operation of the enunciative function" (*Archaeology* 117). The subject position is not determined by biochemistry or by social forces such as greed, honor, beauty, or love. It is determined by systems of symbolic representation, the material manifestation of which is present to us in the form of documents and artifacts—texts. As we shall see, Oswald's status as a negative Libran is not so much due to the media as it is a result of the contradictions that constitute his relationship to the world, contradictions that cannot be resolved because no ground for resolution exists outside the myths they have given birth to.

The most consistent representation of Oswald's subject position is the role of assassin planned for him by Win Everett. When he first conceives of the plan to fake an assassination of Kennedy, Win realizes that they will need an assassin. However, in considering the "shooter," Win knows that he can do the "whole thing with paper. . . . script a person . . . out of ordinary pocket litter" (28). As the plan develops, Win instructs T. J. Mackey to find "a model . . . a name, a face, a bodily frame they might use to extend their fiction into the world" (50). However, this paper position is not simply a role that Oswald will adopt. Actually the "scripted person" exists on the same level with Oswald. Oswald's beliefs, his desires, and dreams are all "scripted"; they all exist as texts—documentary evidence, so much pocket litter. At one point in the novel, Oswald tries to obtain a Cuban visa. He appears at the Cuban embassy with all his papers. When they turn him down, he thinks "documents are supposed to provide substance for a claim or a wish. A man with papers is substantial" (357). Win understands that there is no difference between a scripted Oswald and the "real thing" and makes plans accordingly: "If he thinks he's operating on the left, pro-Castro, pro-Soviet, whatever his special interest, we'll help him select a fantasy" (4–75). But Win has to convince more than Oswald of this role; investigators will be looking into this man: "His gunman would appear behind a strip of scenic gauze. You have to leave them with coincidence, lingering mystery. This is what makes it real" (147).

Win's thoughts allow us to realize that he, too, has been "scripted" by an ideology. But Oswald remains the most emphatic example in *Libra* of existing as a subject position. However, this subject position is extremely complex. At one point in the novel, Oswald tries to start his own branch of Fair Play for Cuba. The headquarters denies him official sanction, but he "didn't need New York's backing to open an office. He had his rubber stamping kit. All he had to do was stamp the committee's initials on a handbill or piece of literature. Stamp some numbers and letters. This makes it true" (313). At the same time that he is a simulacral Fair Play branch director he is recruited by the FBI to work as an informant. In this case, he would fake interest in a right-wing group in New Orleans, gain their confidence, and report their activities and plans. One of the main operations of this group consists in gathering information on liberals in the area. Oswald suggests to them that he set up a Fair Play for Cuba branch as a means of attracting liberals and finding out what plans they have. In addition, the right-wing group has been contacted by Mackey and told to accept Oswald because they want to keep tabs on him. Thus the right-wing group fakes an interest in Oswald who fakes an interest in them while faking his role as informant for the FBI. The conclusion to the simulacral chess match is that everyone ends up doing what he was going to do anyway, but because of all these false maneuverings, the quotidian becomes simulacral.

After this vertiginous whirl of roles and identities, we are not surprised when Oswald begins discovering himself in everything. Headlines in the newspaper are secret messages to him. Rifles in the Book Depository building are meant as a signal for him; "everything that happened was him" (385). Oswald plays his role so well for the conspirators because he is the role. Then again, he is no more the role than they are the manipulators of the plan. The plan and his role are the consequence of the historical forces that have shaped the rules determining what they see and say about themselves. The fact that all of them believe in the myth of the loner not only gives shape to their plan and allows Oswald to fall right into place for them, but it creates the possibility of such a plan in the first place. If the conspirators did not follow this myth, they never would have seen the possibility of executing such a plot outside the authority and power of the CIA. Thus, Oswald's subject position does not make any clearer what kind of person he was, or what kind of people the conspirators were. It does, however, illuminate the invisible laws in our culture that determine what we see and say. Clearly these rules have much in common with the episteme as DeLillo understands it. The rules eschew any essential grounding; and by not providing any path to the real, these rules set the scene for the appearance of the negative Libran, the "sheer possibility" of plot and person.

As we have seen, part of this position is created by the myth of the loner; part of the role is also created by the complementary ethos/mythos of secrecy. In the ideology of the Cold War, the individual is perceived as a source for information that might help destroy or protect the government. All ideologies depend on the management of information. As Oswald discovers, this management of information through subject positions takes the form of myths about and an ethics of secrets. In the myth of the loner, secrecy is represented as both source and protection of the subject's individuality. Similarly, in the myth of American independence, secrets help to protect our autonomy and freedom. Obviously, in its protective role, secrecy must protect against something. That threatening something is of course the projected other.

Win Everett reveals the role that secrets play in the myth of the "loner," one of the most important subject positions in the ideology of American government. He regrets that his daughter is not more careful about sharing her secrets: " 'My little girl is generous with secrets. I wish she weren't, frankly. Don't secrets sustain her, keep her separate, make her self-aware?' " (26). Perhaps the best response to Win's rhetorical question comes from Oswald, the man Win will "create" as a presidential assassin. Oswald finds the small room of the loner in the most isolated section of the trains in New York's subway system. Oswald seems to fulfill Win's prescription for individual distinction and self-awareness in his secret subway rides: "He was riding just to ride. The noise had a power and a human force. The dark had a power. . . . The view down the tracks was a form of power. It was a secret and a power. The beams picked out secret things" (13). Yet this power of secrecy is impossible to maintain, just as the solitude of the lone individual is impossible to maintain. People must live in the world: "Never again in his short life, never in the world, would he feel this inner power, rising to a shriek, this secret force of the soul in the tunnels under New York" (13).

Win also discovers too late that power and secrets are simply not in the control of an individual. He devises a secret plot to bring power back to the anti-Castro movement, a movement he put in motion toward the Bay of Pigs. The secret plot he devises must be shared in order to be fulfilled. He wants to set up a hit on the President of the United States and make it look like Castro's forces did it. Of course the plan is to miss the President—just wound a secret service agent or two. At first, Win is vitalized by his secret plan, as he tells his fellow conspirators, " 'secrets are an exalted state, almost a dream state. They're a way of arresting motion, stopping the world so we can see ourselves in it. . . . there's something vitalizing in a secret' "(26). Win must realize, just as Oswald must, that he cannot "stop the world," cannot avoid the world. That world continues to swirl around these men, forming their plans, shaping their perceptions, determining their fate. Win must realize that his plan is a plot, as we shall see, determined by the governmental institutions, the discursive formations that have shaped not only his consciousness but the way he "speaks the world." Win comes to regret his secret plot; at the point where he realizes that it is out of his control, has always been out of his control, he understands that this plot has a logic of its own, a logic that moves irresistibly toward death. Win's attempt to stop the world, to create a perfect structure that might give him control of his environment, leads to an end even more extreme than the ends reached by the plotters of perfect structures in DeLillo's other novels. Win finally joins the long list of the dead linked to the assassination.

Win Everett's fatal involvement with secrets parallels the fatality of the secrets kept by the Happy Valley Farm Commune in *Great Jones Street*. In both instances the "vitalizing" secret concerns a plot to gain power. For Happy Valley, this means the power to maintain and increase their presence in New York City. As we have seen, for Win this means the power to oust Castro and regain what is "rightfully ours." The plot Happy Valley creates develops a relentless logic of its own. It demands that those who are suspected of working against the commune are guilty, that those who are pursued and caught must be killed. By the same token the fatal logic of Win's plot becomes apparent when it is taken over by T. J. Mackey. But this too is a misconception. Secrets and plots are not taken over by a person, just as they are not created by a person. *Libra* insists that "secrets build their own networks" (22). Win takes this a step further. He fears that the plot he's hatched is heading deathward; he feels a "foreboding that the plot would move to a limit, develop a logical end" (221). The course of events leading up to the assassination does not begin, according to Mackey, with Win's plot but at the moment when JFK put out a hit on Castro, for at that moment " 'he put himself in a world of blood and pain' " (302). Given the historical circumstances of the failure at the Bay of Pigs, Kennedy's personal vendetta against Castro, and that aspect of the myth of the American loner that insists on individual responsibility, " 'someone has to die. It is very much a part of our thinking that Jack is the one' " (303). This logic is so pervasive and is such a determining factor in the perceptions of these men that they interpret Kennedy's planned route through Dallas, which will take him right by Oswald's place of work, as an example of "the force of this driving logic" (361). Even Win regretfully acknowledges the "deathward-tending logic of a plot" (363).

The plot to assassinate Kennedy engenders a second and a third plot. The second plot exists in the attempt to narrate the events of the assassination. The third plot is the narrative contained in *Libra*. Indeed, *Libra* represents all three plots. We have seen how Win Everett and T. J. Mackey represent the first plot. Nicholas Branch represents the second plot. If Everett and Mackey allow us to see the imperative logic of the ideology that interpellates them, then Branch allows us to see how the contradictions of the assassination gave rise to a new ideology, a new way of imagining our relations to objects in our world, in a word, a new episteme. Because, as Lentricchia points out, *Libra* insists that the assassination is not about Lee Harvey Oswald but about determining features in American culture, the contradictions we find in Oswald and in the plot disrupt the pat stories and myths we use to understand ourselves. Because these contradictions run so deeply into the fabric of our cultural sense of who we are, they demand an ideology that runs even more deeply. Or, rather than deep, this new ideology is characterized by an unparalleled breadth. This is the ideology that determines Branch's investigation, the ideology that determines our chaotic perceptions of the world today. The novel implies that the version of the world that informs our government's practices and dominates our episteme intends to account for every detail of existence. It employs a totalizing discourse, a discourse of rational examination and explanation. *Libra* clearly indicates that this penchant for total explanation leads, in fact, to total chaos. We simply cannot account for every detail, every nuance. Yet this is exactly the mission Branch has set for himself; rather it is the mission that the CIA has assigned to him.

Branch virtually lives in a room filled to the ceiling with evidence generated by the assassination. For fifteen years Branch has toiled in a small room where "the stacks {of folders} are everywhere. The legal pads and cassette tapes are everywhere. The books fill tall shelves along three walls and cover the desk, a table and much of the floor. There is a massive file cabinet stuffed with documents so old and densely packed they may be ready to ignite spontaneously" (14). The law of probability demands that so much information is bound to contain contradictions, inconsistencies, "mystery." Branch feels that he "must study everything"; he cannot dismiss anything because he "is in too deep to be selective" (59). At first he dismisses the disturbingly large number of violent deaths associated with the assassination by telling himself that "he

242 ♦ CHRISTOPHER M. MOTT

is writing a history, not a study of the ways in which people succumb to paranoia" (57). He does not think it necessary to "invent the grand and masterful
scheme, the plot that reaches flawlessly in a dozen directions" (58). Yet in the
same thought he "sees how the assassination sheds a powerful and lasting
light, exposing patterns and links, revealing this man to have known that
one, this death to have occurred in curious juxtaposition to that" (58).
Because "the stuff keeps coming," Branch wonders if he ought to despair of
ever getting to the end. After fifteen years of work he has "precious little" finished prose. Because of the pressure applied by the CIA to account for and
resolve all the paradoxes, contradictions, and inconsistencies that threaten the
CIA myth of the lone operative and the lone gunman, Branch finds it "impossible to stop assembling data" (59). Indeed, as long as he subscribes to a single version of incidents that presents itself as a seamless and comprehensive
whole in a culture where contradictions increase by the moment he will never
finish the research, let alone the narrative.

Branch's failure to master the data, to write the secret history of the
assassination, leads him to conclude that "powerful events breed their own
network of inconsistencies. The simple facts elude authentication. . . .
[Branch] concedes everything. He questions everything, including the basic
suppositions we make about our world of light and shadow, solid objects and
ordinary sounds, and our ability to measure such things, to determine weight,
mass and direction, to see things as they are, recall them clearly, be able to say
what happened" (300). Because DeLillo has taken these words directly from
"American Blood," we are tempted to attribute this attitude and state of
affairs to him. However, *Libra* itself is our evidence that it is otherwise with
DeLillo. In fact, Branch seems to function as a kind of mirror figure to the
sensibility of the novel. Clearly *Libra* does "say what happened," at the same
time the novel disavows any claim to truth, to seeing "things as they are."
Indeed, in the "Author's Note" DeLillo claims that *Libra* "makes no claim to
literal truth." The text does not aspire to the condition of a totally comprehensive narration of the assassination. It admits to being selective, to choosing those elements that seem most obvious and most conducive to a narrative, to the construction of a plot.

By acknowledging its limitations and yet insisting on its power to
explain, to create a "way of thinking" that helps us to understand these puz-
zling events, *Libra* fulfills the function and value of the historical narrative,
which is, according to Hayden White, to give "coherence, integrity, fullness
and closure to real events" (*Content* 24). The narrative calls attention to its
status as a created form, a form with explanatory power in Oswald's feelings
about his "Historic Diary." After making an entry at the end of his stay in
Russia, Oswald believes that he has "closed out" a "major era" in his life. The
entry "validated the experience, as the writing of any history brings a persuasion and form to events" (211). This phrase introduces DeLillo's charac-

teristic ambiguity into the text. At the same time that the passage endorses historical narrative it calls that narrative into question. That is, because Oswald believes that the writing of history brings "form and persuasion" to events, and because he has just convinced himself that he was a false defector—just as he will be a false informer, false right-winger, false left-winger—we begin to suspect the kind of "persuasion" he finds in writing history. It should never be mistaken for the Truth, yet it should be taken for a legitimate account.

Thus, the point of *Libra* for DeLillo is not to establish some all-encompassing tome of truth but to record a fully realized treatment of the assassination according to some consistent and fully developed view of it. In the author's note to *Libra,* DeLillo tells us that

> In a case in which rumors, facts, suspicions, official subterfuge, conflicting sets of evidence and a dozen labyrinthine theories all mingle, sometimes indistinguishably, it may seem to some that a work of fiction is one more gloom in a chronicle of unknowing.
>
> But because this book makes no claim to literal truth, because it is only itself, apart and complete, readers may find refuge here—a way of thinking about the assassination without being constrained by half-facts or overwhelmed by possibilities, by the tide of speculation that widens with the years.

Perhaps Hayden White best captures DeLillo's project: in *Libra,* and its difference from Branch's. White believes that a historical narrative

> can be judged solely in terms of the richness of the metaphors which govern its sequence of articulation. Thus envisaged, the governing metaphor of an historical account could be treated as a *heuristic rule which self-consciously eliminates certain kinds of data from consideration as evidence.* The [writer] operating under such a conception could thus be viewed as one who . . . seeks to exploit a certain perspective on the world that does not pretend to exhaust description or analysis of all the data in the phenomenal field. (*Tropics* 46)

DeLillo and White share a sense that we must try to represent our past—no matter how distant—but they are suspicious of representation. They reject the idea that history can be represented in some comprehensive and final version. *Libra* achieves what few other accounts of the assassination even attempt: a narrative that suggests that the bickering to establish the truth of that event is moot, especially in contrast to the possibility of learning something significant about our cultural orientation to our past and ourselves. DeLillo's novel does not claim that the events it relates are true, but it does insist that the rhetoric and ideology it exposes have worked insidiously upon this nation. Fictionalizing these fictions may be our best hope to understand and change the forces that create our world and our selves.

Works Cited

DeLillo, Don. "American Blood." *Rolling Stone.* 8 Dec. 1983: 21–22, 24, 27–28, 74.
———. Interview with Anthony DeCurtis. *South Atlantic Quarterly* 89 (1990): 281–304.
———. *Libra.* New York: Viking, 1988.
Foucault, Michel. *The Archaeology of Knowledge and the Discourse on Language.* Trans. A. M. Sheridan Smith. New York: Pantheon, 1972.
Lentricchia, Frank. "Don DeLillo." *Raritan,* Spring 1989: 1–29.
White, Hayden. *The Content of the Form: Narrative Discourse and Historical Representation.* Baltimore: Johns Hopkins UP, 1987.
———. *Tropics of Discourse: Essays in Cultural Criticism.* Baltimore: Johns Hopkins UP, 1978.

Can the Intellectual Still Speak?
The Example of Don DeLillo's *Mao II*

Silvia Caporale Bizzini

The great danger to avoid is the self-isolating nature of critical discourse.
—Jean Starobinski

When Roland Barthes wrote and published his "The Death of the Author," he cast doubts upon one of the chief mainstays of Western culture. With the disappearance of the Author—I'd rather understand this death not as disappearance but as fragmentation—the status of the so-called universal intellectual (obviously male, white and middle- or upper-class) was also indirectly questioned. This—together with other economic, social and political factors—led to the crisis in which part of the intelligentsia is now living and that some are using not only to discredit the individual figure of the intellectual but also to account for a society whose roots seem to be ahistorical or deeply mythical, in which, as in the case of the Holocaust or Italian Fascism, history can be cancelled and rewritten as the revisionists please.

But if the author and the subject are now, even though with a certain difficulty and some resistance, reconstructing themselves in a different way—and I think of the birth of different forms of identity that, with the help of history, Foucault was starting to theorise some time before his death—what is happening to the intellectual? Can some writers still consider themselves to be committed intellectuals? Or perhaps we should ask: does it mean anything now to talk about a writer as a committed intellectual? Must we classify literature as "unproductive," and for this reason declare the death of intellectuals as writers because they do not fulfil the requirements of a society which is more and more predisposed to the most vulgar, conservative and dangerous technocracy? The concern of this paper is to argue that the intellectual as writer—and I consider the writer as a specific intellectual—is still important, alive and somehow necessary in our contemporary social context. For this reason, in the following section I will introduce the Foucauldian concept of specific intellectual and the Barthesian idea of the writer as intellectual before, in

Originally published in *Critical Quarterly* 37, no. 2 (1995): 104–17. Copyright © The Editors of *Critical Quarterly*. Reprinted by permission.

the third part of this paper, relating the idea of the writer as specific intellectual to Don DeLillo's *Mao II*.

In *Mao II,* DeLillo faces up to most of the contradictions which are present in contemporary society and culture, and through the peculiar structure of the book helps us to enter a world mainly ruled by pictures and violence. The society in which the writer-protagonist of the book lives hidden from everybody is dominated by postmodern *pastiche,* images and spectacle. I find DeLillo's writing interesting not only because it represents a committed criticism of contemporary culture and society but also because this criticism is carried out within a text where the frustrated quest for identity of the American hero merges with the representation of a postmodern world which DeLillo synthesises in the portraits that Andy Warhol did of Mao Tse-tung, Marilyn Monroe and Gorbachev, icons of a society where images and myth prevail. The hero, in spite of his desperate quest, and in betrayal of the American tradition, is incapable of finding a new identity—let alone his old one—and ends up dying on a boat where nobody knows him while going from Greece to Lebanon. From the West to the East.

DeLillo's main character thus offers us an opportunity to start reflecting on the relation that writing maintains with subjectivity without, at the same time, losing sight of a committed vision of writing itself. I am not going to go back to the idea of the universal intellectual—although I think that DeLillo from time to time does consider yielding to the temptation; what I want to stress rather is how DeLillo's text manages to reflect the transformation of the idea of the writer as a universal intellectual into the idea of the writer as a specific intellectual.

At the beginning of the 1970s Michel Foucault started to develop in a more detailed way his theory of power relations. His interest was framed not only within his own philosophical and intellectual project but, at the same time, reacted to the concerns of a society which was changing quickly. It was the same society that during May 1968 had abruptly woken up and that for a long time believed in the chance of a real transformation of the existing structures without realising that the international failure of the student movement was leading to the frustration of unfulfilled promises and to the consequent terrorist abjection.[1] Gilles Deleuze, in an interview with Foucault on the role of intellectuals, declared that the figure who until then had been considered to be a theorist could not be seen any more as a subject and as a result of this the intellectual was not to be seen any more as the "representative consciousness" of society: "For us the intellectual theorist has ceased to be a subject, a representing and representative consciousness . . . there is no longer any representation, there is only action, theory's action, the action of practice in the relationships of networks."[2]

It was in this context, and in relation to his criticism of traditional Western epistemology, that Foucault started to connect more firmly the role that the intellectual and culture play in the frame of the power relations that construct the subject. His can be considered one of the answers to the collapse of the classical theorisation of, for example, the Sartrean universal intellectual in the post-war period. Foucault rejects this idea because he considers that it is directly related to the idea of the existence of an absolute Truth with its corresponding essentialist and universal subject. In the Foucauldian philosophical project there is no epistemological justification to support the idea of the existence of an intellectual figure who can be considered to be *the* universal thinking subject. On the contrary, the Foucauldian specific intellectual is not interested in speaking on behalf of other people. Each intellectual works in her or his own field to give the various social groups the tools which will enable them to speak for themselves and according to their different needs. The role of the intellectual has diversified[3] together with the multiple foci in which Foucauldian power relations act within the social network. All intellectuals belong to this chain, that is to say to the power/knowledge relationship, and their role as specific intellectuals is to resist the idea which portrays them as the "consciousness and eloquence" of Western epistemology.

But what about Roland Barthes? How does he situate the intellectual within the cultural scene and with respect to the death of the author? I think that the discourse on intellectuals in the Barthesian text also answers the need to fragment and burst open the inner structures of writing as one possible answer to the logic of Western epistemology. In many of Barthes's later texts the necessity of staying outside the system and breaking all that ties our culture to the culture of stereotype is evident.

According to Barthes, the universal intellectual is what is left of the heritage of a past time when his word had a prophetic meaning and represented the voice of authority.[4] With the death of the author, this charismatic, and indeed androcentric, figure disappears. If for Foucault this gave way to the birth of the specific intellectual, for Barthes the disappearance has been definitive, and he declares that the only thing left by the intellectual is his spoor: "Les optimistes disent que l'intellectuel est un 'témoin.' Je dirais plutôt qu'il n'est qu'une 'trace.' "[5]

I would argue that this affirmation has to be understood as a fragmentation of the idea of the intellectual and not as the confirmation of his death. The "death of the author" describes not a disappearance but the birth of different subjectivities that manifest themselves, for example, in the questioning and opening of the Canon. Nevertheless I should stress that Barthes's analysis of intellectuals includes his concern with language ("Disons simplement que je suis sans doute la trace d'un intérêt historique pour le langage; et aussi la trace de multiples engouements, modes, termes nouveaux"[6]). For this reason it might be interesting to approach the Barthesian intellectual through the criticism of meaning that Barthes developed in his cultural project from the very beginning (and which remained as a firm point of reference till the end of his life). The Barthesian writer, that is to say, acts in a system based on a very clearly specified number of rules that are defined by the mythology of culture. The myth, according to Barthes, is a message which society creates within a specific historical frame and afterwards uses to build up the structures of stereotypes. Multiple languages are used simply to repeat the same Discourse. It could be said that they function like the Foucauldian commentary:

> car le mythe est une parole choisie par l'histoire: il ne saurait surgir de la "nature" des choses. Cette parole est un message. Elle peut donc être bien autre chose qu'orale; elle peut être formée d'écritures ou de representations: le discours écrit, mais aussi la photographie, le cinéma, le reportage, le sport, les spectacles, la publicité, tout cela peut servir de support à la parole mythique.[7]

Myth does not lie. (It would be very difficult for a picture to lie, just to mention an example which reminds us of the last Barthesian text, *Camera Lucida;* the person who is looking at that picture knows perfectly well that she is looking at something which exists or has existed somewhere.) What we can ask at this point though is how can the myth—which is the language of a specific historical moment[8]—become such a powerful instrument of cultural control? According to Barthes this is because the myth tends to transform itself into nature, that is to say into the essence. Within his framework of power relations Foucault developed the idea of the specific intellectual; so how does Barthes face the task of fighting against the creation of multiple discourses which transform myth from historical product into the essence, that is to say into something that never changes and is always identical to itself? His solution, as we all know, lies in the subversive potential of the literary text. And to understand this we have to refer to the impossibility of the existence of the literary text outside ideology. Barthes argues that no text can exist outside the limits imposed by the ideological apparatuses. The subversion of the text, in other words, consists in its capacity to flourish within this frame and at the same time to be able to create its own *chiaroscuro,* to change the perspective we get of the known phenomenological world and present it in a way[9] which is *different,* and I give to this adjective all the connotations that are present in both Barthesian and Foucauldian texts.

For Barthes as for Foucault, then, history assumes an important role in the definition of what it means to be an intellectual. "The writer is always on the blind spot of system, adrift; he is the joker in the pack, a *mana,* a zero degree, the dummy in the bridge game: necessary to the meaning (the battle), but himself deprived of fixed meaning; his place, his (exchange) *value,* varies according to the movements of history, the tactical blows of the struggle; he is asked all and/or nothing."[10]

Mao II is the story of a famous, much-admired writer who can no longer find a satisfying place in contemporary society; it is for this reason that he decides to hide while he tries to write his last book. The writer feels displaced as an intellectual, and his writing loses the capacity of representing his *chiaroscuro* in a world which is dominated by terrorism. Each character symbolises an aspect of a society which apparently has lost all unity but which, paradoxically, is moving in a single direction. The book that Bill Gray is writing is a text which, significantly, he thinks will never be finished:

> The language of my books has shaped me as a man. There's a moral force in a sentence when it comes out right. It speaks the writer's will to live. The deeper I become entangled in the process of getting a sentence right in its syllables and rhythms, the more I learn about myself. I've worked the sentences of this book long and hard but not long and hard enough because I no longer see myself in the language.[11]

Language does not give back to the writer the image of himself he was used to seeing. Bill has lost control of the grammatical structures and the lexicon ("On the stage of the text, no footlights: there is not, behind the text, someone active [the writer] and out front someone passive [the reader]; there is not a subject and an object.")[12] The situation that Bill is going through can thus be interpreted as the result of questioning the very idea of authorship. It is for this reason that Bill feels he is not capable of publishing his book; he cannot do it because he feels that it is not *his* writing any more. And the work of revision that he carries out day by day is absolutely useless: the text keeps on slipping from his grasp. And so Bill decides to leave his hiding place and agrees to be photographed by Brita, a professional photographer who only takes pictures of writers. He is slowly capitulating to the pressures of the outside world and he tells Brita so in these words: "There's a curious knot that binds novelists and terrorists. In the West we become famous effigies as our books lose the power to shape and influence. Do you ask your writers how they feel about this?" (*MII,* 41). In this quotation two ideas that will become the backbone of the novel appear: the relation between terrorists and writers and that between writers and images.[13]

Why after so many years of isolation does Bill Gray decide to publish his photograph and not his book? As we already know, Bill has a conflictive relation with his novel, that is to say with the text he is writing. This text does not recognise him as the "Author" but as somebody that Barthes defined as a "white card" or as the Joker. When Bill feels that he has lost his identity as a writer (and above all as a committed writer), what he desperately needs is another identity. The camera can give him what he needs at this moment, an image which is able to tell him that, in spite of everything, he still exists as Bill Gray, the writer. This is what Barthes writes in *Camera Lucida:* "Now, once I feel myself observed by the lens, everything changes: I constitute myself in the process of 'posing,' I instantaneously make another body for myself, I transform myself in advance into an image."[14]

For this reason Bill gives up his privacy and agrees to be transformed into an image and, significantly, the person who does it is a woman photographer who left her previous field of research (in the poor outskirts of town) to devote herself to going around the world taking pictures of writers. Through her job the impossibility of writing is transformed into a collection of images of people who write:

> It took me a long time to find out what I wanted to photograph. I came to this country it's fifteen years. To this city actually. And I roamed the streets first day, taking pictures of city faces, eyes of city people, slashed men, prostitutes, emergency rooms, forget it, I did this for years [. . .] But after years of this I began to think it was somehow, strangely—not valid [. . .] Then you know what you want to do at last [. . .] I will just keep on photographing writers, every one I can reach, novelists, poets, playwrights [. . .] This is what I do now. Writers. (*MII*, 24)

If we keep on following Barthesian thought we could even say that the image transforms the referents[15]—which in our case are represented by the portrayed writers—into a simulacrum of what they used to mean at another historical moment. In other words, I think that the idea that we receive from the picture of the writer can be related to a representation of death, to something that has already disappeared and does not exist any more: the author is dead and can only come back to us through a photograph, that is to say through an image that has been emptied of any other meaning ("He said, 'The book is finished but will remain in typescript. Then Brita's photos appear in a prominent place. Timed just right. We don't need the book. We have the author,' " *MII*, 71). Images occupy quite an important place in the narrative of *Mao II* and in one way or another all the characters relate to them. (In *Camera Lucida* Roland Barthes stresses the overwhelming presence of images in our society with the following words: "I see photographs everywhere, like everyone else, nowadays: they come from the world to me, without my asking: they are only 'images,' their mode of appearance is heterogeneous."[16])

In fact DeLillo's novel establishes a unity among the different parts into which it is divided through the world of images and their tendency to transform every human action into spectacle. In the first part, for example, Bill Gray lives with two young persons who take care of him and look after the house, Scott and Karen. Karen lives obsessed by images and the news is the only thing she watches on television; she watches it without the sound, she simply looks and is not interested in listening. She is only interested in seeing because as Guy Debord writes with his usual irony "Spectacle has mixed with reality and has irradiated it."[17] Karen's gaze is, obviously, subjective and her personal experience reflects what she absorbs from the totality of the images that reach her. For this reason, while she is watching the news on the student rebellion in China in May 1989, Karen simply notices the enormous portrait of Mao Tse-tung, the same portrait that her friend Scott keeps in his bedroom and which is a reproduction of the famous one done by Andy Warhol:

> They show the portrait of Mao up close, a clean new picture, and he has those little mounds of hair that bulge out of his head and the great wart below his mouth and she tries to recall if the wart appears on the version Andy drew with a pencil that she has on the wall in the bedroom at home. Mao Zedong. She likes that name all right. But it is funny how a picture. It is funny how a picture what? She hears a car alarm go off in the street. (*MII*, 177–8)

In the last part of the novel, "In Beirut," the enormous tragedy a whole nation is going through is mediated and described through the images that Brita sees from the window of her car. The language that DeLillo uses is dry and the sentences are short; there are no comments on people or the despair produced by war, just a list of images of people and of the war that merge with the ads: "The streets run with images. They cover walls and clothing— pictures of martyrs, clerics, fighting men, holidays in Tahiti" (*MII*, 229).

Bill tries to rebel against all this, above all for himself, and for this reason accepts the proposal that his editor Charlie Everson makes to him to talk on behalf of a young poet who has been kidnapped by a Maoist group in Beirut; but the press conference that Charlie thinks of organising in London is, as well, mere spectacle: "I want one missing writer to read the work of another. I want the famous novelist to address the suffering of the unknown poet. I want the English-language writer to read in French and the older man to speak across the night to his young colleague in letters. Don't you see how beautifully balanced?" (*MII*, 98).

The London meeting fails because a bomb explodes in the place that the British police had chosen for the conference. Nonetheless, it is in London that Bill starts to relate to a mysterious man, George, an intellectual who lives in Athens and who is the contact with the terrorists in Beirut. Bill Gray decides to reject the publicity, runs away from London and flies to Athens to go on acting on his own. In Athens he meets George and it is during a conversation that the two men hold in George's place that all the main elements present in the novel converge; in a few, solid, vigorous pages the intellectual, and through him the terrorists, face up to the writer.

By going away from London and from the press conference Charlie Everson had organised, Bill tries to rebel against the society which transforms everything into spectacle and himself into the image of a writer; he tries to take back his own destiny and so demonstrate to himself that he still exists as a committed intellectual. Little by little, his quest for his lost identity becomes desperate. From his point of view, the strength of ideas has fallen to the force of violence and if, on the one hand, the author is dead, on the other hand, authoritarianism has won the battle because it has been able to transform itself into something spectacular.

Bill and George represent two sides of contemporary culture. The writer and the terrorist are two mythical figures within our cultural codes who through the dynamics of history see their roles and places completely changed in contemporary society. If the writer has lost the power to influence the social fabric with his work, then the terrorist has learnt to use the society of spectacle and of images in his favour. Bill's fear and doubts are patent and materialise in the following quotation where we can sense his nostalgia for the writer/intellectual who used to be society's conscience:

> "For some time now I've had the feeling that novelists and terrorists are play-ing a zero-sum game." "Interesting. How so?" "What terrorists gain, novelists lose. The degree to which they influence mass consciousness is the extent of our decline as shapers of sensibility and thought. The danger they represent equals our own failure to be dangerous." "And the more clearly we see terror, the less impact we feel from art." (*MII*, 129–30)

George here uses the verb *to see* to refer to terror, but terror belongs to the sphere of feelings and we should *feel* it and not *see* it. Once more the act of see-ing and the gaze are presented as basic elements in the balancing game the two men are playing while the ghosts of unknown hostages—whose pictures can be transformed into a lethal weapon—are fluctuating between them: "Gain the maximum attention. Then probably kill you ten minutes later. Then photo-graph your corpse and keep the picture handy for the time when it can be used most effectively" (*MII*, 165). The dialectical confrontation between Bill and George shifts between two different levels: while the first talks of contents, the second never stops relating the content to the image. Guy Debord, in his *Comentarios sobre la sociedad del espectáculo,* not only attacks passionately the theo-rists of the end of history but stresses how the society of images has become a basic element in undermining the bases of all historical thought, and a danger-ous backward step to a mythical conception of human events: "The valuable advantage that spectacle has obtained from situating history outside the law, from sentencing all recent history to clandestinity and helping to forget, in gen-eral terms, the historical spirit of society means, in the first place, hiding its own history: the movement of its recent conquest of the world."[18]

The myth as history is patent in the defence that George makes of the terrorist and the use of real violence. Images are the only weapon left to those who, according to George, fight in the name of justice: "But this is precisely the language of being noticed, the only language the West understands. The way they determine how we see them" (*MII*, 157). Then he goes back to compare the writer's job to the role that terrorists play in contemporary soci-ety: "It's the novelist who understands the secret life, the rage that underlies all obscurity and neglect. You're half murderers, most of you" (*MII*, 158).

Bill's answer reflects the refusal of an absolute Truth and of a figure who can eventually become a kind of God and a creator of Truth, something that holds the right of life and death over other people. In this context, to deny the immutable meaning that myth gives to the figure of the terrorist as defender of truth, whatever the cost, means to become aware of the role of history and to deny that any image is "natural" ("No. It's pure myth, the terrorist as solitary outlaw. These groups are backed by repressive governments. They're perfect little totalitarian states. They carry the old wild-eyed vision, *total destruction and total order*," *MII*, 158). Facing up to a discourse that tries to transform him into something that he absolutely rejects, Bill is obliged to go back to his writing as the only possible answer. Bill's rebellion materialises in the attempt to give back to the hostage an identity that is not the one that images suggest: "He could have told George he was writing about the hostage to bring him back, to return a meaning that had been lost to the world when they locked him in the room" (*MII*, 200).

The real tragedy described in the novel, then, is that the captured poet is used by everyone—nobody is interested in him as a human being. George theorises on the hostage's position, the terrorists think of him simply as a means to obtain something for their cause and Bill, in his own way, does the same. None of these people talk of the poet as a person; each of them sees him in an absolute way, whether as the price that society has to pay for a cause or as a way of recovering a lost identity. Bill's interest is thus directed not towards the prisoner but towards an idea in danger, the idea of the writer as intellectual and thinking being: "You put a man in a room and lock the door. There's something serenely pure here. Let's destroy the mind that makes words and sentences" (*MII*, 161).

So the contemporary writer/intellectual is represented by three different points of view: those of the author as *deus ex machina* (an idea that, as we will see, still lives on in Mao's works); of the writer who has lost his identity and the meaning of his work; and of the silenced writer about whom nobody worries and of whom, by the end of the novel, nothing will be left but a faded unimportant memory.

Mao Tse-tung's writings are the materialisation of the idea of the Author as creator of meaning, a concept that George shares and considers of basic importance for the development of a revolutionary thought: "There are different ways in which words are sacred [. . .] Mao said this. And he wrote and he wrote. He became the history of China written on the masses. And his words became immortal. Studied, repeated, memorized by an entire nation"; "Incantations. People chanting formulas and slogans" (*MII*, 161–2).

Here we have the discourse of what is considered true; in this case it is the interpretation that George gives of Mao's discourse which is repeated until it becomes the only valid one, that is to say the Discourse of the Same. For this reason, this discourse becomes a myth and takes for granted an ahistorical and immortal dimension: *sacred* is how George defines it. What is sacred and mythical has to be accepted as a dogma; it deletes history and lays the theoretical bases of Discourse One: "The Little Red Book of Quotations. The book was the faith that people carried everywhere" (*MII*, 161).

George is looking for—and defends—the elimination of difference: he wants an ideology in which unity can be encountered and totality analysed. If we see things from this point of view, from the perspective of any totalitarian discourse (or from the perspective of other so-called democratic discourses[19]), we should not be surprised that the only viable project is the terrorist one, that is to say the discourse of the elimination of difference either through assassination by the terrorist or by a State that declares itself democratic: "It's an idea. It's a picture of Lebanon without the Syrians, Palestinians and Israelis, without the Iranian volunteers, the religious wars. We need a model that transcends all the bitter history. *Something enormous and commanding. A figure of absolute being*" (*MII*, 158; my emphasis).

The resistance which Bill Gray opposes to this authorial figure—who eventually becomes a kind of God in whose name the destiny of a whole people can be changed and assassination and kidnapping justified from a theoretical point of view—is not enough. Bill's cry of protest ("Do you know why I believe in the novel? It's a democratic shout. Anybody can write a great novel [. . .] One thing unlike another, one voice unlike the next. Ambiguities, contradictions, whispers, hints. And this is what you want to destroy," *MII*, 159) gets lost in a society dominated by rules which regulate the spectacle and transform everything into an image.

As Charlie Everson had already done in London, Bill decides to run away from George's logic and face alone what he will find in Lebanon, but he does not get to Beirut because, as I have already noted, he dies on the ferry. His quest for identity ends up a complete failure. The famous writer who used to live hidden from everybody disappears. On the ferry somebody steals all his documents and what is left of him is just a nameless corpse on a boat and a series of pictures. At the end of his life, and without looking for it, Bill Gray is transformed into the thing that he had wanted to avoid: a silent image with a writer's name.

The hostage, the writer silenced by violence, also disappears in the oblivion of the society of spectacle that continuously needs new emotions and new scandals. It is Brita who takes an interest in the man while she is taking pictures of Abu Rashid, boss of the terrorists who had kidnapped him, and the answer she gets is blood-curdling:

> "What happened to the hostage?" [. . .] He says, "We have no foreign sponsors. Sometimes we do business the old way. You sell this, you trade that. Always there are deals in the works. So with hostages. Like drugs, like weapons, like jewelry, like a Rolex or a BMW. We sold him to the fundamentalists." Brita thinks about this. "And they are keeping him," she says. "They are doing whatever they are doing." (*MII*, 235)

The writer, and together with the writer the intellectual, apparently has not survived contemporary culture. The overwhelming message of violence and the annihilation of any feature which might bring us to accept difference and multiplicity seem to be the only thing left. The boys who surround Abu Rashid, for example, keep their faces constantly covered, but they do not do so to protect themselves from being recognised and put into jail but in order to demonstrate that they accept the uniformity that their boss's ideology demands of them: "The interpreter says, 'The boys who work near Abu Rashid have no face or speech. Their features are identical. They are his features. They don't need their own features or voices. They are surrendering these things to something powerful and great' " (*MII*, 234).

In spite of a progressive sense of defeat that pervades the reader as he or she goes on reading the book, I think that DeLillo's novel can be read as a text with, to use Barthes's words, a literary subversive potential. In *Mao II* Don DeLillo manages to give life to his own game of lights and shadows and gives the reader a perspective of the various clichés of contemporary society and culture. In our case the writer is the intellectual who acts in a specific context—the text. The intellectual who in the novel is obviously unable to change or influence society and is silenced by circumstances that are already out of control, on the other hand keeps on talking and writing through the hand of DeLillo himself. His novel, which is such a hard and desperate one, demonstrates that the writer has to write and through his or her writing develops a criticism of the meaning—or of the lack of it—not only of the false multiplicity of discourses that has been created by the society of spectacle, but of myth and of the so-called end of history as well. It is in this sense that I understand Frank Lentricchia's words[20] on DeLillo's capacity to shape his own *chiaroscuro* within the frame of history and of ideology without losing sight of the necessity of questioning the dangerously mythical and ahistorical society that some contemporary critics, theorists and politicians are helping to define.

DeLillo's use of history as a subversive tool with which he manages to represent an*other* reality, questions and presents from a different perspective the official versions and rules that the society of spectacle imposes on the viewer—or the reader in our case—and makes me think both of Barthesian writers' capacity to depict their own *chiaroscuro* within a specific ideology, and the role that the Foucauldian specific intellectuals play within the power/ knowledge relation. The capacity that DeLillo shows in *Mao II* to use and relate to one another concepts such as history, subjectivity and writing, while opening a new and different perspective, synthesises and lumps together the Barthesian and the Foucauldian ideas of what an intellectual should be:

> The role of an intellectual is not to tell others what they have to do [. . .] The work of an intellectual is not to shape others' political will; it is through the

analysis that he carries out in his [sic] own field, to question over and over what is postulated as self-evident, to disturb people's mental habits, the way they do and think things, to dissipate what is familiar and accepted, to reexamine rules and institutions and on the basis of this reproblematization (in which he carries out his specific task as an intellectual) to participate in the formation of a political will (in which he has his role as citizen to play).[21]

Notes

1. Just to give an example of the political climate of the end of the seventies in Italy I want to quote some phrases from an interview published in the Italian weekly magazine *Panorama* (25 August 1991) on the occasion of the release of Renato Curcio, founder of the Red Brigades. The person who speaks (his name is not mentioned in order to protect him from any possible retaliation) used to be a close associate of General Dalla Chiesa (assassinated together with his wife and the members of his escort by the Mafia) and gives a chilling list of people who were assassinated by the terrorists when Curcio was first put into jail and before the trial: "on the 10th [of March 1978] his comrades killed Rosario Bernardi, officer of the anti-terrorist brigade. On the 16th they kidnapped Aldo Moro and killed the five men of his escort. On the 11th of April the prison warder Lorenzo Cotugno was assassinated. On the 20th they killed Marshal Franco Di Cataldo. On the 9th of May they liquidated the President of the Christian Democracy [Aldo Moro]. On the 22nd they massacred the police inspector Antonio Esposito," p. 49, my translation.

2. Gilles Deleuze, "Intellectuals and Power" (Interview Michel Foucault—Gilles Deleuze), in *Language, Counter-Memory, Practice: Selected Essays and Interviews by Michel Foucault*, ed. Donald F. Bouchard (Ithaca: Cornell University Press, 1977), 206–7.

3. "This task [. . .] is also an attempt to locate the intellectual's freedom at the point of his/her limitations—the point at which desire meets with processes of subjectivization, the place where identity forms," Karlis Racevskis, "Michel Foucault, Rameau's Nephew and the Question of Identity," in *The Final Foucault*, eds. James Bernauer and David Rasmussen (Cambridge, MA: The MIT Press, 1988), 31.

4. "H-L: Il fut un temps où les intellectuels se prenaient, se pensaient comme le 'sel de la terre' . . . R.B.: Je dirais pour ma part qu'ils sont plutôt le déchet de la société. Le déchet au sens strict, c'est-à-dire ce qui ne sert à rien, à moins qu'on le recupère [. . .] En un certain sens, les intellectuels ne servent à rien," Roland Barthes, "A quoi sert un intellectuel?," in *Le grain de la voix. Entretiens* 1962–1980 (Editions du Seuil: Paris, 1981), 256.

5. Ibid., 257.

6. Id.

7. Roland Barthes, "Le mythe, aujourd'hui," in *Mythologies* (Paris: Editions du Seuil, 1957), 194.

8. ". . . on peut concevoir des mythes très anciens, il n'y en a pas d'éternels; car c'est l'histoire humaine qui fait passer le réel â l'état de parole, c'est elle et elle seule qui règle la vie et la mort du langage mythique. Lointaine ou non, la mythologie ne peut avoir qu'un fondement historique, car le mythe est une parole choisie par l'histoire: il ne saurait surgir de la 'nature' des choses," Roland Barthes, "Le mythe, aujourd'hui," *Mythologies*, 194.

9. "There are those who want a text (an art, a painting) without a shadow, without 'the dominant ideology'; but this is to want a text without fecundity, without productivity, a sterile text (see the Myth of the Woman without a Shadow). The text needs its shadow: this shadow is *a bit* of ideology, *a bit* of representation, *a bit* of subject: ghosts, pockets, traces, necessary clouds: subversion must produce its own chiaroscuro," Roland Barthes, *The Pleasure of the Text* (New York: Hill and Wang, 1975), 32.

10. Ibid., 35.

11. Don DeLillo, *Mao II* (1991; London: Vintage, 1992), 43. From now on I will refer to DeLillo's novel as *MII*, with the page number.

12. Roland Barthes, *The Pleasure of the Text*, 16.

13. See Douglas Keesey's *Don DeLillo* (New York: Twayne, 1993), 177–93.

14. Roland Barthes, *Camera Lucida* (London: Vintage 1993), 10.

15. "And the person or thing photographed is the target, the referent, a kind of little simulacrum, any *eidolon* emitted by the object, which I should like to call the *Spectrum* of the photograph because this word retains, through its root, a relation to 'spectacle' and adds to it that rather terrible thing which is there in every photograph: the return of the dead," ibid., 9.

16. Ibid., 16.

17. Guy Debord, *Comentarios sobre la sociedad del espectáculo* (Barcelona: Anagrama, 1990), 20; my translation.

18. Ibid., 27; my translation.

19. "In all the places where spectacle reigns the only organized forces are the ones that want the spectacle. For this reason, none of them can be an enemy of what exists, nor can they transgress the *omertà* that involves everything. That disturbing conception, which ruled for two hundred years, according to which a society could be open to criticism and transformable, reformed or revolutionary is over. And this has not been obtained with the appearance of new reasonings but simply because reasonings have become useless. With this result we will measure, more than the social welfare, the terrible strength of the networks of tyranny," ibid., 34; my translation.

20. "In [. . .] their historical rigor, I suspect, lies their political outrage: the unprecedented degree to which they prevent their readers from gliding off into the comfortable sentiment that the real problems of the human race have always been about what they are today," Frank Lentricchia, "Introduction," *New Essays on White Noise* (Cambridge: Cambridge University Press, 1991), 6.

21. Michel Foucault, "The Concern for Truth," in Lawrence D. Kritzman (ed.), *Michel Foucault: Politics, Philosophy, Culture* (London: Routledge, 1988), 265.

Excavating the Underworld of Race
and Waste in Cold War History:
Baseball, Aesthetics, and Ideology

JOHN N. DUVALL

> What's a ball game to make us feel like this?
>
> Prologue, *Underworld*

Don DeLillo has long been fascinated with crowds and people's collective urge to be a part of something larger than themselves, to surrender to a power that would explain the felt alienation of their lives and to protect them from a recognition of their own mortality. *Mao II* with its frightening evocations of crowds—a mass wedding ceremony performed by Reverend Moon at Yankee Stadium, the suffocation of people pressed against a restraining fence at a soccer game, and the mass hysteria at the Ayatollah Kohmeini's funeral—had been DeLillo's most extensive treatment of this matter. Yet his depiction of a thoroughly American crowd in "The Triumph of Death," the prologue of *Underworld,* pushes the issue further through an examination of baseball as an aesthetic ideology that participates in masking the hidden costs of America's Cold War victory and in erasing race and class difference.

DeLillo's eleventh novel was published on the forty-sixth anniversary of the third and deciding playoff game for the 1951 National League pennant. *Underworld*'s lengthy prologue recreates the action on that day at the Polo Grounds. This game is famous for Bobby Thomson's "Shot Heard 'Round the World," his two-out, ninth-inning, three-run homer that lifted the New York Giants to victory over their arch-rival, the Brooklyn Dodgers. DeLillo uses the Dodgers-Giants rivalry to figure a different us-them binary. If a New Yorker's identity (at least those who were not loyal to the Yankees) in the early 1950s could be read in part by whether that individual was a Dodgers'

An earlier, shorter version of this essay that considers only what is now the prologue of *Underworld* appeared as "Baseball as Aesthetic Ideology: Cold War History, Race, and DeLillo's 'Pafko at the Wall,' " *Modern Fiction Studies* 41, no. 2 (1995): 285–313. © 1995. Purdue Research Foundation. The essay was revised and expanded for this volume and appears by permission of the Johns Hopkins University Press and the author.

or a Giants' fan, then American identity more fully in that same period was shaped in its opposition to the Soviet Union. What makes the metaphorical relationship clear is the historical significance of this date in history that DeLillo explores. On this day, the Soviet Union exploded their second atomic weapon, a fact that confirmed for U.S. intelligence that the Soviets had nuclear capability.

In *Underworld* DeLillo explores a massive irony: if America remembers October 3, 1951, it is for the Thomson home run and not its significance in Cold War history. Yet the confirmation of Soviet nuclear capability meant that the United States now had an adversary powerful enough to sustain post–World War II paranoia about threats to America's sovereignty. Beginning with this last moment of postwar confidence in our exclusive possession of nuclear weapons, DeLillo ranges over American history from the 1950s to the early 1990s and charts this history's effects on his characters. In doing so, he attempts nothing short of an analysis of the paranoia in American national identity during the Cold War period. One technique DeLillo uses to structure his novel is to trace the history of the ball Thomson hit.

Unlike his ninth novel, *Libra,* which explores conspiracies surrounding the assassination of President Kennedy, *Underworld* looks at more everyday paranoia. The various plots of the novel converge on the current owner of the Thomson ball, Nick Shay, who at the end of the Cold War is an executive for a waste-management firm living in Phoenix. But even as Nick grows up in an Italian American neighborhood in Brooklyn, waste is a metaphor for his life. As a 17-year-old, he has a brief affair with his high school math teacher's wife and later kills a friend through a thoughtless action. After rehabilitation in reform school, Nick enters the mainstream of middle-class life and rises to professional success. In the present-time of the novel, mid-1992, he faces a personal crisis in his wife's affair with his best friend. The strangeness of living in the aftermath of the Cold War is neatly represented by a business dinner Nick attends at a restaurant in Dodger stadium in Los Angeles. Unlike the immediacy of the raucous New York crowd of the prologue, a glass wall now separates Nick and his dining companions from the crowd watching the Dodgers play the San Francisco Giants. Both the United States–Russia and the Dodgers-Giants oppositions mean something very different now than in 1951. Old loyalties and beliefs are rendered archaic. Just as the Dodgers and the Giants left New York to tap into the lucrative West Coast market, so too has the relation between America and Russia been rewritten by market forces.

The novel's title resonates in a number of ways. Nick is always uncertain whether his father, a small-time numbers runner who disappeared suddenly, was the victim of underworld violence. The most persistent meaning of "underworld," however, is the volume of waste generated by American consumer culture. When Nick at one point finds himself in a mall boutique devoted exclusively to selling a seemingly endless variety of condoms—both male and female, flavored, glow-in-the-dark—we discover an apt metaphor for the underworld of American consumption: what we experience as freedom of choice is in large part the carefully researched construction of consumer identity by Madison Avenue. If an archaeology of Cold War America is ever to be performed, the novel suggests, it must take place in the massive land-fills near our urban areas. DeLillo argues that, perhaps as much as the prolif-eration of nuclear weapons, the proliferation of consumerism and disposable goods was a key weapon in America's Cold War arsenal. Even as he makes explicit the link between nuclear and consumer waste, DeLillo depicts yet another underworld, the homeless of New York City, who fall outside of American consumerism (as well as, therefore, the space of American advertis-ing) and thus give the lie to the cornerstone assumption of American ideol-ogy—that we are a classless society.

One other connotation of "underworld" directs the reader to aesthetics and artistic renderings of nightmarish spaces. DeLillo's characters encounter previous representations of apocalypse, from *The Triumph of Death* (which gives DeLillo's prologue its title) by sixteenth-century painter Pieter Bruegel, to a 1970s artist's showing on a wall of televisions the Zapruder film of the Kennedy assassination, continuously looped, to a screening of *Unterwelt,* a supposedly lost silent science fiction film depicting a distopian future by Russian director Sergei Eisenstein. The novel's characters, who live in the recent American past, frequently experience these earlier artistic visions as foreshadowings of nuclear annihilation.

It is precisely the foregrounding of the power of the image in the novel, particularly the infinitely reproducible image (the Bruegel painting, for example, is experienced only through its reproduction in *Life* magazine), that invites a reading of imagistic aura in light of Walter Benjamin's famous essay "The Work of Art in the Age of Mechanical Reproduction." For Benjamin, aura is a negative concept because it cloaks the work of art in its cultic and ritual function.[1] He speaks approvingly of the way technologies of mass reproduction destroy the aura of the high-culture work of art, since that aura fetishizes origin: if high-quality prints of the *Mona Lisa* can be infinitely reproduced and disseminated, it is no longer necessary to travel to the Louvre and stand in hushed respect before timeless genius. Benjamin, of course, hoped that film and photography could recuperate aura in a Marxist context (to politicize the aesthetic), but in the epilogue of his essay, Benjamin, a first-hand observer of Hitler's National Socialists, notices that in the Nazi appro-priation of culture, it is not just art but the media "which is pressed into the production of ritual values."[2] Far from simply destroying aura, the techniques of reproduction (particularly the newly emerging electronic media) could reconstruct a specious aura. If Hitler could construct an aura by using news-reels and radio to amplify the impact of his parades, rallies, and sporting events, then there was a link between mass reproduction and the manipula-tion of the masses.[3] For Benjamin, then, one of the defining features of fascism is its ability to transform political conflict and class struggle into objects of aesthetic contemplation.

In DeLillo's postwar America, there is no Führer figure attempting to manipulate the masses; nevertheless, there operates what might be termed a postmodern, decentralized totalitarianism in which the mass media—linked especially to advertising—constructs an aura around popular culture events. Obviously the anti-Semitic violence of National Socialism cannot be equated with advertising in American culture; nevertheless, Benjamin's uneasiness with German fascism's aestheticizing the political speaks to DeLillo's portrayal of American consumer culture, a culture in which he repeatedly finds political and economic matters overwhelmed by aesthetics. It is precisely baseball fans' auratic identification with the game that DeLillo makes problematic as it raises a question: Why on a particular day in our history—October 3, 1951—does one cultural event, a baseball game, eclipse a moment crucial to the construction of the Cold War?

Ty Cobb's Better Boys

In July 1947, the *Rotarian* published the legendary Ty Cobb's article "Batting Out Better Boys," which urges parents to get their sons involved in baseball and cities to invest in facilities for little league baseball to keep boys from going bad. The piece begins as an autobiographical reminiscence. Against his father's wishes, Cobb plans to leave home to try out for a Sally League club; the evening before Cobb leaves, father and son are reconciled and Cobb receives the patriarchal blessing. Through hard work, then, Cobb rises to stardom in the major leagues. Clearly in the tradition of American self-reliance, the family history related here bears little relation to the historical record. Cobb's father, W. H., a rural schoolmaster, had little tolerance for Ty, who was not interested in his father's plans for him to attend college and become a doctor or a lawyer; their relationship at times verged on hatred.[4] Cobb later reproduced this father-son relationship with his son, Ty Jr.: "Cobb and his son became totally alienated from each other. . . . In obvious ways, Cobb's relationship with Ty, Jr., paralleled what his own relationship with W. H. had been and might have become . . . if his father had lived."[5] W. H. did not live, however, because a little over a year after Cobb entered professional baseball, W. H., armed with a pistol and intent on catching his wife with her lover, was shot and killed by Cobb's mother as he attempted to enter their bedroom window.[6] Cobb's rewriting of his personal history within the frame of the blissful nuclear family is an index of the way that the history of baseball is a mythical history, intimately tied to the American mythos of capital. Cobb, a notoriously vicious player well-known for spiking opponents, ends his essay with a list of lessons he claims that baseball teaches "any lad." These are, predictably enough, hard work ("if he's to succeed at the game, or at anything, he's got to buckle down, practice endlessly, and study not only himself, but every man he plays with and comes up against") and courage ("you've first got to drive all fear out of your system"). In the development of an American character, one lesson stands out: baseball "can teach a boy . . . to calculate his risks, and to take 'em. Nothing ventured, nothing gained, goes for baseball as for anything else."[7] Baseball does not simply bat out better boys but also better future citizens of a capitalist economy, men who will work hard to earn money that they will then courageously risk in studied investments. Such procapitalist implications coming from Cobb are not surprising considering his own successful risk; when Coca-Cola stock first went public, he invested heavily and thus was for years the wealthiest former professional baseball player.[8]

In the following issue of the *Rotarian,* one writer's enthusiasm for baseball seems to know no bounds; he suggests an international baseball league with teams from around the world to ensure future world peace on the assumption that "no time would be found for war if our leaders had important baseball games to discuss."[9] The writer stresses that he is not being facetious but believes "that serious world problems may be solved by genuine interest in friendly international athletic competition, wholly devoid of politics, economics, and war."[10] This author writes with typical American forgetfulness of history; Hitler's 1936 Olympics were nothing if not a spectacle of politics. Nevertheless, this piece typifies the jingoistic spirit surrounding coverage of baseball, as further evidenced by a spate of articles on the resurgence of baseball in Japan.

"Japan's at Batto Again," appearing in *Collier's* almost on the second anniversary of America's atomic bombing of Hiroshima and Nagasaki, notes that baseball has displaced sumo wrestling as Japan's number one spectator sport and is quite frank about baseball's cultural mission:

> Our military-government people are pleased by the baseball boom. They don't think that baseball in itself will make the Japanese any more democratic than it did before the war. But compared with the schools' old military drill, it's practically Jeffersonian. Our physical-education experts are actively propagandizing for more baseball everywhere, working in particular and with great success to popularize a one-out game for hurried city youngsters.[11]

Interesting here is the totally unproblematized presentation of cultural imperialism. What to do with an essentially undemocratic race? Give them a cultural-aesthetic form that is American and democratic ("practically Jeffersonian"), even if that inherently democratic form will be unable to overcome the cultural-biological imperative. A twofold forgetfulness of history appears in this article. First, although the professional league suspended play in 1943, the amateur game flourished in Japan throughout the war. The article under-plays this on the grounds that the Japanese league president is intent on "Americaniz[ing] the game completely" by encouraging players and fans to act more like their American counterparts; that is, to argue with the umpire, to openly express emotion over the game—in effect, to stop acting like Japanese.[12] The second point rests more on this writer's assumption that a form of government and an economic system—democracy and capitalism—are one and the same; this assumption ignores the way capitalism worked in Hitler's Germany. The one-out game advocated by American phys-ed people adds an unintentional and odd twist to Ty Cobb's lessons in baseball and cap-ital—production over process. A one-out game allows more "complete" games to be played, which in terms of productivity sends a message that more is better.

And baseball's productivity appears almost to have the power to rebuild Japan from the ground up. Norman Cousins, then editor of the *Saturday Review of Literature,* employs literary license to title his 1949 article; the old popular song about baseball player King Kelly ("Slide, Kelly, Slide") becomes "Slide, Fujimura, SLIDE!" The article begins with Cousins on a tour of Hiroshima with the city's mayor:

> This baseball sand lot in Hiroshima was little more than a mile from the spot where the atom bomb exploded four years ago. It was too far out to show much effect of the big blast. Only one of the dozen Japanese boys who were batting the ball around carried the telltale marks of an atomic burn—on the back of his neck. Except for that single detail, which a knowing eye alone would have caught, it might have been on a diamond off Main Street instead of one 12,000 miles from home.[13]

Cousins is in town to see a professional baseball game and, in a characteristic gesture of postwar articles on baseball in Japan, compares the skill level of Japanese professionals to their American counterparts. Cousins's verdict? "The playing was on a level somewhere between Double A and Triple A ball." Although praising the talent of Japanese infielders, Cousins notes a lack of power in hitting, particularly a lack of home run power: "Despite the high score, there were only three or four long hits that were good for two bases or better."[14] The Japanese lack of power hitting is oddly linked to America's atomic power; American postwar confidence is related to our exclusive pos-session of "the big blast"—where home run and atom bomb metaphorically merge most emphatically, as we shall see, in *Underworld*.[15] The Japanese lack of power is related to size (a comforting lack from an American perspective), even if Cousins's conversation with an American manager reveals that "the Jap players he [the manager] is meeting this trip are taller, heavier, and faster" than before.[16] Stranger still to Cousins is that when one player actu-ally does belt out a grand-slam home run, the fans do not respond with appropriate enthusiasm. An interpreter explains that the Japanese prefer a close contest, and this home run put the contest out of reach for the opposing team; somehow the Japanese fans Cousins sees do not fathom the American notion of competition, a need to "nuke" the opponent/enemy rather than just defeat them. Despite the implied inferiority of the Japanese as a race because of their lack of power hitting and their misunderstanding of some of the rituals of fandom, the underlying message of James's and Cousins's articles is clear: in Japan, baseball bats out better boys.

OCTOBER 3, 1951: BASEBALL HOOVERS THE AURA

In *Underworld,* DeLillo unpacks much of the ideological baggage surrounding America's game. The action of the prologue is perceived mainly from three alternating angles of vision, each of which serves to show how baseball's auratic function masks crucial political realities: from the announcer's booth comes the self-reflexive thoughts of a historical figure, Russ Hodges, the radio voice of the Giants, as he broadcasts the game; in Leo Durocher's box seats, three cultural icons—Jackie Gleason, Frank Sinatra, and J. Edgar Hoover— watch the game with famous New York barman Toots Shor; and, far removed from the announcer's booth and the box seats, a 14-year-old African American youth watches the game from the left-field seats. All three strands work together to show how baseball serves in popular culture a function equivalent to T. S. Eliot's high-culture tradition: baseball, like Eliot's poetic tradition, is an aestheticized space that allows the reader/viewer to experience a sense of transcendence, a removal into a realm of the timeless and universal; in short, like Eliot's tradition, baseball's tradition is ahistorical.

DeLillo plays the odd grouping of Shor, Gleason, Sinatra, and Hoover simultaneously for comic and nostalgic effects: between rounds of beer, Gleason pleases surrounding fans by doing bits from his new television show, *The Honeymooners,* that would air for the first time two nights later; Hoover worries that Gleason will start teasing him about being short. Their presence at the game might be ludicrous—a bit of postmodern excess—if there were not much about the grouping that is plausible, especially regarding Hoover, who initially seems most anomalous in the group. In "The Power of History," an essay that appeared shortly before the publication of *Underworld,* DeLillo in fact claims that he "learned" that the "foursome had been present at the ballgame."[17]

Despite the humor surrounding this group, it is the introduction of Hoover that allows the novel to comment on the way global politics become aestheticized, so much so that the history of the Cold War nearly disappears from American consciousness. DeLillo draws our attention to this when an FBI agent brings Hoover the news of the Soviet Union's detonation of a second atomic device. The novel is historically accurate on this point, and DeLillo has spoken recently about the "sense of history" he experienced in his discovery of the front page of the October 4 edition of the *New York Times,* which bears a dual headline: the left side telling of Bobby Thomson's home run; the right side, in typeface of the same pitch, announcing the Russian atomic bomb.[18] We have, it seems, a tale of two blasts—Bobby Thomson's three-run blast and the Russian atomic blast. The Russian blast will give Hoover the "ammunition" to pursue even more fully his anticommunist agenda, for it is this second explosion that confirms Russian nuclear capability.[19] It is hardly an exaggeration to say that on this day the Cold War becomes fully viable. Yet in American consciousness, Cold War history is overwhelmed by baseball legend.[20]

Each of the major angles of vision on the game is represented at the moment of Ralph Branca's home run pitch to Thomson; Hoover's perspective, however, is particularly noteworthy for its engagement with the aesthetic past. In the shower of paper falling from the stands, a page from *Life* magazine falls on Hoover's shoulder, which then catches his eye as he starts to brush it off. It is a color reproduction of Bruegel's *The Triumph of Death;* this "landscape of visionary havoc and ruin" becomes the object of extended close study for Hoover as time seems to slow while Thomson rounds the bases:

> It covers the page completely and must surely dominate the magazine. Across the red-brown earth skeleton armies on the march. Men impaled on lances, hung from gibbets, drawn on spoked wheels fixed to the top of bare trees, bodies open to the crows. Legions of the dead forming behind shields made of coffin lids.[21]

Even after Thomson has scored and the fans pour onto the field, Hoover still contemplates "the meat-blood-colors and massed bodies," which become in his mind a figuration of nuclear apocalypse. Looking up from Bruegel's images, Hoover sees the confusion and moiling of celebrants on the field, and they become indistinguishable to him from the ravaged sinners he has been scrutinizing on the page.

Hoover is an apt figure for DeLillo's consideration of protofascist impulses in American culture. In *White Noise,* if Professor Jack Gladney, chair of the Department of Hitler Studies, teaches a course in "the continuing mass appeal of fascist tyranny," it is because DeLillo himself is the real student of the subject.[22] In 1951, Hoover was the chief of what amounted to a kinder, gentler American Gestapo, a secret police with almost unchecked power to use electronic surveillance to spy on American citizens. It may be useful to note here the third major story on the front page of the *New York Times* the day after the big game: under the headline of the Giants' win is a photo of Leo Durocher hugging Bobby Thomson; balancing the page, under the headline of the Soviet blast is a photo of Philip Jessup denying Senator Joseph

McCarthy's charges of communist sympathies at a Senate Foreign Relations subcommittee. The Dodgers-Giants game is played a year and half after McCarthy's famous charges about the 205 communists working in the State Department. McCarthy's biggest problem, of course, was that he had no list and so turned to Hoover, a friend since he arrived in Washington in 1947, for help in keeping the issue alive. McCarthy became a media star, but Hoover made it happen by supplying the senator with embarrassing information about individuals, often illegally obtained and consisting largely of gossip and rumor too insubstantial for the Justice Department to act on.[23]

Although Hoover is a relatively minor character in the novel as a whole, he does reappear in part 5, "Better Things for Better Living through Chemistry: Selected Fragments Public and Private in the 1950s and 1960s." In an episode from November 1966, DeLillo explores the fallout from the American policy of the containment of communism—the Vietnam War and the protest at home against the war. These scenes have Hoover attending Truman Capote's Black and White Ball, a mix of celebrity from all walks of political, artistic, and sporting life. DeLillo emphasizes particularly Hoover's well-known, long-time personal relationship with Clyde Tolson, Hoover's top aid at the FBI. Recent biographical work strongly implies Hoover's homosexuality, but in DeLillo's telling, despite a clear homoeroticism between Hoover and Tolson, Hoover is celibate. His celibacy and refusal to act on his sexual urges in fact is central to his power over others, a power that frequently turned on Hoover's uncovering others' sexual behaviors. Imagining a celibate Hoover allows DeLillo to parallel J. Edgar Hoover to another character, Sister Alma Edgar, a Catholic nun, who is as obsessed with ferreting out sin as Hoover is with uncovering the secrets of those under his surveillance. Both are anal and paranoid, deeply fearing contamination from crowds. Just as Hoover is a crucial perspective in the prologue, Sister Edgar is integral to the epilogue, a point I will return to later.

BETTER BOYS BAT BACK

If *Underworld* illustrates the dangerous tendency of baseball to aestheticize and erase international politics, it also comments on the way baseball can participate in a mystification of racial politics within America. Against the fame and aura of the celebrities the novel portrays, there is the anonymity of Cotter Martin, a black member of the underclass, who along with a crowd of other black and white teenagers jumps the gates to get into the Polo Grounds for the big game. Cotter is marked by an American ideology of equality and justice, even if he has not experienced them directly. Cotter, quite simply, believes in baseball and to believe in baseball is to believe in America. In part, this belief comes from his home life. His older sister, Rosie, in 1964 travels from New York to participate in a civil rights protest in Jackson, Mississippi. The event turns violent when the National Guard gas and beat the crowd, which includes "white nuns marching with black ministers" (523). Even as things begin to turn ugly, the speaker who has been exhorting the marchers onward tells them in a deeply ironized moment: "I'm saying there's nothing in the world to worry about despite the evidence all around you. Because any-time you see black and white together you know they are joined in some effort of betterment. Says so in the Constitution" (524). The violence of this later moment of failed interracial cooperation shatters the innocence of the mixed-race crowd of youthful gate jumpers at the ballgame who work together to defeat the stadium cops with their nightsticks.

Reinforcing Cotter's sense of America would be his experience at school. Growing up within the American public educational system means an expo-sure to a particular ideological matrix that includes *Senior Scholastic*. In *Scholastic*'s 1950 article "Baseball, the Great Americanizer," a not-too-subtle mes-sage parallel to that in "Japan at Batto Again" and "Slide, Fujimura, SLIDE!" appears. A photograph in the lower left-hand corner of the article's opening page shows a group of six Japanese boys, all around seven to nine years old. One boy stands at the plate, bat at the ready, waiting for a pitch, while an adult Caucasian, crouched in the catcher's position, smiles benevolently on the scene; the caption reads: "Shoeless Japanese youngsters, coached by GI catcher, knock 'em over the fence."[24] The caption is ironic since these spindle-legged children clearly lack the power to hit home runs, and the white man, who even in his crouch is as tall as his players, seems to be smiling at the cap-tion's humor. If we can only get to this alien race when they are children, the image asserts, there is hope for the future. The assumption in the article's title clearly plays off a notion of America as melting pot: if baseball is the great Americanizer that can produce a homogenized world culture, then of course American culture itself already has been fully homogenized, and no class or race differences really matter.

Yet much about the way Cotter is delineated marks his racial and class status. After he has found a seat in the left-field stands, he is made conscious of his race by a flashy peanut vendor who deftly catches the coins people toss his way:

> It's a thrill-a-minute show but Cotter feels an obscure danger here. The guy is making him visible, shaming him in his prowler's den. Isn't it strange how their common color jumps the space between them? Nobody saw Cotter until the vendor appeared, black rays phasing from his hands. One popular Negro and crowd pleaser. One shifty kid trying not to be noticed. (20)

One person who notices Cotter is Bill Waterson, a middle-aged white archi-tect. Bill recognizes Cotter as a gate-crasher from his nervousness yet engages the youth in conversation, and they start to recognize a shared experience;

both have taken the day off (from school, from work) to watch the big game. Realizing they are both Giants fans, Bill and Cotter develop a friendship over the course of the game, an ostensible bonding between two males who can appreciate individually talented players within baseball's larger tradition. Cotter's racial and class identity, through Bill's big-brotherly attention, seems to melt away as the game wears on.

When the baseball Thomson hits breaks the plane of the outfield wall giving the Giants victory, however, we leave the space of fictionalized history and enter historicized fiction. The illusion of a timeless aesthetic space in which racial differences don't matter dissolves as Cotter and Bill scramble to recover the ball Thomson hit. In the scuffle, Cotter wrests the ball from someone who he moments later realizes is Bill. This struggle over the white ball also takes on overtones of the white domination of the sport in 1951, a domination that was soon to end. Although the color bar in the major leagues officially had been broken by Jackie Robinson in 1947, African American players in this game—Robinson, Willie Mays, and Roy Campanella—are as much interlopers on the field as Cotter Martin was in the stands. (One might highlight "officially" in the previous sentence, since some African American players who could pass as white almost certainly played in the major leagues prior to Robinson; persistent rumors about racial heritage plagued Babe Ruth, and the most violent incident in Ty Cobb's career occurred when a heckler in the stands called him "a half-nigger.")[25]

Bill pursues Cotter for many blocks—arguing, pleading, cajoling. Bill offers to buy the ball, but when Cotter won't sell the ball, baseball's position as the great Americanizer unravels. Bill, like Cotter, believes in baseball, but from the subject position of a middle-class white male, Bill's belief means something different than Cotter's. And what Bill does believe is reflected in the words of Ty Cobb and the American GI's smile:

> I look at you scrunched up in your seat and I thought I'd found a pal. This is a baseball fan, I thought. Not some delinquent in the streets. You seem dead set on disappointing me. Cotter? Buddies sit down together and work things out. . . . Now tell me what it's going to take to separate you from that baseball, son. (56)

Baseball, Bill knows, is supposed to bat out better boys, and the understanding he hopes for, of course, is that Cotter will recognize the white man's property interest in the ball. Just as the U.S. military was using baseball to insure American interests, Bill assumes that baseball stabilizes middle-class hegemony. When Cotter asserts that "the ball's not yours, it's mine" (56), Bill's condescendingly avuncular tone ceases and the chase begins in earnest, as Bill with increasing rage pursues the youth until they reach Harlem, when the middle-aged man now realizes he sticks out as much as Cotter had in the ballpark.[26]

What Bill fails to realize is the contradictory nature of the discourse surrounding (and constituting his belief in) baseball; that is, the very sport that is supposed to ensure the stability of the status quo—of America as a world superpower, of middle-class hegemony at home and of the subjection of the racial other (the Japanese, the African American)—also is supposed to teach courage, independence, and risk taking. And what are Cotter's gate-crashing and struggle over the ball but examples of Ty Cobb's lessons? DeLillo's Cotter thus exposes the constitutive contradiction of postwar baseball rhetoric—is he a better boy because he embodies the virtues Cobb's game supposedly advocates, or is he a bad boy because he is not saved by baseball and thus fails to recognize his place?

DeLillo's presentation of Cold War politics and racial matters finds historical confirmation in an excerpt of testimony before Congress by Jackie Robinson that *Life* published August 1, 1949, as its editorial under the title "Negroes Are Americans: Jackie Robinson Proves It in Words and on the Ball Field." Robinson's testimony speaks to the perceived threat in Paul Robeson's statement in Paris the week before that asserted that American blacks would never fight for the United States against Russia. The most assertive moment in Robinson's "editorial" comes when he gently insists that "the American public ought to understand . . . that because it is a Communist who denounces injustice in the courts, police brutality and lynching, when it happens, doesn't change the truth of the charges. . . . Negroes were stirred up long before there was a Communist party, and they'll stay stirred up long after the party has disappeared—unless Jim Crow has disappeared by then as well."[27] But Robinson quickly turns to one of America's oldest rhetorical gestures—freedom of religion: "I am a religious man. Therefore, I cherish America where I am free to worship as I please, a privilege which some countries do not give" (22). In short, we (America) are free; they (the Soviet Union) are not. This is precisely what the editors of *Life* (who frame Robinson's words within their own) seize on, and the piece is finally more interesting for their frame and the accompanying images than for Robinson's defense of black Americans' loyalty. Robinson ends by saying that "we [African Americans] can win our fight [against discrimination] without the Communists and we don't want their help"; immediately following, the editors add this coda: "When he had finished someone in the audience called out, 'Amen!' So say we" (22). The "we" here is more than the editors of *Life,* since the audience they represent is white, middle-class America. The editors moralize on the differences between bad black/good black, between the ungrateful communist Robeson and the patriotic American Robinson. Robeson, whose "honors . . . never endeared America to him," is overwhelmed by Robinson, "a four-letter man at college," "an intensely respectable man who takes proper pride in his handsome family and in his success as the first Negro admitted to major-league baseball" (22). The photos of the two men, along with the captions, are telling: "Singer Robeson" before microphones, declaiming in Paris;

"Second Baseman Robinson" sliding home in Brooklyn. The images themselves double the text: they, the communists, have ideology; we have baseball.

Although Cotter Martin fades from the novel after the prologue, DeLillo continues his mediation on the impact of race in three chapter-length sections that fall between major divisions of the novel. Taken together, they form a coherent linear narrative that focuses on the immediate fate of the Thomson ball, from Cotter's return home on October 3, 1951, to the sale of the ball by his father, Manx, early the next morning to a fan waiting in line to buy World Series tickets. In the first of these sections, Cotter, who needs a note to explain his absence from school, tells his father about the game and the ball. Manx, as father of an impoverished family, immediately sees the potential to sell the ball. Although Cotter does not want to sell the ball, Manx takes it when his son falls asleep. The remaining two sections record Manx's efforts to sell the ball.

It is in the sale of the ball that DeLillo reiterates the ideological function of baseball to mask race and class difference. After being rebuffed by several people—for even Manx knows he sounds fraudulent since he has no way to document his claim that he has the Thomson ball—Manx discovers a father and son in the ticket line. In the course of the deal, Manx and the other man, Chuck Wainwright, emphasize what is common between them—particularly their fatherhood. However, everything in the encounter is racialized. For example, Chuck is persuaded by the logic that Manx, as an African American, would not be believed by the Giants' management if he showed up at their offices to sell them the ball. And at a key moment in the deal, when Chuck passes his whiskey flask to Manx, Manx must wait to see whether Chuck will wipe the rim before drinking again.

Early in the novel the reader learns that Nick Shay, the current owner of the Thomson ball, paid $34,500 for the memento, despite the missing link in the lineage of the ball—every owner of the ball (Chuck and several others) is known back to October 4, 1951, but no connection to the original owner can be made. Manx sells the ball—and surely his son's trust—for $32.45.

UNDERWORLD'S ART: FROM AESTHETICIZED
POLITICS TO POLITICIZED AESTHETICS

If the treatment of Hoover's and Cotter's perspectives create a critical purchase on the historical past, then DeLillo's presentation of the radio announcer, Russ Hodges, serves to make the critique relevant to our equally historical present. DeLillo's critique in many ways parallels Jean Baudrillard's in "The Order of Simulacra."[28] Starting from Walter Benjamin and Marshall

McLuhan, Baudrillard shifts away from a Marxist analysis of technology as a productive force and toward an interpretation of technology "as medium" or expressive form.[29] Taken to its extreme, "the medium is the message" becomes Baudrillard's hyperreal, where the "contradiction between the real and the imaginary is effaced."[30] Hodges is an artist figure who contemplates the constructive nature of his discourse. Prior to the game he recalls his father's taking him to the Dempsey-Willard fight in Toledo; what he takes as a "measure of the awesome" is clearly made so for him by its media representation: "When you see a thing like that [fight], a thing that becomes a newsreel, you begin to feel you are a carrier of some solemn scrap of history" (16). In the age of the electronic media, Hodges's words reveal, an event has not entered history unless it is represented by that technology.

Here is an announcer who is calling what has become marked over the years as one of baseball's most "authentic" games, a game that over time has acquired an aura—which DeLillo's fiction unavoidably adds to even as it problematizes that aura. During the course of the game, Hodges recalls his years in Charlotte doing simulated broadcasts of Washington Senators baseball games, "announcing" games he did not attend as the events came over the wire. His thoughts reveal that he, like DeLillo in *Underworld*,

> liked to take the action into the stands, inventing a kid chasing a foul ball, a carrot-top boy with a cowlick (shameless, ain't I) who retrieves the ball and holds it aloft, this five-ounce sphere of cork, rubber, yarn, horsehide and spiral stitching, a souvenir baseball, a priceless thing somehow, a thing that seems to recapitulate the whole history of the game every time it is thrown or hit or touched. (26)

Hodges's recollections of simulated broadcasts, of course, call attention to the simulation DeLillo performs in calling up a long-ago game. The very fact that a recording of Hodges's broadcast exists is a fluke of mechanical reproduction, as DeLillo points out, because someone in Brooklyn decides to tape the game "and this will turn out to be the only known recording of Russ's famous account of the final moments of the game" (48). But the specificity of Hodges's remembering how he could create something out of the mere fact of a foul ball—figuring the winner of the scramble to recover the ball as the archetypal white boy—points to the way DeLillo challenges such mythologizing of baseball and America through his rendering of Cotter Martin's securing the ball Thomson hit.

Hodges, who thinks disparagingly of his simulated broadcasts in contrast to the glory of doing "real baseball" (25), misses a key point; namely, he still performs the same order of simulation in his broadcast of the game even when he is present because he still must flesh out all the details for his listeners for the game to rise above the level of mere facts and statistics. Yet the mediation of radio, both for Hodges and his listeners, has become as invisible as an FBI wiretap. When a media form comes to seem transparent, when its role in the construction of aura is experienced paradoxically as an unmediated mediation, then we have entered, the novel suggests, the realm of the postmodern, technological sublime. But now the setting is no longer contemporary America, as it was in *White Noise,* but rather the American past. Indeed, DeLillo seems to be moving away from a strictly Baudrillardian notion of the orders of simulacra as he locates American culture's immersion in mediation progressively earlier, first in *Libra* (set in the early 1960s) and now in *Underworld*'s evocation of the 1950s.

But if Hodges is, on the one hand, DeLillo's ironized self-figuration, he also points toward the political figure whose media career began by doing simulated broadcasts of baseball games—Ronald Reagan.[31] Hodges's participation in the mythologizing of baseball parallels President Reagan's use of a mythological American past. Whenever he waxed anecdotal, Reagan, as Michael Rogin points out, seemed either unable or unwilling to distinguish between Hollywood movies and American history.[32] Reagan's conflation of film and history serves to embody a central contradiction of his presidency: despite the rhetoric of a classless society, the 1980s saw class differences sharpen. As the nostalgia president, Reagan attempted to return us to the prosperity of a mythologized, depoliticized 1950s, a 1950s that DeLillo in *Underworld* takes pains to show is altogether political and relevant to an understanding of the post–Cold War moment.

Moving out from the prologue, it becomes clear that Hodges is only one instance of the reflexive figuration of the artist in the novel. The older woman of Nick's affair in 1952 is Klara Sax, who after this episode leaves her husband and daughter in order to pursue art. She achieves fame in the 1960s through a pop art that constructs art out of the junk people have thrown away. In this way, Klara's and Nick's careers oddly reflect one another—both are waste managers. Nick's job, in essence, is to convince people that industrial and consumer waste does not exist by improving the technologies for the discreet removal of the visible traces of that waste. Like Nick, Klara makes invisible the waste of consumer culture, but with a twist. Klara's largest project, which is still ongoing in the present time of the novel, is a continuation of the recycling of junk that originally made her famous. Taking an unused portion of a military base in the Arizona desert, Klara, along with a large group of volunteers under her direction, paints in rainbow colors the decommissioned B-52s that previously had carried the nuclear payload that could have annihilated humanity. With so vast a canvas, only an aerial view fully reveals the scope of this project—230 airplanes painted so far, the work continuing. Nick and his wife view this installation from a hot air balloon and sense the postmodern sublime:

> The piece had a great riverine wash, a broad arc of sage green or maybe mustard green with brushy gray disturbances, and it curved from the southeast

corner up and across the north edge, touching nearly a third of the massed air-craft, several planes completely covered in the pigment—the work's circulat-ing fluid, naming the pace, holding the surface together. (125)

Nick wonders "if the piece was visible from space like the land art of some lost Andean people" (126). Not merely hiding the detritus of American cul-ture as Nick does (a thing surely dangerous to Americans' environmental awareness in and of itself), Klara in her waste management turns these B-52s into a site of aesthetic contemplation. Klara does have a political awareness; speaking to a reporter, she likens the post–Cold War moment to the end of World War II: "The one difference is we haven't actually fought a war this time. We have a number of postwar conditions without a war having been fought" (69–70). At the same time Klara emphasizes the aesthetic: "This is an art project, not a peace project" (70). Klara's art finally points to the impli-cation of avant-garde art in the structures of high culture. This is not a peo-ple's art, since only a very few people have the economic means to view this massive installation.

If Russ Hodges and Klara Sax serve as DeLillo's reminder of the dangers of aestheticizing the political, then a third artist figure, Ismael Muñoz, repre-sents the possibility of politicizing the aesthetic. Known as Moonman in the 1970s, he is famous in the underground world of New York graffiti artists for his distinctive designs on subway cars. Against Klara, who is an insider in the world of New York art circles, Ismael maintains his outsider status throughout his career, despite attempts of the art world to find him for a showing of his work when graffiti art was in vogue in the 1970s. His very name, which sug-gests simultaneously the biblical and Herman Melville's Ishmael, confirms the marginality he embodies through his class, race, and sexual orientation.

Like Klara, Ismael in the post–Cold War moment has an ongoing instal-lation known as The Wall, which he and his crew use to commemorate the deaths of underclass children in New York. Ismael's Wall becomes a central focus of *Underworld*'s epilogue. That the title of this epilogue is "Das Kapital" is surely another form of directed intertextuality, one that urges a Marxian perspective on the relation of the aesthetic image to the economic forces of capitalism. Unlike Klara's remote and inaccessible art, Ismael's is part of the urban landscape. When a particularly violent death occurs, the rape and mur-der of a homeless girl, Esmeralda, Ismael's Wall is given "two and a half sec-onds" of CNN coverage (816) as part of the media attention to this crime. What makes the news coverage particularly eerie is that Ismael and his crew see the moment on their television, which is powered by a generator that is itself powered by one of Ismael's crew members pedalling a bicycle:

They gawk and buzz, charged with a kind of second sight, the things they know so well seen inside out, made new and nationwide. They stand there smeared in other people's seeing. Then the anchorwoman comes on. They tell

Willamette to pedal faster man because the picture is beginning to fade and the anchorwoman's electric red hair is color-running from her head in a luminous ring, which makes her all the more amazing, and she describes their lives to them in a bell-tone virgin voice, a woman so striking of feature she makes the news her own. . . . (816–17)

This moment, functioning again in Baudrillard's hyperreal, suggests the ability of mass media to construct a powerful imagistic aura, one that seems to draw its power by draining the energy from other images, such as Ismael's political art.

At this point in the epilogue, DeLillo turns to an aesthetic image apparently linked to the supernatural and a revelation, an image that might counter the false aura of the television broadcast. Crowds begin to gather each evening to witness a billboard where an image of the murdered child appears briefly whenever a subway train illuminates the back of the billboard. It is in this moment that DeLillo's homage to Thomas Pynchon's *The Crying of Lot 49* becomes clearest. Waste has been a dominant motif in *Underworld,* and the very word resonates with Pynchon's pairing of waste with the possibility of revelation, for in *Lot 49* waste is also an acronym (We Await Silent Tristero's Empire) of the dispossessed who use a centuries-old underground postal system to communicate. In *Underworld,* DeLillo's dispossessed await the train that apparently brings them the revelation that Pynchon's characters so desire.

It is symbolically appropriate that J. Edgar Hoover's double, Sister Edgar, should be our angle of vision. If J. Edgar meditates in the prologue on Breugel's *The Triumph of Death,* Sister Edgar provides in the epilogue a knowing perspective on the imagery represented by the advertisement:

a vast cascade of orange juice pouring diagonally from the top right into a goblet that is handheld at lower left—the perfectly formed hand of a female caucasian of the middle suburbs. Distant willows and vaguish lake view set the social locus. But it is the juice that commands the eye, thick and pulpy with a ruddled flush that matches the madder moon. And the first detailed drops splashing at the bottom of the goblet with a scatter of spindrift, each fleck embellished with the finicky rigor of some precisionist painting. What a lavishment of effort and technique, no refinement spared—the equivalent, Edgar thinks, of medieval church architecture. And the six-ounce cans of Minute Maid arrayed across the bottom of the board, a hundred identical cans so familiar in design and color and typeface that they have personality, the convivial cuteness of little orange-and-black people. (820)

Rather than the triumph of death, capitalism, in the form of advertising, celebrates the triumph of consumption, which is the denial of death. That this billboard is erected in an area of urban poverty underscores the ideological function of advertising that represents the middle class as the unquestioned norm.

Over and above the issue of technique and advertising's appropriation of the category of public art, the implications that reside in the gorgeous image of orange juice are highly freighted in the symbolic logic of the novel and suggest waste in many forms. While serving in Vietnam, Nick's brother, Matt, notices the black drums at the edge of the camp and learns that planes were

> spraying the jungles with a herbicide stored in black drums that had identifying orange stripes. . . .
> The drums resembled cans of frozen Minute Maid enlarged by a crazed strain of DNA. And the substance in the drums contained, so the rumor went, a cancer-causing agent. (463)

Reflecting on his war experience in the summer of 1974, Matt reiterates the link between the image of orange juice and waste when he wonders "how can you tell the difference between orange juice and agent orange if the same massive [distribution] system connects them at levels outside your comprehension?" (465). Returning to DeLillo's description of the Minute Maid billboard, it is possible to see the racial underside of the image. Against the white hand that is a metonymy for the white middle class is the crowd of "little orange-and-black people" that the cans suggest. These little people are simultaneously the Vietnamese victims of Agent Orange and people of color in the United States who fall outside the parameters of middle-class consumption. More broadly, if Agent Orange was a weapon used in a local "hot" war during the Cold War, then orange juice—as a site of capitalism's appropriation of the aesthetic image to construct an American identity that transforms political freedom into freedom of consumer choice—was surely part of America's Cold War effort.[33]

Despite Sister Edgar's conviction that the source of the revelation is God, the novel strongly implies that Ismael is responsible for the image of Esmeralda appearing in the billboard's orange juice advertisement. That the image depends on the headlights of a subway train points to the fact that Ismael's first art was marking subway cars. When Sister Edgar arrives to witness the miracle, she notices Ismael and his crew in attendance. In his earlier avatar as Moonman, Ismael liked to be in the crowds at the subway stations to see the responses of people to his art. Perhaps most tellingly, the punishment for those caught marking cars in the 1970s, as Ismael knows, had been to wash those cars in orange juice, since the acid in the juice dissolved the paint.

When the first train approaches, Sister Edgar experiences the revelation felt by the crowd; she hears the "holler of unstoppered belief" and sees "a dozen women clutch their heads, they whoop and sob, a spirit, a godsbreath passing through the crowd" (821). Eight minutes later with the next train's arrival, Edgar sees Esmeralda's face take shape under the rainbow of bounteous juice and above the little suburban lake and there is a sense of someone living in the image, an animating spirit—less than a tender second of life, less than half a second and the spot is dark again. (822)

Here it seems is a subversion of advertising's colonization of the aesthetic. Ismael's discovery of a new aesthetic technique that simultaneously subverts specious aura while producing authentic aura is not the anarchist miracle of Pynchon's Jesus Arrabal but the miracle of an outsider art that stays a half-step ahead of the near total control of the image by multinational capital. But just a half-step. In a few days the crowds begin to spiral out of control and threaten social order. When the crowds return one night, they see only a blank billboard advertising itself as *"Space Available"* (824).

DeLillo seems to use these various artist figures to think about his own position as a novelist. Aware that his own vast fictional canvas—*Underworld*, after all, is 827 pages—may render his art as remote from contemporary cognizance as Klara's desert installation, DeLillo earlier has addressed in *Mao II* his concern that the novelist's role in culture has been usurped by the terrorist. The figure of Ismael, the outsider artist whose work assaults the viewer, represents the terrain of cognitive terrorism within which DeLillo wishes to work. Although the final word of the novel is "Peace," *Underworld* is not a peace project; it is an attempt to construct fully historicized art.

The epilogue's exploration of the possibility of authentic aesthetic aura makes the conclusion of the novel's prologue deeply ironic. The game is over, but many fans remain in the stands and on the field. Russ has finished his interviews in the locker rooms and is preparing to leave when his producer, Al, remarks:

"Mark the spot. Like where Lee surrendered to Grant or some such thing."
Russ thinks this is another kind of history. He thinks they will carry something out of here that joins them all in a rare way, that binds them to a memory with protective power. . . . Isn't it possible that this midcentury moment enters the skin more lastingly than the vast shaping strategies of eminent leaders, generals steely in their sunglasses—the mapped visions that pierce our dreams? Russ wants to believe a thing like this keeps us safe in some undetermined way. (59–60)

What DeLillo's Hodges describes here is what Benjamin identifies as aura. The sense of a protective power Hodges experiences is what is pernicious in Benjamin's view, for the false aura of sport masks not only the politics of Cold War America but also the most fundamental reality of life, personal mortality. Hodges's reflections continue:

This is the thing that will pulse in his brain come old age and double vision and dizzy spells—the surge sensation, the leap of people already standing, that bolt of noise and joy when the ball went in. This is the people's history and it has flesh and breath that quicken to the force of this old safe game of ours. And fans at the Polo Grounds today will be able to tell their grandchildren, younger fans here today—they'll be the gassy old men leaning into the next century and trying to convince anyone willing to listen, pressing in with medicine breath, that they were here when it happened. (60)

The veneration of origin and celebration of athletic genius serves to displace personal mortality, recontextualizing it in the space of a timeless tradition. To the extent that the Dodgers-Giants game has an immortal life, the fans who witnessed the game participate in that immortality; if one is present at the constructive moment of aura—or so this quasi-religious logic runs—then one is always part of that aura.

Benjamin's sense that mechanical reproduction could be used to construct aura in mass culture that would aestheticize the political has become in DeLillo's contemporary America more pervasive than Benjamin ever could have imagined. It matters not whether one seeks escape into a timeless tradition by contemplating the relation between the 1951 Dodgers-Giants playoff series and the 1998 Braves-Yankees World Series or by meditating on the relative value of metaphysical versus Romantic poetry. The point here is something more than that baseball in its quasi-religious function is the opiate of the American masses. In the mass media's reflection of the masses back to themselves, there is a structuring of subjectivity conducive to an ahistorical formalist contemplation of the media forms themselves. When people seek a surrender to a transcendent power, the Führer figure will always appear to emerge, if only as pure media construct.

Seen from a more fully historicized perspective, the final image of *Underworld*'s prologue serves as an apt figuration of American reality after 1951. A drunk on the field, participating in the postgame celebration begins to run the bases. As the man approaches second, Hodges and his friend "see that he is going to slide and they stop and watch him leave his feet"; for those watching this celebrant, "all the fragments of the afternoon collect around his airborne form. Shouts, bat-cracks, full bladders, and stray yawns, the sand-grained manyness of things that can't be counted" (70). The fragments that can't be counted include Cold War politics and race-class difference. Postwar America, with its exaggerated sense of exceptionalism, is the suspended drunk of the postgame celebration, the text suggests. The drunk is frozen in the last moment of euphoria over American long-ball power, our exclusive possession of the big blast.

A different portion of the epilogue balances the prologue, bringing the reader full circle by traveling to an old nuclear test site in Kazakhstan. A Russian entrepreneur has brought Nick to the exact spot of the 1951 atomic blast that had made the Soviet Union a superpower. Nick is there to witness a test for the potential commercial use of underground nuclear explosions—the elimination of hazardous wastes (including nuclear waste) from first-world countries. The losers of the Cold War will "clean up" by literally cleaning up for the winners. This visit to post–Cold War Russia is chilling for two reasons. First, DeLillo shows the way Russian culture is attempting to ape the worst of Western consumerism. In a Russian bar called the Football Hooligan, where paid doubles of Lenin, Marx, and Trotsky mix with the crowd, Nick senses the force of multinational capital:

> Foreign investment, global markets, corporate acquisitions, the flow of infor-mation through transactional media, the attenuating influence of money that's electronic and sex that's cyberspaced, untouched money and computer safe sex, the convergence of consumer desire—not that people want the same things, necessarily, but that they want the same range of choices. (785)

The bar represents Fredric Jameson's postmodern, a space wherein previously articulated styles blur in a dizzying confusion that erases the specificity of time and place.

The second and more disturbing view of the former Soviet Union is Nick's visit to a local clinic for the unacknowledged and in some instances grotesquely disfigured victims of nuclear testing. The victimization is not limited to a single generation, since genetic mutations have increased the cancer rates of this population's children and grandchildren. Here is waste that cannot be managed, and we are reminded that these people are as much war casualties as were those killed in any of the local "hot" wars (Vietnam, Afghanistan) during the period of U.S.-Soviet rivalry.

In his eleventh novel, DeLillo urges Americans to acknowledge the cost, both in personal identity and world resources, of our Cold War victory. He further suggests that although the threat of nuclear holocaust may have receded, a secular apocalypse may be at hand if multinational corporations do succeed in turning the entire world into a homogenous consumer culture. In our accelerating rate of consumption, we are producing the underworld that will consume us. America may have "won" the Cold War but at what price? From individual families buying fallout shelters in the 1950s to Reagan's "Star Wars" Strategic Defense Initiative in the 1980s, much of America's real and symbolic capital has been spent in the maintenance of a definition, our ability to distinguish ourselves from our Cold War Other, the Soviet Union. The demise of Reagan's Evil Empire and the end of the Cold War means that the master "us-them" binary of the 1950s—the United States versus the Soviet Union—can no longer mask racial division in America. Violence in the age of electronic reproduction—the video record of the police beating of Rod-ney King and the assault on Reginald Denny—makes it all too clear that America's problems of race and class cannot be sanitized (*pace* Ken Burns and his epic treatment of baseball on PBS) by a mythologized history of our great American pastime. *Underworld* may not ensure the production of a "solid historiographic formation on the reader's part" that Jameson requires before he will grant any political vocation to contemporary historical fiction (and perhaps one may wonder why any cultural text should have to shoulder such a burden alone).[34] However, fiction such as DeLillo's opens a site wherein historical thinking becomes possible.

Notes

1. Walter Benjamin, *Illuminations* (New York: Harcourt, 1955), 225–26. For a number of readers, Benjamin seems nostalgic for the loss of aura in the work of art. And indeed for a dialectical thinker such as Benjamin, it is not unusual to discover contradictory impulses within the same essay. But for my purposes, I emphasize that part of Benjamin that welcomed the destruction of aura in classical art in order to embrace the mechanically reproduced arts (such as film) that might serve the aims of political communication. In doing so, I follow Richard Wolin's *Walter Benjamin: An Aesthetic of Redemption* (Berkeley: University of California Press, 1994); see 187–97. The migration of aura from the high-culture artifact to mass culture is one bridging concept linking modernism and postmodernism that Andreas Huyssen examines in his discussion of Benjamin's relation to the Frankfurt School in *After the Great Divide: Modernism, Mass Culture, Postmodernism* (Bloomington: Indiana University Press, 1986), 152–56.

2. Benjamin, 243.

3. Benjamin, 253.

4. Charles Alexander, *Ty Cobb* (New York: Oxford University Press, 1984), 11–16.

5. Alexander, 215–16.

6. In Alexander's account, Cobb's mother, Amanda, supposedly had taken a lover. When this rumor reached W. H., he told Amanda on August 8, 1905, that he would be gone farming for several days. That night, armed with a revolver, he returned home, climbed to the roof and attempted to enter his and his wife's bedroom window. The window—and indeed all the house—was closed and locked, despite daytime temperatures in the nineties. Amanda apparently was aware of her husband's design. She fired a shotgun through the window and "after what witnesses later described as a considerable interval, she fired again" (21).

7. Alexander, 12.

8. Cobb became a commercial spokesman for Coca-Cola in 1908 and "eventually came to own 20,000 shares" of the company's stock (see Alexander, 155). Although he had diversified investments, his main holdings in Coca-Cola and GM "held up through the Depression years," and through shrewd investment, Cobb's personal income doubled during the 1930s (Alexander, 214).

9. Wade V. Lewis, "Substitute Play for War," *Rotarian,* August 1947, 4.

10. Lewis, 52.

11. Weldon James, "Japan's at Batto Again," *Collier's,* August 2, 1947, 46.

12. James, 44.

13. Norman Cousins, "Slide, Fujimura, SLIDE!" *Collier's,* November 5, 1949, 28.

14. Cousins, 54.

15. In his second novel, *End Zone,* DeLillo explores in depth the way the language of football and that of nuclear strategy are at times indistinguishable.

16. Cousins, 55.

17. Don DeLillo, "The Power of History," *New York Times Magazine,* September 7, 1997, 62. DeLillo, however, does not reveal his source for this information. Whether it can be documented that these four men attended the ballgame, it is true that the late FBI director

enjoyed both New York entertainments and the company of celebrities. As Curt Gentry (*J. Edgar Hoover: The Man and His Secrets* [New York: Norton, 1991]) points out, from the late 1930s and throughout the 1950s Hoover spent most of his weekends in New York, where on Saturday night he frequented Toots Shor's before ending up at Walter Winchell's table at the Stork Club (217), which makes the possibility of Hoover attending the game with Shor less fantastic. As Gentry further notes, "Given Hoover's public persona of strict morality, it was assumed that those he honored with his friendship were models of probity. On the contrary according to a top aide, 'Hoover didn't associate with people unless he had something on them' " (384). One of the people the head of the FBI "had something on" was Frank Sinatra, on whom Hoover had maintained a file since February 26, 1947 (Gentry, 333).

18.   DeLillo, "Power," 60.

19.   Clearly Hoover didn't need Russian nuclear capability to be anticommunist; he had made his career as a law enforcement agent fighting the red menace at least since his involvement in the deportation of Emma Goldman in 1919 (see Gentry, 84).

20.   An odd example of the construction of American cultural memory occurs in a particular episode of the 1970s sitcom version of the Korean War, *M*A*S*H;* the characters first listen to the Dodgers-Giants game and then later see Thomson hit his home run on a newsreel. Presumably that same newsreel would detail the Soviet blast, yet this piece of history—surely pertinent to anyone serving in the Korean War—is invisible.

21.   Don DeLillo, *Underworld* (New York: Scribner, 1997), 41. All subsequent references to the novel are to this edition.

22.   Don DeLillo, *White Noise* (New York: Penguin, 1985), 25.

23.   Gentry, 377–82.

24.   Herman L. Massin, "Baseball, the Great Americanizer," *Senior Scholastic,* May 3, 1950, 10.

25.   In 1911, Cobb went into the stands in New York and viciously attacked Claude Lueker, a man with one hand, who shouted the slur at Cobb; after knocking Lueker down, Cobb repeatedly stomped on him with his spikes (See Alexander, 105).

26.   In some respect, DeLillo's treatment of Bill and Cotter serves to revise the author's unproblematic depiction of the relation between another white member of the middle class and another 14-year-old minority figure; this earlier pair reminds us too that DeLillo writes *Underworld* from the implicated position of a baseball fan. In his first novel, *Americana* (New York: Penguin, 1989), the moment experienced as most authentic by the jaded television executive David Bell in his trip through an otherwise unauthentic American West occurs when he and a Native American youth play catch in the desert: "I picked up one of the gloves, a very old Luke Appling model. I spat into the palm and pounded it a few times." The page-long description of this male bonding through baseball ends with David briefly in touch with himself through the exertion: "Sweat was collecting at my navel and I would rub it off with my right hand and then rub my hand in the dirt and wipe off the sticky dirt on my pants and blow on my hand then, drying it further, and then lean back and heave another long arching fly into the mouth of the sun" (359).

27.   Jackie Robinson, "Negroes Are Americans," *Life,* August 1, 1949, 22.

28.   Several critics usefully link DeLillo's fiction to Baudrillard's theory of simulation. On *White Noise,* see John Frow, "The Last Things before the Last: Notes on *White Noise,*" in *Introducing Don DeLillo,* ed. Frank Lentricchia (Durham, N.C.: Duke University Press, 1991), 175–91; see also Leonard Wilcox, "Baudrillard, DeLillo's *White Noise* and the End of Heroic Narrative," *Contemporary Literature* 32 (1991): 346–55.

29.   Jean Baudrillard, *Simulations* (New York: Semiotext[e], 1983), 99.

30.   Baudrillard, 142.

31.   Michael Paul Rogin, *Ronald Reagan, the Movie* (Berkeley: University of California Press, 1987), 11.

32.   See Rogin, 1–43.

33. DeLillo completes the symbolism surrounding orange juice by having Charles Wainwright, an advertising account executive and the man who bought the Thomsom ball from Manx Martin, imagine in 1961 an ad campaign for Minute Maid that similarly stresses visual appeal by showing "juice splashing in a glass" (532).

34. Fredric Jameson, *Postmodernism, or, The Logic of Late Capitalism* (Durham, N.C.: Duke University Press, 1991), 24.

Everything Is Connected:
Underworld's Secret History of Paranoia

PETER KNIGHT

Elevated to a principle of national policy in the McCarthy years of the Cold War, and then reappropriated as an indispensable attitude of the counter-culture in the 1960s, paranoia has become one of the defining characteristics of postwar American politics and culture. In the words of Don DeLillo (once hailed as the "chief shaman of the paranoid school of fiction" [Towers 6]), this is the period in which "paranoia replaced history in American life" (qtd. in O'Toole). As many commentators have pointed out recently, there are very good reasons why conspiratorially infused paranoia should no longer have a hold over the collective imagination, not the least of which is the end of the Cold War and all its attendant anxieties about communist infiltration and mutually assured nuclear destruction. Yet in the last decade it has come to seem that paranoia and conspiracy theories are everywhere: a brief sampling from the last couple of years might include the Oklahoma bombing; the crash of TWA flight 800; the runaway success of *The X-Files;* the self-consciously titled summer 1997 Hollywood blockbuster *Conspiracy Theory;* the inclusion of the very term "conspiracy theory" for the first time in the 1997 supplement to the *OED;* the public declaration by Martin Luther King's family that his death was part of a government conspiracy; and even Hillary Clinton's assertion on national television that "a vast right-wing conspiracy" was against the President. Elaine Showalter's recent book *Hystories* speaks to the common perception there is a "plague of paranoia" spreading through western society. Just when you thought it was safe, the emergence of new fears and fantasies (summed up by President Bush's infamous announcement of a "New World Order") has paradoxically meant a return to the dominance of conspiracy thinking in American life.

A similar conundrum arises in the new world order of American fiction. On the one hand, as Michael Wood suggests, Thomas Pynchon's *Mason and Dixon* and DeLillo's *Underworld* are "post-paranoid" epics: DeLillo's *Libra,* Wood pronounced, was "perhaps the last really good novel of the great age of

Originally published in *Modern Fiction Studies* 45, no. 3 (1999): 811–36. © 1999. Purdue Research Foundation. Reprinted by permission of the Johns Hopkins University Press.

282

American paranoia," an age that "faded away somewhere in the early nineties" ("Post-Paranoid" 3). On the other hand, other critics accused *Underworld* of having an unnecessarily paranoid structure, of hinting at connections where none exist; for instance, James Wood, writing in the *New Republic,* declared that *Underworld* "proves, once and for all, the incompatibility of paranoid history with great fiction" ("Black Noise"). So, just when we might expect paranoia to have gone beyond its sell-by date in that six-floor book depository of postwar American literature containing Pynchon, William Burroughs, Norman Mailer, and DeLillo, it seems that *Underworld* has brought the topic out of storage and back onto the shelves.

How can we explain what looks like the simultaneous disappearance and recrudescence of paranoia, in both American literature and society? In this essay I suggest that DeLillo's monumental new novel presents the materials for constructing a secret history of paranoia over the last half-century, which in turn can help explain some of these paradoxes. In brief, *Underworld* revises the anatomy of popular American paranoia that DeLillo has conducted in his previous novels, pushing back the inquiry before the assassination of President John F. Kennedy, which had previously served as the watershed event in his work, and reaching ahead into the as yet unconfigured world beyond the end of the Cold War.

PLOTTING THE ASSASSINATION

The assassination of President Kennedy and its surrounding culture of conspiracy have haunted DeLillo's career as a writer. Its influence and iconography are present in one form or another throughout his work, from the drive through Dealey Plaza in the final scene of *Americana,* to the underground screening of the Zapruder footage in *Underworld.* He admits that "it's possible I wouldn't have become the kind of writer I am if it weren't for the assassination," but its influence remained subterranean until addressed directly in *Libra* (qtd. in DeCurtis 47–48). For many Americans a conspiratorial worldview came to be taken for granted in the decades following the political assassinations of the 1960s and the revelations about the nefarious activities of government agencies that emerged in the investigations of the 1970s. It has become commonplace to back-date a loss of innocence and a distrust of the authorities to what DeLillo has called "the seven seconds that broke the back of the American century" (*Libra* 181). In *Underworld,* at the mid-1970s New York underground art-scene screening of the Zapruder footage of the Kennedy assassination, the audience experiences both a sense of shock (at seeing for the first time endlessly looped versions of what until then had been hidden from the American public), and a cynical sense of having already carried this ultimate snuff movie inside their heads. In a sense, then, it was only in the paranoid atmosphere of the late 1960s and the post-Watergate period of disillusion that a certain form of countercultural paranoia—and DeLillo's writing—could take shape.

As much as *Libra*'s version of the Kennedy assassination is shaped by conspiracy, secret histories, and a sense of a hidden order behind the visible, it is also framed in terms of randomness and disorder, chaos, and coincidence. The taut, ruthless plotting of the renegade CIA conspirators is unraveled by the accidental intrusion of Lee Harvey Oswald into their ready-made plans, an aberration in the inexorable unfolding of the plot of history.[1] In the larger scheme of American history, for DeLillo the assassination belatedly comes to function as "an aberration in the heartland of the real" (*Libra* 15): "I think we've all come to feel that what's been missing over these past twenty-five years is a sense of manageable reality. Much of that feeling can be traced to that one moment in Dallas" (qtd. in DeCurtis 48).

The Kennedy assassination might indeed have set the American public to thinking that everything is connected in a sinister fashion. But that paranoid realization is ultimately experienced as a loss of connectedness, a fall into a postmodern sense of epistemological—and social—fragmentation. For the cast of amateur conspiracy theorists, secret historians, decoders, and readers that populate DeLillo's novels, the Kennedy assassination and its impossibly complex proliferation of data produce an overwhelming sense of paranoia, such that eventually everything is suspect, even reality itself. It is an event that in hindsight becomes the symbolic cause of what might be termed a postmodern hermeneutic of suspicion. It is retrospectively posited as the origin of a skepticism that produces not only a distrust of the narratives of the authorities (most notably, the *Report* prepared by the Warren Commission), but also a distrust of the authority of narrative itself, or, in Lyotard's classic formulation of postmodernism, an "incredulity toward metanarratives" (xxiv).

The hermeneutic of suspicion (for which *The X-Files* has supplied the corporate slogan—Trust No One™) has come to be taken for granted in much recent critical and creative thought.[2] It is an attitude that DeLillo has learned in part by studying de-realized media events like the shooting of President Ronald Reagan, and later projected back onto the Kennedy assassination as its symbolically necessary causal origin. In DeLillo's preliminary survey of presidential assassinations published by *Rolling Stone* in 1983, he describes the shooting of Reagan by John Hinckley (a "self-created media event") as "pure TV, a minicam improvisation" ("American" 24). In comparison, the horrifying spectacle of President Kennedy's head exploding has in theory the power to shock, but, in the underground screening in *Underworld*, it too becomes endlessly repeated and decomposed, subsumed into the routinized cynicism of a paranoia that has lost its critical, countercultural edge.

Secure Paranoia

It is significant, however, that there is a measure of nostalgia in DeLillo's ret-rospective plotting of the Kennedy assassination as an inaugural event in the society of the spectacle, the limit case of modernist solidity before politics finally gave way to postmodern simulation.[3] Through a parallel mechanism of nostalgia, the recreation in *Underworld* of the 1951 Giants/Dodgers base-ball game confirms and extends DeLillo's argument that the Kennedy assas-sination marks the watershed between an older faith in the communal experi-ence of a "manageable reality" and a sense of uncontrolled suspicion towards events that are entirely subsumed within the postmodern logic of the com-modified image. Brian Glassic, waste manager and amateur pundit, counter-poises Thomson's home run against the Kennedy assassination, another "shot that was heard around the world": "When JFK was shot, people went inside. We watched TV in dark rooms and talked on the phone with friends and rel-atives. We were all separate and alone. But when Thomson hit the homer, people rushed outside. People wanted to be together. Maybe it was the last time people spontaneously went out of their houses for something" (DeLillo, *Underworld* 94).

If the Thomson homer was an event experienced together in public, then the Kennedy assassination marked the emergence of the substitute and isolated community of a national (and global) television audience—think of the scene in *Libra* with Beryl Parmenter, the CIA operative's wife, endlessly watching the reruns of the "live" death of Lee Harvey Oswald.[4] In compari-son, the unrepeatable and more distant memory of the Thomson home run takes on a far greater stability and solidity than the Kennedy assassination, which by now has dissolved into endless repetitions, not of the raw event itself, but of its mediated and commodified versions.[5]

In *Underworld* the division between a before and an after is not some-thing that is immediately recognizable by the characters at the time, but is strategically projected backwards through the lens of nostalgia. The novel does not evoke nostalgia for a Norman Rockwell-esque version of the 1950s—a view that is thoroughly satirized in the Jell-O section, which links together the domestic innocence of suburbia with the military economy that underpins it. Rather, it calls up an earlier form of paranoia that in retrospect can seem oddly comforting. For example, visiting a nuclear test site in Kazakh-stan, Nick Shay feels a "kind of homesickness" (793) for the 1950s brand-name products left on the shelf of a recreated American home destined for destruction. This is a homesickness not so much for the "safe" domesticity of the 1950s as for the paranoia of the nuclear age, whose obsessive dedication to murderous detail can almost seem touching in an age when, with the pri-vatization of public responsibility, the paranoically intimate interest of the state in the daily lives of its citizens—even for sinister purposes—has begun to disappear. In a similar fashion, when they meet again after four decades, Klara Sax voices her suspicion to Nick that "life [took] an unreal turn at some point" (73), an echo of DeLillo's long-running preoccupation with the post-1960s "aberration in the heartland of the real." She goes on to explain how as a young woman during the 1960s she used to watch mysterious lights in the sky and wanted to believe that they were from B-52 bombers carrying their nuclear cargo: "War scared me all right but those lights, I have to tell you those lights were a complex sensation. Those planes on permanent alert, ever present you know, sweeping the Soviet borders, and I remember sitting out there rocking lightly at anchor in some deserted cove and feeling a sense of awe, a child's sleepy feeling of mystery and danger and beauty" (75).

Looking back from beyond the end of the Cold War (she is now turning those decommissioned planes into an artwork), her past fear comes to seem paradoxically appealing:

> Now that power is in shatters or tatters and now that those Soviet borders don't even exist in the same way, I think we understand, we look back, we see ourselves more clearly, and them as well. Power meant something thirty, forty years ago. It was stable, it was focused, it was a tangible thing. It was greatness, danger, terror, all those things. And it held us together, the Soviets and us. Maybe it held the world together. You could measure things. You could measure hope and you could measure destruction. Not that I want to bring it back. It's gone, good riddance. But the fact is. (76)

In an age when power has become unstable, unfocused, and intangible, Klara expresses a fondness for the certainties of four decades ago, while also recognizing the misery of living under the shadow of such terror. Marvin Lundy, the baseball collector, likewise argues that "the Cold War is your friend": "It's the one constant thing. It's honest, it's dependable. Because when the tension and the rivalry come to an end, that's when your worst nightmares begin. All the power and the intimidation of the state will seep out of your personal bloodstream" (170). These characters express what has now become a widespread nostalgic yearning, which is less for the constrictions of the containment culture of the 1950s than for the more manageable certainties of Cold War anxiety. In comparison with the insecure paranoia that DeLillo presents as an effect of the Kennedy assassination, the secure paranoia of the Cold War years takes on a comforting solidity.[6]

Where DeLillo's previous novels have given narrative shape to the shifting, spiraling paranoia of postmodernity, *Underworld* presents an outline of an earlier notion of paranoia as a source of stability. The novel offers several explanations for the nature of Cold War paranoia. Its characterization of nuclear fear as paradoxically a form of security is in line with a standard interpretation of American paranoia as a psychic strategy for maintaining a stable sense of identity, whether on the individual or the national level.[7] In *Underworld,* for example, we hear J. Edgar Hoover speculate during the ballgame that a form of national consensus is not so much a result of a natural unity as a product of there being a definite and coherent enemy: "Edgar looks at the faces around him, open and hopeful. He wants to feel a compatriot's nearness and affinity. All these people formed by language and climate and popular songs and breakfast foods and the jokes they tell and the cars they drive have never had anything in common so much as this, that they are sitting in the furrow of destruction" (28). Paranoia in the Cold War "displaces religious faith" (241) with "radioactivity, the power of alpha particles and the all-knowing systems that shape them, the endless fitted links" (251), becoming in effect the glue that cements the nation together.

Underworld suggests that paranoia is not merely a strategic belief (whether spontaneously emerging from below or cynically imposed from above) which serves to forge a sense of national consensus at precisely the time when it was beginning to come under internal threat from the collapse of the traditional white middle-class male hegemony. DeLillo's novel also devotes many pages to the psychic damage inflicted by the nuclear age, to the "hundred plots [that] go underground, to spawn and skein" (51). Even though the presentation of Cold War paranoia is suffused with nostalgia, there is still recognition that this mentality was at best a defense mechanism that exacted a high price in both individual and national terms. In his drug-enhanced state of paranoia at a "bombhead" party in the mid-1970s, Matt Shay hears a colleague intone in a cartoon Prussian accent, "You can never underestimate the willingness of the state to act out its own massive fantasies" (421), though later, when Matt looks at a photograph of Nixon, he wonders whether "the state had taken on the paranoia of the individual or was it the other way around" (465). In *Underworld* paranoia comes to represent a genuine psychic disturbance of the state whose "power and intimidation" have seeped their way into the "personal bloodstream" of its citizens, from Lenny Bruce's mantra "We're all gonna die!" during the Cuban missile crisis to Sister Edgar's obsessive use of latex gloves to protect her from the "submicroscopic parasites in their soviet socialist protein coats" (241).

Some of the novel's explanations are less than convincing. The portrayal of Hoover, for example, amounts to a clumsy psychologizing of history, suggesting a reading of Cold War paranoia not as a sense-making strategy that takes its meaning from the culture at large, but as the emanation of a personal pathology writ large. The reader is left to suppose that the emergence of paranoia in the collective imagination is in part a result of Hoover's projecting his own internal weaknesses and thwarted desires onto the external scene of American society. He is portrayed as germophobic, "the man who has an air-filtration system in his house to vaporize specks of dust" (50), who fears "the sense of infiltration" (557) more than the bomb and is as paranoid about maintaining intact personal boundaries as he is about national borders. And in what reads like a return to pop-Freudian theories of paranoia as a result of repressed homosexuality, Hoover is also presented as a closet queen who spies on his faithful companion in bed and delights in wearing a leather bikers' mask to a ball. This explanation of the source of popular paranoia as a manifestation of the psychosexual disturbance of the nation's leaders is unconvincing, though the portrait of Hoover is not so inaccurate.[8] Instead, a populace's interest in conspiracy theories is less a result of the externalization of repressed internal conflicts than the internalization into narrative form of very real—though not immediately visible—conflicts in the social realm. Likewise, the line that the postwar obsession with conspiracies is merely a substitute for the loss of religion is less than convincing. Though undoubtedly part of the reshaping of popular forms of knowledge in the postwar period, the secularization of American culture is only part of a larger story involving (in Jürgen Habermas's phrase) an increasing "legitimation crisis" of many traditional forms of authority, one manifestation of which is a conspiratorial questioning of the word of government experts such as the Warren Commission.

DIETROLOGY

Even though *Underworld*'s portrait of paranoia in the 1950s as a national pathology is at times heavy-handed, the novel nevertheless sketches an intriguing and suggestive picture of more recent modes of conspiracy thinking. Despite the fixation on the Bomb, throughout its 827 pages and its half-century span, *Underworld* maintains a texture of everyday fear that exceeds the rigidifying, bipolar logic of the Cold War and its accompanying Manichaean anxieties. Many characters in the novel experience moments of low-level paranoia that are not directly connected to the overt concern with the nuclear threat (and might instead be seen as more in tune with a foreign policy of "low intensity conflict"). For example, Ismael Muñoz, also known as the graffiti artist Moonman 157, worries that the gallery world's sudden desire to buy his art is merely a plot by the authorities to trap him. An old man on a street corner in Harlem rants about the pyramid on the dollar bill. Marvin Lundy speculates that Greenland either doesn't exist at all or is being kept secret for a reason. Sims, Nick Shay's colleague, floats the possibility that the government is altering the census reports on the number of black people in America. Sister Edgar dismisses popular suspicions that the government introduced AIDS into the ghetto, believing instead that "the KGB was behind this particular piece of disinformation" (243). Albert Bronzini is tempted by the rumor that the moon landings were faked in a Hollywood studio. And many characters feel the pull of numerology, and the number thirteen in particular. These fears speak of a bewildering world controlled along the lines of race, class, gender, and economic forces beyond anyone's control.

The obsession with secrets is an indication that the restricted access to knowledge in supposedly public institutions like NASA is less a matter of pure epistemological skepticism than it is a question of power. Likewise, everyday tactics such as conspiratorial forms of numerology can perversely come to make sense in a society in which numbers are always the bottom line, and in which "voodoo economics" becomes official policy. As with previous DeLillo novels, conspiracy theory becomes an everyday attitude, a provisional but ever-present way of making sense of the world and giving narrative shape to fears that are more a reflection of the society at large than one's personal psychopathology.

In *Underworld* many forms of paranoid thinking work outside the conventional modes of conspiracy theory. On one of his trips to track down the missing link in the Thomson home run saga, Marvin Lundy visits the Conspiracy Theory Café in San Francisco, a place filled with "books, film reels, sound tapes, official government reports in blue binders." Given Marvin's predilection for wild conspiratorial theories, it is perhaps surprising that he "waved the place off" as a "series of sterile exercises." He does so because he believes that "the well-springs were deeper and less detectable, deeper and shallower both, look at billboards and matchbooks, trademarks on products, birthmarks on bodies, look at the behavior of your pets" (319). For both Marvin and the novel as a whole, the hidden story of recent history is not to be found buried in government files, waiting to be pieced together into a coherent story of shadowy conspirators. Instead it is to be found in the daily ephemera and vast entanglement of multinational consumer capitalism, both more obvious because it is omnipresent, and less detectable because it is so much taken for granted.

The exchanges between Sims and Nick about the real story of the mysterious garbage boat likewise offer a revealing contrast between a straightforward version of conspiracy theory and a more fluid, multiplicitous, and hesitant mode of paranoid belief. Sims suggests to Nick that their theories about the underworld involvement of the Mafia and the CIA are part of a recognizable conspiratorial worldview:

> "There's a word in Italian. *Dietrologia*. It means the science of what is behind something. A suspicious event. The science of what is behind an event."
> "They need this science. I don't need it."
> "I don't need it either. I'm just telling you."
> "I'm an American. I go to ball games," he said.
> "The science of dark forces. Evidently they feel this science is legitimate enough to require a name."
> "People who need this science, I would make an effort to tell them we have real sciences, hard sciences, we don't need imaginary ones."
> "I'm just telling you the word. I agree with you, Sims. But the word exists."

"There's always a word. There's probably a museum too. The Museum of Dark Forces. They have ten thousand blurry photographs. Or did the Mafia blow it up?" (280)

There are several revealing touches in this exchange. On the one hand, Nick resolutely dismisses this kind of post-Watergate explanation as somehow inappropriate for America (he insists that "History was not a matter of missing minutes on the tape" [82]), yet he alone maintains a conspiracy theory about his father's disappearance. On the other hand, though Sims seems to be trying to give his conspiratorial speculations the weight and precision of an exact science, it is noticeable that he seems uncommitted to his belief: "He liked saying this even more. Not that he believed it. He didn't believe it for half a second but he wanted me to believe it, or entertain the thought, so he could ridicule me. He had a hard grin that mocked whatever facile sentiments you might be tempted to shelter in the name of your personal conspiracy credo" (280).

If Sims takes the idea of dietrology only half seriously here, then later in the novel he presents in earnest his theory that the census reports have been doctored, with the result that Nick reminds him, "We're not, remember, we don't have a word, you and I, for the science of dark forces. For what is behind an event. We don't accept the validity of this word or this science" (335). Sims floats dietrological possibilities and then retracts them, hiding behind layers of irony too complex to unmask. In his world there is no longer a stable, monolithic "personal conspiracy credo" which one can adhere to unswervingly, only a temporary and strategic form of self-reflexive paranoia.

Sims's theories are presented as both undeniably plausible and yet probably false, in the same way that Matt's bombhead colleague makes out a convincing case about the unwitting use of "downwinders" in nuclear tests, only to deny the claims at the end of the conversation. In both the former Soviet Union and the Nevada desert, such experiments are presented as an "open secret," paradoxically something that everyone knows but that is officially denied. The paranoid beliefs of both Sims and Matt's colleague hover between the serious and the ironic, never quite coalescing into the rigid logic of a dietrological worldview. When Detwiler tries to persuade Nick and Sims that the garbage boat might be carrying CIA heroin, it is not because of any particular facts he knows, but because "it's stupid not to believe it" (289), or, as DeLillo puts it elsewhere, "paranoia in some contexts is the only intelligent response" ("American" 24). After all the revelations about government and corporate malfeasance ("Knowing what we know," says Jesse Detwiler, that "everything's connected" [*Underworld* 289]), a self-conscious and sophisticated expectation of a conspiracy comes both to be taken for granted and held at arm's length. One can never be paranoid enough, but a secure, single-minded faith in paranoia—either in the form of a McCarthyite political expediency or a countercultural reaction against such abuses of power—is no longer an option. In a similar fashion, one of the young volunteers on Klara's project to paint decommissioned bombers in the desert tells Nick of the joke about the end of the Cold War that is making the rounds of the camp: "the whole thing is a plot to trick the West" (81). She laughs at the joke, but admits that "no one seems sure that it's a joke." In *Underworld* conspiracy theories become not so much items of irrefragable faith as tentative gestures toward understanding the unknown, provisional forms of representation that can only approximate the "deeper and less detectable" (319) wellsprings of power. The novel tunes in to the transition in American paranoia over the last four decades from an inflexible and monolithic belief structure in a personalized cabal, to a contradictory, ironic, and self-reflexive appropriation of the language of conspiracy theory as a populist way of making sense of larger social and political changes.

In many ways these shifting, subterranean beliefs operate in precisely the opposite way to conventional explanations of what I have been calling secure paranoia. They can hardly be said to maintain a stable sense of self, whether personal or national, since they offer at best a fleeting suggestion of a shadowy and fragmented force that offers no coherent sense of a nameable enemy—and hence little possibility of an integral personal or national identity. In Sims's discussion, he hints at connections between CIA heroin smuggling, nuclear waste management, and the Mafia, but, departing from standard presentations of conspiracy theories, he doesn't develop an extended and documented narrative of how "They" might link together, or what "Their" purpose might be. Nor does he attribute ruthlessly efficient agency to the supposed conspirators. Conspiracy theorists are frequently attacked for failing to understand the intellectual challenge of the social sciences, namely that history is the effect of abstract forces rather than individual (conspiring) agents. In contrast, *Underworld* creates a sense that there are larger forces in our lives over which we have no control, but which refuse to coalesce for more than a moment into a recognizable conspiracy theory—and only then merely as a half-serious approximation of those unthinkably complex and hence unrepresentable forces. In effect, the novel develops a notion of conspiracy without conspiring, its reconfigured paranoia an appropriate response to the bewildering complexities of the current world in which everything is connected but nothing adds up.

THE WHOLE THING IS A PLOT TO TRICK THE WEST

How are we to account for this broad shift from secure to insecure paranoia? If the need to plot such a division is an effect of the nostalgia of the present, then what is it about the present that creates such a need? The obvious answer is the end of the Cold War. In publicity interviews DeLillo reinforced the explicit emphasis of *Underworld* on the Cold War and its uncertain aftermath, using many of the same formulations as Klara Sax within the novel. "I don't think there's any clear sense," DeLillo comments, "of what the ending of the Cold War meant, and what it's going to mean": "We're in between two historical periods, the Cold War and whatever it is that follows it. I'm not sure that this is what follows it. This may just be the interim. I think we're just beginning to wonder what happened, and what didn't happen" (qtd. in Williams, "Everything").

DeLillo goes on to discuss how the nuclear threat paradoxically produced, for all its restrictiveness, a "sense of limits we don't have any more," a "kind of ceiling against which other things were measured" (qtd. in Williams, "Everything"). But *Underworld* contains clues to a less visible but ultimately more convincing account of the disorienting instabilities of the New World Order. The spectacular end of the Cold War and its attendant reconfiguration of national boundaries, the novel suggests, are but an effect of the far more significant and ongoing, underground reshaping of the global economy. The end of the Cold War presents itself as a belated, convenient, and dramatic explanation for what is documented in subterranean ways throughout the novel. It is in some ways a red herring, a distraction from what is really going on, the flip side of the joke making the rounds at Klara's art project in the desert, that the whole thing is merely a plot to trick the West.

We can make more sense of the shift from secure to unstable paranoia if we read it in part as the way of making sense of and giving expression to changes in American society which are a result, not so much of the sudden collapse of the Berlin Wall, as of the gradual transition from a Fordist to a post-Fordist economy. In *Underworld,* Nick expounds upon the changes in the world's economy, borrowing phrases from Viktor Maltsev, the executive of a toxic waste trading company in the former Soviet Union:

> Foreign investment, global markets, corporate acquisitions, the flow of information through transnational media, the attenuating influence of money that's electronic and sex that's cyberspaced [. . .]. Some things fade and wane, states disintegrate, assembly lines shorten their runs and interact with lines in other countries. This is what desire seems to demand. A method of production that will custom-cater to cultural and personal needs, not to cold war ideologies of massive uniformity. And the system pretends to go along, to become more supple and resourceful, less dependent on rigid categories. (785–86)

At first sight a post-Fordist mode of production would seem to promote a fluidity of desire and identity that is commendable in comparison with the "rigid categories" and "massive uniformity" of "cold war ideologies." But the globalized economy as it appears in *Underworld* is not only uncontrolled in practice but in theory uncontrollable, a system that can only "pretend to go along" with the desires of its participants, with its specialization of production leading paradoxically to a transnational "planing away of particulars" (as Nick puts it [786]). The flip side of the loss of "rigid categories" and "massive uniformity" of the Cold War period is the loss of the sense of control over national (not to mention individual) economic destiny that allowed governments to guarantee the social contract between the state, capital, and labor. The absence of a Fordist sense of stability and security now manifests itself in popular conspiracy culture, such as the accusations of UN-controlled black helicopters flying in secret over the U.S. These popular narratives of world conspiracy and suspicion that the government is betraying its people to alien forces begin to make sense in the age of NAFTA, downsizing, job insecurity, and the erosion of the welfare state. The nostalgia many characters in *Underworld* feel for the stable paranoia of the Cold War might therefore be read instead as a displaced and timely nostalgia for the older—though no less scary—secure paranoia of Fordism.

The real secret history of paranoia in *Underworld,* then, is not the simple story of the replacement of bomb-induced fears by newer anxieties resulting from the fragmentation of those former geopolitical certainties. It is instead an underground current of increasing awareness and consternation that slowly everything is becoming connected. In the architecture of the novel there is far more continuity than the end-of-the-Cold-War hypothesis would suggest. It is also noteworthy that, if the beginnings of the Cold War nuclear terror are present in the novel through the dramatic simultaneity of the two "shots that are heard around the world," then the fall of the Berlin Wall, the equally symbolic end of the Cold War, is almost entirely absent from *Underworld*. Instead DeLillo offers glimpses, sometimes metaphorical, at other times literal, of the increasing interconnectedness of social and economic relationships within a global economy.

Underworld repeatedly explores how "all technology refers to the bomb" (467) in the postwar period, tapping into the underground currents that link civilian and military hardware. The "October 8, 1957" section dwells not just on the shared futuristic language of brand names and weaponry, but also on the unsettling physical resemblance between domestic and military products: young Eric masturbates into a condom "because it had a sleek metallic shimmer, like his favorite weapons system" (514); his mother doesn't like one of her Jell-O molds because it was "sort of guided missile-like" (515); her loaf of bread is "strontium white" (516); and the vacuum cleaner is "satellite-shaped" (520).

Matt Shay, a systems analyst involved in bomb production, has a moment of insight into those interlocking systems of production and consumption: "He was thinking about his paranoid episode at the bombhead party the night before. He felt he'd glimpsed some horrific system of connections in which you can't tell the difference between one thing and another, between a soup can and a car bomb, because they are made by the same people in the same way and ultimately refer to the same thing" (446). In Vietnam Matt experiences another sudden flash of insight, when he notices that "the drums [of agent orange] resembled cans of frozen Minute Maid enlarged by crazed strains of DNA" (463). What at first appears to be merely a visual resemblance, the product of a bombed-out mind, years later becomes a troubling ethical question as Matt waits for the sun to rise in the desert while he contemplates leaving his bomb-related job: "how can you tell the difference between orange juice and agent orange if the same massive system connects them at levels outside your comprehension?" (465). Matt comes to sense that "everything connects in the end, or only seems to, or seems to only because it does" (465). His access to the deep-forged linkages between seemingly unconnected areas of the economy that are "outside your level of comprehension" is through a series of verbal and visual associations. Matt's subliminal awareness that "everything connected at some undisclosed point down the line" (408) is a long way from a hyperbolically conspiratorial expose of the misdealings and hidden mutual interests of the wartime and peacetime economies. It is also a long way from the traditional form of systems analysis in which he was trained, since, with the interpenetration of the logic of the market into every last enclave of social life, there is no way to separate out self-contained systems.

Although the force field of the military industrial complex is not mapped in detail in *Underworld,* its metaphoric convergences offer an alternative and subtextual history of the emergence of a globalized economy, which uses public funds for private profit, in contrast to the novel's manifest interest in the end of the Cold War. The catalogue of brand names and intersecting vested business interests runs from the set-piece about simonizing the car in the breezeway during the 1950s to the complicated transnational operation run by Viktor Maltsev to dispose of toxic waste using converted nuclear weapons in the 1990s ("Tchaika is connected to the commonwealth arms complex, to bomb-design laboratories and the shipping industry" [788]). The continuity of these forms of interconnectedness throughout the time span of the novel suggests that the overt ideological struggle of the Cold War was merely a sideshow for what was—and still is—literally business as usual.

MINUTE MAID ORANGE JUICE

Though some of the connections in *Underworld* can be inserted into a coherent narrative of the quasi-conspiratorial collusion of hegemonic interests in the globalized economy, there are many others that refuse to be assimilated so easily. Take the example of the Minute Maid drums. In the passages quoted above, the link between weapons and domestic goods, though operating more at an emblematic than a factual level, nevertheless taps into the plausible suggestion that both are part of a larger system of production. But what are we to make of the other references to orange juice in the novel? In passing we learn that Chuckie Wainwright's ad-agency father is daydreaming about the Minute Maid account on the day he decides to give the baseball to his ungrateful son—who later ends up in Vietnam. And, in the novel's transcendent ending, the image of the street kid Esmeralda appears on a billboard underneath a poster for—what else?—Minute Maid orange juice.

It is precisely these forms of strange connection, however, which led some reviewers to attack the novel for being unnecessarily paranoid. James Wood and Richard Williams separately argue that the novel ends up replicating the paranoid worldview of a figure like Hoover, such that "*Underworld* surrenders fiction to the mysticism it should repel" (Williams). In a similar vein, Michael Dibdin concludes that DeLillo's novel "ultimately offers a hollow confirmation of the paranoid fears it addresses by being overtly manipulated from start to finish." In many ways these criticisms repeat a long-standing objection to fictions of conspiracy. Christopher Lasch, for example, takes issue with Pynchon's brand of literary paranoia for "hiding the obvious behind a veil of obscurity": in Lasch's view, Pynchon misses the "open secret" of society's faults by becoming too caught up with the trivia of conspiracy theories (159). More broadly, Fredric Jameson characterizes conspiracy theory as "the poor person's cognitive mapping in the postmodern age." It is a "degraded figure of the total logic of late capital," a displaced and distorted representation which, in his view, merely serves to mystify the real social relations at work ("Cognitive" 355).

In a certain sense, the bewildering connectedness of *Underworld* can indeed be read as a symptom of the crisis in "cognitive mapping" that Jameson outlines. Yet the novel is full of many different instances of interconnectedness, only some of which intimate vast threatening forces beyond our control. Taken together, they cannot be dismissed as simple conspiracy theories. There are strange parallels, some of which are appropriately thematic: Sister Edgar and Marvin Lundy echo Hoover's germophobia with their latex gloves (Erica, the 1950s housewife, similarly has a passion for her "rubberoid" gloves); Hoover and Albert Bronzini both have an interest in Bruegel; there is Pafko at the wall in the baseball game, the Berlin Wall and the Wall in the Bronx with its commemorative mural of fallen residents; Nick and Klara are both involved, though in different ways, with the recycling of waste, and both visit at different times the Watts Towers in Los Angeles; Nick's betrayal of Klara's marriage in the 1950s is repeated with a difference when it is Nick as a married man who engages in infidelity with the woman at the swingers' convention, and reversed when Nick's wife has an affair with his friend Brian Glassic; and in their respective sons' homes there are Albert's dying mother and much later Nick's dying mother. Examples of quirky doublings that are harder to classify include the references to the Fred F. French building, noticed by Klara from a rooftop in the 1970s, which reminds her of the punch line in a tale about double-dating in a car with her friend Rochelle back in her adolescence, and it is—of course—the building where ad executive Charles Wainwright works. Also there is the blackout of the northeastern seaboard, experienced by Nick when he returns to New York after many years' absence, and referred to by Sims as his comparison point when talking about the underreporting of the numbers of black people in the USA. There are subtle synchronicities, with the main armature of the book provided by the front-page pairing of the Thomson home run and the Soviet nuclear bomb test, the two shots that were heard around the world. But there is also, for instance, the scene where Marvin and his wife, chasing a lead in the story of the baseball in San Francisco, are waiting for the arrival of Chuckie Wainwright's ship from Alaska, but instead all they find is the infamous shit-filled garbage boat. There are odd repetitions and coincidental allusions: the taxi-driving volunteer on the desert art project mentions the Texas Highway Killer, the home movie video of whose murderous activities is watched at different times by Nick, Matt, and old Albert Bronzini, while Nick's teenage son develops a belated obsession for the Highway Killer through a website (he also incidentally later becomes hooked on the Esmeralda website). Similarly, the issue of *Time* magazine featuring Klara crops up in several of the characters' homes, and heroin is a feature of the lives of George the waiter, Nick's wife Marian, and Lenny Bruce. Despite the novel's sprawling form, there is an unsettling economy of characters, coupled with an intertwining of many different lives. For example, the 1960s garbage guerrilla Detwiler, who orchestrates the raid on Hoover's trash can, later shows up as a waste consultant and colleague of Nick Shay in the 1990s. Klara was also at Truman Capote's Black and White ball, which is interrupted by the garbage guerrillas. Readers learn in passing that the next project of Jane Farish, a BBC producer working on a story about waste for which she is interviewing Nick, is a documentary about Klara. And Moonman 157, the young graffiti artist sought by Klara's agent, turns out to be Ismael, the leader of a scrap-metal gang in the Bronx whom Sister Edgar relies upon for protection. But more than anything, in a series of virtuosic developments, there is a central strand of uncanny coincidences and convergences, with one part of the novel's fictional world intruding upon another. Klara is the organizer of an art project in the 1990s, which involves painting decommissioned bombers in the desert. The project is called Long Tall Sally (the name, incidentally, of an erotic goods store in San Francisco that Marvin the baseball collector passes), and it takes its title from the nose painting on a particular plane, which turns out to have been the one in which Chuckie Wainwright flew during the Vietnam war. Nick visits Klara in the desert, some four decades after their brief affair in the Bronx; he is now the owner of the legendary baseball. Meanwhile, his brother, Matt, who worked on bomb systems in the desert, was an image analyst for bombing missions in Vietnam like those flown by Chuckie. And, just to complete the complex system of connections, Matt's chess coach as a child was none other than Albert Bronzini, Klara's first husband.

Taken individually, many of these connections are perhaps no more than the usual thematic concentration of a well-composed work of fiction (DeLillo talks about the well-crafted construction of the text in interviews), but taken together they amount to an extended demonstration of the hypothesis—at times even the faith—that everything is connected.[9] *Underworld*'s revised version of paranoia is concerned with representing not just the conspiratorial concatenations of power and influence made visible in a dietrological account, but the deeper linkages that refuse to yield their hidden import so easily. It suggests that what is wrong with the usual forms of conspiracy theory is not that they connect too many factors but that they don't connect enough.

The structure of *Underworld* takes to a new level DeLillo's attempt to map the impossibly complex interactions in the age of globalization between individuals and larger social and economic forms that resemble but exceed the logic of conspiracy theory. Though *Libra* is explicitly concerned with conspiracies and secrets at a political level, it also evinces a fascination with all the coincidences that are in some way connected with the assassination, but which cannot be subsumed into a simple plot, whether fictional or conspiratorial. In the *New York Times* interview, DeLillo explains how the true meaning of the Warren Commission Report ("the novel James Joyce would have written if he'd moved to Iowa City and lived to be a hundred" [DeLillo, *Libra* 181]) was not its revelations about any conspiracy plot, significant though they were, but the accidental insight it affords into the otherwise invisible interweavings of the vast social—and textual—fabric of America: "There are endless aspects, endless connections, between Jack Ruby and organized crime and anti-Castro groups and on and on forever. And these links and connections would have been totally unrevealed if there had not been an assassination. That's what the assassination did; it cast a strong light on a part of the culture that nobody was aware of" (qtd. in Remnick).

In a parallel fashion, the labyrinthine path of the Bobby Thomson baseball in *Underworld* offers DeLillo a way of shedding light on vast areas of American culture normally omitted in other inquiries. Some of the most remarkable passages in the novel consist merely of lists of the hands through which the home run baseball has passed, forming an evocative litany of desires and frustrations that cannot be reduced to a socioeconomic analysis. In this way, DeLillo's quasi-conspiratorial presentation of coincidences and connections is not so much, as Jameson would have it, a failed or "degraded" mapping of contemporary society, as an attempt to capture some of the complexities which might well be left out of what Jameson considers the most important story, namely the "single vast unfinished plot" of class struggle (Jameson, *Political* 19).

Sometimes the subterranean connections are indeed sinister, combining with other facts and rumors to suggest how decentered and intentionless forces conspire to control people's lives. But these connections also exceed the inexorable stranglehold of power and surveillance. The proliferation of small-scale rhizomatic entanglements of meaning are part of "some curious neuron web of lonely-chrome America" (DeLillo, *Underworld* 84), which operates not outside of but in the interstices between the binary gridwork of power that dominates the Cold War years.[10] In the novel's final pages, for example, Sister Edgar experiences both a quasi-spiritual transcendence through the ultimate connectivity of the web (she too comes to understand that "everything is connected in the end" [826]), and also the apocalyptic horror of finding the nuclear holocaust endlessly repeated on a website (not forgetting, of course, that the decentered infrastructure of the Internet was invented as a failsafe in the event of nuclear attack). *Underworld* remains resolutely dialectical in its engagement with the paranoid logic of the globalized economy in the information age.

Although *Underworld* is structured by the principle that everything is connected, what is striking about the novel is how confusing and fragmented its narrative is. We learn about connections belatedly, haphazardly, in passing, since the different strands of the novel's converging plots are not presented in a linear, chronological fashion. Causes are presented long after their relevant effects, out of sequence, such that part of the frustration—and the delight— in reading the novel is piecing together the complex relations between its many different parts. That everything is connected remains, for the reader as much as for the novel's characters, a subliminal suspicion and an act of discovery, rather than a tritely proven observation. DeLillo seems to be experimenting with different ways to represent connectedness, trying to find a narrative grammar that can do justice to the kind of question that troubles Matt when he begins to realize that his neat mathematical equations of systems analysis fail to capture the fissiparous multiplying of effects:

> Everything connected at some undisclosed point down the systems line. This caused a certain select disquiet. But it was a splendid mystery in a way, a source of wonder, how a brief equation that you tentatively enter on your screen might alter the course of many lives, might cause the blood to rush through the body of a woman on a tram many thousands of miles away, and how do you define this kind of relationship? (408–09)

Underworld is an attempt to define this kind of relationship through an exploration of the dialectic of connectedness, both the disquiet and the wonder. Its narrative structure gestures towards the complex connections and convergences that operate underneath the heavy-handed conspiratorial coagulations of the military-industrial-media complex.

In conclusion, DeLillo's new novel can be read alongside other contemporary discourses of interconnectedness that have emerged since the 1960s.[11] As much as "everything is connected" is the operating maxim of encyclopedic fictions like *Underworld,* it is also the slogan of recent conspiracy theorists who have come to develop Grand Unified Theories of all history which link together individual stories into one all-encompassing plot. "Everything Is Connected to Everything Else" is also, according to Barry Commoner's *The Closing Circle* (a seminal analysis of the environmental crisis), the "First Law of Ecology," a science which constitutes a new mode of representation responsive to the previously invisible global interaction of "natural" and industrial forces (13). (It is no coincidence that *Underworld* repeatedly returns to the topic of waste.) The emergence of ecology, chaos theory, and new forms of economics inspired by notions of complexity similarly emerge alongside (and sometimes from) the historical combination of proto–New Age mysticism and an increasing awareness that older forms of economic analysis could no longer account for the impossibly complex interdependencies of world trade. And finally, the excessive boosterism of the digital industry and the technoparanoid rantings of net-heads all attempt to come to terms with and come up with terms for the insatiable connectivity of cyberspace. DeLillo's new novel, then, is both a product of and a creative response to the New World Order of connectedness that has reshaped the history of the last half-century. Its mutation of the rigid grammar of conspiracy theory into a decentered circuit of interplotted relationships moves beyond a simple shift from secure to insecure paranoia. *Underworld* strategically hacks into the current resurgence of conspiracy thinking that emerges paradoxically at the end of the Cold War, while at the same time rewiring and upgrading that popular epistemology for post-paranoid times.

Notes

1.   Skip Willman argues cogently that DeLillo's novel creates a stance of social critique by pitting conspiracy theories against contingency theories of historical causation. On the one hand, the novel creates a Marxist sense of social necessity in its portrait of Oswald, in contrast to the Warren Commission's "contingency theory" of Oswald as a misfit, a lone gunman—an aberration, as it were, in the normal functioning of America. Conversely, *Libra* rejects a model of society and history shaped by ruthlessly efficient covert agents by resolutely insisting on the contingency at the heart of the assassination.

2.   In her introduction to *Novel Gazing: Queer Readings of Fiction*, Eve Kosofsky Sedgwick makes the case that it is time for critical theory to move beyond its paranoid obsession with endlessly unmasking the hidden violence of society.

3.   In *Simulacra and Simulations*, Jean Baudrillard presents an account of the translation of political power into its simulation. For Baudrillard, the Kennedy assassination only comes to take on the contours of "originality" with the discovery of its fake copies: "Power can stage its own murder to rediscover a glimmer of existence and legitimacy. Thus with the American presidents: the Kennedys are murdered because they still have a political dimension. Others—Johnson, Nixon, Ford—only had a right to puppet attempts, to simulated murders. But they nevertheless needed that aura of an artificial menace in order to conceal that they were nothing other than mannequins of power" (23–24).

4.   In *Postmodernism, or, The Cultural Logic of Late Capitalism*, Fredric Jameson makes the argument that the significance of the Kennedy assassination as an inaugural moment of the

1960s was less a result of its dramatic interruption of democratic politics than its role in the constitution of a national (televisual) public sphere based on the consumption of mediated images (355–56).

5. And as I was completing this essay in 1998, the Zapruder family licensed the release of a new, computer-enhanced video version of the famous footage, while the federal government entered into lengthy negotiations about buying the rights, if not the actual footage, for the National Archives for huge sums of money from the Dallas dressmaker's descendents.

6. In my account of a shift from secure to insecure paranoia, I am drawing on Andrew Tudor's analysis in *Monsters and Mad Scientists: A Cultural History of the Horror Movie.*

7. See, for example, David Brion Davis's introduction to *The Fear of Conspiracy: Images of Un-American Subversion from the Revolution to the Present.*

8. Regarding the putative connection between homosexuality and paranoia, it is important to realize, as Sedgwick points out, that "a chain of powerful, against-the-grain responses to Freud's argument [. . .] has [recently] established the paranoid stance as a uniquely privileged one for understanding not—as in the Freudian tradition—homosexuality itself, but rather precisely the mechanisms of homophobic and heterosexist enforcement against it" ("Introduction" 277).

9. In a recent interview, DeLillo contests that "there wasn't a great deal of manipulation," though he does concede that "there are some links, more or less buried, that one doesn't expect will be very easily spotted." He goes on to discuss how, in addition to the "technological connections," there are "curious connections between the characters that I would say are bits of artistic stitching more than anything else." DeLillo talks about the coincidence of Klara and Nick both visiting the Watts Towers, and admits, "it doesn't really mean very much," it's just "part of the book's pattern of repetition, which gives it a certain structural unity." But then he confesses that "it becomes, to me, fairly important" (qtd. in Williams, "Everything").

10. John McClure argues persuasively that DeLillo's fiction exhibits a fascination with secrets and mystery which, no longer available in the spaces of romance outside the rationalizing systems of modernity, are now to be found *"within* the intricate fabric woven by a now global economic order, in the mysterious zones produced by the system itself" (119).

11. For further discussions of discourses of interconnectedness, see Nigel Clark; Sadie Plant; and Jodi Dean, 145–52.

Works Cited

Baudrillard, Jean. *Simulacra and Simulations.* 1981. Trans. Sheila Faria Glaser. Ann Arbor: U of Michigan P, 1994.

Clark, Nigel. "Earthing the Ether." *Cyberfutures: Culture and Politics on the Information Superhighway.* Ed. Ziauddin Sardar and Jerome R. Ravetz. New York: New York UP, 1996. 90–110.

Commoner, Barry. *The Closing Circle: Nature, Man, and Technology.* New York: Knopf, 1971.

Conspiracy Theory. Dir. Richard Donner. Warner Bros., 1997.

Davis, David Brion. *The Fear of Conspiracy: Images of Un-American Subversion from the Revolution to the Present.* Ithaca: Cornell UP, 1971.

Dean, Jodi. *Aliens in America: Conspiracy Cultures from Outerspace to Cyberspace.* Ithaca: Cornell UP, 1998.

DeCurtis, Anthony. " 'An Outsider in This Society': An Interview with Don DeLillo." *Introducing Don DeLillo.* Ed. Frank Lentricchia. Durham: Duke UP, 1992. 43–66.

DeLillo, Don. "American Blood: A Journey through the Labyrinth of Dallas and JFK." *Rolling Stone* 8 Dec. 1983: 21–22, 24, 27–28, 74.

———. *Americana.* Boston: Houghton, 1971.

―――. *Libra.* New York: Viking, 1988.

―――. *Underworld.* New York: Scribner's, 1997.

Dibdin, Michael. "Out to Get Us." Rev. of *Underworld,* by Don DeLillo. *Sunday Times* (London) 4 Jan. 1998.

Habermas, Jürgen. *Legitimation Crisis.* 1973. Trans. Thomas McCarthy. London: Heinemann, 1976.

Jameson, Fredric. "Cognitive Mapping." *Marxism and the Interpretation of Culture.* Ed. Cary Nelson and Lawrence Grossberg. Basingstoke: Macmillan, 1988. 347–58.

―――. *The Political Unconscious: Narrative as a Socially Symbolic Act.* Ithaca: Cornell UP, 1981.

―――. *Postmodernism, or, The Cultural Logic of Late Capitalism.* Durham: Duke UP, 1991.

Lasch, Christopher. *The Minimal Self: Psychic Survival in Troubled Times.* New York: Norton, 1984.

Lyotard, Jean-François. *The Postmodern Condition: A Report on Knowledge.* 1979. Trans. Geoff Bennington and Brian Massumi. Manchester: Manchester UP, 1986.

McClure, John. *Late Imperial Romance.* London: Verso, 1994.

O'Toole, Fintan. "And Quiet Writes the Don." *Irish Times* 10 Jan. 1998.

Plant, Sadie. "The Virtual Complexity of Culture." *FutureNatural: Nature/Science/Culture.* Ed. George Robertson, et al. London: Routledge, 1996. 203–17.

Pynchon, Thomas. *Mason and Dixon.* New York: Holt, 1997.

Remnick, David. "Profile of Don DeLillo." *New Yorker* 15 Sep. 1997: 42–48.

Sedgwick, Eve Kosofsky, ed. *Novel Gazing: Queer Readings of Fiction.* Durham: Duke UP, 1997.

―――. "Introduction: Queerer than Fiction." *Studies in the Novel* 28.3 (1996): 277–80.

Showalter, Elaine. *Hystories: Hysterical Epidemics and Modern Culture.* New York: Columbia UP, 1997.

Towers, Robert. "From the Grassy Knoll." Rev. of *Libra,* by Don DeLillo. *New York Review of Books* 18 Aug. 1988: 6–7.

Tudor, Andrew. *Monsters and Mad Scientists: A Cultural History of the Horror Movie.* Oxford: Blackwell, 1987.

Williams, Richard. "Books of Discrimination." Rev. of *Underworld,* by Don DeLillo. *Guardian* (London) 8 Jan. 1998.

―――. "Everything under the Bomb." Interview with Don DeLillo. *Guardian* (London) 10 Jan. 1998.

Willman, Skip. "Traversing the Fantasies of the JFK Assassination: Conspiracy and Contingency in Don DeLillo's *Libra.*" *Contemporary Literature* 39.3 (1998): 405–33.

Wood, James. "Black Noise." *New Republic* 10 Nov. 1997.

Wood, Michael. "Post-Paranoid." Rev. of *Underworld,* by Don DeLillo. *London Review of Books* 5 Feb. 1998: 3.

Awful Symmetries in Don DeLillo's *Underworld*

Arthur Saltzman

At the conclusion of *White Noise,* Don DeLillo abandons the surviving citizens of Blacksmith to a vivid, unprecedented, and profoundly baffling sky. Day after day, people are drawn to the overpass for a clear vantage of an ambiguous epic of the atmosphere. The sky positively swarms with intention: colors breed and evolve; light descends in complicated arcs and grades. The unspoken consensus is that the sky is "powerful and storied," but whether that power represents an incantation or a threat, or how encouraging the stories are that it implies, remains in doubt. Thus the witnesses waver between enchantment and dread, until they settle into introversion, diffidence, and, finally, silence. "What else do we feel? Certainly there is awe, it is all awe, it transcends previous categories of awe," but because no one can react with confidence, much less interpret the redefined horizon, this transcendence seems more of a terminal than a point of departure.[1]

The impasse has largely to do with the obscure malevolence behind that sky, with the etiology of the marvelous. For the fact is that this elevated display comes in the wake of the "airborne toxic event," whose chief enlightenment has had to do not with sublime ascension but with mortality. Indeed, like the poisonous plume itself, which so frustrated both official reports and civilian definitions, this renovated sky is an optical (if not reliably visionary) counterpart of white noise. Here is made visible the ghostly "ambient roar" of advertising and military jargon, televisions and computer terminals, political speeches and tabloids. Although some of its viewers are determined to see the sky as a wholesome meditation instead of a precipitous muddle, it is significant that the novel ends with a parallel phenomenon: the rearrangement of shelves in the supermarket, whose altered patterns and "smeared," resistant data create "agitation and panic in the aisles," then a "fragmented trance," leading to "an aimless and haunted mood."[2] Out of their shared desperation, people pull back from the edge as best they can, composing intricate click songs with keystrokes and television remotes, returning to the consoling blur of the familiar, bright packages, and content "to dwell in the syntonic dome of well-engineered voices."[3]

This essay was written especially for publication in this volume and is included here with the permission of the author.

But the fact remains that this indeterminate sky presides, and its calamitous source diffracts whatever vague inspiration may be taken from it. The contentions and language of Guy Debord in *The Society of the Spectacle* may be effectively applied to these conditions. For Debord, a spectacle is not an escape from but an eruption of reality; the inaccessibility of its meaning represents the mystical expansion of the commodity culture, which supplants understanding with addiction, contemplation with fetishism. Hence the sky at the close of *White Noise* is yet another airborne toxic event, another dishonorable discharge, another aspect of the dictatorship of manufactured ambiguity. It is just consumption brought to a higher altitude. ("Everything seeks its own heightened version," we learn in *Mao II*.)[4] Sinister claims upon the absolute, airborne toxic events, whether they are technologically, politically, or linguistically constituted, are like society's guilty dreams. They are at once the shameless exhibition, volatile essence, and inevitable excrescence of a decadent status quo.

It is more than a matter of semantics, after all, to relate sublime radiance to radiation or visionary experience to visibility alone. To adapt Debord's words, the spectacle is not a breach but an expansion of society's "real unreality": "In form as in content the spectacle serves as total justification for the conditions and aims of the existing system."[5] As in DeLillo's *Ratner's Star,* in which scientists discover that a signal from outer space actually originated on earth, we are observing a reflection of a society in-toxic-ated with itself. Therefore, "the spectacle is essentially tautological, for the simple reason that its means and its ends are identical. It is the sun that never sets on the empire of modern passivity. It covers the entire globe, basking in the perpetual warmth of its own glory."[6] It unifies not through the distribution of insight but by the demand for fervency and capitulation. What DeLillo refers to in *The Names* as "the conscious hovering sum of things" is revealed as "the locus of illusion and false consciousness."[7]

Not by virtue of its sacredness or promise of illumination but because of the compulsion to wonder it initiates, the spectacle represents "the material reconstruction of the religious illusion," serving as "a technological version of the exiling of human powers in a 'world beyond.' "[8] There is no denying DeLillo's interest in a realm that stands apart from the contamination he so consistently locates in all human practices and institutions. ("Fuck you. Show some amazement," Brian Glassic fires back at Nick Shay when his companion does not muster sufficient appreciation of the ingenuity and variety on display at a condom emporium.)[9] The problem lies in trying to establish transcendence in a commodified heaven.

One of the most intriguing thematic paths in DeLillo's latest novel, *Underworld,* tracks the status of that realm. The profundity of *Underworld* is undeniable; its massive erudition, enterprising lyricism, and sociopolitical reach compel us to include it along with Thomas Pynchon's *Gravity's Rainbow,* William Gass's *The Tunnel,* and David Foster Wallace's *Infinite Jest* among the chief "meganovels" in contemporary American fiction. There is arguably a sort of sublimity inherent in the sheer entrepreneurial scope of such novels; however else we respond to them, we cannot help but respect what Emily Dickinson called "A Wilderness of Size."[10] But whereas all of these novels share a rich enlistment in the trappings and details of the real-world depictions, *Underworld* displays a particular, consistent concern with what may lie beyond. By interrogating the accessibility and the merit of transcendental moments, *Underworld* focuses and extends an interest that appears throughout DeLillo's fictions.

Several such opportunities emerge in *Underworld,* and a paradox unites them: what are we to make of a transcendence that betrays its debt to the corruption from which it presumably establishes a pure and epiphanic distance? A baseball flies off the bat of Bobby Thomson and leaves the Polo Grounds as a Holy Grail; the image of a murdered girl seems magically to weep through light flashing off a billboard; a miracle Web site is founded on the World Wide Web. When it is revealed that transcendence is tethered, that it derives from the same veiled precincts and secret systems as produce advertising logos, political espionage, or nuclear waste, awe primarily becomes a repudiation of analysis, a satori too expensive to embrace. Paradoxically, "capital burns off the nuance in a culture" (785), but capital investment is consistently promoted as a means of restoring that nuance, as if "the convergence of consumer desire" were a description equally suitable to the awestruck as to the incorporated or the cyberspaced.[11] There may be "guilt in every dosed object" near Ground Zero (792), but there is also enchantment, not to mention, for those attuned to the Big Picture, real prospects for profit.

To further prepare for DeLillo's treatment of awe in *Underworld,* let us return to the sensation in *White Noise* that "it is all awe, it transcends previous categories of awe." First, it is necessary to point out that this awe comes prior to revelation rather than in reponse to it; in fact, it is awe that *substitutes* for revelation. *Ratner's Star* warns against succumbing to "the fool's rule of total radiance" (438), which is also an apt phrase for paranoia;[12] as William S. Burroughs wrote in *Cities of the Red Night,* a paranoid is "a man in possession of all the facts."[13] But the sovereign mood in this "new category" of awe is prerevelatory, or nonrevelatory. There is a deep stir in the works, but there is no edification in this awe-beyond-awe apart from the conviction that "[w]e're part of the aura."[14] The sheer indefiniteness of the vision, which neither imposes nor excludes any interpretation, is what makes it so appealing, and so sinister. For while poisonous clouds make for supremely elastic symmetries and, therefore, invite our collaboration in the making of meaning, what authenticates them beyond the size of the crowd exposed to them? We are stunned, left gaping but no wiser, nor more holy. Incipience stalls, leaving white noise, white space, and the dubious prospect repeatedly noted in *Great Jones Street:* "Evil is moving toward void."[15]

It may be futile to expect DeLillo to provide closure and domestication of meaning in the sublime when he cannot locate them on the ground. As *Libra* shows, for example, it is impossible to contain the documentary evidence regarding the Kennedy assassination, much less anything so extratextual as the truth of the matter. Totalization, whether prompted by religious, political, or reading experience, is a messianic fantasy that, if left to prosper, may prove as dangerous as any conspiracy it is designed to solve.[16]

The title *Underworld* connotes the subterranean, something on the order of Ralph Ellison's "lower frequencies" in *Invisible Man;* whatever dim iniquity or dull roar derives from the underworld is decidedly earthly. (Ruin nests above and below in DeLillo's fiction, in both turreted clouds and buried drums.) For all the oblique cults, codes, and abstractions operating there, it implies a repository of base materialism and, to borrow from George Bataille, the seduction of waste in all of its obscenity and formlessness.[17] Ecstasies in *Underworld,* for however long they are sustainable, require the repression of the underworld, but the novel's higher climes are eventually implicated along with its sullen depths. Instead of the achievement of a sustaining belief, there is a surrender to man-made magnitude: "The faith of suspicion and unreality. The faith that replaces God with radioactivity, the power of alpha particles and the all-knowing systems that shape them, the endless fitted links" (251).

To be sure, one of the most intense experiences of exaltation in *Underworld* appears to endorse rather than repudiate material waste. As three "waste specialists" perch at the brink of an immense landfill, that dense and utterly terrestrial site imbues them with "a certain drastic grandeur, a kind of greatness, maybe."[18] In response to the statistics regarding how much methane would be recovered to power the vicinity, they experience "a weird elation, a loyalty to the company and the cause." "The sight of this thing, the enormous gouged bowl lined with artful plastic" competes with "the red-tailed hawks transparent in the setting sun and the spring stalks of yucca tall as wishing wands" as "oddly and equally beautiful in a way" (285). Disclaimers like "a kind of," "maybe," "in a way," "weird," and "oddly" seem naturally to arise from this liminal zone where desert landscape and human enterprise, design and debris, secretly intersect.[19] Underground radiation, underground gases, underground enterprises that no conventional map confirms—such things consign Nick Shay to hushed tones. In referring to the philosophy of Whiz Co, the firm sponsoring their desert conference on The Future of Waste (and nothing else and none of us has so reliable a claim on posterity), Nick Shay employs the "grave and layered word" *Weltanschauung* "because somewhere in its depths there is a whisper of mystical contemplation that seems totally appropriate to the subject of waste" (282). Instead of achieving sufficient escape velocity to leave the world and its detritus behind, mysticism succumbs to gravity and invests in waste. Paradise is subject to the same digestive processes as everything else.

From the redefinition of waste as something ominous and magical comes the presumption that waste facilities may be promoted as temples. Detwiler, who is called the visionary member of this threesome, confidently predicts a lucrative fallout of bus tours and postcards once garbage "sanctuaries" are granted the majestic architecture and publicity their mystery merits. "Don't underestimate our capacity for complex longings," he insists (286). People hunger to assemble in *Underworld,* as if ballparks and waste facilities, irradiated testing grounds and the World Wide Web were all sites where collective bargaining for the mystical could be conducted. We are eager to esteem what we do not control or comprehend.[20] Hence, the notorious garbage barge, a Flying Dutchman for the century's end, which moves through *Underworld* in search of a permanent home, represents the blame progress trundles behind it; it is the vagrant all society turns away from, still bearing responsibility. But at the same time, it is our most intimate legend, and it is rich with mythic intensity. Waste is feared and extolled as "the secret history, the underhistory" by Viktor Maltsev (791), a contemporary trading company executive for Tchaika (meaning "seagull," after that persistent follower of garbage) who has seen the stakes between East and West change over the decades from armaments to computer chips. And technology remains the hero and the prime suspect of that secret history: nuclear energy creates contaminated nuclear waste, which military scientists (or is it scientific militants?) attempt to vaporize with nuclear explosions.[21] This god is great enough to contain opposing personalities of savior and destroyer and thereby only increases its command over the congregation.

Along with rumors of conspiracy and toxic waste, awe is another growth industry. In response to his suspicion of Dylar, his death fears, and the erosion of faith in the American experiment, Jack Gladney's colleague assures him, "We still lead the world in stimuli."[22] DeLillo makes much the same point in *Players,* in which Lyle Wynant constantly surfs television channels in a random search for "fresh image-burns."[23] Saturation is another sort of void. As "the linked grids lap around you," it becomes harder and harder to extract pure figure from polluted ground, if such a pure figure may be confidently posited in the first place. The "enfolding drone of the computers and fax machines" in *Underworld* does not isolate the authentic from the slosh of stimuli; it imitates and increases the blear (806).

As in *White Noise,* awe in *Underworld* arises apart from conventional sacred observance or structured ritual. One of the first mentions of awe in the novel comes from Klara Sax, whose compulsions run to the transformation of obsolete B-52s, thus repositioning them through composition and paint (and the efforts of her cult-like team of collaborators) into works of art. When she recalls her history of response to strategic bombers and the luminous panorama they once provided, aesthetic and religious inspirations seem easily to conspire. She scripts a belief that what she saw coming out of the high haze must have been B-52s "[b]ecause I wanted to believe that's what we were seeing. B-52s. War scared me all right but those lights, I have to tell you those lights were a complex sensation." It was a sensation at once intimate and distant, invasive and aloof. Add to that the omniscience of unidentifiable powers perpetually presiding over Soviet borders—the valley of the shadow of death, circa mid-1950s—and what results is "a sense of awe, a child's sleepy feeling of mystery and danger and beauty" (75). And so we have the airfield as canvas and reliquary.

However, there are some complications interfering with this epiphany. To begin with, Klara admits that she deliberately foisted her own needs upon that original vision, further refracting "the refracted light from an object way up there." Like the corporate mysteries that inflect the language of waste managers, the objects that refract the light participate in something as insistently secular as the military-industrial complex. But rather than wishing to convince herself of some purer source, Klara "decided" and "wanted to believe" that this visionary gleam came from those bombers and, more to the point, that their mission was wholesome, that their maneuvers were benedictory. Second, the sense of security attending her sleepy, childlike wonder came from respect for power—namely, the authoritative balance predicated upon the dynamic tensions of the Cold War (76). Klara's nostalgia for the stability lost in the collapse of the Soviet empire, which more or less duplicates J. Edgar Hoover's neurotic philosophy of how enemies bring one another to "deep completion" (51), rather dispenses with the spiritual aspects of supervening power.[24] Klara's description of the transcendental undergoes a crucial bit of editing, as the "mystery and danger and beauty" that initially constituted her awe changes into the "greatness, danger, terror" of geopolitics (76). Force becomes not the exercise or the guarantee of divine will but the thing to be idolized itself, notwithstanding its source. It should be a questionable consolation that whatever disruptions may be due to the end of the Cold War, the production of data goes unstintingly on.

Ineffability sacralizes and shrouds the object of worship. Just like the very God who goes nameless as He is approximated by a thousand names, worldly forces are everywhere evident and nowhere precisely defined. As the poet Pattiann Rogers concludes in "Fractal: Repetition of Form over a Variety of Scales,"

> God is a process, a raveled nexus
> forever tangling into and around the changing
> form of his own moment—pulse and skein,
> shifting mien, repeating cry
> of loss and delivery.[25]

Everything shimmers in *Underworld,* so divine radiance and lethal rads are hard to distinguish from one another. It is a guided missile, not God, that is described as "infallible," "precise," "saintly and sun-tipped," manifesting in a ball of fire that "haloes out above its column of smoke and roar, like some nameless faceless whatever," and making one "want to be a Catholic" (515).[26] A "language of circumspection and tact" suits our psalms, our politics, and our paranoia alike. In E. L. Doctorow's *The Book of Daniel,* it is argued that the failure to make connections leads to complicity with powers that must be conscientiously opposed; in DeLillo's novel, connections press relentlessly upon us, and it is the failure to make distinctions that undoes us personally, politically, and linguistically. Thus Matt Shay feels that he has "glimpsed some horrific system of connections in which you can't tell the difference between one thing and another, between a soup can and a car bomb, because they are made by the same people in the same way and ultimately refer to the same thing" (446). If everything carries the same visionary potential, it may be because everything carries the same taint. The dominant mood in *Under-world* is edginess; an "odd mortality clings to every object" (804), rising from the suburban barbecues, contaminating the carefully separated recyclables.[27]

Meanwhile, the words perpetrated in the wake of any given airborne toxic event themselves constitute an airborne toxic event, which may be the subtlest and most fundamental form of complicity in *Underworld.* Imitating the screech of feedback from an electric guitar, which "is what happens when part of a system's output is returned to the input" (463), what DeLillo refers to in another novel as "the screech and claw of the inexpressible" results when language strains to signify in the relentless grasp of uncertainty.[28] Certain words may be swaddled in euphemism, banned, or buried like toxic waste, but eventually they emerge, along with all the secret testing and silenced testimony, "seeping invisibly into the land and air, into the marrowed folds of the bone" (803).

As corporations and the CIA bid for the Infinite, the "higher condition" merges with the devastation. When Matt Shay tells his lover about some of the emergencies and fatalities associated with the vast system he serves, Janet replies, "You make it sound like God. Or some starker variation thereof. Go to the desert or tundra and wait for the visionary flash of light, the critical mass that will call down the Hindu heavens, Kali and Shiva and all the grimacing lesser gods" (458). As the denizens of *Underworld* hunt down the luster, the chance that a flash of light may be from an atomic blast instead of a heavenly host is less pertinent than its irresistibility. The mushroom cloud from an atomic blast fascinates better than any painting or poem; the discharge blown from power-company smokestacks is "gorgeous" (470). The desert "sensitives" murmur strange words about psychic wars, and the boundary between rapturous insight and chemically induced hallucination fades.[29] And it is this convergence of everything that rises—missiles and media bulletins and messianic chants setting the sky afire—that leaves us faithless yet believing anything. Because nothing can be penetrated, nothing is afforded the luxury of irrelevance. Or as one experienced observer of governmental cover-ups puts it, "Nothing you can believe is not coming true"

(802). Not that prostrating ourselves before the opacity of events will save us. It may prove fatal to stare at an inscrutable sun: "Om does not rhyme with bomb. It only looks that way" (466).[30] On the other hand, how do we know that exposure to high levels of radon may not cure blindness, diabetes, or cancer? Jeff Shay, Nick's son, discovers the rumor on a "miracle web-site" and "smirks shyly, either because he thinks it's funny or because he thinks it's funny and he believes it" (806). As the condition is put in *Mao II,* "Only shallow people insist on disbelief."[31]

When Matt examines a dot on a bit of film footage from Vietnam, he determines, "It was a truck or a truck stop or a tunnel entrance or a gun emplacement or a family grilling burgers at a picnic" (463). The confusion of the imperative and the ordinary, of the clandestine and the mundane, is irreducible; revelation is not a matter of better focus or higher fidelity. "A dot was a visual mantra, an object that had no properties": whether that dot is the "jewel in the heart of the lotus" or Ground Zero remains obscure (464). As for the black drums near the perimeter of the compound, they "resembled cans of frozen Minute Maid enlarged by a crazed strain of DNA" and contained, "so the rumor went, a cancer-causing agent" (463). Once again, homely images (cans of frozen Minute Maid) are not resistant to inflationary forces. "And how can you tell the difference between orange juice and agent orange if the same massive system connects them at levels outside your comprehension?" (465). Household appliances mimic the shapes of sleek modern rockets and satellite designs. The FBI fills dossiers with the results of ransacked garbage because there is nothing that does not reveal us, or at least there is nothing that can be said for sure is not germane. In 1957, the same shape and sheen are figured into Jello molds, Jayne Mansfield's breasts, the bullet bumpers of the family car, an erection sheathed in a latex condom, and a surface-to-air missile. Does salvation or disaster reside in these coincidences? Light, language, private life, public perception, and heaven itself seem bent to darker methods than anyone in *Underworld* can confidently penetrate—not systems analysts, not street preachers, not J. Edgar Hoover.

Under these conditions, it is no wonder we are addicted to wonder. Few of DeLillo's characters are so skeptical of the source that they will not surrender to any large-scale phenomenon that will have them. As she endures routine, abandonment, and hard times in the Bronx of the early 1950s, Nick and Matty's mother thinks, "There are times when you want to stop working at faith and just be washed in a blowing wind that tells you everything" (757). Bombs as well as God may speak out of such a wind, but what a relief to be awed, to drop her duties and her knitting and let the world go. As a boy, little Matty Shay and his classmates at Catholic school eagerly obeyed Sister Edgar's directions during duck-and-cover drills. "The only thing that mattered was the abject entreaty, the adoration of the cloud of all-power—forty softly throbbing bodies arrayed along the walls" (728). Before what authority do the children adopt these postures? The government, God, death, the

Bomb, and Sister Edgar are inseparable for them—they are all vague, incontrovertible powers. We are typically depicted in *Underworld* as "drained, docile, soft in our inner discourse, willing to be shaped, to be overwhelmed," so "easy retreats, half beliefs" are sufficient to win us over (826). Accordingly, supplication becomes its own inspiration, justification, and reward.

Yet vaunted blasphemies are blasphemies still. What happens once psychic endowments are exposed as repercussions of technological ventures gone wrong? Ismael Muñoz, a notorious graffiti artist of the Bronx tenements, is only half-ironic when he conflates sources of faith: "Some people have a personal god, okay," he tells Sisters Edgar and Gracie. "I'm looking to get a personal computer. What's the difference?" (813). The encounter takes place near the squatters' memorial wall on which are spray-painted angels commemorating the deaths of children due to drugs, AIDS, or abuse. But it is the death of Esmeralda Lopez that precipitates a vision that awakens believers from all stripes to crisis. Raped and thrown to her death from a roof, Esmeralda regularly appears before rapt crowds and eager media, temporarily turning the neighborhood into an urban Fatima. As a commuter train passes,

> The headlights sweep the billboard and she [Sister Edgar] hears a sound from the crowd, a gasp that shoots into sobs and moans and the cry of some unnameable painful elation. A blurted sort of whoop, the holler of unstoppered belief. Because when the train lights hit the dimmest part of the billboard a face appears above the misty lake and it belongs to the murdered girl. A dozen women clutch their heads, they whoop and sob, a spirit, a godsbreath passing through the crowd. (821)

It is a taut community of seeing—an outdoor Mass—at once charged, hopeful, and afraid. People gather to bask and consider. They "gawk and buzz" before a vision that exceeds crafted utterance (817), recalling both "the screech and claw of the inexpressible" when primordial anticipation rode modern technology out in *Ratner's Star* and the failure of words in face of the freighted sky at the end of *White Noise*.[32]

The feeling that something immense is about to detonate is its own incentive, whether the occasion is a mythic home run, an atmospheric miracle, or an atomic blast. In *Underworld,* as in previous DeLillo fictions, some private grief, deprivation, or duress underwrites and projects upon ambiguous circumstances the possibility of grace. DeLillo's assorted crowds are connected by the same trajectory of compulsion.[33] Cynics as well as cultists, venture capitalists as well as desert sensitives, crave a higher condition. Or as poet Albert Goldbarth puts it, "Maybe a God, / even a God of terrible vengeance, is less frightening / than floating through physics."[34]

Sister Gracie offers a rational dismissal of the Esmeralda phenomenon: it is not a prophetic illumination but a trick of the light. The billboard is not heaven's scrim. Her conclusion is that they are witnessing the pentimento surfacing of part of an old layer of advertisement onto this one. It is, in short, a "technical flaw" fanned into epiphanic proportions by desire alone. Put another way, it is another visual mantra; and as it happens, orange juice, which played a vital role in the purported Agent Orange conspiracy earlier in the novel, reasserts itself here, for the current billboard ad is for Minute Maid Orange Juice. (Evidently, everything that is *buried* must converge, too, in *Underworld.*) The fleeting image of Esmeralda coaxed from, or superimposed upon, the orange juice ad shows religious and commercial urgencies coalescing once again. Thus Esmeralda has been translated into Minute Maid, which suggests either the apotheosis of a product line or the reduction of the star of a contemporary passion play into a company shill.

But Sister Edgar reasons not the need. Her belief has been faltering, and intimations of immortal forces may offer a reprieve from "the gut squalor of our lives" (810). Thus she is not stayed by the orange caution tape, although here "the very orange of the living juice" (824) counsels caution instead of adulation—caution enforced by civil servants and common sense. In a world of ruse, ruin, and delusion, Sister Edgar misses "the serenity of immense design" whose very ambiguity makes it impregnable to the dreadful possibility "that all creation is a spurt of blank matter that chances to make an emerald planet here, a dead star there, with random waste between" (817).

But the next evening there is nothing to see. The sign has been whited out, the lights of the train reveal nothing, and only the words *Space Available* remain to recall that random cosmos Sister Edgar quails from. This is not the white of purity achieved but the white that heaps and tasks Melville's Ahab, or that so appalls Frost in "Design," or that shrouds annihilation in Stevens's "The Snow Man." It is like the white space on the map where the Kazakh Test Site is "unlocated," an absent presence for blast analysts to reflect on (789). The crowd is left in shambles, not knowing anymore where to aim their supplications. Devotion turns to open-ended speculation, which is something like an automatic contribution to the soul's escrow: "Is the memory thin and bitter and does it shame you with its fundamental untruth—all nuance and wishful silhouette? Or does the power of transcendence linger, the sense of an event that violates natural forces, something holy that throbs on the hot horizon, the vision you crave because you need a sign to stand against your doubt?" (824).

The impenetrability of the event—it cannot be explicated—may also be viewed as the permeability of the event—no one can refute speculations about it. John McClure maintains that "the porous, polyvocal, imprecise, and transitory quality of the 'new formations' DeLillo depicts, then, guarantees us that they cannot become coercive and carceral institutions,"[35] which is to say that the sacred is made all the more hospitable and permissive by virtue of its freedom from established practices and precedents. On the other hand, however, when the possibility arises that, say, virulent corporations or secular chemistry is responsible for the event that arrests and consolidates us, secrecy masquerades as spirituality. Pining after direction, we can become the victims, not the beneficiaries, of a dead-end enchantment.

"Most of our longings go unfulfilled," Nick Shay decides, taking stock of his responsibilities, possessions, and compromises. "This is the word's wistful implication—a desire for something lost or fled or otherwise out of reach" (803). But in the case of the vanished Esmeralda sightings, the congregants have to improvise. Sister Edgar struggles to keep her grip on the vision in the wake of homely explanations and the evacuation of the befuddled masses. She holds on to that beleaguered image of Esmeralda; she remakes the remembered odor of jet fuel into "the incense of her experience," which is also an adhesive "that keeps the moment whole" and the "fellowship of deep belief" intact (824). In short, Sister Edgar is not immune to the woven moment, the orchestral sensation.[36] And so her rapture seems to verify the commiseration between the holy and the unwholesome. Then she dies, as if choosing the very moment of quickened conviction to point her properly God-ward.

What actually happens to Sister Edgar is unclear, so the way that the afterlife is characterized in *Underworld* seems to have much in common with cyberspace. Perhaps heaven is just that: an infinity of miracle Web sites, in which the innocent and the corrupt connect. "The real miracle is the web, the net, where everybody is everywhere at once," Nick insists (808), and the possibility of a real miracle trumps suspicions occasioned by entrapping terms like "web" and "net," as well as those caused by the sense of being in "the grip of systems" that exceed our understanding (825)—a trademark sensation throughout DeLillo's fiction. We may imagine in this world without end Esmeralda, Sister Edgar, J. Edgar Hoover, Jimmy Costanza (Nick and Matt Shay's shady father, who abandoned the family one day without word or trace), and "Interactive Sonya" in a conjugal bliss of online ether.[37]

Does being online increase the potential for intimacy, or does it isolate us more effectively, consigning us to lonely rooms? Like nuclear fusion, which can blow us apart even as its implications unite the globe, the computer impacts us in contradictory ways. It neither forgets nor discriminates. It is an awesome synthesis of miracle and mass horror, promoting divinity and devastation simultaneously. It has no center and all circumference: "Is cyberspace a thing within the world or is it the other way around? Which contains the other, and how can you tell for sure?" (826). *Underworld* ends without answering these questions. Fates are left open, motives uninterpreted, culprits undetected, sacred and profane puzzles unresolved. There are just more resonances to add to "the thick lived tenor of things" (827).

Resonance is key testimony on behalf of enchantment. Paul Maltby sees DeLillo's fiction as affirming the regenerative possibilities of vision despite the radically suspicious nature of postmodern sensibilities. According to Maltby, the tendency of postmodern writers to expose visionary moments as delusions owing to literary convention or linguistic logocentrism does not account for their sincere handling in DeLillo's works. Tabloid stories and brand names provide "a flow of spiritually charged meaning" that belies their commercial attachments and that no irony can entirely dispose of.[38] In other words, the obsolescence of transcendence may be debatable, but the urge toward it is not. And yet, DeLillo continues to indict the material culture from which our intrigue derives. Consequently, DeLillo transforms George Will's notorious contention that the novelist is a "bad citizen" into not only a political prescription but also a metaphysical premise.[39] This double vision, as it were, is evident in DeLillo's paradoxical assertions that "fiction rescues history from its confusions" and that his work "has always been informed by mystery; the final answer, if there is one at all, is outside the book. My books are open-ended."[40]

Describing the recovered Eisenstein film that shares the title of the novel, DeLillo writes, "Of course the film was strange at first, elusive in its references and filled with baroque apparitions and hard to adapt to—you wouldn't want it any other way" (429). If sacredness may be said to inhere anywhere in *Underworld*, it may be in the conscientiousness of our appraisal. In Eisenstein's *Unterwelt*, "Arguments are raised and made, theories drift across the screen and instantly shatter—there's a lot of opposition and conflict" (429). This results in a sense of "rhythmic contradiction," which does not resolve our longing. Instead, "[y]ou look at the faces on the screen and you see the mutilated yearning, the inner divisions of people and systems, and how forces will clash and fasten, compelling the swerve from evenness that marks a thing lastingly" (444). In DeLillo's *Underworld*, lives intersect and braid, etymologies overlap and deepen, and data pour endlessly in. The novel's last word is "Peace," but it is hard to tell whether "Peace" results from the contention that "[e]verything is connected in the end" (826) or whether it is just a wish for release from that sentence.

Perhaps what DeLillo is implying is that it is fatal to be satisfied with a brilliant delirium or with wandering aimless and agog. In *Mao II,* the adoring followers of the Reverend Moon are described as "a nation . . . founded on the principle of easy belief."[41] Indeed, it is tantalizing always to receive an answer to yearning, especially when it is always the same answer of blessed commandment. In *Underworld,* Klara Sax recalls Louise Nevelson's having told her that the point of art was to return the canvas or a piece of wood to its "virgin state, and this was the great and frightening thing" (386). Conversely, the great and frightening thing in DeLillo's fiction may be that virginity is always already betrayed. Contaminated, we make temples out of garbage; we pray into a lavish, trammeled sky.[42] DeLillo promotes a kind of psychic brinkmanship—an availability to strange provocations that does not sacrifice a probing intelligence because it cannot afford to.[43] It is at best a difficult, complicated peace that concludes *Underworld*—a wakeful, wary awe that bursts previous categories of awe. Then again, in this pageant of intersection and entropy, you wouldn't want it any other way.

Notes

1.   Don DeLillo, *White Noise* (New York: Alfred A. Knopf, 1984), 324–25.
2.   DeLillo, *White Noise,* 325–26.
3.   Don DeLillo, *Great Jones Street* (Boston: Houghton Mifflin, 1973), 61.
4.   Don DeLillo, *Mao II* (New York: Viking, 1991), 44.
5.   Guy DeBord, *The Society of the Spectacle,* trans. Donald Nicholson-Smith (New York: Zone Books, 1995), 13.
6.   DeBord, 15.
7.   Don DeLillo, *The Names* (New York: Alfred A. Knopf, 1982), 123; DeBord, 12.
8.   DeBord, 18.
9.   Don DeLillo, *Underworld* (New York: Scribner, 1997), 110. Further page references to this novel are noted parenthetically in the text.
10.   Emily Dickinson, "There is a finished feeling" (J. 856), in *Emily Dickinson: The Complete Poems,* ed. Thomas H. Johnson (London and Boston: Faber and Faber, 1960), line 4.
11.   Some of the "misshapens" living near the old Soviet test site wear T-shirts left over from a gay celebration in Europe and distributed to them as part of a business ploy gone horribly awry, as have their own bodies (800). Marketing and human deformity are both responses to nuclear fallout.
12.   Don DeLillo, *Ratner's Star* (New York: Alfred A. Knopf, 1976), 438.
13.   Quoted in John Kuehl, *Alternate Worlds: A Study of Postmodern Antirealistic American Fiction* (New York and London: New York University Press, 1989), 237.
14.   DeLillo, *White Noise,* 13.
15.   DeLillo, *Great Jones Street,* 88.
16.   See DeLillo, *Mao II,* 159.
17.   Yve Alain Bois and Rosalind E. Krauss, *Formless: A User's Guide* (New York: Zone Books, 1997), 29–31.
18.   Indeed, near the end of the novel the Shays visit the local landfill whose rising methane "produces a wavering across the land and sky that deepens the aura of sacred work" (810). Perhaps reverence for the waste we produce can by some logic work backwards to cover its producers.
19.   Nick thinks of his coming to the desert in terms of overexposure to an open, irradiated landscape and a white, invidious sky (341). Later in the novel, too, the secret Pocket where special weapons are tested is identified by a litany of blanks. The wind coming out of the Organ Mountains turns the sky "an odd dangerous gray that seemed a type of white gone mad" (402). Again, whiteness seems less pure than predatory, and most unsettling for what it conceals.
20.   Nick's brother, Matt, recalls the impact that reading a book by a medieval mystic had upon him. *The Cloud of Unknowing* convinced him to correlate God's power with His unknowability. Again, impenetrability not only confirms power and awesomeness, it actually activates those capacities. And like God, earthly sources of mystery, from buried chemical sites to weeping billboards to boardrooms, persist through rumor and disqualify available vocabularies (295–97).
21.   Similar logical circularity may be found in *White Noise,* in that the technology that produced the airborne toxic event is rumored to have produced a toxin-eating microbe that can eliminate the chemical plume. Faith in technology alters and rallies, outflanking disqualification. Accordingly, "we began to marvel at our own ability to manufacture awe" (*White Noise* 153). Meanwhile, in *Underworld,* Klara Sax has a related insight regarding those mutated insects in movies of the fifties: "all radioactive and seeking revenge . . . these creatures not only come from the bomb but displace it" (430).
22.   DeLillo, *White Noise,* 189.
23.   Don DeLillo, *Players* (New York: Alfred A. Knopf, 1977), 16.

24. Nick Shay's recollection of the Bronx version of Klara, who temporarily took the boy as a furtive lover, focuses on her misaligned jaw, which created "the kind of erotic flaw that makes you want to lose yourself in the imbalance" (75). That comment provides a punning echo of the fear of being lost in the imbalance she herself is about to disclose as motivation for her current work in progress. Meanwhile, Klara's and Hoover's references to the "secure" paranoia of Cold War binarism complicates the Burroughs quotation by suggesting nostalgia for a grand Manichean narrative that seems easier to read than the New World Order in which "[e]verything connected at some undisclosed point down the systems line" (408). In short, DeLillo's characters are paranoid about losing the paranoia they know.

25. Pattiann Rogers, "Fractal: Repetition of Form over a Variety of Scales," in *Eating Bread and Honey* (Minneapolis: Milkweed, 1997), lines 34–38.

26. Arising from snug suburban confines, as affirmed by a waxed Ford Fairlane convertible in the driveway, chicken mousse salad, and monogamy, this wish to be Catholic is as likely to represent a desire to emulate the missile's impact as to defend against it.

27. The threat also echoes from *White Noise* during the Gladneys' rummaging through their possessions: "Things, boxes. Why do these possessions carry such sorrowful weight? There is a darkness attached to them, a foreboding" (6).

28. DeLillo, *Ratner's Star,* 22. A confession from *Ratner's Star* reads: "There is something in the space between what I know and what I am and what fills this space is what I know there are no words for" (370). The slipperiness of the referents in that statement is at once grammatical, scientific, and metaphysical. The notion of some "G-dash-D beyond G-dash-D" (217) dashes against premises there are no words for and, despite the plethora of specialized jargon brought by the expert population of Field Experiment One, cannot be talked about effectively.

29. The old Soviet test grounds, however, betray rapture. There is nothing to see at Ground Zero but the contaminated plain. Anticipation goes unanswered: "No ascending cloudmass, of course, or rolling waves of sound. Maybe some dust rises from the site and maybe it is only afternoon haze and several people point and comment briefly and there is a flatness in the group, an unspoken dejection, and after a while we go back inside" (799). Instead of ecstasy, there is the flat affect of the landscape and its witnesses alike.

30. At the end of the novel, a downloaded replay of a Soviet explosion above the Arctic Ocean in 1961 is likewise confused with a vision of God (826). It is available on a Web site devoted to the history of the testing of thermonuclear devices—the ultimate bomb-site, as it were.

31. Don DeLillo, *Mao II,* 132.

32. Robert Lowell wrote in "Epilogue" that the painter's vision "trembles to caress the light" (line 8), and indeed, Sister Edgar believes that "all heaven trembles when a soul swings in the wind" (811). Visionary faith asks that these "tremblings" conspire.

33. "At the edge of every disaster," we read in *Great Jones Street,* "people collect in affable groups to whisper away the newless moments and wait for a message from the front" (254). An alternative assessment is provided by Kenneth Auchincloss, "The Year of the Tear," *Newsweek,* 29 December 1997–5 January 1998. Auchincloss discounts the "event grief" occasioned when the media play up the death of a princess or the killing of a child, for "emotions of this sort hardly count as feelings at all; they're a form of participation." People are just "exuberan[t] at being part of the show" (40). This cautionary reasoning, which denigrates such groups as examples of our self-indulgent culture, could apply to the hysterical gatherings at the billboard.

34. Albert Goldbarth, "Reality Organization," in *Heaven and Earth: A Cosmology* (Athens: University of Georgia Press, 1991), 101–3.

35. John McClure, "Enchantment without Enclosure: Don DeLillo's Postsecular Turning," conference paper delivered at "Don DeLillo: At the Edges of Perception," Rutgers University, 26 March 1998.

316 ◆ ARTHUR SALTZMAN

36.   For contrast, see the "confession" of Sister Hermann Marie in *White Noise,* who calls conventional Christian belief a sham. According to her testimony, her dedication is a pretense nuns adopted to help pacify a frightened population (318–20).

37.   "Sure, you can find pornography on the Internet. But you can also find God," begins a report on how many religious groups have taken to high-tech means of spreading the Word. Depending on one's point of view, these virtual sanctuaries either reduce spiritual searches to chat and diminish given religions for the sake of increasing their market shares, or they represent, in the words of Jennifer Cobb, the author of *Cybergrace: The Search for God in the Digital World,* an emerging "noosphere," a new psychic layer surrounding the earth (quoted in Leslie Miller, "Finding On-line Faithful Revives Religious Groups," *USA Today,* 25 March 1998, D1–2.) In this vein we may recall Sister Edgar's refutation of Sister Gracie's argument that visiting the site of the Esmeralda apparitions represents an abdication of good religion and good sense. Sister Edgar says that, tabloid fodder or not, this is an important, powerful event. "People go there to weep, to believe" (819).

38.   Paul Maltby, "The Romantic Metaphysics of Don DeLillo," *Contemporary Literature* 37, no. 2 (1996): 266–67. Maltby goes on to trace DeLillo's solidarity with Romantic conceptions of and reverence for the Sublime (269–71). He concludes by saying that this persistent concern (he focuses on *White Noise, The Names,* and *Libra*) qualifies any definition of DeLillo as an exemplary postmodern writer. But if we view the *combination* of fervency and jaundice regarding metaphysical matters as true to the plight of contemporary man, it is possible to treat DeLillo as a crucial representative of postmodernism.

39.   Frank Lentricchia, "The American Writer as Bad Citizen," in *Introducing Don DeLillo,* ed. Frank Lentricchia (Durham, N.C., and London: Duke University Press, 1991), 3–4.

40.   Don DeLillo, "An Outsider in This Society," interview with Anthony DeCurtis, in *Introducing Don DeLillo,* 55–56.

41.   DeLillo, *Mao II,* 7.

42.   See Belden Lane, *Landscapes of the Sacred* (New York: Paulist Press, 1988). Belden writes of how ritual can make even manufactured places seem hallowed grounds. For those appropriately attuned, the godly may be proximate in urban landscapes, building sites, or hydroelectric plants, and these may be just as able as pastoral spaces to generate awe and prayer (24–25).

43.   In *Mao II,* a line that grabs Bill Gray from the Sears Roebuck Catalog could be used as a motto for deliberated fascination: "Measure your head before ordering" (201).

Index

♦

317

The Volume Editors

♦

Hugh Ruppersburg is associate dean of Arts and Sciences and professor of English at the University of Georgia. He is the author of *Voice and Eye in Faulkner's Fiction* (1983), *Robert Penn Warren and the American Imagination* (1990), and *Reading Faulkner: Light in August* (1994). He has edited three collections of Georgia writing: *Georgia Voices: Fiction* (1992), *Georgia Voices: Non-Fiction* (1994), and *Georgia Voices: Poetry* (2000). His teaching and research interests include modern American literature, the novel, and film. He has published essays on Faulkner, Warren, John Irving, Jack Kerouac, John Kennedy Toole, James Wilcox, Thomas Wolfe, and others, as well as on film. He is married to Patricia Smith Ruppersburg, a jeweler and metal smith. They are the parents of three sons, Michael, Charles, and Max.

Tim Engles teaches at Eastern Illinois University. He has written on the works of Don DeLillo, Tim O'Brien, Gloria Naylor, Chang-rae Lee, and Alice Walker. He specializes in twentieth-century and Asian American literature, critical race theory, and whiteness studies.

The General Editor

♦

Dr. James Nagel, J. O. Eidson Distinguished Professor of American Literature at the University of Georgia, founded the scholarly journal *Studies in American Fiction* and edited it for 20 years. He is the general editor of the Critical Essays on American Literature series published by Macmillan, a program that now contains more than 130 volumes. He was one of the founders of the American Literature Association and serves as its executive coordinator. He is also a past president of the Ernest Hemingway Society. Among his 17 books are *Stephen Crane and Literary Impressionism, Critical Essays on* The Sun Also Rises, *Ernest Hemingway: The Writer in Context, Ernest Hemingway: The Oak Park Legacy,* and *Hemingway in Love and War,* which was selected by the *New York Times* as one of the outstanding books of 1989 and which has been made into a major motion picture. Dr. Nagel has published more than 50 articles in scholarly journals and has lectured on American literature in 15 countries. His current project is a book on the contemporary short story cycle.